曾智明"曾子学术基金"科研成果

山东大学曾子研究所科研成果

曾子研究院科研成果

儒家文明协同创新中心（山东大学）研究成果

曾子文化丛书

《论语》通解

通解

Lunyu
Tongjie

曾振宇 主编

蔡杰 陈萌萌 注译

人民出版社

责任编辑:宫　共
封面设计:胡欣欣

图书在版编目(CIP)数据

《论语》通解/曾振宇 主编;蔡杰,陈萌萌 注译. —北京:人民出版社,2024.4
ISBN 978-7-01-026418-9

Ⅰ.①论…　Ⅱ.①曾…②蔡…③陈…　Ⅲ.①《论语》-注释②《论语》-
译文　Ⅳ.①B222.22

中国国家版本馆 CIP 数据核字(2024)第 058415 号

《论语》通解

LUNYU TONGJIE

曾振宇　主编

蔡　杰　陈萌萌　注译

人民出版社 出版发行
(100706　北京市东城区隆福寺街 99 号)

北京中科印刷有限公司印刷　新华书店经销

2024 年 4 月第 1 版　2024 年 4 月北京第 1 次印刷
开本:710 毫米×1000 毫米 1/16　印张:26　字数:373 千字

ISBN 978-7-01-026418-9　定价:106.00 元

邮购地址 100706　北京市东城区隆福寺街 99 号
人民东方图书销售中心　电话 (010)65250042　65289539

| 曾振宇 |

　　中国著名儒学专家，儒学研究领域"泰山学者"。山东省社会科学名家。山东大学二级教授，山东大学儒学高等研究院教授、博士生导师、史学博士，山东大学儒学高等研究院原副院长、曾子研究院院长。山东省第9、10、11届政协委员。美国康涅狄格大学访问学者、布莱恩特大学访问学者。中国哲学史学会曾子研究会会长，国际儒联理事。专业为儒学与中国思想史。

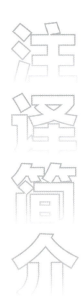

| 蔡 杰 |

福建漳州人，清华大学哲学博士，山东大学儒学高等研究院副教授、硕士生导师，入选山东大学青年学者未来计划（2023—2027），兼任中华孔子学会理事。主要研究方向为：中国经学、宋明理学与儒家伦理学。

序　言

　　"四书"是国学经典。所谓"经典"，意味着时间的长河慢慢将文本中有永恒意义的东西筛选出来，并将非本质的成分滤除。简言之，经典永远具有现代性价值。从汉代开始，《论语》便成为人人诵读的蒙学教材。第一部由外国人翻译的《论语》英译本，由拉丁文转译而来，初版于康熙三十年（1691）；马歇曼（Joshua Marshman，1768—1837）于1809年出版的《论语》英文节译本，乃第一部直接由中文直译的《论语》英译本；第一部中国人翻译的英译本，则是辜鸿铭于1898年出版的译本。迄至今日，"四书"英译本已不下十余种。

　　不同的哲学与文化形态需要沟通与互鉴。相互学习、"美美与共"，各民族历史文化传统中优秀成分才能升华为全世界人人共享的文明成果。在各种英译本"四书"基础上，让全世界各国读者对"四书"的理解有进一步的提升，是本丛书的努力方向，也是本丛书特点所在。我们分别择选出几种有代表性的"四书"译本，从概念、文句和翻译风格等等方面加以比较、分析和点评，冀望读者在阅读过程中，对"四书"的领悟与把握有所深化。譬如，在《论语》一书中，众多弟子问"什么是仁?"孔子的回答都不一致。在大多数语境中，孔子立足于伦理学与工夫论层面讨论"为仁之方"，而非逻辑学意义上的"仁是什么?"但是，在逻辑学和道德哲学层面，孔子自己是否对"仁是什么"存在一个哲学的思考和逻辑上的定义？这是我们今天颇感兴趣的话题。实际上，孔子仁论不属于认识论层面的概念，也不仅仅是道德论层面的概念，而应该将其视为审美境界的概念。孔子仁学重心不在于从认识论维度界说"仁是什么"，也不单纯在道德层面表述"应该""如何"，而是更多地关注心与性合一、身与心合一。换言之，天与人合一。这种审美境界的仁学，对外在客观必然性已有所超越，其中蕴含自由与自由意志的色彩。由此而来，也给历代学者如何准确翻译"仁"这一核心概念产生了很大的挑战。理雅格将"仁"译为"true virtue"（真正的美德），辜鸿铭将"仁"译为"moral character"（符合道德的性格）。读者不仅仅是阅读者，也是文本创作者。在阅读作者研究成果的同时，必然提升对"四书"思想的整体认识。

六朝时期的鸠摩罗什曾经感叹道："但改梵为秦，失其藻蔚，虽得大意，殊隔文体。有似嚼饭与人，非徒失味，乃令呕哕也。"①鸠摩罗什的感叹蕴涵诸多困惑与无奈，"依实出华"是译者矻矻以求的奋斗目标，也是阅读者期望之所在。

是为序。

曾振宇

2023 年 7 月 25 日于山东大学

---

① 慧皎撰、汤用彤校注：《高僧传》卷二，中华书局 1992 年版，第 53 页。

目　录

学而篇第一

【原文】1.1　子曰[1]："学[2]而时习[3]之，不亦说乎？有朋[4]自远方来，不亦乐[5]乎？人不知[6]而不愠，不亦君子[7]乎？"

【译文】孔子说："学了，又在适当的时候演习所学到的内容，不也很愉快吗？有志同道合的人从远处来，不也快乐吗？人家不理解我，我却不怨恨，不也是君子吗？"

【英译】The Master said："Is it not pleasant to learn with a constant perseverance and application？Is it not delightful to have friends coming from distant quarters？Is he not a man of complete virtue，who feels no discomposure though men may take no note of him？"

【注释】

[1] 子：中国古代对于有地位、有学问的男子的尊称，有时也泛称男子。《论语》书中"子曰"的子，主要是指孔子。理雅格、刘殿爵翻译为"The Master"；辜鸿铭译为"Confucius"。

[2] 学：孔子在这里所讲的"学"，主要是指学习周代的礼、乐、诗、书等文化典籍。

[3] 时习：在周秦时代，"时"字用作副词，意为"在一定的时候"或者"在适当的时候"。朱熹在《四书章句集注》中把"时"解释为"时常"。"习"，指演习礼、乐，复习诗、书，含有温习、实习、练习的意思。

[4] 有朋：一本作"友朋"。包咸注"同门曰朋"，即同在一位老师门下学习的叫朋，也就是志同道合的人。理雅格、刘殿爵、辜鸿铭均译为

"friends"，指"朋友"，并未突出"同学""志同道合"之意。

[5] 乐：与"说（悦）"有所区别。朱熹《集注》引程子之说，悦在内心，乐见于外。

[6] 人不知：此句没有说明人不知道何事何物，缺少宾语。知，是理解的意思。人不知，是说别人不理解自己。理雅格本将"不知"译为"take no note of him"，"不知"更侧重"不注意""不了解"；辜鸿铭本将"不知"译为"not noticed of men"，同样侧重"不注意"；刘殿爵本补上"知"的宾语"abilities"，认为他人所不了解的是"自己的能力"；韦利将"不知"译为"unrecognized"，意为"未被认出的、未被认可的"。笔者认为此处译为"understand"更为恰当。

[7] 君子：指人格高尚、道德品行兼好之人。"君子"一语，广见于先秦典籍，《周易·乾》："九三，君子终日乾乾，夕惕若厉，无咎。"《诗经·周南·关雎》："窈窕淑女，君子好逑。"《尚书·虞书·大禹谟》："君子在野，小人在位。"理雅格将君子译为"The superior man"；刘殿爵、韦利将其译为"gentleman"，强调君子的高贵身份和良好教养；辜鸿铭译为"wise man"，侧重君子的智慧。刘殿爵、韦利的译文更佳，突出了君子的德行维度。笔者认为将君子译为"gentleman"，较难体现儒家君子德行高尚的特征，此处或译为"a man of noble character"（品德高尚的人）更为恰当。

【原文】1.2　有子[1]曰："其为人也孝弟[2]，而好犯上[3]者，鲜矣；不好犯上，而好作乱者，未之有也[4]。君子务本[5]，本立而道[6]生。孝弟也者，其为仁之本[7]与！"

【译文】有子说："为人孝顺父母，敬爱兄长，却喜好冒犯上级，这种人是很少的；不喜欢触犯上级，却喜欢造反作乱，这种人从来没有过。君子专心致力于根本，根本确立了，大道就会产生。孝顺父母，敬爱兄长，这就是'仁'的基础吧！"

【英译】The philosopher Yu said, "They are few who, being filial and fraternal，are fond of offending against their superiors. There have been none，who，not liking to offend against their superiors，have been fond of stirring up confusion. Gentleman bends his attention to foundation. That being established，all practical courses naturally grow up. Filial piety and fraternal submission，-are they not the foundation of all benevolent actions?"

【注释】

[1] 有若（前518—?），有氏，名若，字子有（一说字子若），世称"有子"，孔门七十二贤之一。孔子去世后，弟子们思慕孔子，曾因有若似孔子，而群起推举其为师，并以师礼事之。

[2] 弟，通"悌"，指弟对兄的恭敬态度。孝弟是孔子特别重视的两种美德，善事父母曰孝，善事兄长曰弟。理雅格本译为"filial and fraternal"，即"孝顺友爱"；辜鸿铭与刘殿爵采用直译，分别为"Is a good son and a good citizen""good as a son and obedient as a young man"，其中辜本认为"悌"这一行为的主体是"良好公民"，刘本认为行为主体是"顺从的年轻人"；韦利直译为"behave well towards their parents and elder brother"，"孝悌"即为"与父兄保持良好行为"。理雅格与韦利的翻译体现出"孝悌"属于家庭伦理范畴，更为准确恰当。

[3] 犯上：犯，冒犯、干犯。上，指在上位的人。

[4] 未之有也：此为"未有之也"的倒装句型。古代汉语的句法规律，否定句的宾语若为代词，一般置于动词之前。

[5] 务本：务，专心、致力于。本，根本。理雅格将"本"译"radical"，即"根本的、彻底的"；刘殿爵译为"roots"，指根、根源；韦利本以"树干"喻"本"，译为"trunk"；辜鸿铭将"本"理解为重要的、基础的，即"foundation"。此处辜鸿铭的译文更为恰当。

[6] 道：孔子提倡的仁道，即以仁为核心的整个道德思想体系及其在实际生活的体现。理雅格将道译为"practical courses"，侧重实践过程中的具

体法则；刘殿爵与韦利将道直译为"way"，侧重解决问题的方法和途径；辜鸿铭本将其译为"wisdom"，道不是具体的路径和方案，而是抽象的智慧和道德。笔者认为"道"作为传统儒家的核心概念，难以从其他语言中找到一个完全恰当的词来概括，作为专有名词的"道"音译为"Tao"并加以注释更为恰当。

[7] 为仁之本：仁是孔子思想的最高范畴，又是伦理道德准则。为仁之本，是指行仁以孝悌作为开端。

【原文】1.3　子曰："巧言令色[1]，鲜仁矣。"

【译文】孔子说："那种花言巧语、装出和颜悦色的样子，这种人的仁心就很少了。"

【英译】The Master said, "Fine words and an insinuating appearance are seldom associated with true virtue."

【注释】

[1] 巧言令色：朱熹注曰："好其言，善其色，致饰于外，务以说人。"巧和令都是美好的意思。此处意为装出和颜悦色的样子。理雅格将"巧言"译为"fine words"，意为"美好的言论"；韦利将其译为"clever words"，指聪明的言论，没有体现贬义色彩；刘殿爵译为"cunning words"，突出了"巧言令色"中的"狡猾"之义；辜鸿铭将其译为"plausible"，强调看似有道理实则无道理的"花言巧语"。上述译本相较，刘殿爵与辜鸿铭的翻译更为恰当。

【原文】1.4　曾子曰[1]："吾日三省[2]吾身——为人谋而不忠[3]乎？于朋友交而不信[4]乎？传不习乎？"

【译文】曾子说："我每天多次反省自己，为别人办事是不是尽心竭力了呢？同朋友交往是不是做到诚实可信了呢？老师传授给我的学业是不是复习了呢？"

【英译】The philosopher Tsang said，"I daily examine myself on three points：whether，in transacting business for others，I may have been not faithful；whether，in intercourse with friends，I may have been not sincere and trustworth；whether I may have not mastered and practiced the instructions of my teacher."

【注释】

[1] 曾子（前505—前435），姒姓，曾氏，名参，字子舆，鲁国南武城（今山东嘉祥）人，孔子晚年弟子之一。倡导以"孝恕忠信"为核心的儒家思想，"修齐治平"的政治观，"内省慎独"的修养观，"以孝为本"的孝道观，具有极其宝贵的社会意义和实用价值。曾子参与编撰《论语》，撰写《大学》《孝经》《曾子十篇》等作品。曾子在儒学发展史上占有重要的地位，后世尊为"宗圣"，成为配享孔庙的四配之一，仅次于颜渊。

[2] 三省，意为多次反省。

[3] 忠：朱熹注："尽己之谓忠。"此处指对人应当尽心竭力。理雅格将"忠"译为"faithful"，即"忠实的、忠诚的"；韦利译为"loyal"，同为"忠诚、忠贞"之义；刘殿爵将其译为"do my best"，侧重在完成他人托付时尽最大努力；辜鸿铭译为"conscientiousness"，强调君子在"为人谋"过程中应具备责任心。

[4] 信，诚实之谓信。要求人们按照礼的规定相互守信，以调整人与人之间的关系。理雅格将其译为"sincere"，即"真诚的、诚恳的"；韦利译为"true to my word"，意即"信守我的诺言"，强调"信"中重诺守诺的义素；刘殿爵译为"trustworthy"，即"值得信赖的"；辜鸿铭译为"sincerity and trustworthiness"，兼顾"信"中"真诚"与"值得信任"的义素。辜鸿铭此处翻译更为全面恰当。

【原文】1.5 子曰："道千乘之国，敬事[1]而信，节用而爱人[2]，使民以时。"

【译文】孔子说："治理一个拥有一千辆兵车的国家，就要严谨认真地办理国家大事而又恪守信用，节约财政开支而又爱护官吏臣僚，役使百姓不可误其农时"。

【英译】The Master said，"To rule a country of a thousand chariots，there must be reverent attention to business，and sincerity；economy in expenditure，and love for men；and the employment of the people at the proper seasons."

【注释】

[1] 敬：表示对待所从事的事务要谨慎专一、兢兢业业。理雅格与刘殿爵均将"敬"翻译为"reverent"，形容君子处事应当是"虔敬的、恭敬的"；辜鸿铭译为"serious"，侧重对待事物应当是严肃的、重视的；韦利译为"strictly"，即"严格、严厉"之义。上述译本相较，reverent 更为契合《论语》原义。

[2] 爱人：古代"人"的含义有广义与狭义的区别。广义的"人"，指一切人群；狭义的"人"，仅指士大夫以上各个阶层的人。此处的"人"与"民"相对而言，可见其用法为狭义。理雅格译为"love for men"，"爱"的对象是普遍的人类全体；韦利译为"shows affection towards his subject in general"，即"总体上表现出对他的对象的喜爱"；刘殿爵译为"love your fellow men"，强调对同胞的爱。杨伯峻此处译为"爱护官吏"，体现出"人"与"民"的差别，各英译本均忽略此处差别。

【原文】1.6　子曰："弟子[1]入[2]则孝，出则弟，谨[3]而信，凡爱众，而亲仁[4]。行有余力，则以学文[5]。"

【译文】孔子说："弟子们在父母跟前，就孝顺父母；出门在外，要顺从师长，言行要谨慎，要诚实可信，寡言少语，要广泛地爱众人，亲近那些有仁德的人。如此躬行实践之后，还有余力的话，再去学习《诗》《书》等文献。"

【英译】The Master said，"A youth，when at home，should be filial，and，abroad，respectful to his elders. He should be earnest and truthful. He should overflow in love to all，and cultivate the friendship of the good. When he has time and opportunity，after the performance of these things，he should employ them in polite studies."

【注释】

[1] 弟子：一般有两种意义：一是年纪较小，为人弟和为人子的人；二是指学生。这里是第一种意义上的"弟子"。

[2] 入：古代时父子分别住在不同的居处，学习则在外舍。《礼记·内则》："由命士以上，父子皆异宫。"入是入父宫，指进到父亲住处，或说在家。各译本此处均译为"at home"。

[3] 谨：寡言少语称之为谨。理雅格本译为"earnest"，意即"认真的、诚挚的"，该翻译没能突出"严谨、慎重"的义素。刘殿爵译为"sparing of speech"，侧重言论的有所保留和谨慎。韦利译为"be cautious in giving promises"，强调君子在作出承诺时应谨慎认真。辜鸿铭译为"circumspect"，突出"谨"的"严谨认真"和"全面周到"。上述译本相较，辜鸿铭的翻译较为全面。

[4] 仁：仁即仁人，有仁德之人。敦煌写本皇侃《论语义疏》作"人"，刘殿爵译本从之。理雅格、刘殿爵将"亲仁"译为"cultivate the friendship of the good"，强调与好人建立友交。辜鸿铭译为"Intimate with men of moral character"，即君子应当与具有道德品质的人保持亲近关系，该翻译凸显了"仁"的道德内涵。

[5] 文：古代文献，此处主要是指诗、书、礼、乐等文化知识。

【原文】1.7 子夏[1]曰："贤贤易色[2]；事父母，能竭其力；事君，能致其身[3]；与朋友交，言而有信。虽曰未学，吾必谓之学矣。"

【译文】 子夏说："一个人能够看重贤德，改易平常容色；侍奉父母，能够竭尽全力；服侍君主，能够献出自己的生命；同朋友交往，说话诚实恪守信用。这样的人，尽管他自己说没有学习过，我一定说他已经学习过了。"

【英译】 Tsze-hsia said, "A person can value virtue, change the usual appearance, and applies it as sincerely to the love of the virtuous; if, in serving his parents, he can exert his utmost strength; if, in serving his prince, he can devote his life; if, in his intercourse with his friends, his words are sincere: -although men say that he has not learned, I will certainly say that he has."

【注释】

[1] 卜商（前507—前400），姒姓，卜氏，名商，字子夏，南阳郡温邑（今河南温县）人，名列"孔门七十二贤"和"孔门十哲"之一，以"文学"著称。

[2] 贤贤：第一个"贤"字作动词用，尊重之意。贤贤即尊重贤者。易有两种解释：一是改变的意思，即尊重贤者而改变好色之心；二是轻视的意思，即看重贤德而轻视女色。理雅格译为"Withdraws his mind from the love of beauty"，"易"是改变之意，即"使他的心不再爱美"；辜鸿铭译为"love worthiness in man as he loves beauty in woman"，即"爱人的价值，就像爱美色一样"，这一翻译忽视了"易"的意义；刘殿爵译为"shows deference to men of excellence by putting on the right countenance"，即"用正气的样子对待有才能的人"，此处"易"侧重"改变"，即面对贤者时改变了自己的容色。

[3] 致其身：致，意为"献纳""尽力"，把生命奉献给君主。理雅格译为"devote his life"，辜鸿铭译为"give up his life"，上述译本将"致身"理解为"献出自己的生命"。

【原文】1.8 子曰："君子不重[1]，则不威；学则不固[2]。主忠信[3]。无[4]友不如己[5]者。过，则勿惮改。"

【译文】孔子说："君子，不庄重就没有威严；学习可以使人不闭塞；要以忠信为主，不要同与自己不同道的人交朋友；有了过错，就不要怕改正。"

【英译】The Master said, "If the scholar be not grave, he will not call forth any veneration, and his learning will not be solid. Hold faithfulness and sincerity as first principles. Have no friends not equal to yourself. When you have faults, do not fear to abandon them."

【注释】

[1] 重：庄重、自持。理雅格、刘殿爵译为"grave"，即"严肃的，庄重的"，语气情感更为庄严肃穆；辜鸿铭译为"serious"，即"认真的"，语气相对较轻。

[2] 学则不固：有两种解释：一是作坚固解，与上句相连，不庄重就没有威严，所学也不坚固；二是作固陋解，喻人见闻少，学了就可以不固陋。理雅格译为"his learning will not be solid"，即"所学不坚固"；刘殿爵译为"inflexible"，强调对待学问不是"固守己见的、顽固的"；韦利译为"lack firm ground"，认为君子如果"不重不威"，其学问就"缺少坚固的基础"；辜鸿铭译为"remain permanent"，"固"强调学问知识是"坚固的"，能够"保持永久"。

[3] 主忠信：以忠信为主。理雅格、辜鸿铭译为"Hold faithfulness and sincerity as first principles"，即以忠诚为首要原则，体现了"主"的"首要、为主"之义。

[4] 无：通毋，"不要"。

[5] 不如己：一为不如自己；二为不类似自己："不如己者，不类乎己，所谓'道不同不相为谋'也。"理雅格译为"friends not equal to yourself"，即和自己不相似、不同道的朋友；辜鸿铭译为"not as yourself"，即和自己

"不类似";刘殿爵译为"not as good as you",即"不如自己"。理雅格、辜鸿铭把"如"翻译为"类似",更为符合孔子原意。

【原文】1.9 曾子曰:"慎终[1],追远[2],民德归厚矣。"

【译文】曾子说:"谨慎地对待父母的去世,恭敬地追念久远的祖先,那么百姓的德性会日趋敦厚老实。"

【英译】The philosopher Tsang said,"Let there be a careful attention to perform the funeral rites to parents,and let them be followed when long gone with the ceremonies of sacrifice;then the virtue of the people will resume its proper excellence."

【注释】

[1] 慎终:人死为终,指父母的去世。孔安国注:"慎终者丧尽其哀。"

[2] 追远:远指祖先。孔安国注:追远者祭尽其敬。理雅格译为"Let them be followed when long gone with the ceremonies of sacrifice",即"让他们在祭奠仪式中被追念",此处"远"指代上文的"父母";刘殿爵译为"let not sacrifice to your remote ancestors be forgotten","远"指的是"遥远的先祖";辜鸿铭将"远"译为"distant past",指"遥远的过去",并未突出"祖先"之义。

【原文】1.10 子禽[1]问于子贡[2]曰:"夫子至于是邦也,必闻其政,求之与?抑与之与?"子贡曰:"夫子温、良、恭、俭、让[3]以得之。夫子之求之也,其诸异乎人之求之与?"

【译文】子禽问子贡说:"老师到了一个国家,总是预闻这个国家的政事。(这种资格)是他自己求得呢,还是人家国君主动给他的呢?"子贡说:"老师温良恭俭让,所以才得到这样的资格,(这种资格也可以说是求得的),但他求的方法,或许与别人的求法不同吧?"

【英译】Tsze-ch'in asked Tsze-Kung saying,"When our master

comes to any country，he does not fail to learn all about its government. Does he ask his information？ or is it given to him？" Tsze-Kung said，"Our master is benign，upright，courteous，temperate，and complaisant and thus he gets his information. The master's mode of asking information，-is it not different from that of other men？"

【注释】

[1] 陈亢（约前 508—前 430），字子元，一字子禽，又字子亢，春秋时顿子国（今项城市南顿镇）人。

[2] 端木赐（前 520—前 456），复姓端木，字子贡，春秋末年卫国黎（今河南省鹤壁市浚县）人。孔门十哲之一，善于雄辩，办事通达，曾任鲁国、卫国的丞相，还善于经商，是孔门弟子中的首富。

[3] 温、良、恭、俭、让：温顺、善良、恭敬、俭朴、谦让。这是孔子的弟子对他的赞誉。

【原文】 1.11　子曰："父在，观其志；父没，观其行；三年[1]无改于父之道[2]，可谓孝矣。"

【译文】 孔子说："当他的父亲在世时，要观察他的志向；在他的父亲去世后，要考察他的行为；若是他对他父亲的合理部分长期保持不变，这样的人可以说是尽到孝了。"

【英译】 The Master said，"While a man's father is alive，look at the bent of his will；when his father is dead，look at his conduct. If for three years he does not alter from the way of his father，he may be called filial."

【注释】

[1] 三年：经过一个较长的时间而已，不一定仅指三年的时间。理雅格、辜鸿铭、韦利、刘殿爵均译为 "three years"，保留了《论语》原貌。

[2] 道：有时候是一般意义上的名词，无论好坏、善恶都可以叫作道。

但更多时候是积极意义的名词，表示善的、好的东西。这里表示"合理内容"的意思。理雅格、刘殿爵均译为"the way"，保留"道"的本义，直译为"方式、方法"；韦利译为"carry on the household exactly as in his father's day"，即"像他父亲在世时那样操持家业"，强调在管理家族上继承祖辈遗志；辜鸿铭将"道"译为"principles"，即"原则、准则"。

【原文】1.12　有子曰："礼[1]之用，和为贵。先王之道[2]，斯为美；小大由之。有所不行，知和而和，不以礼节之，亦不可行也。"

【译文】有子说："礼的应用，以和谐为贵。上古圣明君主的治国方法，值得称赞的地方就在这里，他们大小事情都遵循这个准则。但是如果有时候行不通，就为和谐而和谐，不以礼仪准则来加以节制，也是不可行的。"

【英译】The philosopher Yu said, "In practicing the rules of propriety, a natural ease is to be prized. In the ways prescribed by the ancient kings, this is the excellent quality, and in things small and great we follow them. Yet it is not to be observed in all cases. If one, knowing how such ease should be prized, manifests it, without regulating it by the rules of propriety, this likewise is not to be done."

【注释】

[1] 礼：儒家的"礼"，既指"周礼"、礼节、仪式，也指"天理之节文，人事之仪则"，同时还有人的德性的维度。理雅格译为"The rules of propriety"，即"礼仪规范"；韦利、刘殿爵译为"ritual"，侧重礼的"仪式、典礼"维度，具有宗教属性；辜鸿铭译为"art"，同时指出"礼"这一概念很难在其他语言中找到同义词汇。此处论"礼"更侧重具体的仪制，理雅格的翻译较为恰当。

[2] 先王之道：指尧、舜、禹、汤、文、武、周公等古代帝王的治世

之道。

【原文】1.13　有子曰："信近于义[1]，言可复[2]也。恭近于礼，远[3]耻辱也。因[4]不失其亲，亦可宗[5]也。"

【译文】有子说："讲信用要符合于义，（符合于义的）话才能实行；恭敬要符合于礼，这样才能远离羞辱；所依靠的不失为可以亲近的人，也是可以效法的。"

【英译】The philosopher Yu said, "When agreements are made according to what is right, what is spoken can be made good. When respect is shown according to what is proper, one keeps far from shame and disgrace. When the parties upon whom aman leans are proper persons to be intimate with, he can make them his guides and masters."

【注释】

[1] 义：义是儒家的伦理范畴，是指思想和行为符合一定的标准。理雅格、韦利、辜鸿铭将"义"翻译为"what is right"，即指按照正确的标准来行事；刘殿爵将"义"翻译为"being moral"，凸显了"义"作为儒家伦理范畴所具有的道德属性。

[2] 复：实践。朱熹《集注》云："复，践言也。"理雅格译为"spoken can be made good"，即"说出的话可以得到很好的践行"；刘殿爵译为"be repeated"，即"重复"之意，误解了此处"复"的意涵；韦利译为"fulfil"，即"完成、履行、执行"之意；辜鸿铭译为"keep your word"，强调符合道义的诺言才能被遵守履行。

[3] 远：动词，使动用法，使之远离的意思，此外亦可以译为避免。

[4] 因：依靠、凭藉。理雅格译为"leans"，意为"倚靠"；韦利将该句译为"marry one who has not betrayed her own kin"，即"嫁给一个没有背叛过自己亲人的人"，该译文将"因"理解为"姻"，似有误。

[5] 宗：主、可靠，又解释为"尊敬"。理雅格译为"make them his guides and masters"，即"要使他们作他的领路人"；刘殿爵译为"as the head of the clan"，即让有德的人"作氏族的首领"；韦利译为"present her to your ancestors"，即"把她（指上文姻亲）献给你的祖先"，"宗"在此处被理解为"祖先"，该说似有误。

【原文】1.14　子曰："君子食无求饱，居无求安，敏于事而慎于言，就[1]有道[2]而正焉，可谓好学也已。"

【译文】孔子说："君子，饮食不求饱足，居住不求舒适，做事敏捷，说话谨慎，到有美德的人那里去匡正自己，这样可以说是好学了。"

【英译】The Master said，"He who aims to be a man of complete virtue in his food does not seek to gratify his appetite，nor in his dwelling place does he seek the appliances of ease；he is earnest in what he is doing，and careful in his speech；he frequents the company of men of virtue and learning that he may be rectified：-such a person may be said indeed to love to learn."

【注释】

[1] 就：靠近、看齐。理雅格译为"The company of"，即"与……为同伴"。

[2] 有道：指有道德的人。理雅格将"道"译为"principle"，即"原则、行为准则"；韦利译为"The way"；辜鸿铭将"道"具象化为"virtue and learning"，即美德和学识。辜鸿铭的翻译更契合儒家对"尊德性"和"道问学"的孜孜以求。

【原文】1.15　子贡曰："贫而无谄[1]，富而无骄，何如？"子曰："可也；未若贫而乐，富而好礼者也。"子贡曰："《诗》云：'如切如磋，如琢如磨'[2]，其斯之谓与？"子曰："赐也，始可与言

《诗》已矣，告诸往而知来者[3]。"

【译文】子贡说："贫穷而能不谄媚，富有而能不骄傲自大，怎么样?"孔子说："这也算可以了。但是还不如虽贫穷却乐于道，虽富裕而又好礼之人。"子贡说：《诗》中说'要像对待骨、角、象牙、玉石一样，切磋它，琢磨它'，就是讲的这个意思吧?"孔子说："赐呀，你能从我已经讲过的话中领会到我还没有说到的意思，举一反三，我可以同你谈论《诗》了。"

【英译】Tsze-kung said,"What do you pronounce concerning the poor man who yet does not flatter,and the rich man who is not proud?"The Master replied,"They will do；but they are not equal to him,who,though poor,is yet cheerful,and to him,who,though rich,loves the rules of propriety."Tsze-kung replied,"It is said in the Book of Poetry,'As you cut and then file,as you carve and then polish.'-The meaning is the same,I apprehend,as that which you have just expressed."The Master said,"With one like Ts'ze,I can begin to talk about the odes. I told him one point,and he knew its proper sequence."

【注释】

[1] 谄：巴结、奉承。理雅格译为"flatter"，即"奉承、讨好、使高兴"；韦利译为"cadging"，形容卑贱地"讨要、乞讨"；刘殿爵译为"obsequious"，即"谄媚的、奉承的"。此处译为 obsequious 更符合《论语》原义。

[2] 如切如磋，如琢如磨：此二句见《诗经·卫风·淇澳》。有两种解释：一说切磋琢磨分别指对骨、象牙、玉、石四种不同材料的加工，否则不能成器；一说加工象牙和骨，切了还要磋，加工玉石，琢了还要磨，有精益求精之意。

[3] 告诸往而知来者：诸，同之；往，过去的事情；来，未来的事

情。理雅格译为"I told him one point，and he knew its proper sequence"，即"我告诉他一点，他就知道该怎么说了"，侧重举一反三之义；辜鸿铭译为"understand how to apply the moral"，强调能够"理解如何运用道德"，忽略了原文中"往"和"来"之意；刘殿爵译为"Tell such a man something and he can see its relevance to what he has not been told"，即"告诉这样的人一些事情，他能看出它与他没有被告知的事情的相关性"，凸显原文"往"和"来"的翻译。此处刘殿爵本更忠实于《论语》文本原貌。

【原文】1.16　子曰："不患人[1]之不己知，患不知[2]人也。"

【译文】孔子说："不怕别人不了解自己，只怕自己不了解别人。"

【英译】The Master said，"I will not be afflicted at men's not knowing me；I will be afflicted that I do not know men."

【注释】

[1] 人：指有教养、有知识的人，而非民。

[2] 知：理解、了解。理雅格译为"knew"；辜鸿铭译为"understand"。know 指知道了人或事的存在，可能并不了解其成因、影响、结果等；understand 语气更重，指清晰地明白人和事，或深入了解成因、结果、影响，译为 understand 更为恰当。

为政篇第二

【原文】2.1　子曰："为政以德[1]，誓如北辰，居其所而众星共[2]之。"

【译文】孔子说："通过修养自身的品德来治理政事，就会像北极星那样，自己居于一定的方位，而群星都会环绕在它的周围。"

【英译】The Master said, "He who exercises government by means of his virtue may be compared to the north polar star, which keeps its place and all the stars turn towards it."

【注释】

[1] 为政以德：以，用的意思。此句是说统治者应以道德进行统治，即"德治"。理雅格、刘殿爵将"德"译为"virtue"，即"德性、美德"，拉丁文 virtus 是古希腊文 ἀρετή 的对译词，ἀρετή 本身指"卓越""力量"，柏拉图与亚里士多德用以指称"德性"或"美德"。辜鸿铭将"德"译为"moral sentiment"，即"道德情操"，韦利译为"moral force"，即"道德力量"。英文 morality 源自拉丁文 mōrālitās（"方式""特征""品格"）。拉丁文 mōrālitās 源自拉丁文形容词 mōrālis（"与行为方式有关的"）。拉丁文形容词 mōrālis 源自拉丁文名词 mōs（"行为方式""习惯"）。同样的行为以相同或类似方式（mos）完成，就会形成习惯（mores）。习惯（mores）被确立后，就具有法则（lex）的力量。因此，英文 morality 意义上的"道德"蕴含了"法则"（lex）观念。基于 virtue（"德性"）观念的道德哲学是希腊传统的道德哲学，基于 morality（"道德"）观念的道德哲学是基督教传统的道德哲学。前

者突出人性的自我成全，后者强调律法对自由意志的规制。

[2] 共：同"拱"，环绕的意思。

【原文】2.2 子曰："《诗》[1]三百，一言以蔽之，曰'思无邪'[2]。"

【译文】孔子说："《诗经》三百篇，可以用一句话来概括它，就是'思想纯正'。"

【英译】 The Master said, "In the Book of Poetry are three hundred pieces，but the design of them all may be embraced in one sentence 'Having no depraved thoughts.'"

【注释】

[1] 诗，指《诗经》一书，此书实有305篇，三百只是举其整数。

[2] 思无邪：此为《诗经·鲁颂》上的一句，无邪，一解为"纯正"，一解为"直"。刘殿爵译为"swerving not from the right path"，即"不偏离正确的道路"，强调道路的正确；辜鸿铭、韦利、理雅格均直译为"没有邪恶的思想"，强调《诗经》主旨的纯正无邪。

【原文】2.3 子曰："道[1]之以政，齐[2]之以刑，民免而无耻；道之以德，齐之以礼，有耻且格[3]。"

【译文】孔子说："用法制禁令去引导百姓，使用刑法来约束他们，老百姓只是求得免于犯罪受惩，却失去了廉耻之心；用道德教化引导百姓，使用礼制去统一百姓的言行，百姓不仅会有羞耻之心，而且也会守规矩。"

【英译】 The Master said, "If the people be lead by laws，and uniformity sought to be given them by punishments，they will try to avoid the punishment，but have no sense of shame. If they be guide by virtue，and uniformity sought to be given them by the rules of propriety，they will have the sense of shame，and moreover will become good."

【注释】

[1] 道：清刘宝楠《论语正义》："正义曰：'道'如'道国'之道，谓教之也。《礼·缁衣》云：'教之以德，教之以政。'文与此同。汉祝睦碑：'导济以礼。'皇本两'道'字并作'导'。《释文》：'道，音导。下同。'《说文》：'导，导引也。'此义亦通。"可见"道"有两种解释，一为"引导"；二为"治理"，朱子在《四书章句集注》中释其为"引导"。理雅格译为"be lead"，即"被领导、被引导"；刘殿爵译为"guide"，同样侧重"带领、引导"；辜鸿铭将该句译为"If in government you depend upon laws"，即"如果你在政府中依赖法律"，该译文忽略了"道"的意涵；韦利译为"govern"，侧重"管理、治理"。lead 可以表示"领导""带路"，含有领导者走在前面，而把被领导者控制在自己的权威之下，或被领导者处于秩序井然的状态中的意思。因此我们认为，此处译文 guide 较为恰当。

[2] 齐：马融注为"齐整之以刑罚"；朱熹解为"齐，所以一之也"；杨伯峻译为"整顿、约束"。理雅格将"齐"译为"uniformity"，强调刑罚所要求的统一性、一致性，更贴近朱熹的解释；辜鸿铭、韦利、刘殿爵译为"keep order""keep them in line"，侧重通过政刑来约束百姓"保持秩序"。

[3] 格：朱熹《四书章句集注》："格，至也。言躬行以率之，则民固有所观感而兴起矣，而其浅深厚薄之不一者，又有礼以一之，则民耻于不善，而又有以至于善也。一说，格，正也。《书》曰：'格其非心。'"可见"格"两种解释：一为"至"，二为"正"。刘殿爵译为"reform"，强调"改革、革新"，辜鸿铭、理雅格、韦利等人忽略了"格"字的翻译。

【原文】 2.4 子曰："吾十有[1]五而志于学，三十而立[2]，四十而不惑，五十而知天命，六十而耳顺[3]，七十而从心所欲不逾矩。"

【译文】 孔子说："我十五岁立志于学习；三十岁能够自立；四十岁能不被外界事物所迷惑；五十岁懂得天命；六十岁能正确对待各种言论，

不觉得逆耳；七十岁能随心所欲而不越出规矩。"

【英译】The Master said，"At fifteen，I had my mind bent on learning. At thirty，I stood firm. At forty，I had no doubts. At fifty，I knew the decrees of Heaven. At sixty，my ear was an obedient organ for the reception of truth. At seventy，I could follow what my heart desired，without transgressing what was right."

【注释】

[1] 有：同"又"。

[2] 立：站得住的意思。三十而立指人在三十岁左右知晓礼仪，做事有分寸，也表示人在三十岁前后应当有所成就。刘殿爵译为"I took my stand"；理雅格翻译为"I stood firm"；韦利译为"I had planted my feet firm upon the ground"，上述译本均将"立"直译为"双脚稳稳地踩在地上"。辜鸿铭意译为"I formed my opinions and judgment"，即"我形成了自己的观点和判断"。

[3] 耳顺：耳顺出自《论语·为政》："子曰：'六十而耳顺'。"是六十岁的代称，也可以称耳顺之年。是指个人的修行成熟，没有不顺耳之事。听得进逆耳之言，詈骂之声也无所谓，无所违碍于心。一般而言，指对那些于己不利的意见也能正确对待。理雅格将"耳顺"译为"my ear was an obedient organ for the reception of truth"，即"耳朵能够顺从地接受真理"，"顺"在这里被译为顺从；辜鸿铭将"耳顺"译为"I could understand whatever I heard without exertion"，即"我不费力气就能听懂所听到的一切"，"顺"在这里更强调认知和理解能力层面的轻而易举；韦利译为"I heard them with docile ear"，即"我用温顺的耳朵听他们说话"，"顺"在这里被译为"温顺"，没有翻译出"顺耳"之意。上述"耳顺"的英译，均未翻译出"正确对待那些于己不利的意见"之意。

【原文】2.5　孟懿子[1]问孝。子曰："无违。"樊迟[2]御，子告之曰："孟孙问孝于我，我对曰，无违。"樊迟曰："何谓也?"子曰："生，事之以礼；死，葬之以礼，祭之以礼。"

【译文】孟懿子问什么是孝，孔子说："孝就是不要违背礼。"后来樊迟给孔子驾车，孔子告诉他："孟孙问我什么是孝，我回答他说不要违背礼。"樊迟说："不要违背礼是什么意思呢?"孔子说："父母活着的时候，要按礼侍奉他们；父母去世后，要按礼埋葬他们、祭祀他们。"

【英译】Mang I asked what filial piety was. The Master said, "It is not being disobedient." Soon after, as Fan Ch'ih was driving him, the Master told him, saying, "Mang-sun asked me what filial piety was, and I answered him, - 'not being disobedient.'" Fan Ch'ih said, "What did you mean?" The Master replied, "That parents, when alive, be served according to propriety; that, when dead, they should be buried according to propriety; and that they should be sacrificed to according to propriety."

【注释】

[1] 孟懿子：鲁国的大夫，三家之一，姓仲孙，名何忌，"懿"是谥号。其父临终前要他向孔子学礼。

[2] 樊迟：姓樊名须，字子迟。孔子的弟子，比孔子小46岁。他曾和冉求一起帮助季康子进行革新。

【原文】 2.6 孟武伯[1]问孝。子曰："父母唯其疾之忧。"[2]

【译文】孟武伯向孔子请教孝道。孔子说："做父母的只是为孝子的疾病发愁。"

【英译】Mang Wu asked what filial piety was. The Master said, "Parents are anxious lest their children should be sick."

【注释】

[1] 孟武伯：孟懿子的儿子，名彘。"武"是他的谥号。

[2] 本章是孔子对孟懿子之子问孝的答案。对于这里孔子所说的父母唯其疾之忧，历来有三种解释：1. 父母爱自己的子女，无所不至，唯恐其有疾病，子女能够体会到父母的这种心情，在日常生活中格外谨慎小心，这就是孝。2. 做子女的，只需父母在自己有病时担忧，但在其他方面就不必担忧了，表明父母的亲子之情。3. 子女只要为父母的病疾而担忧，其他方面不必过多地担忧。理雅格译为 "parents are anxious lest their children should be sick"，强调孝子应当使父母少为自己感到忧心，韦利同样持这种观点。刘殿爵译为 "give your father and mother no cause for anxiety other than illness"，即除了疾病之外，不要过多地让父母忧心。辜鸿铭译为 "Think how anxious your parents are when you are sick"，意为 "想想当你生病时，你的父母是多么的焦虑"。

【原文】2.7　子游[1]问孝。子曰："今之孝者，是谓能养。至于犬马，皆能有养[2]；不敬，何以别乎？"

【译文】子游问什么是孝，孔子说："如今所谓的孝，只是说能够赡养父母而已。然而即便犬马都能够得到饲养，如果不存心孝敬父母，那么赡养父母与饲养犬马又有什么区别呢？"

【英译】Tsze-yu asked what filial piety was. The Master said，"The filial piety nowadays means the support of one's parents. Dogs and horses can be bred；without reverence，what is there to distinguish the one support given from the other？"

【注释】

[1] 言偃（前 506—前 443），字子游，又称叔氏，常熟人，"孔门七十二贤"中较少的南方弟子，擅长"文学"。

[2] 至于犬马，皆能有养：一是说狗守门、马拉车驮物，也能侍奉人；二是说犬马也能得到人的饲养。理雅格支持第一种解释，译为 "dogs and horses likewise are able to do something in the way of support"，即"但是狗和

马同样能够做一些支持的事情"；辜鸿铭、刘殿爵、韦利等人的译本均支持第二种翻译，即犬马也能得到人的饲养，所以仅仅在物质上赡养父母是不够的。

【原文】2.8　子夏问孝。子曰："色难[1]。有事，弟子服其劳[2]；有酒食，先生[3]馔，曾是以为孝乎？"

【译文】子夏问什么是孝，孔子说："（作为子女要尽孝）最不容易的就是对父母和颜悦色。仅仅是有了事情，儿女替父母去做，有了酒饭，让父母吃，难道认为这样就算是孝了吗？"

【英译】Tsze-hsia asked what filial piety was. The Master said, "The difficulty is with the countenance. If，when their elders have any troublesome affairs，the young take the toil of them，and if，when the young have wine and food，they set them before their elders，is this to be considered filial piety？"

【注释】

[1] 色难：色，脸色。难，不容易的意思。理雅格译为"The difficulty is with the countenance"，强调始终保持好的面容、表情是困难的，刘殿爵、辜鸿铭也持这种观点；韦利译为"It is demeanour that is difficult"，侧重行为举止上的难易始终保持良好，并不仅仅局限在面容表情上。"色"在中国古代多侧重容色、脸色，邢昺注为"和颜悦色是为难也。又内则云父母之所下气怡声，是孝子当和颜色顺辞令也"，"色"在这里指面容表情，而非行为举止，韦利的翻译没有体现出"色"的本义。

[2] 服劳：服，从事、担负。服劳即服侍、侍奉。

[3] 先生：先生指长者或父母；前面说的弟子，指晚辈、儿女等。

【原文】2.9　子曰："吾与回[1]言终日，不违[2]，如愚。退而省其私[3]，亦足以发，回也不愚。"

【译文】孔子说："我整天给颜回讲学，他从来不提反对意见和疑问，像个蠢人。等他退下之后，我考察他私下的言论，发现他对我所讲授的内容有所发挥，可见颜回其实并不蠢。"

【英译】The Master said，"I have talked with Hui for a whole day，and he has not made any objection to anything I said；as if he were stupid. He has retired，and I have examined his conduct when away from me，and found him able to illustrate my teachings. He is not stupid."

【注释】

[1] 颜回（前521—前481），曹姓，颜氏，名回，字子渊，鲁国都城人（今山东曲阜市），尊称"复圣"，孔门"七十二贤"之首。孔子对颜回称赞最多，他是孔子最得意的门生。

[2] 不违：不提相反的意见和问题。

[3] 退而省其私：考察颜回私下里与其他学生讨论学问的言行。理雅格译为"I have examined his conduct when away from me"，"私"即颜回不在孔子身边时的行为。

【原文】2.10　子曰："视其所以[1]，观其所由[2]，察其所安[3]。人焉廋[4]哉？人焉廋哉？"

【译文】孔子说："（要了解一个人）应看他言行的动机，观察他所走的道路，考察他安心干什么，这样的人怎么能隐藏得了呢？这样的人怎么能隐藏得了呢？"

【英译】The Master said，"See what a man does. Mark his motives. Examine in what things he rests. How can a man conceal his character? How can a man conceal his character?"

【注释】

[1] 所以：所做的事情。

[2] 所由：所走过的道路。理雅格、辜鸿铭译为"mark his motives"，将"由"理解为动机、心境；韦利译为"means"，强调追求目标时所采取的方式、方法；刘殿爵将"由"直译为"path"，即"路径""道路"之义。我们认为此处刘殿爵的翻译更为恰当。

[3] 所安：所安的心境。本文主要讲如何了解别人的问题。孔子认为，对人应当听其言而观其行，还要看他做事的心境，从他的言论、行动到他的内心，全面了解观察一个人，那么这个人就没有什么可以隐埋得了的。对于"察其所安"一句，理雅格译为"Examine in what things he rests"，"安"即为其休息时的样子；辜鸿铭译为"find out his tastes"，"安"即为个人的兴趣喜好；韦利译为"discover what brings him content"，"安"即为让个体感到满足的事物；刘殿爵译为"examine where he feels at home"，"安"强调个体感到如同在家般的轻松自在。

[4] 廋：隐藏、藏匿，多译为"hidden"或"conceal"。

【原文】2.11　子曰："温故而知新[1]，可以为师矣。"

【译文】孔子说："在温习旧知识时，能有新体会、新发现、就可以当老师了。"

【英译】The Master said，"If a man keeps cherishing his old knowledge，so as continually to be acquiring new，he may be a teacher of others."

【注释】

[1] 温故而知新：故，已经过去的。新，刚刚学到的知识。

【原文】2.12　子曰："君子不器[1]。"

【译文】孔子说："君子不像器具那样，只有某一方面的用途。"

【英译】The Master said，"The accomplished scholar is not a utensil."

【注释】

[1] 器：器具。皇侃《义疏》云："此章明君子之人不系守一业也……君子当才业周普，不得如器之守一也。"君子是孔子心目中具有理想人格的人，他应该担负起治国安邦之重任。对内可以妥善处理各种政务；对外能够应对四方，不辱君命。所以，孔子说，君子应当博学多识，具有多方面才干，不只局限于某个方面，因此，他可以通观全局、领导全局，成为合格的领导者。这种思想在今天仍有可取之处。理雅格认为该句意为"博学的学者不是一件器皿"，此处"君子"译为"The accomplished scholar"，侧重君子在学识上的广博，"器"直译为"utensil"，理雅格此处采取直译，并未补充"君子不器"背后的意蕴。辜鸿铭将该句译为"A wise man will not make himself into a mere machine fit only to do one kind of work"，即"智慧的人不会把自己变成只适合做一种工作的机器"，"君子"在这里意即"智慧的人"，"器"译为"机器"。《说文解字》训"器"为"皿也。象器之口，犬所以守之"，"器"是器皿、器具之意，辜氏将"器"译为"machine"，违背了古代"器"的含义。刘殿爵将该句译为"The gentleman is no vessel"，即"君子不是容器"。相比而言，辜鸿铭的译文翻译出了"君子不器"一句的内涵，但在对"器"这一概念的理解上，理雅格与刘殿爵的翻译更为恰当。

【原文】 2.13　子贡问君子。子曰："先行其言而后从之。"[1]

【译文】 子贡问怎样做一个君子。孔子说："对于你要说的话，先实行了，再说出来。"

【英译】 Tsze-Kung asked what constituted the superior man. The Master said，"He acts before he speaks，and afterwards speaks according to his actions."

【注释】

[1] 朱熹《集注》引用周氏说："先行其言者，行之于未言之前，而后从之者，言之于既行之后。"孔子认为，作为君子，不能只说不做，而应先

做后说。只有先做后说，才可以取信于人。

【原文】2.14　子曰："君子周而不比[1]，小人[2]比而不周。"

【译文】孔子说："君子团结忠诚而不与人勾结，小人结党营私而不团结忠信。"

【英译】The Master said，"The superior man is catholic and not partisan. The base person is partisan and not catholic."

【注释】

[1] 何晏《集解》引孔安国说："忠信为周，阿党为比。"朱子《集注》："周，普遍也。比，偏党也。皆与人亲厚之意，但'周'公而'比'私耳。"理雅格作为传教士，此处对"周"的翻译体现出鲜明的宗教色彩：里氏将"周"译为"catholic"，即"广泛的，包罗万象的"，该词另有"天主教的"之义；理雅格此处从朱说，将"周"理解为"普遍"而非"忠信"。刘殿爵将"周而不比"译为"enter into associations but not cliques"，即君子"加入社团，但不拉帮结派"。辜鸿铭译为"Impartial and not neutral"，即君子是"公正但不是（不带感情色彩的）中立"，辜氏将"比"理解为不带任何感情色彩的不偏不倚，体现出其认为君子的中庸之道应当是带有个人情感的。韦利将该句译为"A gentleman can see a question from all sides without bias"，认为该句是从看待和解决问题的角度，告诫君子应该全面看待问题，不应当具有偏见。此处刘殿爵与辜鸿铭的翻译，更为契合《论语》本旨。

[2] 小人：指士阶层以下的平民，也指道德水平低下的人。理雅格译为"mean man"，指邪恶吝啬的人；刘殿爵、韦利直译为"small man"，没有体现出"小人"一词隐含的在地位和道德层面的低下；辜鸿铭译为"fool"，即"愚蠢的、傻的"。儒家以"小人"指代品行道德低下的人，此处译为"Vile Character"或"base person"更为恰当。

【原文】2.15　子曰："学而不思则罔[1]，思而不学则殆[2]。"

【译文】孔子说："只读书学习而不思考问题，就会罔然迷失；只思考求索而不读书学习，就会疑惑疲怠。"

【英译】The Master said，"Learning without thought is labor lost；thought without learning is perilous."

【注释】

[1] 罔：迷惑，迷惘而无所得。辜鸿铭、理雅格译为"labor lost"，以俚语化的"白费劲"解释"罔"，忽略了"迷惘"的义素。刘殿爵译为"bewildered"，强调"困惑的、迷惘的"；韦利译为"He who learns but does not think is lost"，认为人只学习但不思考，就会像如有所失一样。上述译本相较，刘殿爵的翻译更为精到明白。

[2] 殆：朱子《集注》释为疑惑、危险。何晏《集解》曰："不学而死，终卒不得，徒使人精神疲怠。"皇侃《义疏》："又若不广学旧文而唯专意而独思，则精神疲怠，而于所业无功也。"可见历史上该词有"危险"和"疲怠"两种解释。理雅格、辜鸿铭、韦利均从朱说，译为"perilous"或"dangerous"，即"危险的，艰险的"。

【原文】2.16　子曰："攻乎异端[1]，斯害也已。"

【译文】孔子说："攻击与自己不同的学说观点，这样就会有弊端了。"

【英译】The Master said，"The study of strange doctrines is injurious indeed！"

【注释】

[1] 何晏注："攻，治也。善道有统，故殊途而同归。异端，不同归者也"。王闿运《论语训》："攻，犹伐也。先进篇曰：'鸣鼓而攻之。'道不同不相为谋，若必攻去其异己者，既妨于学，又增敌忌，故有害也。"此章诸说纷纭，莫衷一是，笔者比较《论语》中凡用"攻"字，均作"攻伐"解，如"小子鸣鼓而攻之"，"攻其恶，毋攻人之恶"，不应此处独训为"治理"。

理雅格、辜鸿铭译为"study"侧重"治理"之意；刘殿爵译为"attack a task"、韦利译为"set to work"，强调"开始工作"。上述英译本均沿袭何晏、朱熹一脉，将"攻"解释为"治理"，而非翻译为"攻击、反对"之意。

【原文】2.17　子曰："由[1]！诲女[2]知之乎！知之为知之，不知为不知，是知[3]也。"

【译文】孔子说："由，我教给你的话，你明白了吗？知道就是知道，不知道就是不知道，这才是真智慧。"

【英译】The Master said，"Yu，shall I teach you what knowledge is？When you know a thing，to hold that you know it；and when you do not know a thing，to allow that you do not know it；-this is wisdom."

【注释】

[1] 仲由（前542—前480），字子路，又字季路，鲁国卞（今山东泗水县）人。"孔门十哲"之一，"二十四孝"之一。仲由性情刚直，好勇尚武，跟随孔子周游列国，做孔子的侍卫。后做卫国大夫孔悝的蒲邑宰，以政事见称。

[2] 女，同"汝"，你，多用于称同辈或后辈。

[3] 知：陆德明《经典释文》：知如字，又音智。郑玄、孔颖达皆读此经为"不知为不知，是智也"。"知"在这里不同于上文，是"智慧"之意。理雅格、刘殿爵、韦利将"是知也"的"知"译为"knowledge"，将"知"译为"知识"；辜鸿铭译为"understanding"，强调"理解、领会"了道理。笔者认为此处译为"wisdom"，更能体现儒家哲学中"智"的含义。

【原文】2.18　子张[1]学干禄[2]。子曰："多闻阙[3]疑，慎言其余，则寡尤。多见阙殆，慎行其余，则寡悔。言寡尤，行寡悔，禄在其中矣。"

【译文】 子张要学谋取官职的办法。孔子说："要多听，有怀疑的地方先放在一旁不说，其余有把握的，也要谨慎地说出来，这样就可以少犯错误。要多看，有怀疑的地方先放在一旁不做，其余有把握的，也要谨慎地去做，就能减少后悔。说话少过失，做事少后悔，官职俸禄的道理就在这里面了。"

【英译】 Tsze-chang was learning with a view to official emolument. The Master said，"Hear much and put aside the points of which you stand in doubt，while you speak cautiously at the same time of the others：-then you will afford few occasions for blame. See much and put aside the things which seem perilous，while you are cautious at the same time in carrying the others into practice：then you will have few occasions for repentance. When one gives few occasions for blame in his words，and few occasions for repentance in his conduct，he is in the way to get emolument."

【注释】

[1] 颛孙师（前504—?），复姓颛孙、名师，字子张，春秋战国时期陈国人，"孔门十二哲"之一。颛孙师为人勇武，清流不媚俗，被孔子评为"性情偏激"，但广交朋友。

[2] 干禄：干，求的意思。禄，即古代官吏的俸禄。干禄就是求取官职。理雅格译为"official emolument"，即"公职薪俸"；辜鸿铭译为"preferment"，即地位官职上的"晋升"；韦利将"干禄"视为专有名词，直译为"The song Ganlu"（"干禄"这首诗）；刘殿爵译为"official career"，即"宦途、仕途"之意。上述诸家译本相较，理雅格的翻译更为遵循文本原貌，刘殿爵的翻译清晰反映出了"求干禄"的含义。

[3] 阙：缺。此处意为放置在一旁。

【原文】 2.19 哀公[1]闻曰："何为则民服？"孔子对曰："举直

错诸枉^[2]，则民服；举枉错诸直，则民不服。"

【译文】鲁哀公问："怎样才能使百姓服从呢？"孔子回答说："把正直无私的人提拔起来，把邪恶不正的人置于一旁，老百姓就会服从了；把邪恶不正的人提拔起来，把正直无私的人置于一旁，老百姓就不会服从管理了。"

【英译】The Duke Ai asked，saying，"What should be done in order to secure the submission of the people?" Confucius replied，"Advance the upright and set aside the crooked，then the people will submit. Advance the crooked and set aside the upright，then the people will not submit."

【注释】

[1] 哀公：姓姬名蒋，哀是其谥号，鲁国国君。

[2] 举直错诸枉：举，选拔的意思。直，正直公平。错，同措，放置。枉，不正直。《黄氏日抄》云："错者，置也。如贾谊'置诸安处则安'之类。错诸者，犹云举而加之也。举直而加之枉者之上，是君子在位，小人在野，此民之所以服。举枉者而置于直之上，是小人得志，君子失位，此民之所以不服。"《论语述何》："举直错诸枉，则民服。举正直之人措之枉曲之上，贵教化也。"刘宝楠《论语正义》："诸，之也。言投于下位也。案春秋时世卿持禄，多不称职，贤者隐处，有仕者亦在下位，故此告哀公以举措之道。直者居于上，而枉者置之下位，使其贤者得尽其才，而不肖者有所受治。亦且畀之以位，未甚决绝，俾知所感奋，而犹可以大用。"

【原文】2.20　季康子^[1]问："使民敬、忠以劝^[2]，如之何？"子曰："临之以庄，则敬；孝慈^[3]，则忠；举善而教不能，则劝。"

【译文】季康子问道："要使老百姓对当政的人尊敬、尽忠而努力做事，该怎样去做呢？"孔子说："你用庄重的态度对待老百姓，他们就会尊敬你；你做到孝顺、慈祥，百姓就会尽忠于你；你选用善良的人，又教育能力差的人，百姓就会互相勉励，加倍努力了。"

【英译】Chi K'ang asked how to cause the people to reverence their ruler，to be faithful to him，and to go on to nerve themselves to virtue. The Master said，"Let him preside over them with gravity；- then they will reverence him. Let him be final and kind to all；then they will be faithful to him. Let him advance the good and teach the incompetent；-then they will eagerly seek to be virtuous."

【注释】

[1] 季康子：姓季孙名肥，康是他的谥号，鲁哀公时任正卿，是当时政治上最有权势的人。

[2] 劝：勉励。这里是自勉努力的意思。

[3] 孝慈：一说当政者自己孝慈；一说当政者引导老百姓孝慈。皇侃疏引江熙云："言民法上而行也。上孝慈，民亦孝慈。孝于其亲，乃能忠于君。求忠臣必于孝子之门也。"皇侃采用前者，即统治者做到孝慈，民众进而效仿。理雅格译为"Let him be final and kind to all"，即统治者要求百姓做到孝慈；刘殿爵译为"Treat them with kindness"，即统治者对待百姓仁慈；韦利、辜鸿铭对该句的翻译则侧重统治者应身先士卒做到"孝慈"，为百姓起到表率作用，该种理解更为恰当。

【原文】2.21　或谓孔子曰："子奚不为政？"子曰："《书》[1]云：'孝乎惟孝，友于兄弟，施于有政[2]。'是亦为政，奚其为为政？"

【译文】有人对孔子说："你为什么不从事政治呢？"孔子回答说："《尚书》上说：'孝是孝敬父母，友爱兄弟，把这孝悌的道理施于政事。'这也是从事政治，又要怎样才算是为政呢？"

【英译】Some one addressed Confucius，saying，"Sir，why are you not engaged in the government？" The Master said，"What does the Shu-ching say of filial piety？'You are final，you discharge your brotherly duties. These qualities are displayed in government.' This then also constitutes the exercise of government. Why must there be that-making one be in the government?"

【注释】

[1] 指《尚书》。理雅格译为 "Shu-ching"，刘殿爵译为 "The book of history"，韦利译为 "The books"，辜鸿铭译为 "book of records"。

[2] 施于有政：把这孝悌的道理施于政事。施，一作施行讲，一作延及讲。"施于有政"一句出自《尚书》还是孔子，历来存疑。宋翔凤《四书释地辨证》引上文引书作"于"，下"施于有政"作"于"，是夫子语显有"于""于"字为区别；包慎言《论语温故录》："后汉书郅恽传郑敬曰：'虽不从政，施之有政，是亦为政。'玩郑敬所言，则'施于有政，是亦为政'，皆夫子语。"其说并是。东晋古文误连"施于有政"为书语，而云"克施有政"，非也。包氏又云："《白虎通》云：'孔子所以定五经何？孔子居周末世，王道陵迟，礼义废坏，彊凌弱，众暴寡，天子不敢诛，方伯不敢问，闵道德之不行，故周流冀行其道，自卫反鲁，知道之不行，故定五经以行其道。故孔子曰："书云：'孝于惟孝，友于兄弟，施于有政。'是亦为政也。"依《白虎通》说，则孔子之对或人，盖在哀公十一年后也。五经有五常之道，教人使成其德行，故曰'施于有政，是亦为政。'"

【原文】 2.22　子曰："人而无信[1]，不知其可也。大车无輗[2]，小车无軏[3]，其何以行之哉？"

【译文】 孔子说："一个人不讲信用，是根本不可以的。就像大车没有輗、小车没有軏一样，它靠什么行走呢？"

【英译】 The Master said, "I do not know how a man without truthfulness is to get on. How can a large carriage be made to go without the crossbar for yoking the oxen to, or a small carriage without the arrangement for yoking the horses?"

【注释】

[1] 信，是儒家传统伦理准则之一。孔子认为，信是人立身处世的基点。《论语》中，信的含义有两种：一是信任，二是诚信。理雅格译为"truthfulness"，强调个体在与人交往中应做到"真实、坦率"，辜鸿铭译为"good faith"，即"诚实、真挚"。可见理雅格与辜鸿铭更侧重"信德"的诚信、真实维度。刘殿爵译为"untrustworthy"，"人而无信"即"人不值得被信任"，更强调人际关系中的相互信任。《论语》的《子张》《阳货》《子路》等篇中，都提到信的美德。

[2] 輗：古代大车车辕和横木衔接的活销。

[3] 軏：古代车上置于辕前端与车横木衔接处的销钉，与大车之輗同用而异名。

【原文】2.23 子张问："十世[1]可知也？"子曰："殷因[2]于夏礼，所损益[3]，可知也；周因于殷礼，所损益，可知也。其或继周者，虽百世，可知也。"

【译文】子张问孔子："今后十世的礼乐制度可以预先知道吗？"孔子回答说："商朝继承了夏朝的礼乐制度，所减少和所增加的内容是可以知道的；周朝又继承商朝的礼乐制度，所废除的和所增加的内容也是可以知道的。将来有继承周朝的，即使一百世以后的情况，也是可以预先知道的。"

【英译】Tsze-Chang asked whether the affairs of ten generations after could be known. Confucius said，"The Yin dynasty followed the regulations of the Hsia；where in it took from or added to them may be known. The Chau dynasty has followed the regulations of Yin；where in it took from or added to them may be known. Some other may follow the Chau，but though it should be at the distance of a hundred generations，its affairs may be known."

【注释】

[1] 世：古时称 30 年为一世。也有的把"世"解释为朝代。理雅格此处直译为"ten ages"；刘殿爵、韦利、辜鸿铭直译为"ten generations"。相比而言，"generation"更凸显了"世代"之义。

[2] 因：因袭、沿用、继承。辜鸿铭译为"adopted"，即"接受、采取"前代的礼乐制度；理雅格、韦利译为"followed"，强调"继承"和"沿袭"；刘殿爵译为"built on the rites of the yin"，即"在殷商基础上建立礼仪"。上述译文相较，将"因"译为"follow"更能体现汉语本义。

[3] 损益：减少和增加，即优化、变动之义。理雅格直译为"take from or add"，辜鸿铭译为"modification"，即"修改、变动的内容"。

【原文】 2.24　子曰："非其鬼[1]而祭之，谄也。见义[2]不为，无勇也。"

【译文】 孔子说："不是你应该祭的鬼神，你却去祭它，这就是谄媚。见到应该挺身而出的事情，却袖手旁观，就是怯懦。"

【英译】 The Master said, "For a man to sacrifice to a spirit which does not belong to him is flattery. To see What ought to be done and not to do it is want of courage."

【注释】

[1] 鬼：一是指鬼神，二是指死去的祖先。郑玄注曰："人死曰鬼。非其祖考而祭之者，是谄求福也。""鬼"为"人鬼"，即自己的先祖。韦利、刘殿爵据此译为"ancestor"，即自己"亡故的祖先"。另有说法认为此处"鬼"泛指鬼神，《礼记·曲礼》云："天子祭天地，祭四方，祭山川，祭五祀，岁徧。诸侯方祀，祭山川，祭五祀，岁徧。大夫祭五祀，岁徧。士祭其先。凡祭，有其废之，莫敢举也；有其举之，莫敢废也。非其所祭而祭之，名曰淫祀。淫祀无福。"朱熹《四书章句集注》亦认为"非其鬼，谓非其所当祭之鬼。"可见"鬼"即为鬼神之义。基于此，理雅格、辜鸿铭译为

"spirit"，泛指灵魂、鬼神。

[2] 义：《论语集解》注："义，所宜为"。符合于仁、礼要求的，人应该做的事就是义。理雅格、韦利、辜鸿铭译为"what is right"，即"正确的事"；刘殿爵译为"what ought to be done"，即自己应当做的事。二者相比，刘殿爵本更为符合儒家对"义"的理解。

八佾篇第三

【原文】3.1　孔子谓季氏[1]，"八佾[2]舞于庭，是可忍[3]也，孰不可忍也？"

【译文】孔子谈到季氏，说："在他的家庙的庭院里用八佾奏乐舞蹈，如果这样的事情都可以被容忍，还有什么是不能容忍的？"

【英译】Confucius said of the head of the Chi family, who had eight rows of pantomimes in his area, "If he can bear to do this, what may he not bear to do?"

【注释】

[1] 季氏：指当时执掌鲁国大权的三桓之一，鲁国正卿季孙氏，即季孙意如。

[2] 古时一佾 8 人，八佾就是 64 人，据《周礼》规定，只有周天子才可以使用八佾，诸侯为六佾，卿大夫为四佾，士用二佾。季氏是正卿，只能用四佾。"八佾"一般被译为"eight rows"，即八行。

[3] 可忍：一说可以狠心，《贾子·道术》云"反慈为忍"；一说可以容忍，朱熹《四书章句集注》："或曰'忍，容忍也。'盖深疾疾之辞。"理雅格译为"bear"，即"忍受、容忍"；刘殿爵译为"be tolerated"、韦利译为"be endured"，均为"可以容忍"之意。上述英译本在对《论语》本章"忍"的理解上，更倾向于将其译为"容忍"。

【原文】3.2　三家[1]者以《雍》[2]彻[3]。子曰："'相维辟公，天子穆穆'[4]，奚取于三家之堂?"

【译文】 孟孙氏、叔孙氏、季孙氏三家在祭祖完毕撤去祭品时，也命乐工唱《雍》这篇诗。孔子说："（《雍》诗上这两句）'助祭的是诸侯，天子严肃静穆地在那里主祭'，怎么能用在这三家的庙堂里呢?"

【英译】 The three families used the Yungode，while the vessels were being removed，at the conclusion of the sacrifice. The Master said，"'Assisting are the princes；the son of heaven looks profound and grave'；what application can these words have in the hall of the three families?"

【注释】

[1] 三家：鲁国当政的三家：孟孙氏、叔孙氏、季孙氏。他们都是鲁桓公的后代，又称"三桓"。

[2] 《雍》：《诗经·周颂》中的一篇。古代天子祭宗庙完毕撤去祭品时唱这首诗。

[3] 彻：本义同"撤"，撤除、撤去，指祭祀完毕撤除祭品。

[4] 相维辟公，天子穆穆：《诗·周颂·雍》中的两句。相，助。维，语助词，无意义。辟公，指诸侯。穆穆：庄严肃穆。

【原文】 3.3　子曰："人而不仁[1]，如礼何? 人而不仁，如乐[2]何?"

【译文】 孔子说："一个人没有仁德，他怎么能实行礼呢? 一个人没有仁德，他怎么能运用乐呢?"

【英译】 The Master said，"If a man be without the virtues proper to humanity，what has he to do with the rites of propriety? If a man be without the virtues proper to humanity，what has he to do with music?"

【注释】

[1] 仁：《说文》："仁，亲也。从人，从二。"本义是对人友善、相

亲。《论语·颜渊》："樊迟问仁。子曰：'爱人。'"后来发展为含义广泛的道德范畴，如儒家提倡"仁爱""仁政"等。理雅格译为"the virtues proper to humanity"，即"人类应有的美德"；辜鸿铭译为"moral character"，即"道德品质"；韦利译为"A man who is not good"，较为宽泛地译为"一个不好的人"；刘殿爵译为"benevolent"，即"仁慈的、乐善好施的"。"仁"是儒家特有的、内涵丰富的道德范畴。《说文》："仁，亲也。从人，从二。"本义是对人友善、相亲。《论语·颜渊》："樊迟问仁。子曰：'爱人。'""仁"后来发展为含义广泛的道德范畴。刘殿爵译为"benevolent"，仅侧重"仁"慈善、仁爱的层面，未能凸显仁德作为儒家道德体系上位概念的地位。

[2] 乐是表达人们思想情感的一种形式，在古代，它也是礼的一部分。礼与乐都是外在的表现，而仁则是人们内心的道德情感和要求，所以乐必须反映人们的仁德。孔子就把礼、乐与仁紧紧联系起来，认为没有仁德的人，根本谈不上什么礼、乐的问题。此处各译者均将"乐"翻译为"music"。

【原文】3.4　林放[1]问礼[2]之本。子曰："大哉问！礼，与其奢也，宁俭；丧，与其易[3]也，宁戚。"

【译文】林放问什么是礼的根本。孔子回答说："你问的问题意义重大，就礼节仪式的一般情况而言，与其奢侈，不如节俭；就丧事而言，与其仪式上治办周备，不如内心真正哀伤。"

【英译】Lin Fang asked what was the first thing to be attended to in ceremonies. The Master said，"A great question indeed！In festive ceremonies，it is better to be sparing than extravagant. In the ceremonies of mourning，it is better that there be deep sorrow than in minute attention to observances."

【注释】

[1] 林放（前552—前480），字子丘（邱），春秋末鲁国人，故里在今山东新泰市放城镇。

[2]"礼"的本义是举行礼仪、祭神求福。中国古代社会，礼常常作为行为规则、道德规范和各种礼节的总称，在政治、文化和社会生活中占有重要的地位。理雅格译为"ceremonies"，即"仪式、典礼、礼节"；辜鸿铭译为"art"，即"艺术活动"；韦利译为"ritual"，强调宗教层面的仪式、典礼。孔子认为，礼节仪式只是表达礼的一种形式，但礼不能只停留在表面仪式上，更重要的是要从内心和感情上体悟礼的根本，符合礼的要求。辜鸿铭译为"艺术活动"，没有凸显"礼"具有仪制维度和道德维度的特质。

[3] 易：治理。指有关丧葬的礼节仪式办理得很周到，如《孟子·尽心上》"易其田畴"，因此这里译为"仪文周到"。刘殿爵此处译为"indifference"，即"漠不关心的"，用以与"戚"（即悲伤）形成对比，并未突出"易"的"周到"之义。韦利译为"fear"，认为丧礼与其出自恐惧，不如出自哀伤的情感。理雅格、辜鸿铭在这里均译为"than in minute attention to observances"，即"比专注于仪式更重要"。可见各译本在此处均采取意译，没有凸显"易"的本义。

【原文】3.5   子曰："夷狄[1]之有君，不如诸夏[2]之亡[3]也。"[4]

【译文】孔子说："夷狄尚且有君长上下之分，不像中原国家反而没有上下之分。"

【英译】The Master said，"The rude tribes of the east and north have their princes，and are not like the States of our great land which are without them."

【注释】

[1] 夷狄：古代中原地区的人对周边地区的贬称，谓之不开化，缺乏教养，不知书达礼。理雅格、辜鸿铭、韦利译为"the rude tribes of the east and north"，即"东方和北方的野蛮部落"；刘殿爵译为"barbarians tribes"，即"野蛮人部落"，没有凸显东方和北方的方位。

[2] 诸夏，指中原地区。

[3] 亡：同无。古书中的"无"字多写作"亡"。

[4] 夷狄之有君，不若诸夏之亡也：皇侃《义疏》云："言中国所以尊于夷狄者，以其名分定而上下不乱也。周室既衰，诸侯放恣，礼乐征伐之权不复出自天子，反不如夷狄之国尚有尊长统属，不至如我中国之无君也。"朱子《集注》引程子之说："夷狄且有君长，不如诸夏之僭乱，反无上下之分也。"据此，有君指有君长、有尊卑上下之分。杨氏《疏证》认为"夷狄之有君"指的是楚庄天、吴王阖闾等，君指贤明的君主，此说亦通。敦煌本皇侃《义疏》无"也"字。

【原文】3.6 季氏旅[1]于泰山。子谓冉有[2]曰："女弗能救[3]与？"对曰："不能。"子曰："呜呼！曾谓泰山不如[4]林放乎？"

【译文】季孙氏去祭祀泰山。孔子对冉有说："你难道不能劝阻他吗？"冉有说："不能。"孔子说："唉！难道说泰山神还不如林放知礼（竟然会接受这种僭越的祭祀）吗？"

【英译】The chief of the Chi family was about to sacrifice to the T'ai mountain. The Master said to Zan Yu，"Can you not save him from this?" He answered，"I cannot." Confucius said，"Alas！Can it be said that Taishan God is not as good as Lin Fang to know the ceremony，and will accept this arrown sacrifice?"

【注释】

[1] 旅：祭名。祭祀山川为旅。当时，只有天子和诸侯才有祭祀名山大川的资格。各本均译为"sacrifice"。

[2] 冉有：字子有，通称"冉有"，也称"冉求"，尊称"冉子"，鲁国人，孔门"七十二贤"之一，以政事见称。曾担任季氏宰臣，所以孔子责备他。

[3] 救：挽求、劝阻的意思，这里指谏止。此处该本均译为"save"，即"挽救、拯救"，没有体现冉有对季氏的劝谏阻止意味。

[4] 曾谓泰山不如林放乎：理雅格译为"T'ai mountain is not so discerning as Lin Fang"，即"泰山不像林放那么眼光敏锐"；辜鸿铭译为"The spirit of the great mountains is not as Lin Fang"，即"高山的灵魂不如林放"；韦利译为"mountain Tai to be ignorant of matters that even LinFang enquires into"，即"泰山对连林放都了解的事一无所知"。我们认为，此处译为"Can it be said that Taishan God is not as good as Lin Fang to know the ceremony，and will accept this arrown sacrifice"，更符合孔子语气。

【原文】3.7　子曰："君子无所争。必也射[1]乎！揖[2]让而升，下而饮。其争也君子。"

【译文】孔子说："君子没有什么可与别人争的事情。如果有的话，那就是射箭比赛了。比赛时，先相互作揖谦让，然后上场。射完后，又相互作揖再退下来，然后登堂喝酒。这样的争，其实是君子之争。"

【英译】The Master said，"The student of virtue has no contentions. If it be said he cannot avoid them，shall this be in archery? But he bows complaisantly to his competitors；thus he ascends the hall，descends，and exacts the forfeit of drinking. In his contention，he is still the Chun-Tsze."

【注释】

[1]《周礼·保氏》："养国子以道，乃教之六艺：一曰五礼，二曰六乐，三曰五射，四曰五御，五曰六书，六曰九数。"礼指礼节，乐指音乐，射指射箭技术，御指驾驶马车的技术，书指书法，数指计算、数学的技法。

[2] 揖：拱手行礼，表示尊敬。此处各译本均译为"bow"，即"鞠躬"之意。

【原文】3.8　子夏问曰："巧笑倩兮，美目盼兮[1]，素以为绚兮。何为也?"子曰："绘事后素。"[2] 曰："礼[3]后乎?"子曰："起予者商也！[4]始可与言《诗》矣。"

【译文】 子夏问孔子："笑得真好看啊，美丽的眼睛真明亮啊，用素粉来打扮啊。这几句话是什么意思呢？"孔子说："这是说先有白底，然后画画。"子夏又问："那么，是不是说礼也是后起的事呢？"孔子说："商，你真是能启发我的人，现在可以同你讨论《诗经》了。"

【英译】 Tsze-hsia asked，saying，"What is the meaning of the passage.'The pretty dimples of her artful smile！The well-defined black and white of her eye！The plainground for the colors？'" The Master said，"The business of laying on the colors follows the preparation of the plain ground." "Ceremonies then are a subsequent thing？" The Master said，"The person who inspired my understanding of rites was Shang . Now I can begin to talk about the odes with him."

【注释】

[1] "巧笑倩兮，美目盼兮"，出自《诗经·卫风·硕人》。

[2] 绘事后素：绘，画。素，白底。孔子认为，外表的礼节仪式同内心的情操应是统一的，如同绘画一样，质地不洁白，不会画出丰富多彩的图案。

[3] 礼：古代在祭祀活动中逐步形成的规范，演变为古代社会的等级制度，以此相适应的行为准则和道德规范。"礼"引申为指这些行为准则和道德规范。祭祀神灵往往是有一套严格而隆重的仪式的，所以"礼"引申指"礼节""礼仪"。理雅格译为"Ceremonies"，即"仪式、典礼"；辜鸿铭译为"art"，即"艺术"；韦利、刘殿爵译为"rites"，即"礼数、仪节"。学界通常将《礼记》译为"book of rites"，将"礼部"译为"ministry of rites"，可见此处将"礼"译为"rites"更为恰当。

[4] 起予者商也：起，启发。予，我，孔子自指。商，子夏名商。子夏从孔子所讲的"绘事后素"中，领悟到仁先礼后的道理，受到孔子的称赞。理雅格将"起"译为"bring out my meaning"，即"说出我的意思"，这

一翻译没能体现"起"的"启发"之义。辜鸿铭译为"you have given me an idea"，即"你给了我一个主意"。韦利意译为"bear me up"，即"扶我一把"，比喻子夏的观点给了孔子引导和帮助。刘殿爵译为"Thrown light on the text for me"，指子夏帮助孔子"理清了文本"。实际上，礼指对行为起约束作用的外在形式，素则指行礼的内心情操，即仁。孔子这里的启发并不仅仅局限在文本层面，而是经由子夏一言，更为深刻地理解了礼与仁之间的关系。因此笔者认为，该句译为"The person who inspired my understanding of rites was Shang"较为合适。

【原文】3.9　子曰："夏礼，吾能言之，杞[1]不足征也；殷礼，吾能言之，宋[2]不足征也。文献[3]不足故也。足，则吾能征之矣。"

【译文】孔子说："夏朝的礼，我能说出来，（但是它的后代）杞国不足以证明我的话；殷朝的礼，我能说出来，（但它的后代）宋国不足以证明我的话。这都是由于文字资料和熟悉夏礼和殷礼的人不足的缘故。如果足够的话，我就可以得到证明了。"

【英译】The Master said, "I could describe the ceremonies of the Hsia dynasty, but Chi cannot sufficiently attest my words. I could describe the ceremonies of the Yin dynasty, but Sung cannot sufficiently attest my words. They cannot do so because of the insufficiency of their records and wise men. If those were sufficient, I could adduce them in support of my words."

【注释】

[1] 杞：春秋时国名，是夏禹的后裔，在今河南杞县一带。

[2] 宋：春秋时国名，是商汤的后裔，在今河南商丘一带。

[3] 文献：文，指历史典籍；献，指贤人。理雅格译为"records and wise men"，即流传下来的记录材料和智者；辜鸿铭译为"literary monument"，即文字记录材料，该译文忽略了"献"的古义；韦利译为

"documents and learned men"，即"文献与学者"。《尔雅·释言》："献，圣也。"朱熹《四书章句集注》："文，典籍也；献，贤也。"马端临《文献通考》："凡一话一言，可以订典故之得失，证史之是非者，则采而录之，所谓献也。"可见古汉语中，"文"指文献史料，"献"指有才有德的贤人，辜鸿铭译本忽略了"献"的含义。

【原文】3.10　子曰："禘[1]自既灌[2]而往者，吾不欲观之矣[3]。"

【译文】孔子说："对于行禘礼的仪式，从第一次献酒以后，我就不愿意看了。"

【英译】The Master said，"At the Ti sacrifice，after the pouring out of the libation，I have no wish to look on."

【注释】

[1] 禘：古代只有天子才可以举行的祭祀祖先的非常隆重的典礼。理雅格译为"The great sacrifice"，即"盛大隆重的祭祀"；刘殿爵、辜鸿铭音译为"Ti sacrifice"，并在注释中解释禘礼是只有周天子才能举行的仪典；韦利译为"Ancestral Sacrifice"，即"祖先的祭祀"。将禘礼译为"盛大的祭祀"或"祖先的祭祀"，难以直观体现禘礼是只能由周天子举行的仪式，无法反映孔子对当时礼崩乐坏状况的不满。因此辜鸿铭、刘殿爵直接音译"禘礼"，并在注解中解释禘礼，该种翻译较为可取。

[2] 灌：禘礼中第一次献酒。各译本此处均译为"libation"，即"奠酒祭神仪式"。

[3] 孔子不想观礼的原因，历来大体有三种说法。第一种是孔安国注："既灌之后，列尊卑，序昭穆。而鲁逆祀，跻僖公，乱昭穆。故不欲观之矣。"昭穆，就是指在祭祀的时候这些祖先排列的次序，要有先后的顺序。太祖、始祖摆在中间，左为昭，右为穆。昭穆讲究次序。不能排错，依次排列。如果排错，就使尊卑、长幼、上下序位错乱。在禘礼中，用酒灌地来降

神之后，要"列尊卑，序昭穆"，可是鲁国讲逆祀，顺序是错乱的。第二种说法是朱熹注，《论语集注》引唐朝的大儒赵伯循说，"鲁之君臣，当此之时，诚意未散，犹有可观。自此以后，则浸以懈怠而无足观矣。盖鲁祭非礼，孔子本不欲观，至此而失礼之中又失礼焉，故发此叹也。"朱子说鲁国的君臣在行禘礼的时候，是去祭祀宗庙，祭祀周公，在行祭礼的时候还有诚意，所谓"诚意未散"。祭礼的关键是诚，有诚敬心，虽然有一些不符合礼，像前面孔安国所说的乱昭穆、逆祀，还可以看一看，是因为还有诚意。自灌之后，当行用酒灌地求神之礼的时候，这已经懈怠了，即毫无诚意，自然无足观。第三种说法是刘宝楠《论语正义》中，引《礼经》和参考诸儒的批注，刘宝楠说鲁国特别受周天子之赐，可以在周公庙里举行祭祀只有天子才能用的禘礼，这是为了感念周公，但后来其他国君的宗庙都用这种禘礼，这是不符合礼的。这种礼只有在周公庙里才能举行，因为周公是得到周成王特别恩赐，才能享受这种礼，其他国君的宗庙不能用这种礼，所以孔子不想去看。

【原文】 3.11　或问禘之说[1]。子曰："不知也；知其说者之于天下也，其如示诸斯乎！"指其掌。

【译文】 有人问孔子关于举行禘祭的规定。孔子说："我不知道。知道这种规定的人，对治理天下的事，就会像把这东西摆在这里一样容易吧！"（一面说一面）指着他的手掌。

【英译】 Some one asked the meaning of the great sacrifice. The Master said，"I do not know. He who knew its meaning would find it as easy to govern the kingdom as to look on this！"pointing to his palm.

【注释】

[1] 理论、道理、规定。禘之说，意为关于禘祭的规定。理雅格、辜鸿铭译为"The meaning of the great sacrifice"，即"重要祭礼的意义"；刘殿爵译为"The theory of the ti sacrifice"，即"禘礼的理论"；韦利译为"an explanation of the Ancestral Sacrifice"，即"对祖祭的解释"。此处孔子认为，

谁懂得禘祭的规定，谁就可以归复混乱的"礼"了。

【原文】3.12 祭如在，祭神如神在。子曰："吾不与祭，如不祭。"

【译文】祭祀祖先就像祖先真的在面前，祭神就像神真的在面前。孔子说："我如果不亲自参加祭祀，那就和没有举行祭祀一样。"

【英译】He sacrificed to the dead，as if they were present. He sacrificed to the spirits，as if the spirits were present. The Master said，"I consider my not being present at the sacrifice，as if I did not sacrifice."

【原文】3.13 王孙贾[1]问曰："与其媚于奥[2]，宁媚于灶[3]，何谓也？"子曰："不然；获罪于天，无所祷也。"

【译文】王孙贾问道："（人家都说）与其奉承奥神，不如奉承灶神。这话是什么意思？"孔子说："不是这样的。如果得罪了天，那就没有地方可以祷告了。"

【英译】Wang-sun Chia asked，saying，"What is the meaning of the saying，'It is better to pay court to the furnace then to the southwest corner?'" The Master said，"Not so. He who offends against Heaven has none to whom he can pray."

【注释】

[1] 王孙贾：卫灵公的大臣，时任大夫。

[2] 奥：这里指屋内位居西南角的神。理雅格译为"pay court to the furnace then to the southwest corner"，即向西南角祷告；刘殿爵译为"The southwest corner of the house"，即"屋内西南角"；韦利译为"pay court to the shrine"，即"向佛龛祈祷"。上述译文均未体现出"奥"指的是房屋西南角神明。辜鸿铭译为"The god of the house"，即"房屋的神"。可见辜鸿铭译本更为忠实《论语》原义。

[3] 灶：这里指灶旁管烹饪做饭的神。各本均译为"stove"，即"火灶"之义。

【原文】3.14　子曰："周监[1]于二代[2]，郁郁[3]乎文哉！吾从周。"

【译文】孔子说："周朝的礼乐制度借鉴于夏、商二代，是多么丰富多彩啊。我遵从周朝的制度。"

【英译】The Master said，"Chau had the advantage of viewing the two past dynasties. How complete and elegant are its regulations！I follow Chau."

【注释】

[1] 监：同鉴，借鉴。孔子认为历史是不能割断的，后一个王朝对前一个王朝必然有承继沿袭。理雅格译为"viewing the two past dynasties"，"监"即"观察"；韦利译为"survey"，即"考察、调查"之义。上述两版翻译没有体现出"监"的"借鉴"之意。刘殿爵译为"have before it the example of the two previous dynasties"，即"在它之前有前两个朝代的例子"，周代是继承效仿了夏代和商代的经验，在此基础上建立了周礼。

[2] 二代：指夏代和周代。

[3] 郁郁：丰富、浓郁之意。理雅格译为"complete and elegant"，即"完整优雅的"；辜鸿铭译为"splendidly rich"，即"华丽丰富的"；韦利译为"how great a wealth of culture"，即"多么丰富的文化"；刘殿爵译为"resplendent"，即"光辉的、华丽的"。

【原文】3.15　子入太庙[1]，每事问。或曰："孰谓鄹人[2]之子知礼乎？入太庙，每事问。"子闻之，曰："是礼也。"

【译文】孔子到了太庙，每件事都要问。有人说："谁说此人懂得礼呀，他到了太庙里，什么事都要问别人。"孔子听到此话后说："这就是礼呀！"

【英译】The Master，when he entered the grand temple，asked about everything. Some one said，"Who say that the son of the man of Tsau knows the rules of rites！He has entered the grand temple and asks about everything."The Master heard the remark，and said，"This is a rule of rites."

【注释】

[1] 太庙：君主的祖庙。鲁国太庙，即周公旦的庙，供鲁国祭祀周公。理雅格、韦利、刘殿爵译为"The grand temple"，即"宏伟的寺庙"；辜鸿铭译为"the state cathedral"，即"国家大教堂"，并补充"Ancestral Temple of the reigning prince"，即"在位君主的祭祖庙宇"。辜鸿铭译本体现出"太庙"的祭祖功能，较为符合史实。

[2] 鄹：鲁国地名，在今山东省曲阜市东南。孔子的父亲做过鄹大夫，所以这里称为鄹人。

【原文】3.16 子曰："射不主皮[1]，为力不同科[2]，古之道也。"

【译文】孔子说："比赛射箭，不在于穿透靶子，因为各人的力气大小不同。自古以来就是这样。"

【英译】The Master said，"In archery it is not going through the leather which is the principal thing；because people's strength is not equal. This was the old way."

【注释】

[1] 皮：用兽皮做成的箭靶子。主皮，指射穿皮候。

[2] 科：等级。"射"是周代贵族经常举行的一种礼节仪式，孔子在这里所讲的射箭是一种比喻，意即只要肯学习有关礼的规定，不管学到什么程度，都是值得肯定的。

【原文】3.17　子贡欲去告朔[1]之饩羊[2]。子曰:"赐也! 尔爱[3]其羊,我爱其礼。"

【译文】子贡提出去掉每月初一告祭祖庙用的活羊。孔子说:"赐,你爱惜那只羊,我却爱惜那种礼。"

【英译】Tsze-Kung wished to do away with the offering of a sheep connected with the inauguration of the first day of each month. The Master said,"Ts'ze,you love the sheep; I love the ceremony."

【注释】

[1] 告朔:朔,农历每月初一为朔日。告朔,古代制度,天子每年秋冬之际,把第二年的历书颁发给诸侯,告知每个月的初一日。诸侯接受后将其藏之祖庙,每逢初一(朔日)就杀一活羊祭庙。

[2] 饩羊:祭祀用的活羊。

[3] 爱:爱惜、舍不得。理雅格译为"love",即"爱、喜爱";辜鸿铭译为"save",即"保留、俭省";韦利译为"grudge",即"怨恨"之义,该译文失当;刘殿爵将"我爱其礼"意译为"I am loath to see the disappearance of the rite."即"不愿意看到礼仪被破坏"。上述译文相较,辜鸿铭译本凸显了"可惜、舍不得"之义,更忠实于文本原义。

【原文】3.18　子曰:"事君尽礼,人以为谄[1]也。"

【译文】孔子说:"按照礼节去侍奉君主,别人却以为这是谄媚。"

【英译】The Master said,"The full observance of the rules of propriety in serving one's prince is accounted by people to be flattery."

【注释】

[1] 孔子一生要求自己严格按照周礼的规定事奉君主,这是他的政治伦理信念。但却受到别人的讥讽,认为他是在向君主谄媚。辜鸿铭将"谄"译为"servile",即"过分屈从的";理雅格译为"flattery",即"奉承的";韦利译为"sycophant",即"谄媚者、奉承者";刘殿爵译为"obsequious",

即"谄媚的"。

【原文】 3.19　定公[1]问："君使臣，臣事君，如之何？"孔子曰："君使臣以礼，臣事君以忠[2]。"

【译文】 鲁定公问孔子："君主怎样使唤臣下，臣子怎样事奉君主呢？"孔子回答说："君主应该按照礼的要求去使唤臣子，臣子应该以忠来事奉君主。"

【英译】 The Duke Ting asked how a prince should employ his ministers, and how ministers should serve their prince. Confucius replied, "A prince should employ his minister according to according to the rules of propriety; ministers should serve their prince with faithfulness."

【注释】

[1] 定公：鲁国国君，姓姬，名宋，定是谥号。公元前 509—前 495 年在位。

[2] 忠：理雅格译为"faithfulness"，即"忠诚、诚实"；辜鸿铭译为"loyalty"，即"忠诚的"；刘殿爵将"事君以忠"译为"serve his ruler by doing his utmost"，即"尽心尽力为君主办事"，该译文体现了《论语》中"忠"的"尽己"之义，更加形象严谨。

【原文】 3.20　子曰："《关雎》[1]，乐而不淫[2]，哀而不伤。"

【译文】 孔子说："《关雎》这篇诗，快乐而不放荡，忧愁而不哀伤。"

【英译】 The Master said, "The Kwan Tsu is expressive of enjoyment without being licentious, and of grief without being hurtfully excessive."

【注释】

[1] 关雎：今本《诗经》首篇。此篇写一君子"追求"淑女，思念时

辗转反侧，寤寐思之的忧思，以及结婚时钟鼓乐之琴瑟友之的欢乐。孔子对《关雎》一诗的评价，体现了他的"思无邪"的艺术观。《关雎》是写男女爱情、祝贺婚礼的诗，与"思无邪"本不相干，但孔子却从中认识到"乐而不淫、哀而不伤"的中庸思想，认为无论哀与乐都不可过分，有其可贵的价值。

[2] 淫：过分、失当。理雅格译为"licentious"，即"放肆的"；辜鸿铭译为"sensual"，即"愉悦感官的、肉欲的"；韦利译为"Pleasure not carried to the point of debauch"，即"快乐但没有到放荡的地步"；刘殿爵译为"Wantonness"，即"放纵"。上述译文相较，理雅格、韦利、刘殿爵均强调了"淫"的"放纵、过分"之义；辜鸿铭译本则是将"淫"理解为"肉欲"或"感官欲望"，忽略了"淫"对情感程度的强调。

【原文】3.21　哀公问社[1]于宰我。宰我对曰："夏后氏以松，殷人以柏，周人以栗，曰：使民战栗[2]。"子闻之，曰："成事不说，遂事不谏，既往不咎。"

【译文】鲁哀公问宰我，土地神的神主应该用什么树木，宰我回答："夏朝用松树，商朝用柏树，周朝用栗子树。用栗子树的意思是说：使老百姓战栗。"孔子听到后说："已经做过的事不用提了，已经完成的事不用再去劝阻了，已经过去的事也不必再追究了。"

【英译】The Duke Ai asked Tsai Wo about the altars of the spirits of the land. Tsai Wo replied，"The Hsia sovereign planted the pine tree about them；the men of the Yin planted the cypress；and the men of the Chau planted the chestnut tree，meaning thereby to cause the people to be in awe." When the Master heard it，he said，"Things that are done，it is needless to speak about；things that have had their course，it is needless to remonstrate about；things that are past，it is needless to blame."

【注释】

[1] 社：土地神，祭祀土神的庙也称社。理雅格译为"The spirits of the land"，即"这片土地上的神灵"；辜鸿铭译为"The Titular Genius of the land"，即"这个国家名义上的天才"；刘殿爵译为"The god of earth"，即"大地之神""土神"；韦利译为"The Holy Ground"，即"圣地"。上述英译本中，辜鸿铭译文以"天才"（"Genius"）翻译"神灵"一词，不够精到；韦利将"社神"或"土地神"译为"圣地"，未能体现"社"作为人格神的义素；刘殿爵、理雅格的翻译更为恰当。

[2] 战栗：恐惧，发抖。理雅格译为"cause the people to be in awe"，即"让人们敬畏"；韦利译为"the common people to be in fear and trembling"，即"让普通人恐惧和战栗"；辜鸿铭、刘殿爵则是在"awe"后标注"li"，表明由"栗树"到"战栗"是由于汉语表述相近造成。古时立国都要建立祭土神的庙，选用宜于当地生长的树木做土地神的牌位。宰我回答鲁哀公说，周朝用栗木做社主是为了"使民战栗"。这一说法不当，因而孔子对此加以批评。

【原文】 3.22　子曰："管仲之器小哉！"或曰："管仲俭乎？"曰："管氏有三归[1]，官事不摄，焉得俭？""然则管仲知礼乎？"曰："邦君树塞门[2]，管氏亦树塞门。邦君为两君之好，有反坫[3]，管氏亦有反坫。管氏而知礼，孰不知礼？"

【译文】 孔子说："管仲的器量真是狭小呀！"有人说："管仲节俭吗？"孔子说："他有三处豪华的藏金府库，他家里的管事也是一人一职而不兼任，怎么谈得上节俭呢？"那人又问："那么管仲知礼吗？"孔子回答："国君大门口设立照壁，管仲在大门口也设立照壁。国君同别国国君举行会见时在堂上有放空酒杯的设备，管仲也有这样的设备。如果说管仲知礼，那么还有谁不知礼呢？"

【英译】 The Master said, "Small indeed was the capacity of Kwan

Chung！" Some one said，"Was Kwan Chung parsimonious？" "Kwan，" was the reply，"had the San Kwei，and his officers performed no double duties；how can he be considered parsimonious？" "Then，did Kwan Chung know the rules of propriety？" The Master said，"The princes of States have a screen intercepting the view at their gates. Kwan had likewise a screen at his gate. The princes of States on any friendly meeting between two of them，had a stand on which to place their inverted cups. Kwan had also such a stand. If Kwan knew the rules of propriety，who does not know them？"

【注释】

[1] 三归：有几种不同的说法：1. 根据何晏《集解》引包咸、皇侃《义疏》、邢昺《注疏》等人的说法，古时候称女子出嫁为"归"，管仲娶三个不同姓的女人，所以叫"三归"。2. 朱子《集注》认为三归即三台，指收藏财货的府库，毛奇龄《论语稽求篇》认为此说无依据，不可为训。3. 俞樾《群经评议》驳斥前两种说法，指出于管仲而言当是"三娶"而非"三归"，他认为"三归"指的是三归之家，管仲自朝中归来有三个家可以回去。4. 三处采邑。5. 杨伯峻认为当指向百姓收取的市租。理雅格将"三归"音译为"San Kwei"；辜鸿铭同样采用音义，译为"Sansouci"；刘殿爵译为"three establishments"，管仲拥有"三处府库"或"三处盈利的机构"；韦利则采用第一种说法，将"三归"译为"三娶"，即"three lots of wives"。

[2] 树塞门：树，树立。塞门，在大门口筑的一道短墙，以别内外，相当于屏风、照壁等。理雅格译为"a screen intercepting the view at their gates"，即"一个在门口遮挡视线的屏幕"；辜鸿铭译为"walls built before their palace gates"，即"在宫殿门前建立的影壁"；刘殿爵译为"erect gate-Screens"，即"树立大门的影壁"。

[3] 反坫：古代君主招待别国国君时，放置献过酒的空杯子的土台。理雅格、刘殿爵译为"a stand on which to place their inverted cups"，即"一

个用来放置倒立空杯的支架"；辜鸿铭译为"special buffet"，即"特别的自助"；韦利译为"cup-mounds"，即"杯型土堆"，体现出"反坫"的是土制的特点。上述《论语》英译本相较，刘殿爵、理雅格的版本较为准确。

【原文】3.23　子语鲁大师[1]乐，曰："乐其可知也：始作，翕[2]如也；从[3]之，纯[4]如也，皦[5]如也，绎[6]如也，以成。"

【译文】孔子对鲁国乐官谈论演奏音乐的道理说："奏乐的道理是可以知道的：开始演奏，各种乐器合奏，声音繁美；继续展开下去，悠扬悦耳，音节分明，连续不断，最后完成。"

【英译】The Master instructing the grand music master of Lu said, "How to play music may be known. At the commencement of the piece, all the parts should sound together. As it proceeds, they should be in harmony while severally distinct and flowing without break, and thus on to the conclusion."

【注释】

[1] 大师：大，音 tài 。大师是乐官名。

[2] 翕：合、聚、协调。

[3] 从：放纵、展开。

[4] 纯：美好、和谐，即"harmony"。

[5] 皦：音节分明，即"distinct"。

[6] 绎：连续不断，即"flowing without break"。

【原文】3.24　仪封人[1]请见，曰："君子之至于斯也，吾未尝不得见也。"从者见之。出曰："二三子何患于丧[2]乎？天下之无道也久矣，天将以夫子为木铎[3]。"

【译文】仪这个地方的长官请求见孔子，他说："凡是君子到这里来，我从没有不和他见面的。"孔子的随从学生引他去见了孔子。他出来后（对孔子的学生们）说："你们几位何必为没有官位而发愁呢？天下无道已经很久了，上天将以孔夫子为圣人来号令天下。"

【英译】The border warden at Yi requested to be introduced to the Master，saying，"When men of superior virtue have come to this，I have never been denied the privilege of seeing them." The followers of the sage introduced him，and when he came out from the interview，he said，"My friends，why are you distressed by your master's loss of office？ The kingdom has long been without the principles of truth and right；Heaven is going to use your master as a bell with its wooden tongue."

【注释】

[1] 仪封人：仪为地名，在今河南兰考县境内。封人，系镇守边疆的官。

[2] 丧：失去，这里指失去官职。

[3] 木铎：木舌的铜铃。古代天子发布政令时摇它以召集听众。辜鸿铭译为 "now God is going to make use of your Teacher as a tocsin to awaken the world"，即"现在上天要以孔子作为工具来唤醒世界"，没有具体翻译"木铎"，而是通过意译，直接表述孔子对天下的教化启蒙作用。理雅格、刘殿爵译为 "heaven is going to use your master as a bell with its wooden tongue"，即"上天要把孔子当作钟的木舌用"，这一翻译较为忠实于《论语》原义。韦利译为 "heaven intends to use your Master as a wooden bell"，该本将"木铎"译为 "wooden bell"，即木钟，不符合铜制木舌的形制。

【原文】3.25　子谓《韶》^[1]，"尽美^[2]矣，又尽善^[3]也。"谓《武》^[4]，"尽美矣，未尽善也。"

【译文】孔子评论《韶》乐说："极尽其美了，并且极尽其善。"评论《武》乐说："极尽其美了，但未能极尽其善。"

【英译】The Master said of the Shao that it was perfectly beautiful and also perfectly good. He said of the Wu that it was perfectly beautiful but not perfectly good.

【注释】

[1] 韶：相传是古代歌颂虞舜的一种乐舞。

[2] 美：指乐曲的音调、舞蹈的形式而言。理雅格、刘殿爵、韦利译为"perfectly beautiful"；辜鸿铭译为"The excellence of the physical beauty of harmony"，即"卓越的和谐之美"。

[3] 善：指乐舞的思想内容而言。理雅格、刘殿爵译为"perfectly good"；辜鸿铭译为"The excellence of moral grandeur"，即"卓越的伟大道德"，这一翻译体现出孔子主张艺术作品应对人民群众具有道德教育作用。孔子在这里谈到对艺术的评价问题。他不仅重视艺术的形式美，更强调艺术内容的善和价值导向作用。

[4] 武：相传是歌颂周武王的一种乐舞。

【原文】3.26 子曰："居上不宽，为礼不敬，临丧不哀，吾何以观之哉？"

【译文】孔子说："居于执政地位的人，不能宽厚待人，行礼的时候不严肃，参加丧礼时也不悲哀，这种情况我怎么能看得下去呢？"

【英译】The Master said, "High station filled without indulgent generosity；ceremonies performed without reverence；mourning conducted without sorrow；wherewith should I contemplate such ways？"

里仁篇第四

【原文】 4.1 子曰："里仁为美[1]。择不处仁，焉得知[2]?"

【译文】 孔子说："跟有仁德的人住在一起，才是好的。如果你选择的住处不是跟有仁德的人在一起，怎么能说你是明智的呢?"

【英译】 The Master said，"It is virtuous manners which constitute the excellence of a neighborhood. If a man in selecting a residence do not fix on one where such prevail，how can he be wise?"

【注释】

[1] 里仁为美:《尔雅》云:"里，邑也。"居也，借为动词，里仁指居住在有仁人的地方。郑玄云:"里者，民之所居。居于仁者之里，是为美。求居而不处仁者之里，不得为有知。"皇侃《义疏》曰:"周家去王城百里谓之远郊，远郊内有六乡，六乡中五家为比，五比为间，五间篇族，五族为党，五党为州，五州为乡，百里外至二百里谓之六遂，遂中五家为邻，五邻为里，四里为酂，五那为鄙，五鄙为县，五县为遂。二百里外至王畿五百里之内，并同六遂之制也。仁者，博施济众也。言人居宅必择有仁者之里，所以为美也。里仁为美，则间仁亦美可知也。"邢昺《注疏》云:"里，居也，仁者之所居处，谓之里仁。"理雅格将"美"翻译为"virtuous manners"，即"高尚的举止";辜鸿铭译为"moral life"，即"道德生活";刘殿爵直译为"beautiful"，多指艺术形式上的"美丽、令人愉悦"，没能体现"里仁为美"的美善之义。上述译本相较，理雅格的翻译更为恰当。

[2] 知:同智。此处各家译本均译为"wise"，即"智慧"之义。

【原文】4.2 子曰："不仁者不可以久处约[1]，不可以长处乐。仁者安仁[2]，知者利仁[3]。"

【译文】孔子说："没有仁德的人不能长久地处在贫困中，也不能长久地处在安乐中。仁人是安于仁道的，有智慧的人则是知道仁对自己有利才去行仁的。"

【英译】The Master said，"Those who are without virtue cannot abide long either in a condition of poverty and hardship，or in a condition of enjoyment. The virtuous rest in virtue；the wise desire virtue."

【注释】

[1] 约：穷困、困窘。理雅格译为"poverty and hardship"，即"贫穷与困苦的"；辜鸿铭、韦利译为"adversity"，即"困境"；刘殿爵译为"straitened circumstances"，即"艰苦的环境"。上述译本相较，理雅格译本更为详细地译出了"约"所具有的"穷"和"困"两个义素。

[2] 安仁：安于仁道。理雅格译为"The virtuous rest in virtue"，即"有德者在美德中安居"，辜鸿铭、刘殿爵将"安"译为"at home in"。我们认为，理雅格的翻译较为恰当。

[3] 利仁：认为仁有利自己才去行仁。孔子认为，没有仁德的人不可能长久地处在贫困或安乐之中，否则，他们就会为非作乱或者骄奢淫逸。只有仁者安于仁，智者也会行仁。这种思想是希望人们注意个人的道德操守，在任何环境下都做到矢志不移，保持气节。

【原文】4.3 子曰："唯仁者能好人，能恶人。"

【译文】孔子说："只有那些有仁德的人，才能爱人和厌恶人。"

【英译】The Master said，"It is only the truly virtuous man，who can love，or who can hate，others."

【原文】4.4　子曰："苟志于仁矣，无恶[1]也。"

【译文】孔子说："如果立志于仁，就不会做坏事了。"

【英译】The Master said，"If the will be set on virtue，there will be no practice of wickedness."

【注释】

[1] 恶：有两种解释，第一种，与"善"相对，皇侃《义疏》云："言人若诚能志在于仁，则是为行之胜者，故其余所行皆善无恶行也。"第二种，认为与上一章相接，语义与上一章同，表示厌恶，俞樾《群经平议》即此观点。理雅格译为"wickedness"，辜鸿铭、刘殿爵译为"evil"，均为"邪恶的、不道德的"之义；韦利承接上一章，译为"dislike"，表示厌恶。上一章言："唯仁者，能好人，能恶人。"即是说仁者亦有厌恶之人，若此处"恶"字解作"憎恨、厌恶"，则与上一章矛盾，显然不通。该句主张，只要养成了仁德，那就不会去做坏事，既不会犯上作乱、为非作恶，也不会骄奢淫逸、随心所欲，而是可以做有益于国家、有利于百姓的善事了。

【原文】4.5　子曰："富与贵，是人之所欲也；不以其道得之，不处也。贫与贱，是人之恶也；不以其道得之，不去也。君子去仁，恶乎成名？君子无终食之间[1]违仁，造次[2]必于是，颠沛[3]必于是。"

【译文】孔子说："富裕和显贵是人人都想要得到的，但不用正当的方法得到，就不应去享受；贫穷与低贱是人人都厌恶的，但不用正当的方法去脱离，就不应去摆脱。君子如果离开了仁德，又怎么能叫君子呢？君子没有一顿饭的时间背离仁德的，就是在最紧迫的时刻也必然按照仁德而行，就是在颠沛流离的时候也一定会按照仁德去办事的。"

【英译】The Master said，"Riches and honors are what men desire. If they cannot be obtained in the proper way，they should not be held. Poverty and meanness are what men dislike. If they cannot be avoided in the proper way，they should not be avoided. If a superior man abandon virtue，how can he fulfill the requirements of that name? The superior man does not，even for the space of a single meal，act contrary to virtue. In moments of haste，he cleaves to it. In seasons of danger，he cleaves to it."

【注释】

[1] 终食之间：吃完一顿饭的时间。理雅格译为"The space of a single meal"，刘殿爵译为"as long as it takes to eat a meal"，均是用一餐饭的空隙来比喻时间短暂。

[2] 造次：匆忙、仓促。理雅格、辜鸿铭、刘殿爵、韦利等人均译为"haste"或"hurry"，即"仓促""匆忙"之义。

[3] 颠沛：跌倒在地。韦利直译为"Tottering"，即"蹒跚的、摇摇欲坠的"之义。理雅格译为"In seasons of danger"，即"处在危险中时"；辜鸿铭译为"In moments of danger and peril"，即"在危险的时刻"，两种翻译将"颠沛"引申为遭受挫折陷入困顿、社会动乱不安。上述译本相较，理雅格、辜鸿铭译本的引申义较为忠实地展现了孔子的本意。

【原文】 4.6 子曰："我未见好仁者，恶不仁者。好仁者，无以尚[1]之；恶不仁者，其为仁矣，不使不仁者加乎其身。有能一日用其力于仁矣乎？我未见力不足者。盖有之[2]矣，我未见也。"

【译文】 孔子说："我没有见过爱好仁德的人，也没有见过厌恶不仁的人。爱好仁德的人，是不能再好的了；厌恶不仁的人，在实行仁德的时候，不让不仁德的人影响自己。能有一天把自己的力量用在实行仁德上吗？我还没有看见力量不够的。这种人可能还是有的，但我没见过。"

【英译】 The Master said，"I have not seen a person who loved virtue，or one who hated what was not virtuous. He who loved virtue， would esteem nothing above it. He who hated what is not virtuous，would practice virtue in such a way that he would not allow anything that is not virtuous to approach his person. Is any one able for one day to apply his strength to virtue? I have not seen the case in which his strength would be insufficient. Should there possibly be any such case，I have not seen it."

【注释】

［1］ 尚：胜过、超过。

［2］ 有之：有两种解释，第一种，朱子《集注》云："有之，谓有用力而力不足者。"联系上一句"我未见力不足者"理解。第二种，皇侃《义疏》云："孔子既言无有，复恐为顿诬于世，故追解之。云世中盖亦当有一日行仁者，特是自未尝闻见耳。"应是对"有能一日用其力于仁矣乎"一句的回答，此说更为恰当。理雅格译为"Should there possibly be any such case"，韦利译为"It may well have happened"，上述翻译较为笼统，没有详细点出"有之"所指代的对象。刘殿爵译为"There must be such cases of insufficient strength"，即"一定有力量不足的情况"，该翻译是延续了朱子《四书章句集注》对"有之"的解读。对于代词指称对象造成的歧义，笔者认为在翻译过程中可以采取理雅格、韦利等人的翻译方法，并在注释中阐明中国历代注者对该词的训诂和诠释。

【原文】4.7　子曰："人之过也，各于其党[1]。观过，斯知仁矣。"

【译文】孔子说："一个人的过错，和他的同类人所犯的错误，差不多是相同的。所以考察一个人所犯的错误，就可以知道他是否有仁德。"

【英译】The Master said，"The faults of men are characteristic of the class to which they belong. By observing a man's faults，it may be known that he is virtuous."

【注释】

[1] 党：类别。理雅格译为"the class to which they belong"，即"他们所属的阶级"；刘殿爵译为"type"，即"类型、具有某种类型的人"；韦利译为"every man's faults belong to a set"，即"每个人的错误都从属于一套系统"。此处孔子本意是强调人的过错总与和他相类的一类人所犯错误性质相同，韦利译本没有体现"党"的"同类"之义。该句或译为"A man's faults are always the same as those of his kind"，较为准确。

【原文】 4.8　子曰："朝闻道[1]，夕死可矣。"

【译文】 孔子说："早晨得知了道，就算当天晚上死去也甘心。"

【英译】 The Master said，"If a man in the morning hear the right way，he may die in the evening hear regret."

【注释】

[1] 这句话有多种解释，歧义皆在"闻道"二字上：1."闻道"指听闻真理。朱子《集注》曰："道者，事物当然之理。苟得闻之，则生顺死安，无复遗恨矣。"2."闻道"指闻知天下有道，何晏、皇侃即作此解。皇侃《义疏》云："叹世无道，故言设使朝闻有道，则夕死无恨，故云可矣。"黄式三、程树德皆赞同此说。3.廖名春《〈论语〉"朝闻道，夕死可矣"章新解》认为，"闻道"指达到道、实现理想，"闻"训为"达"。理雅格、韦利、刘殿爵将"道"译为"The way"，辜鸿铭译为"a man has learnt wisdom"，即"一个人已经学到了智慧"。"道"作为中国哲学的重要概念，在海外译介中可音译为"Dao"，并于注释中诠释所在句的"道"的意涵。

【原文】 4.9　子曰："士志于道，而耻恶衣恶食者，未足与议也。"

【译文】 孔子说："士立志于追求道，但又以自己吃穿得不好为耻辱，对这种人是不值得与他谈论道的。"

【英译】The Master said，"A scholar, whose mind is set on truth, and who is ashamed of bad clothes and bad food, is not fit to be discoursed with."

【原文】4.10　子曰："君子之于天下也，无适也，无莫[1]也，义之于比。"

【译文】孔子说："君子对于天下的人和事，没有固定的厚薄亲疏，只是按照义去做。"

【英译】The Master said，"The superior man, in the world, does not set his mind either for anything, or against anything；what is right he will follow."

【注释】

[1] 适、莫：适，借为"敌"字，意为敌对、仇敌。据《释文》，郑玄本即作"敌"，戴氏本亦作"敌"，定州竹简本则作"谪"；莫，据《释文》，郑玄解为贪慕，与"敌"相对。皇侃《义疏》云："范宁曰：'适、莫，犹厚、薄也。'比，亲也。君子与人无有偏颇厚薄，唯仁义是亲。"此说就适、莫的解释与郑玄注相反，但句义相通，亦通。理雅格译为"does not set his mind either for anything, or against anything"，即"他对任何事都不抱好感，也不反对任何事"，可见理雅格是按照皇侃《论语义疏》的解释来翻译该句。韦利将该句译为"A gentleman in his dealings with the world has neither enmities nor affections"，即"君子在与世界打交道时，既没有敌意，也没有感情"，韦利将"适"译为"敌意"，将"莫"译为"热情"，这与郑玄注解释相同。

【原文】4.11　子曰："君子怀[1]德，小人[2]怀土；君子怀刑，小人怀惠。"

【译文】孔子说："君子思虑的是道德，小人思虑的是乡土；君子思虑的是法制，小人思虑的是恩惠。"

【英译】The Master said，"The superior man thinks of virtue；the ordinary man thinks of comfort. The superior man thinks of the sanctions of law；the ordinary man thinks of favors which he may receive."

【注释】

[1] 怀：朱子《集注》解作"思念"，孔安国注、皇侃《义疏》解作"安"。理雅格译为"The superior man thinks of virtue"，即"高尚的人想到美德"；辜鸿铭译为"A wise man regards the moral"，即"智者重视道德"；刘殿爵译为"The gentleman cherishes benign rule"，将"怀"翻译为"珍视的"。上述译本更多倾向朱子之解，将"怀"理解为"安"。韦利译为"Where gentlemen set their hearts upon moral"，即"君子把他们的心安放在道德上"，这一翻译更倾向于孔安国、皇侃之说。

[2] 本句对比"君子"和"小人"不同的人生境界。君子心系天下、胸怀远大，而小人思乡恋土、计较恩惠。但此处的"小人"虽不及君子品行高尚，但表现出来的也无功无过，只是普通百姓的想法和行为罢了。所以，此处若还将"小人"翻译为"a fool""small man"的话，情感语气往往显得过重，我们认为此处译为"ordinary man"或"common people"较为恰当。

【原文】4.12　子曰："放[1]于利而行，多怨[2]。"

【译文】孔子说："凡事都按照利益原则行事，就会招致更多的怨恨。"

【英译】The Master said，"He who acts with a constant view to his own advantage will be much murmured against."

【注释】

[1] 放：同仿，效法，引申为追求。

[2] 怨：别人的怨恨。

【原文】4.13　子曰："能以礼让为国乎？何有^[1]？不能以礼让为国，如礼何^[2]？"

【译文】孔子说："能够用礼让原则来治理国家，那还有什么困难呢？不能用礼让原则来治理国家，那又如何对待礼呢？"

【英译】The Master said, "If a prince is able to govern his kingdom with the complaisance proper to the rules of propriety，what difficulty will he have? If he cannot govern it with that complaisance，what has he to do with the rules of propriety?"

【注释】

[1] 何有：这是春秋时代的常用语，在这里是"有何困难"的意思。黄式三《论语后案》、刘宝楠《论语正义》都说："何有，不难之词。"

[2] 如礼何：在孔子看来，礼并不仅仅是空洞的形式，还必须有礼让的内涵。理雅格译为"If he cannot govern it with that complaisance，what has he to do with the rules of propriety?"即"如果他不能以那种谦恭的态度来管理它，他又与礼仪规则有什么关系呢？"刘殿爵译为"For a man who is unable to govern a state by observing the rites and showing deference，what good can the rites be to him?"即"对于一个人来说，如果他不能通过礼制来治理国家，礼制对他又有什么好处呢？"孔子在这里通过反诘，强调了礼的内涵、礼的态度、礼的情感和思想的重要性，上述译文相比，理雅格的翻译更为贴近《论语》原义。

【原文】4.14　子曰："不患无位^[1]，患所以立。不患莫己知，求为可知也。"

【译文】孔子说："不怕没有官位，就怕自己没有任职的能力。不怕没有人知道自己，只求自己成为有真才实学值得为人们知道的人。"

【英译】The Master said, "A man should say, I am not concerned that I have no place，I am concerned how I may fit myself for one. I am not concerned that I am not known，I seek to be worthy to be known."

【注释】

[1] 位：官位、职位。理雅格译为"place"，即"地点、场所"；辜鸿铭、刘殿爵译为"position"，即"位置、职务、职位"。《论语》此处当指"职位"，辜鸿铭、刘殿爵译本较为准确。

【原文】 4.15　子曰："参乎！吾道一以贯之。"曾子曰："唯。"子出，门人问曰："何谓也？"曾子曰："夫子之道，忠恕[1]而已矣。"

【译文】 孔子说："参啊，我讲的道是由一个基本的思想贯彻始终的。"曾子说："是。"孔子出去之后，同门便问曾子："这是什么意思？"曾子说："老师的道，就是忠恕罢了。"

【英译】 The Master said，"Shan, my doctrine is that of an all-pervading unity." The disciple Tsang replied，"Yes." The Master went out，and the other disciples asked，saying，"What do his words mean?" Tsang said，"The doctrine of our master is to be true to the principles of our nature and the benevolent exercise of them to others，this and nothing more."

【注释】

[1] 忠恕：朱熹《论语集注》释"忠恕"云："尽己之谓忠，推己之谓恕。"其引程子曰："以己及物，仁也；推己及物，恕也。"理雅格将"忠恕"译为"be true to the principles of our nature and the benevolent exercise of them to others"，即"忠实于我们本性中的原则，并将这些原则善意地运用于他人"；辜鸿铭概括为"conscientiousness and charity"两个单词，即"尽责和慈善"；刘殿爵译为"doing one's best and in using oneself as a measure to gauge the likes and dis-likes of others"，即"尽自己最大的努力，并以自己为衡量他人好恶的标准"；韦利概括为"loyalty, consideration"，即"忠诚与体贴"。上述译文相较，理雅格的翻译最为贴近《论语》本意。其实，"尽己"

与"推己"并无实质的差别。"尽己之谓忠",而"忠"实亦是"推其所欲以及于人";"推己之谓恕",而"恕"之"推己"实亦是"尽己"之意。"忠"与"恕"实只一道,故孔子说"吾道一以贯之"。

【原文】4.16 子曰:"君子喻于义,小人喻于利。"[1]

【译文】孔子说:"君子明白大义,小人只知道小利。"

【英译】The Master said, "The mind of the superior man is conversant with righteousness;the mind of the mean man is conversant with gain."

【注释】

[1]"君子喻于义,小人喻于利"是孔子学说中对后世影响较大的一句话,被人们传说。这就明确提出了义利问题。孔子认为,利要服从义,要重义轻利,他的义指服从等级秩序的道德,一味追求个人利益,就会犯上作乱,破坏等级秩序。所以,把追求个人利益的人视为小人。

【原文】4.17 子曰:"见贤思齐焉,见不贤而内自省也。"[1]

【译文】孔子说:"见到贤人,就应该向他学习、看齐,见到不贤的人,就应该自我反省(自己有没有与他相类似的错误)。"

【英译】The Master said, "When we see men of worth, we should think of equaling them;when we see men of a contrary character, we should turn inwards and examine ourselves."

【注释】

[1] 本章谈的是个人道德修养问题。这是修养方法之一,即见贤思齐,见不贤内自省。实际上这就是取别人之长补自己之短,同时又以别人的过失为鉴,不重蹈别人的旧辙,这是一种理性主义的态度,在今天仍不失其精辟之见。

【原文】4.18　子曰："事父母几^[1]谏，谏志不从，又敬不违，劳^[2]而不怨。"

【译文】孔子说："事奉父母，（如果父母有不对的地方）要委婉地劝说他们。自己的意见表达了，见父母心里不愿听从，还是要对他们恭恭敬敬，并不违抗，替他们操劳而不怨恨。"

【英译】The Master said, "In serving his parents, a son may remonstrate with them, but gently；when he sees that they do not incline to follow his advice, he shows an increased degree of reverence, but does not abandon his purpose；and should they punish him, he does not allow himself to murmur."

【注释】

[1] 几：轻微、婉转。理雅格译为"a son may remonstrate with them, but gently"，即"温和地向他们提出忠告"；刘殿爵译为"dissuade them from doing wrong in the gentlest way"，即"用最温和的方式劝阻他们不要做错事"。理雅格、刘殿爵将"几"译为"温和地"。辜鸿铭译为"In serving his parents a son should seldom remonstrate with them"，即"儿子为父母服务时，几乎不向他们提出异议"，"几"被译为"几乎不"。《论语》："子夏问孝，子曰：'色难。'"孔子认为，事父以孝，孝行不是对父母一味地顺从，对父母和颜悦色是最难的。因此理雅格、刘殿爵将"几"翻译成"温和地"较为准确，辜鸿铭此处将"几"翻译为"少""几乎不"，是依据现代汉语习惯进行翻译，违背了《论语》本义。

[2] 劳：辛劳、烦劳。理雅格译为"They punish him, he does not allow himself to murmur"，即"父母惩罚他，他不允许自己抱怨"，理雅格将"劳"译为"惩罚"；辜鸿铭译为"however much trouble they may give him, he should never complain"，即"不管父母给他添多少麻烦，他都不应该抱怨"，"劳"被译为"添麻烦"；刘殿爵译为"you should not complain even if you are distressed"，即"即使你很苦恼，你也不应该抱怨"，"劳"被译为"苦恼、

苦闷"；韦利译为"feel discouraged，but not resentful"，"劳"被译为"气馁"。该句译为"work hard for them without resenting them"，即"为父母操劳而不抱怨"，较为恰当。

【原文】4.19　子曰："父母在，不远游[1]，游必有方[2]。"

【译文】孔子说："父母在世，不出远门；如果不得已要出远门，也必须有一定的去处。"

【英译】The Master said，"While his parents are alive，the son may not go abroad to a distance. If he does go abroad，he must have a fixed place to which he goes."

【注释】

[1] 游：指游学、游官、经商等外出活动。

[2] 方：定、常规、一定的地方。理雅格译为"he must have a fixed place to which he goes"，即"他必须有一个固定的地方去"；辜鸿铭译为"he should let them know where he goes"，即"应该让父母知道自己去了哪里"；刘殿爵译为"your whereabouts should always be known"，即"你的行踪应该一直让父母清楚"；韦利译为"goes only where he has said he was going"，即"告知父母自己要去的地方"。辜鸿铭、韦利、刘殿爵三译本翻译相近，理雅格将"方"译为"固定的地方"，更为忠实《论语》本意。

【原文】4.20　子曰："三年无改于父之道，可谓孝矣。"[1]

【译文】孔子说："能够在父亲去世三年内都不改变父亲定下的行事准则，这样的人可以被称为孝子。"

【英译】The Master said，"If the son for three years does not alter from the way of his father，he may be called filial."

【注释】

[1] 本章内容见于《学而篇》1.11章，此处略。

【原文】4.21　子曰："父母之年，不可不知也。一则以喜，一则以惧。"

【译文】孔子说："父母的年纪，不可不知道，并且常常记在心里。一方面为他们的长寿而高兴，一方面又为他们的衰老而恐惧。"

【英译】The Master said，"The years of parents may by no means not be kept in the memory，as an occasion at once for joy and for fear."

【原文】4.22　子曰："古者言之不出[1]，耻[2]躬[3]之不逮[4]也。"

【译文】孔子说："古代人不轻易把话说出口，因为他们以自己做不到为可耻。"

【英译】The Master said，"The reason why the ancients did not readily give utterance to their words，was that they feared lest their actions should not come up to them."

【注释】

[1] 言之不出：不轻易出言。理雅格译为"not readily give utterance to their words"，即"不轻易说出他们的话"；辜鸿铭译为"Men of old kept silence for fear lest what they said should not come up to what they did"，"言之不出"即"保持沉默"；刘殿爵译为"loath to let their words issue forth"，即"不愿让他们的话传出去"；韦利译为"kept a hold on his words"，即"保持沉默"。孔子赞成"言之不出"一行，是因其一贯主张谨言慎行、不轻易允诺表态，如果做不到，就会失信于人、丧失威信。本章"言之不出"，应理解为"不轻易出言"而非"不愿自己的言论传出"，我们认为理雅格的翻译更为恰当。

[2] 耻：以……为耻。

[3] 躬：自身、自己。

[4] 逮：及、赶上。不逮，意为"做不到"。

【原文】 4.23　子曰："以约[1]失之者鲜矣。"

【译文】 孔子说："因为约束节制自己而犯错的事非常少见。"

【英译】 The Master said，"The cautious seldom err."

【注释】

[1] 约：约束、节制。理雅格此处译为"The cautious"，即"小心谨慎的"，没有翻译出"约束"之义；辜鸿铭译为"He who wants little seldom goes wrong"，即"欲求少的人很少出错"，"约"被理解为"欲求少""约束节制欲望"；刘殿爵译为"It is rare for a man to miss the mark through keeping to essentials"，即"一个人很少因为固守要领而失手"，"约"被译为"固守要领"；韦利译为"Those who err on the side of strictness are few indeed"，即"过分严格而犯错误的人确实很少"，"约"被译为"过分严格"。

【原文】 4.24　子曰："君子欲讷[1]于言而敏[2]于行。"

【译文】 孔子说："君子说话要谨慎，而行动要敏捷。"

【英译】 The Master said，"The superior man wishes to be slow in his speech and earnest in his conduct."

【注释】

[1] 讷：迟钝。这里指说话要谨慎。理雅格、辜鸿铭、刘殿爵译为"slow in speech"，韦利译为"slow in word"，上述英译本均译为"讲话缓慢"。实际上，"讷"虽然是迟钝缓慢之义，但孔子此处是劝勉弟子说话谨慎、三思后行。因此该句译为"A gentleman speaks slowly and carefully"，较为恰当。

[2] 敏：敏捷、快速的意思。理雅格译为"earnest in his conduct"，即"行为认真"；辜鸿铭译为"diligent in conduct"，即"勤奋的行为"；刘殿爵译为"quick in action"，即"行动迅速"。"敏"和"讷"形成对比，"敏"即"迅敏"之义，因此上述译本中，刘殿爵的翻译较为精到。

【原文】4.25　子曰："德不孤，必有邻[1]。"

【译文】孔子说："有道德的人是不会孤立的，一定会有志同道合的人与他相处。"

【英译】The Master said，"Virtue is not left to stand alone. He who practices it will have neighbors."

【注释】

[1] 邻：邻居，引申为伙伴、志同道合的人。

【原文】4.26　子游曰："事君数[1]，斯辱矣；朋友数，斯疏矣。"

【译文】子游说："事奉君主太过烦琐，就会招致侮辱；对待朋友太烦琐，就会被疏远了。"

【英译】Tsze-yu said，"In serving a prince，frequent remonstrances lead to disgrace. Between friends，frequent reproofs make the friendship distant."

【注释】

[1] 数：频繁、烦琐。

公冶长篇第五

【原文】5.1 子谓公冶长[1]，"可妻[2]也。虽在缧绁[3]之中，非其罪也。"以其子妻之。

【译文】孔子评论公冶长说："可以把女儿嫁给他，他虽然被关在牢狱里，但这并不是他的罪过。"于是，孔子就把自己的女儿嫁给了他。

【英译】The Master said of Kung-ye Ch'ang that he might be wived；although he was put in bonds，he had not been guilty of any crime. Accordingly，he gave him his own daughter to wife.

【注释】

[1] 公冶长（前519—前470），复姓公冶，名长，字子芝，山东诸城贾悦镇近贤村人。春秋时期孔子的弟子和女婿，孔门"七十二贤"之一。

[2] 妻：动词，以女嫁人。

[3] 缧绁：捆绑犯人用的绳索，这里借指牢狱。理雅格译为"put in bonds"，刘殿爵译为"In gaol"，辜鸿铭译为"In prison"，韦利译为"suffered imprisonment"，上述译本均为"在牢狱中""被监禁"之意。

【原文】5.2 子谓南容[1]，"邦有道[2]，不废；邦无道，免于刑戮。"以其兄之子妻之。

【译文】孔子评论南容说："国家有道时，他不会被罢免；国家无道时，他也可以免去刑戮。"于是把自己的侄女嫁给了他。

【英译】Of Nan Yung he said that if the country were well governed he would not be out of office，and if it were in governed，he would escape punishment and disgrace. He gave him the daughter of his own elder brother to wife.

【注释】

[1] 南容：姓南宫名适，字子容，孔子的学生，通称他为南容。

[2] 有道：孔子这里所讲的道，是说国家的政治符合最高的和最好的原则。理雅格译为"The country were well governed"，即"国家治理得好"；辜鸿铭译为"order and justice in the government"，即"国家有秩序和正义"；刘殿爵译为"The Way prevailed in the state"，"道"被译为"The Way"；韦利译为"In a country ruled according to the Way"，即"在一个按常理统治的国家"。上述译本相较，辜鸿铭与理雅格的译本较为忠实《论语》原义。

【原文】 5.3　子谓子贱[1]，"君子哉若人[2]！鲁无君子者，斯焉取斯[3]？"

【译文】 孔子评论子贱说："这个人真是个君子呀。如果鲁国没有君子的话，他是从哪里学到这种品德的呢？"

【英译】 The Master said of Tsze-chien，"Of superior virtue indeed is such a man！If there were not virtuous men in Lu，how could this man have acquired this character？"

【注释】

[1] 宓子贱（前521或502—前445），名不齐，字子贱，春秋末年鲁国人，孔门"七十二贤"之一，曾任单父（今山东省菏泽市单县）宰。

[2] 若人：这个，此人。

[3] 斯焉取斯：斯，此。第一个"斯"指子贱，第二个"斯"字指子贱的品德。理雅格译为"how could this man have acquired this character"，即"这个人怎么会有这样的品格呢"；辜鸿铭译为"how that man could have acquired the character he has"，即"那个人是怎么得到他现在的性格"；韦利

译为"how could he have learnt this",即"他如何知道这种道"。上述译本相较,理雅格、辜鸿铭的翻译较为恰当。

【原文】 5.4 子贡问曰:"赐也何如?"子曰:"女,器也。"曰:"何器也?"曰:"瑚琏[1]也。"

【译文】 子贡问孔子:"我这个人怎么样?"孔子说:"你呀,好比一个器具。"子贡又问:"是什么器具呢?"孔子说:"是瑚琏。"

【英译】 Tsze-Kung asked,"What do you say of me,Ts'ze!"The Master said,"You are a utensil.""What utensil?""A gemmed sacrificial utensil."

【注释】

[1] 瑚琏:古代祭祀时盛粮食用的器具。朱子《集注》云:"夏曰瑚,商曰琏,周曰簠簋,皆宗庙盛黍稷之器,而饰以玉,器之贵重而华美者也。"瑚琏是一种竹制缀有玉饰的器皿,用于宗庙祭祀中盛粮食。关于孔子用瑚琏比拟子贡的含义,有几种不同的说法。1.戴望《论语注》云:"喻其材可王左,不当大用。"2.刘宝楠《正义》云:"言女器若瑚琏者,则可荐鬼神,羞王公矣。"3.黄怀信《论语汇校集释》云:"盖言其只能盛黍稷,犹人骂人饭桶,戏辞也。"理雅格译为"A gemmed sacrificial utensil",即"有宝石的祭祀器具";辜鸿铭译为"A rich jewelled work of art",即"华丽的珠宝艺术品";刘殿爵译为"A sacrificial vessel",即"祭祀的容器",并在注释中解释瑚琏是"玉制的";韦利译为"A sacrificial vase of jade",即"用于祭祀的玉质花瓶"。上述译文均体现了瑚琏"饰以玉"且用于祭祀,但没有体现出"宗庙盛黍稷之器",即用于盛放粮食。孔子把子贡比作瑚琏,肯定子贡有一定的才能,因为瑚琏是古代祭器中贵重而华美的一种。但如果与上二章联系起来分析,可见孔子认为子贡还没有达到"君子之器"那样的程度,仅有某一方面的才干。

【原文】5.5　或曰："雍[1]也仁而不佞。"子曰："焉用佞[2]？御人以口给[3]，屡憎于人。不知其仁[4]，焉用佞？"

【译文】有人说："冉雍这个人有仁德但不善辩。"孔子说："何必要能言善辩呢？靠伶牙俐齿和人辩论，常常招致别人的讨厌。冉雍是不是做到仁，我不知道，但何必要能言善辩呢？"

【英译】Some one said，"Yung is truly virtuous，but he is not ready with his tongue." The Master said，"What is the good of being ready with the tongue？ They who encounter men with smartness of speech for the most part procure themselves hatred. I know not whether he be truly virtuous，but why should he show readiness of the tongue？"

【注释】

[1] 雍：姓冉名雍，字仲弓，生于公元前 522 年，孔子的学生。

[2] 佞：能言善辩，有口才。理雅格译为 "not ready with his tongue"，即 "不善于说话"；辜鸿铭译为 "a man of ready wit"，"佞" 即是形容一个人有智慧；刘殿爵译为 "not have a facile tongue"，"佞" 即为 "灵巧的舌头"。

[3] 口给：言语便捷、嘴快话多。理雅格译为 "smartness of speech"，韦利译为 "good talker"，可见上述译本均将 "口给" 理解为 "能言巧辩""善于说话" 的人。

[4] 不知其仁：指有口才者有仁与否不可知。

【原文】5.6　子使漆雕开[1]仕。对曰："吾斯之未能信。"子说[2]。

【译文】孔子让漆雕开去做官。漆雕开回答说："我对做官这件事还没有信心。"孔子听了很高兴。

【英译】The Master was wishing Ch'i-tiao K'ai to enter an official employment. He replied，"I am not yet able to rest in the assurance of this." The Master was pleased.

【注释】

[1] 漆雕开（前 540—前 489），字子开，又字子若，又说作子修，春秋时蔡国人。孔子的学生，漆雕氏之儒的创始人。

[2] 说：同"悦"。

【原文】 5.7　子曰："道不行，乘桴[1]浮于海。从[2]我者，其由与？"子路闻之喜。子曰："由也好勇过我，无所取材[3]。"

【译文】 孔子说："如果我的主张行不通，我就乘上木筏子到海外去。能跟从我的大概只有仲由吧！"子路听到这话很高兴。孔子说："仲由好勇超过了我，这就没有什么可取的了。"

【英译】 The Master said，"My doctrines make no way. I will get upon a raft，and float about on the sea. He that will accompany me will be Yu，I dare say." Tsze-Lu hearing this was glad，upon which The Master said，"Yu is fonder of daring than I am. He does not exercise his judgment upon matters."

【注释】

[1] 桴：用来过河的木筏。理雅格、刘殿爵译为"raft"，即"木筏"；辜鸿铭译为"ship"，即"船"。此处译为 raft 更为恰当。

[2] 从：跟随、随从。

[3] 材：有三种不同的说法：1. 将"材"解作桴材，何晏《集解》云："郑曰：'子路信夫子欲行，故言好勇过我也。无所取材者，言无所取桴材也。子路不解，微言戏之耳。'"2."材"同"哉"，语助词，认为子路除了勇之外，没其他可取之处。何晏《集解》又云："一曰：'子路闻孔子欲乘桴浮海便喜，不复顾望，故夫子叹其勇曰过我，何所复取哉？言惟取于己也。'"古字"材""哉"同耳。3. 说法出自朱熹。朱子《集注》云："材，与裁同，古字借用。桴，筏也。程子曰：'浮海之叹，伤天下之无贤君也。子路勇于义，故谓其能从己，皆假设之言耳。子路以为实然，而喜夫子之与

己，故夫子美其勇，而讥其不能裁度事理，以适于义也。'"理雅格译为"Yu is fonder of daring than I am. He does not exercise his judgment upon matters"，即"由比我更大胆。他对事情不作判断"；辜鸿铭译为"You have certainly more courage than I have；only you do not exercise judgment when using it"，即"你的勇气当然比我大，只是你用勇气的时候没有判断"；刘殿爵译为"Yu is more foolhardy than I. He has not even a supply of timber for his raft"，即"他比我更莽撞，他甚至连做木筏的木料都没有"。刘殿爵的翻译从郑玄的解释；理雅格、辜鸿铭的翻译从程朱的解释："故夫子美其勇，而讥其不能裁度事理，以适于义也。"

【原文】5.8　孟武伯问子路仁乎？子曰："不知也。"又问。子曰："由也，千乘之国，可使治其赋[1]也，不知其仁也。""求也何如？"子曰："求也，千室之邑[2]，百乘之家[3]，可使为之宰也，不知其仁也。""赤[4]也何如？"子曰："赤也，束带立于朝[5]，可使与宾客言也，不知其仁也。"

【译文】孟武伯问孔子："子路做到了仁吧？"孔子说："我不知道。"孟武伯又问。孔子说："仲由嘛，在拥有一千辆兵车的国家里，可以让他管理军事，但我不知道他是不是做到了仁。"孟武伯又问："冉求这个人怎么样？"孔子说："冉求这个人，可以让他在一个有千户人家的公邑或有一百辆兵车的采邑里当总管，但我也不知道他是不是做到了仁。"孟武伯又问："公西赤又怎么样呢？"孔子说："公西赤嘛，可以让他穿着礼服，站在朝廷上，接待贵宾，我也不知道他是不是做到了仁。"

【英译】Mang Wu asked about Tsze-Lu，whether he was perfectly virtuous. The Master said，"I do not know."He asked again，when the Master replied，"In a kingdom of a thousand chariots，Yu might be employed to manage the military levies，but I do not know whether he be perfectly virtuous.""And what do you say of Ch'iu？"The Master replied, "In a city of a thousand families, or a clan of a hundred chariots, Ch'iu might be employed as governor, but I do not know whether he is perfectly virtuous." "What do you say of Ch'ih?" The Master replied, "With his sash girt and standing in a court, Ch'ih might be employed to converse with the visitors and guests, but I do not know whether he is perfectly virtuous."

【注释】

[1] 赋：兵赋，向居民征收的军事费用。理雅格译为"employed to manage the military levies"，将"收缴兵赋"概括译为"治理军队"；辜鸿铭译为"organisation of the army"，即"管理军队"；刘殿爵译为"managing the military levies"，即"管理军队"。

[2] 千室之邑，邑是古代居民的聚居点，大致相当于后来城镇。有一千户人家的大邑。理雅格译为"a city of a thousand families"，即"一千户人家的城市"；辜鸿铭译为"The government of a large town"，即"大城市或小公国"；刘殿爵译为"With a thousand households or in a noble family"。辜鸿铭以"小公国"一以言之，没有突出"千室之邑"的体制大小。上述译本比较，理雅格、刘殿爵译本较为恰当。

[3] 百乘之家：指卿大夫的采地，当时大夫有车百乘，是采地中的较大者。理雅格译为"a clan of a hundred chariots"，即"有一百辆车的军队"；刘殿爵译为"With a hundred chariots"；辜鸿铭将"百乘之家"与"千室之邑"视为同一个问题，没有翻译出二者之间在礼制、等级上的差别。

[4] 公西赤（前509或前519—？），字子华，又称公西华，今河南省濮阳市濮阳县人，孔门"七十二贤"之一，具有杰出的外交能力。

[5] 束带立于朝：指穿着礼服立于朝廷。理雅格译为"with his sash girt and standing in a court"，即"系着腰带站在庭院里"；辜鸿铭简单译为"at court"，即"在朝廷上"；刘殿爵译为"takes his place at court, wearing his sash"，即"系着衣带站在朝堂上"。理雅格将"朝"理解为"庭院"，没有

体现出公西赤从事礼制、外交事务，是站在"朝堂"上。上述译本比较，理雅格、刘殿爵译本较为恰当。

【原文】5.9 子谓子贡曰："女与回也孰愈[1]？"对曰："赐也何敢望回？回也闻一以知十[2]，赐也闻一以知二[3]。"子曰："弗如也；吾与[4]女，弗如也。"

【译文】孔子对子贡说："你和颜回两个相比，谁更好一些呢？"子贡回答说："我怎么敢和颜回相比呢？颜回听到一件事就可以推知十件事，我知道一件事，只能推知两件事。"孔子说："是不如他呀，我同意你说的，是不如他。"

【英译】The Master said to Tsze-Kung, "Which do you consider superior, yourself or Hui?" Tsze-Kung replied, "How dare I compare myself with Hui? Hui hears one point and knows all about a subject；I hear one point, and know a second." The Master said, "You are not equal to him. I grant you, you are not equal to him."

【注释】

[1] 愈：胜过、超过。

[2] 十：指数的全体，旧注云："一，数之数；十，数之终。"理雅格译为"Hui hears one point and knows all about a subject"，即"回听到一点，就知道一个主题的一切"；辜鸿铭译为"When he has learnt one thing he immediately under-stands its application to all cases"，即"当他学会了一件事，他就会立刻明白它在所有情况下的应用"；刘殿爵译为"When he is told one thing he understands ten"，即"告诉他一件事，他就明白十件事"；韦利译为"For Hui has but to hear one part in ten, in order to understand the whole ten"，即"要想了解全部，颜回只需听十分之一的部分"。理雅格与辜鸿铭将"十"理解为"全体、整体"；刘殿爵直译为"十件事"；韦利则将"十"译为"整体"，"一"理解为"十分之一"。上述译本相较，理雅格、辜鸿铭译本较为

恰当。

[3] 二：旧注云："二者，一之对也。"理雅格译为"I hear one point，and know a second"，即"我听到一点，知道另一点"；辜鸿铭译为"When I have learnt one thing I can only follow out its bearing and applications to one or two particular cases"，即"当我学会一件事情时，我只能根据它的意义应用到一两个具体的例子中去"；刘殿爵译为"When I am told one thing I understand only two"，即"别人告诉我一件事，我能明白两件事"；韦利译为"Whereas if I hear one part，I understand no more than two parts"，即"如果我听到一个部分，我能理解两个部分"。上述译本相较，理雅格、辜鸿铭译本较为恰当。

[4] 与：有两种解释。1. 连词，即孔子认为他和子贡都不如颜回；2. 作动词，表示赞同、同意，即孔子赞许子贡能承认自己不如颜回。理雅格译为"I grant you"，即"赞同、同意"之意。刘殿爵译为"Neither of us is as good as he is"，韦利译为"you and I are not equal to him"，刘殿爵与韦利均将"与"理解为连词，即"我和你都不如他"。

【原文】 5.10　宰予昼寝。子曰："朽木不可雕也，粪土[1]之墙不可杇[2]也。于予与何诛[3]？"子曰："始吾于人也，听其言而信其行；今吾于人也，听其言而观其行。于予与改是。"

【译文】 宰予白天睡觉。孔子说："腐朽的木头无法雕刻，粪土垒的墙壁无法粉刷。对于宰予这个人，责备还有什么用呢？"孔子说："起初我对于别人，是听了他说的话便相信了他的行为；现在我对于别人，听了他讲的话还要观察他的行为。在宰予这里，我改变了观察人的方法。"

【英译】 Tsai Yu being asleep during the daytime，The Master said，"Rotten wood cannot be carved；a wall of dirty earth will not receive the trowel. This Yu，what is the use of my reproving him？" The Master said, "At first, my way with men was to hear their words, and give them credit for their conduct. Now my way is to hear their words, and look at their conduct. It is from Yu that I have learned to make this change."

【注释】

[1] 粪土：腐土、脏土。

[2] 杇：抹墙用的抹子。这里指用抹子粉刷墙壁。

[3] 诛：意为责备、批评。

【原文】 5.11 子曰："吾未见刚[1]者。"或对曰："申枨[2]。"子曰："枨也欲，焉得刚？"

【译文】 孔子说："我没有见过刚毅不屈的人。"有人回答说："申枨就是这样的人。"孔子说："申枨这个人欲望太多，怎么能刚毅不屈呢？"

【英译】 The Master said, "I have not seen a firm and unbending man." Some one replied, "There is Shan Ch'ang." "Ch'ang," said the Master, "Is under the influence of his passions; how can he be pronounced firm and unbending?"

【注释】

[1] 刚：刚毅、刚强不屈。理雅格译为"firm and unbending"，即"坚固不屈"；辜鸿铭译为"strong character"，即"坚强的性格"；刘殿爵译为"truly unbending"，即"真正坚定的"；韦利译为"truly steadfast"，即"真正坚定的"。上述译本相较，理雅格的翻译较为恰当。

[2] 申枨：姓申名枨，字周，孔子的学生。

【原文】 5.12 子贡曰："我不欲人之加[1]诸我也，吾亦欲无加诸人。"子曰："赐也，非尔[2]所及也。"

【译文】 子贡说:"我不愿别人强加于我事情,我也不愿强加在别人身上。"孔子说:"赐呀,这就不是你所能做到的了。"

【英译】 Tsze-kung said,"What I do not wish men to do to me,I also wish not to do to men."The Master said,"Ts'ze,you have not attained to that."

【注释】

[1] 加:强加。

[2] 尔:人称代词,你。非尔所及:有两种理解,1.何晏《集解》引孔曰:"非尔所及,言不能止人使不加非义于己也。"即是说人不能阻止别人将非义之事强加在自己身上。2.朱子《集注》云:"子贡言我所不欲人加于我之事,我亦不欲以此加之于人。此仁者之事,不待勉强,故夫子以为非子贡所及。"杨树达《论语疏证》批驳说:"己所不欲,勿施于人,忠恕之道也。行忠恕之道,于才质沉潜者为易,而子贡则高明之才也,故孔子因其自言而姑抑之,亦欲激励之,使其自勉云而。孔子之答问也必因材;子贡有一言终身之问,而夫子以恕教之,亦可证此章之义矣。朱子云:'无加于人为仁,勿施于人未恕,恕则子贡能勉,仁则非所及。'似不免强生分别之病,殆未是也。"理雅格、辜鸿铭译为"you have not attained to that",即"你还没有达到那种境界";刘殿爵译为"That is quite beyond you",即"这不是你能理解的";韦利译为"You have not quite got to that point yet",即"你还没到那个地步"。上述译本均从朱子《集注》的观点。

【原文】 5.13 子贡曰:"夫子之文章[1],可得而闻也;夫子之言性[2]与天道[3],不可得而闻也。"

【译文】 子贡说:"老师讲授的礼、乐、诗、书的知识,我们听得到;老师讲授的人性和天道的理论,我们听不到。"

【英译】 Tsze-kung said,"The Master's personal displays of his principles and ordinary descriptions of them may be heard. His discourses about man's nature，and the way of Heaven，cannot be heard."

【注释】

[1] 文章：有多种说法，1. 何晏《集解》云："章，明也。文采形质著见，可以耳目循也。"邢昺《注疏》类此。2. 皇侃《义疏》云："文章者，六籍也。"3. 朱子《集注》云："文章，德之见乎外者，威仪、文辞皆是也。"4. 戴望《论语注》云："文章，《诗》、《书》、礼、乐。《传》曰：'《诗》《书》义之府，礼乐德之则'。孔子之教人，始于《诗》《书》，终于礼乐，故可得而闻也。"5. 刘宝楠《正义》："据《世家》诸文，夫子文章谓《诗》《书》礼乐也。"理雅格译为"The Master's personal displays of his principles and ordinary descriptions of them"，即"孔子对他的原则的个人展示和对这些原则的普通描述"，"文章"被译为"个人原则"；辜鸿铭译为"The subjects of art and literature"，即"艺术和文学的话题"；刘殿爵译为"accomplishments"，即"成就"；韦利译为"cultural and the outward insignia of goodness"，即"文化和外在的善良"。辜鸿铭强调孔子在艺术文化上的教导，并未翻译出教育的内容是六经；韦利强调孔子在文化和道德上的引导，较近似于朱子《集注》之说；刘殿爵将"文章"理解为孔子在六经校注上的成就，较近似于何晏《论语集解》之说。上述译本相较，辜鸿铭译本较为契合《论语》原义，或译为"The study of the Six Classics and moral cultivation"较为恰当。

[2] 性：人性。《阳货篇》第十七中谈到性。理雅格、刘殿爵、韦利译为"man's nature"，即"人的本性"；辜鸿铭译为"metaphysics"，即"形而上学"。辜鸿铭此处译文不够恰当。

[3] 天道：指自然与人世之间的吉凶祸福关系。《论语》书中孔子多处讲到天和命，但不见有孔子关于天道的言论。理雅格、刘殿爵、韦利译为"the way of Heaven"，即"天道"；辜鸿铭译为"theology"，即"神学"。辜鸿铭此处译文带有西方宗教神学色彩，应从理雅格等人之译。

【原文】5.14　子路有闻，未之能行，唯恐有[1]闻。

【译文】子路在听到一条道理但不能亲自实行的时候，唯恐又听到新的道理。

【英译】When Tsze-Lu heard anything，if he had not yet succeeded in carrying it into practice，he was only afraid lest he should hear something else.

【注释】

[1] 有：通"又"。

【原文】5.15　子贡问曰："孔文子[1]何以谓之'文'也？"子曰："敏而好学，不耻下[2]问，是谓之'文'也。"

【译文】子贡问道："为什么给孔文子一个'文'的谥号呢？"孔子说："他聪敏勤勉而好学，不以向比他地位卑下的人请教为耻，所以给他谥号叫'文'。"

【英译】Tsze-Kung asked，saying，"On what ground did Kung-wan get that title of Wan？"The Master said，"He was of an active nature and yet fond of learning，and he was not ashamed to ask and learn of his inferiors！On these grounds he has been styled Wan."

【注释】

[1] 孔文子：卫国大夫孔圉，"文"是谥号，"子"是尊称。

[2] 下：在己之下的人，朱子与戴望理解为下臣、官位在己之下。钱穆《论语新解》云："以能问于不能，以多问于寡，皆称下问，不专指位与年之高下。"此说更当。吐阿363号墓8/1号写郑本"下"作"夏"，误。理雅格译为"ask and learn of his inferiors"，即"向不如己者请教"；辜鸿铭译为"seek for information from others more ignorant than himself"，即"向比自己更无知的人寻求信息"；刘殿爵译为"seek the advice of those who were beneath him in station"，即"向地位比他低的人征求意见"；韦利译为"pick

up knowledge even from his inferiors"，即"从不如他的人那里学知识"。此处刘殿爵从朱子说，将"下"译为地位低于自己的人，理雅格、韦利则概括为"不如己者"，此种翻译更为恰当。

【原文】5.16 子谓子产[1]，"有君子之道四焉：其行己也恭[2]，其事上也敬[3]，其养民也惠[4]，其使民也义[5]。"

【译文】孔子评论子产说："他有君子的四种道德：自身行为谦恭，事奉君主礼敬，养护百姓有恩惠，役使百姓有法度。"

【英译】The Master said of Tsze-ch'an that he had four of the characteristics of a superior man-in his conduct of himself，he was humble；in serving his superior，he was respectful；in nourishing the people，he was generous；in ordering the people，he was just.

【注释】

[1] 子产：姓公孙名侨，字子产，郑国大夫，做过正卿，是郑穆公的孙子，为春秋时郑国的贤相。本章孔子讲的君子之道，就是为政之道。子产在郑简公、郑定公之时执政 22 年。其时，于晋国当悼公、平公、昭公、顷公、定公五世，于楚国当共王、康王、郏敖、灵王、平王五世，正是两国争强、战乱不息的时候。郑国地处要冲，而周旋于这两大国之间，子产却能不低声下气，也不妄自尊大，使国家得到尊敬和安全，的确是中国古代一位杰出的政治家和外交家。孔子对子产的评价甚高，认为治国安邦就应当具有子产的这四种道德。

[2] 恭：理雅格译为"humble"，即"谦逊的"；辜鸿铭译为"earnest"，即"热心的"；刘殿爵译为"respectful"，即"恭敬的"；韦利译为"courteous"，即"有礼貌的"。上述译本相较，理雅格的翻译较为恰当。

[3] 敬：理雅格译为"respectful"，即"恭敬的"；辜鸿铭译为"serious"，即"严肃的"；刘殿爵译为"reverent"，即"虔诚的"；韦利译为"punctilious"，即"一丝不苟的"。上述译本相较，理雅格的翻译较为恰当。

[4] 惠：理雅格译为"kind"，即"善良的"；辜鸿铭、刘殿爵译为"generous"，即"慷慨的"。上述译本相较，辜鸿铭、刘殿爵的翻译较为恰当。

[5] 义：理雅格、辜鸿铭、刘殿爵、韦利等译本均译为"just"，即"公正的"。

【原文】5.17　子曰："晏平仲[1]善与人交，久而敬之。"

【译文】孔子说："晏平仲善于与人交朋友，相识久了，别人仍然尊敬他。"

【英译】The Master said，"Yen P'ing knew well how to maintain friendly intercourse. The acquaintance might be long，but he showed the same respect as at first."

【注释】

[1] 晏平仲：齐国的贤大夫，名婴。"平"是他的谥号。孔子在这里称赞齐国大夫晏婴，认为他与人为善，能够获得别人对他的尊敬。

【原文】5.18　子曰："臧文仲[1]居蔡[2]，山节藻棁[3]，何如其知也？"

【译文】孔子说："臧文仲藏了一只大龟，藏龟的屋子斗拱雕成山的形状，短柱上画以水草花纹，他这个人怎么能算是有智慧呢？"

【英译】The Master said，"Tsang Wan kept a large tortoise in a house，on the capitals of the pillars of which he had hills made，and with representations of duckweed on the small pillars above the beams supporting the rafters. Of what sort was his wisdom？"

【注释】

[1] 臧文仲：姓臧孙名辰，"文"是他的谥号。因不遵守周礼，被孔子指责为"不仁""不智"。臧文仲不顾周礼的规定，修建了藏龟的大屋子，装

饰成天子宗庙的式样，这在孔子看来就是"越礼"之举了。所以，孔子指责他"不仁""不智"。

[2] 蔡：国君用以占卜的大龟。蔡这个地方产龟，所以把大龟叫作蔡。

[3] 山节藻棁：节，柱上的斗拱。棁，房梁上的短柱。把斗拱雕成山形，在棁上绘以水草花纹。这是古时装饰天子宗庙的做法。理雅格译为"on the capitals of the pillars of which he had hills made，and with representations of duckweed on the small pillars above the beams supporting the rafters"，即"在柱子上刻了小山，在支撑房梁的小柱子上刻了浮萍"；辜鸿铭译为"carvings for a large tortoise"，即"精心雕刻一只大乌龟"；刘殿爵译为"The pillars carved in the shape of hills and the rafter posts painted in a duckweed design"，即"将石柱的柱顶雕刻成山的形状，椽柱则画成浮萍的图案"；韦利译为"The hill pattern on its pillar tops and the duckweed pattern on its king posts"，即"柱子上有山的图案，门柱上有浮萍的图案"。上述译文相较，辜鸿铭译本较为简略，理雅格、韦利、刘殿爵则译出了"山节藻棁"的具体形态。但上述译本均未翻译出"山节藻棁"实际上是古时装饰天子宗庙的仪制，臧文仲僭越礼制这一行为，可以在注释中予以补充。

【原文】5.19　子张问曰："令尹子文[1]三仕为令尹，无喜色；三已[2]之，无愠色。旧令尹之政，必以告新令尹。何如？"子曰："忠矣。"曰："仁[3]矣乎？"曰："未知，焉得仁？"

"崔子[4]弑[5]齐君[6]，陈文子[7]有马十乘，弃而违之。至于他邦，则曰：'犹吾大崔子也。'违之。之一邦，则又曰：'犹吾大夫崔子也。'违之。何如？"子曰："清[8]矣。"曰："仁矣乎？"曰："未知，焉得仁？"

【译文】子张问孔子说："令尹子文多次做楚国宰相，没有显出高兴的样子，几次被免职，也没有显出怨恨的样子。（他每一次被免职）一定把自己的一切政事全部告诉给来接任的新宰相。这个人怎么样？"

孔子说："可算得是忠了。"子张问："算得上仁了吗?"孔子说："不知道。这怎么能算得仁呢?"

子张又问："崔杼杀了他的君主齐庄公之后,陈文子家有四十匹马,全都舍弃不要,离开了齐国,到了另一个国家,他说:'这里的执政者也和我们齐国的大夫崔子差不多。'就离开了。到了另一个国家,又说:'这里的执政者也和我们齐国的大夫崔子差不多。'又离开了。这个人怎么样?"孔子说:"可算得上洁身自好了。"子张说:"可说是仁了吗?"孔子说:"不知道。这怎么能算得仁呢?"

【英译】 Tsze-Chang asked, saying, "The minister Tsze-wan thrice took office, and manifested no joy in his countenance. Thrice he retired from office, and manifested no displeasure. He made it a point to inform the new minister of the way in which he had conducted the government; what do you say of him?" The Master replied. "He was loyal." "Was he perfectly virtuous?" "I do not know. How can he be pronounced perfectly virtuous?"

Tsze-Chang proceeded, "When the officer Ch'ui killed the prince of Ch'i, Ch'an Wan, though he was the owner of forty horses, abandoned them and left the country. Coming to another state, he said, 'They are here like our great officer, Ch'ui,' and left it. He came to a second state, and with the same observation left it also; what do you say of him?" The Master replied, "He was a pure, high-minded man." "Was he perfectly virtuous?" "I do not know. How can he be pronounced perfectly virtuous?"

【注释】

[1] 令尹子文:令尹,楚国的官名,相当于宰相。子文是楚国的著名宰相。

[2] 三已:三,指多次。已,罢免。

[3] 理雅格将"仁"译为"perfectly virtuous",即"（道德上）完全善良的";刘殿爵译为"benevolent",即"仁爱的、仁慈的";辜鸿铭译为"moral character",即"道德品质";韦利译为"good",侧重"善的、好的"。我们认为,此处理雅格的翻译较为恰当。

[4] 崔子:齐国大夫崔杼,曾杀死齐庄公,在当时引起极大反应。

[5] 弑:地位在下的人杀了地位在上的人。

[6] 齐君:即指被崔杼所杀的齐庄公。

[7] 陈文子:陈国的大夫,名须无。

[8] 清:皇侃《义疏》云:"清,清洁也。"朱子《集注》云:"文子洁身去乱,可谓清矣。"理雅格、刘殿爵译为"pure",即"纯洁的";辜鸿铭译为"pure, high-minded man",即"纯洁高尚的人";韦利译为"scrupulous",即"正直的"。据皇侃及朱子说,"清"当为"清高、纯洁"之义,可见理雅格、刘殿爵、辜鸿铭的译本较为忠实《论语》文本。

【原文】5.20 季文子^[1]三思而后行。子闻之,曰:"再斯可矣^[2]。"

【译文】季文子每做一件事都要考虑多次才行动。孔子听到后,说:"考虑两次也就行了。"

【英译】Chi Wan thought thrice, and then acted. When the Master was informed of it, he said, "Twice may do."

【注释】

[1] 季文子:即季孙行父,鲁成公、鲁襄公时任正卿,"文"是他的谥号。

[2] 再斯可矣:第一种认为孔子是称赞季文子,皇侃《义疏》云:"孔子美之,言若如文子之贤,不假三思,唯再思此则可也。"第二种认为孔子贬损季文子,但仍有多种理解,如皇侃《义疏》引季彪曰:"时人称季孙名过其实,故孔子矫之,言季孙行事多阙,许其再思则可矣,无缘乃至三思

也。此盖矫抑之谈耳，非称美之言耳。"又如朱子《集注》引程子曰："为恶之人，未尝知有思，有思则为善矣。然至于再则已审，三则私意起而反惑矣，故夫子讥之。"朱子则曰："季文子虑事如此，可谓详审，而宜无过举矣。而宣公篡立，文子乃不能讨，反为之使齐而纳赂焉，岂非程子所谓私意起而反惑之验欤？是以君子务穷理而贵果断，不徒多思之为尚。"

【原文】5.21　子曰："宁武子[1]，邦有道，则知[2]；邦无道，则愚[3]。其知可及也，其愚不可及也。"

【译文】孔子说："宁武子这个人，当国家有道时，他就显得聪明，当国家无道时，他就装傻。他那种聪明，别人可以做得到，但他那种装傻，别人就做不到了。"

【英译】The Master said, "When good order prevailed in his country, Ning Wu acted the part of a wise man. When his country was in disorder, he acted the part of a stupid man. Others may equal his wisdom, but they cannot equal his stupidity."

【注释】

[1] 宁武子：姓宁名俞，卫国大夫，"武"是他的谥号。

[2] 知：同"智"，智慧、智谋。理雅格译为"wise"，即"智慧的"；辜鸿铭译为"acted as a man of great understanding"，即"表现得很有见地"；刘殿爵译为"Intelligent"，即"聪明的"；韦利译为"wisdom"，即表现出"智慧"。

[3] 愚：这里是装傻的意思。宁武子是一个处世为官有方的大夫。当形势好转，对他有利时，他就充分发挥自己的聪明智慧，为卫国的政治竭力尽忠。当形势恶化，对他不利时，他就退居幕后或处处装傻，以便等待时机。孔子对宁武子的这种做法，基本取赞许的态度。

【原文】5.22　子在陈[1]，曰："归与！归与！吾党之小子[2]狂简[3]，斐然[4]成章，不知所以裁[5]之。"

【译文】孔子在陈国说："回去吧！回去吧！家乡的学生有远大志向，但行为粗率简单；有文采，却还不知道怎样来节制自己。"

【英译】When the Master was in Ch'an，he said，"Let me return！Let me return！My young people at home are ambitious and too hasty. They are accomplished and complete so far，but they do not know how to restrict and shape themselves."

【注释】

[1] 陈：古国名，大约在今河南东部和安徽北部一带。

[2] 吾党之小子：古代以 500 家一为党。吾党意即我的故乡。小子，指孔子在鲁国的学生。理雅格译为 "The little children of my school"，即 "我们学校的学子"；辜鸿铭、刘殿爵译为 "My young people at home"，即 "我家乡的年轻人"。上述译本相较，辜鸿铭等人的翻译更为恰当。

[3] 狂简：志向远大但行为粗率简单。狂：进取；简：大，定州竹简本作 "间"，误。狂简，朱子《集注》解作 "志大而略于事"，皇侃《义疏》、邢昺《注疏》解作志向高远，钱宾四先生引《孟子》："万章问，孔子在陈，曰'盍归乎来，吾党之士狂简，进取不忘其初。'"因而说 "是狂简即谓有志进取"。辜鸿铭译为 "high-spirited and independent"，即 "精神饱满又独立的"；刘殿爵译为 "ambitious"，即 "野心勃勃的"；韦利译为 "headstrong and careless"，即 "任性粗心的"；理雅格译为 "ambitious and too hasty"，即 "野心勃勃但草率行事的"。辜鸿铭译本没有正确理解 "狂简" 之意，刘殿爵仅翻译了 "狂"、忽略了 "简" 的意义，韦利的翻译含贬义，没能翻译出 "狂" 字对青年人志向高远的肯定。上述译本相较，理雅格译本更为忠实《论语》原义。

[4] 斐然：有文采的样子。韦利将该句译为 "They are perfecting themselves in all the showy insignia of culture without any idea how to use them"，即 "他们在各种炫目的文化中不断完善自己，却不知道如何使用它

们"。此处"斐然"用以形容孔子家乡青年人的"文采斐然",韦利此处翻译不够恰当。

[5] 裁：裁剪，节制。吐阿 363 号墓 8/1 写郑本、戴氏本皆作"吾不知所以裁之"，皇本、正平本作"不知所以裁之也"。《史记·孔子世家》亦有"吾"字。裁：剪裁、割正，引申为引导。辜鸿铭译为"have no judgment"，即"没有判断力"；刘殿爵译为"do not know how to prune themselves"，其将"裁"直译为"prune"，即"修剪"；理雅格译为"restrict and shape"，即"限制和约束"。倘若按敦煌本、戴氏本，以及《史记》记载"吾不知所以裁之"，则"裁"的主语应为孔子本人；而各英译本《论语》均为自行补上该句主语，将"吾党之小子"视为"裁"这一行为的发出者。

【原文】5.23　子曰："伯夷、叔齐[1]不念旧恶，怨是用希。"

【译文】孔子说："伯夷、叔齐两个人不记念人家过去的仇恨，怨恨因此也就少了。"

【英译】The Master said, "Po-i and Shu-ch'i did not keep the former wickednesses of men in mind，and hence the resentments directed towards them were few."

【注释】

[1] 伯夷、叔齐：殷朝末年孤竹君的两个儿子。父亲死后，二人互相让位，都逃到周文王那里。周武王起兵伐纣，他们认为这是以臣弑君，是不忠不孝的行为，曾加以拦阻。周灭商统一天下后，他们以吃周朝的粮食为耻，逃进深山中以野草充饥，饿死在首阳山中。

【原文】5.24　子曰："孰谓微生高[1]直？或乞醯[2]焉，乞诸邻而与之。"

【译文】孔子说："谁说微生高这个人直率呢？有人向他讨点醋，（他不说自己没有，）却到邻人家里转讨一点给人。"

【英译】The Master said, "Who says of Weishang Kao that he is upright? One begged some vinegar of him, and he begged it of a neighbor and gave it to the man."

【注释】

[1] 微生高：姓微生名高，鲁国人。当时人认为他为直率。

[2] 醯：醋。

【原文】5.25　子曰："巧言、令色、足恭[1]，左丘明[2]耻之，丘亦耻之。匿怨而友其人[3]，左丘明耻之，丘亦耻之。"

【译文】孔子说："花言巧语，装出好看的脸色，摆出逢迎的姿势，低三下四地过分恭敬，左丘明认为这种人可耻，我也认为可耻。把怨恨装在心里，表面上却装出友好的样子，左丘明认为这种人可耻，我也认为可耻。"

【英译】The Master said, "Fine words, an insinuating appearance, and excessive respect；Tso Ch'iu-ming was ashamed of them. I also am ashamed of them. To conceal resentment against a person，and appear friendly with him；-Tso Ch'iu-ming was ashamed of such conduct. I also am ashamed of it."

【注释】

[1] 足恭：有多重解释。1. 何晏《集解》引孔说云："足恭，便辟貌。"邢昺《注疏》云："便辟其足以为恭……便辟，谓便习盘僻其足以为恭也。"即是说，巧言令色从言语、表情上讨好人，足恭是从双足做出恭敬奉迎的姿势讨好人。2. 邢昺《注疏》云："一曰：足，成也，谓巧言令色以成其恭，取媚于人也。"即是说，巧言令色以成其恭。3. 朱子《集注》云："足，过也。"理雅格译为"excessive respect"，即"过度的尊重"；辜鸿铭译为"studied earnestness"，即"学着认真"；刘殿爵译为"utter servility"，即"绝对的奴性"；韦利译为"a reverence that is only of the feet"，即"对双脚的崇

敬"。上述译本相较，刘殿爵采用意译，理雅格则从朱子说，更为忠实《论语》文本。

[2] 左丘明：姓左丘，名明，鲁国人。是否即是相传为《左传》作者的左丘明仍未有定论，但《左传》作者乃孔子后辈，此处孔子乃是引左丘明以自重，因而左丘明不当是孔子后辈。

[3] 理雅格将该句译为"To conceal resentment against a person，and appear friendly with him"，即"掩饰对某人的怨恨，并对他表现得友好"；辜鸿铭与理雅格翻译相近："To conceal resentment against a person and to make friends with him"；刘殿爵译为"To be friendly towards someone while concealing a sense of grievance"，即"对某人友好，却隐藏着委屈"；韦利译为"Having to conceal one's indignation and keep on friendly terms with the people against whom one feels it"，即"必须隐藏自己的愤怒，并与自己感到愤怒的人保持友好关系"。理雅格、辜鸿铭将"怨"译为"怨恨"，刘殿爵理解为"委屈"，韦利则译为"愤怒"。上述译本相较，理氏翻译更为精到。

【原文】5.26　颜渊、季路侍[1]。子曰："盍各言尔志？"子路曰："愿车马衣轻裘与朋友共敝之而无憾。"颜渊曰："愿无伐[2]善，无施劳[3]。"子路曰："愿闻子之志。"子曰："老者安之，朋友信之，少者怀之。"

【译文】颜渊、子路两人侍立在孔子身边。孔子说："你们何不各自说说自己的志向？"子路说："愿意拿出自己的车马、衣服、皮袍，同我的朋友共同使用，用坏了也不抱怨。"颜渊说："我愿意不夸耀自己的长处，不表白自己的功劳。"子路向孔子说："希望听听您的志向。"孔子说："（我的志向是）让年老的人安心，让朋友们信任我，让年轻的子弟们得到关怀。"

【英译】Yen Yuan and Chi Lu being by his side，The Master said to them，"Come，let each of you tell his wishes." Tsze-Lu said，"I should like，having chariots and horses，and light fur clothes，to share them with my friends，and though they should spoil them，I would not be displeased."Yen Yuan said，"I should like not to boast of my excellence，nor to make a display of my meritorious deeds."Tsze-Lu then said，"I should like，sir，to hear your wishes."The Master said，"They are，in regard to the aged，to give them rest；in regard to friends，to show them sincerity；in regard to the young，to treat them tenderly."

【注释】

[1] 侍：服侍，站在旁边陪着尊贵者叫侍。

[2] 伐：夸耀。理雅格译为"boast of my excellence"，即"吹嘘我的优秀"；辜鸿铭译为"boast of my ability"，即"吹嘘我的能力"；刘殿爵译为"boast of my own goodness"，即"夸耀我的善良"；韦利译为"boast of my good qualities"，即"夸耀我的优秀品质"。此处刘殿爵采用直译法，将"善"译为道德上的善良。但中国哲学中"善"的范畴不仅包含道德判断的"善"，还包涵价值判断的"好"，《论语》此处所"夸耀"的应当是价值维度的"好"，也即理雅格、辜鸿铭等人翻译的"优秀"。

[3] 施劳：施，夸耀；一说为施加。何晏《集解》引孔说云："不以劳事置施他人。"劳，功劳。辜鸿铭将该句译为"be humble in my estimate of what I have done for others"，将"无施劳"理解为"谦虚地估计我为别人所做的事情"；理雅格译为"nor to make a display of my meritorious deeds"，即"不炫耀我的功勋"；刘殿爵译为"impose onerous tasks upon others"，即"把繁重的工作强加于人"。辜鸿铭、理雅格将"施"理解为"夸耀"，刘殿爵则从何晏《集解》说，将"施"翻译为"施加"。

【原文】 5.27 子曰："已矣乎，吾未见能见其过而自讼者也。"

【译文】 孔子说："算了吧，我还没有见过能够看到自己的错误而又能从内心责备自己的人。"

【英译】The Master said，"It is all over. I have not yet seen one who could perceive his faults，and inwardly accuse himself."

【原文】5.28　子曰："十室之邑，必有忠信^[1]如丘者焉，不如丘之好学^[2]也。"

【原文】5.28　子曰："十室之邑，必有忠信[1]如丘者焉，不如丘之好学[2]也。"

【译文】孔子说："即使只有十户人家的小村子，也一定有像我这样讲忠信的人，只是不如我那样好学罢了。"

【英译】The Master said，"In a hamlet of ten families，there may be found one loyal and true as I am，but not so fond of learning."

【注释】

[1]　忠信：韦利译为"loyal and true"，即"忠诚和真实的"；理雅格译为"honorable and sincere"，即"可敬的和真诚的"；辜鸿铭译为"conscientious and honest"，即"严谨的和诚实的"；刘殿爵译为"trustworthy"，即"值得信赖的"。孔子乃至先秦儒家认为，忠信是君子的立身之本，《论语》6次并称"忠信"，即"忠诚信实"之意。上述译本相较，韦利的翻译更为契合《论语》原义。

[2]　孔子坦言自己非常好学，表明他承认自己的德性和才能都是学来的，并不是"生而知之"。

雍也篇第六

【原文】6.1 子曰："雍也可使南面[1]。"

【译文】孔子说："冉雍[2]这个人，可以让他去做官。"

【英译】The Master said，"There is Yung！He might occupy the place of a prince."

【注释】

[1] 古代以面向南为尊位，天子、诸侯和官员听政都是面向南面而坐。本章孔子意为冉雍可以去从政做官治理国家。理雅格译文"occupy the place of a prince"、辜鸿铭译文"made a prince"，均意译为"成为统治者"；刘殿爵、韦利直译为"face south"，即"面向南方"，并在注释中补充解释"南面"的含义。刘殿爵、韦利译本在忠实《论语》文本的基础上，对中国的历史文化典故进行补充说明，这种翻译方式较为全面恰当。

[2] 冉雍（前531—?），字仲弓，春秋末期鲁国人，与冉耕、冉求皆在孔门"十哲"之列，世称"一门三贤"。

【原文】6.2 仲弓问子桑伯子[1]。子曰："可也简[2]。"仲弓曰："居敬[3]而行简，以临[4]其民，不亦不可乎？居简而行简，无乃[5]大[6]简乎？"子曰："雍之言然。"

【译文】仲弓问孔子：子桑伯子这个人怎么样。孔子说："此人还可以，办事简要而不烦琐。"仲弓说："居心恭敬严肃而行事简要，像这样来治理百姓，不是也可以吗？但是居心简单、马马虎虎，又以简要的方法办事，这岂不是太简单了吗?"孔子说:"冉雍，这话你说得对。"

【英译】Chung-kung asked about Tsze-sang Po-Tsze. The Master said, "He may pass. He does not mind small matters." Chung-kung said, "If a man cherish in himself a reverential feeling of the necessity of attention to business, though he may be easy in small matters in his government of the people, that may be allowed. But if he cherish in himself that easy feeling, and also carry it out in his practice, is not such an easymode of procedure excessive?" The Master said, "Yung's words are right."

【注释】

[1] 子桑，即子桑户，又名子桑伯子，鲁人。古代的隐士，与孔子同时，和子舆是朋友，生活崇尚简约。《庄子·大宗师》:"子桑户死，未葬。孔子闻之，使子贡往待事焉。或编曲，或鼓琴，相和而歌曰:'嗟来桑户乎! 嗟来桑户乎! 而已返其真，而我犹为人猗!'"

[2] 简:简要，不烦琐。理雅格译为"He does not mind small matters"，即"不计较小事";辜鸿铭译为"independent"，即"独立的";刘殿爵译为"simplicity of style"，即"简约的行事风格";韦利译为"lax"，即"松弛的、松懈的"。上述译本相较，刘殿爵的翻译更为忠实《论语》原义。

[3] 居敬:持身恭敬，为人严肃认真，严格要求自己。理雅格译为"cherish in himself"，即"珍视自己";辜鸿铭译为"serious with himself"，即"对待自己很严肃";刘殿爵译为"hold oneself in reverence"，即"敬畏自己";韦利译为"scrupulous in his own conduct"，即"对自己的行为谨慎"。我们认为此处辜鸿铭的翻译更为恰当。

[4] 临:面临、面对。此处有"治理"的意思。

[5] 无乃:岂不是。

[6] 大:同"太"。

【原文】6.3　哀公问："弟子孰为好学?"孔子对曰："有颜回者好学，不迁怒[1]，不贰过[2]。不幸短命死矣，今也则亡[3]，未闻好学者也。"

【译文】鲁哀公问孔子："你的学生中谁是最好学的呢?"孔子回答说："有一个叫颜回的学生好学，他从不迁怒于别人，也从不犯同样的过错。不幸短命死了。现在没有那样的人了，没有听说谁是好学的。"

【英译】The Duke Ai asked which of the disciples loved to learn. Confucius replied to him，"There was Yen Hui；he loved to learn. He did not transfer his anger；he did not repeat a fault. Unfortunately，his appointed time was short and he died；and now there is not such another. I have not yet heard of any one who loves to learn as he did."

【注释】

[1] 不迁怒：不把对此人的怒气发泄到彼人身上。

[2] 不贰过："贰"是重复、一再的意思。这是说不犯同样的错误。

[3] 亡：同"无"。

【原文】6.4　子华[1]使于齐，冉子[2]为其母请粟。子曰："与之釜[3]。"请益。曰："与之庾[4]。"冉子与之粟五秉[5]。子曰："赤之适齐也，乘肥马，衣轻裘。吾闻之也：君子周急不继富。"

【译文】子华出使齐国，冉求替他的母亲向孔子请求补助一些谷米。孔子说："给他六斗四升。"冉求请求再增加一些。孔子说："再给他二斗四升。"冉求却给他八十斛。孔子说："公西赤到齐国去，乘坐着肥马，驾着车子，穿着又暖和又轻便的皮袍。我听说过，君子只是周济急需救济的人，而不是周济富人的人。"

【英译】Tsze-hwa being employed on a mission to Ch'i，the disciple Zan requested grain for his mother. The Master said，"Give her a fu." Yen requested more. "Give her a yi，" said the Master. Yen gave her five ping. The Master said，"When Ch'ih was proceeding to Ch'i，he had fat horses to his carriage，and wore light furs. I have heard that a superior man helps the distressed，but does not add to the wealth of the rich."

【注释】

[1] 子华：即公西赤，字子华。

[2] 冉子：冉有，在《论语》书中被孔子弟子称为"子"的只有四五个人，冉有即其中之一。

[3] 釜：古代量名，一釜约等于六斗四升。理雅格、刘殿爵音译为"fu"，辜鸿铭概括为"so much"，韦利将"釜"译为"锅"，即"give her a cauldron full"（给他满满一大锅）。"釜"作为中国古代的量词，其形制容量有准确的规定，此处采取理雅格、刘殿爵的音译法，并在注释中给出"釜"的具体容量，较为恰当。

[4] 庾：古代量名，一庾等于二斗四升。理雅格音译为"yi"，刘殿爵译为"yu"，韦利译为"give her a measure"，即"给她一个量器的量"，此处采取理雅格、刘殿爵的音译法，并在注释中给出"釜"的具体容量，较为恰当。

[5] 秉：古代量名，十六斛。五秉则是八十斛。古代以十斗为斛，所以译为八十石。南宋的贾似道才改为五斗一斛，一石两斛，沿用到民国初年，现今已经废除这一量名。周秦的八十斛合今天的十六石。

【原文】6.5　原思[1]为之宰[2]，与之粟九百，辞。子曰："毋！以与尔邻里乡党[3]乎！"

【译文】原思给孔子家当总管，孔子给他俸米九百，原思推辞不要。孔子说："不要推辞。如果有多的，给你的乡亲们吧。"

【英译】Yuan Sze being made steward of his town by the Master, he gave him nine hundred measures of grain，but Sze declined them.

The Master said，"Do not decline them. May you not give them away in the neighborhoods，hamlets，towns，and villages?"

【注释】

[1] 原思：姓原名宪，字子思，鲁国人。孔子的学生，生于公元前 515 年。孔子在鲁国任司法官的时候，原思曾做他家的总管。

[2] 宰：家宰，管家。理雅格译为 "being made governor of his town"，即 "被任命为他所在城镇的管理者"；辜鸿铭译为 "Was appointed the chief magistrate of a town"，即 "被任命为家乡的管理者"；刘殿爵译为 "steward"，即 "（孔子的）管家"；韦利译为 "Was made a governor"，即 "被任命为统治者"。有史可考，在孔子任大司寇时，原思曾担任孔子的家宰，因此本章刘殿爵的翻译较为忠实《论语》文本。

[3] 邻里乡党：相传古代以五家为邻，25 家为里，12500 家为乡，500 家为党。此处指原思的同乡，或家乡周围的百姓。

【原文】6.6　子谓仲弓，曰："犁牛[1]之子骍且角[2]，虽欲勿用，山川[3]其舍诸?"[4]

【译文】孔子在评论仲弓的时候说："耕牛产下的牛犊长着红色的毛，角也长得整齐端正，人们虽然不想用它作牺牲来祭祀，但是山川之神难道会舍弃它吗?"

【英译】The Master，speaking of Chung-kung，said，"If the calf of a brindled cow has a sorrel coat and well-formed horns，although men may not wish to use it，would the spirits of the mountains and rivers put it aside?"

【注释】

[1] 犁牛：即耕牛。古代祭祀用的牛不能以耕牛代替，耕牛所产的牛犊一般也被认为不配用来祭祀。祭祀用的牛系红毛长角，单独饲养的。

[2] 骍且角：骍，红色。祭祀用的牛，毛色为红，角长得端正。理雅

格译为"be red and homed"，即"红色的且家养的"，该译文没有译出"角"的含义。辜鸿铭概括译为"provided it be well conditioned"，即小牛犊的"条件良好"。刘殿爵译为"have a sorrel coat and well-formed horns"，即"有一层酢浆色的皮毛和形状良好的角"，"sorrel"即"红褐色"。韦利译为"ruddy coated and has grown its horns"，即"红色皮毛并长出了角"。上述译本相较，刘殿爵译本较为忠实《论语》文本。

[3] 山川：山川之神。理雅格、刘殿爵译为"The spirits of the mountains and rivers"，即"山川之灵"。辜鸿铭译为"spirits of the land"，即"土地之灵"。

[4] 寓意像仲弓这样的人才，为什么因为他父亲"下贱"而舍弃不用呢？

【原文】6.7　子曰："回也，其心三月[1]不违仁，其余则日月[2]至焉而已矣。"

【译文】孔子说："颜回这个人，他的心可以在长时间内不离仁德，其余的学生则只能在短时间内做到仁而已。"

【英译】The Master said，"Such was Hui that for three months there would be nothing in his mind contrary to perfect virtue. The others may attain to this on some days or in some months，but nothing more."

【注释】

[1] 三月：指较长的时间，并非实指三个月。理雅格、刘殿爵、韦利译为"three months"，即"三个月"；辜鸿铭译为"months"，泛指"几个月"或较长的一段时间。该处译为"over a longer period of time"较为恰当。

[2] 日月：一日、几日或一月，指较短的时间。理雅格译为"on some days or in some months"，即"在某些日子或某些月"；刘殿爵译为"by fits and starts"，即"断断续续的"。上述译文相较，刘殿爵本采用意译方式，较为精确地译出了"日月"之义。

【原文】6.8　季康子[1]问："仲由可使从政也与？"子曰："由也果[2]，于从政乎何有？"曰："赐也可使政也与？"曰："赐也达[3]，于从政乎何有？"曰："求也可使从政也与？"曰："求也艺[4]，于从政乎何有？"

【译文】季康子问孔子："仲由这个人，可以让他管理国家政事吗？"孔子说："仲由做事果断，对于管理国家政事有什么困难呢？"季康子又问："端木赐这个人，可以让他管理国家政事吗？"孔子说："端木赐通达事理，对于管理政事有什么困难呢？"又问："冉求这个人，可以让他管理国家政事吗？"孔子说："冉求有才能，对于管理国家政事有什么困难呢？"

【英译】Chi K'ang asked about Chung-yu, whether he was fit to be employed as an officer of government. The Master said, "Yu is a man of decision; what difficulty would he find in being an officer of government?" K'ang asked, "Is Ts'ze fit to be employed as an officer of government?" and was answered, "Ts'ze is a man of intelligence; what difficulty would he find in being an officer of government?" And to the same question about Ch'iu the Master gave the same reply, saying, "Ch'iu is a man of various ability."

【注释】

[1] 季康子：他在公元前 492 年继其父为鲁国正卿，此时孔子正在各地游说。8 年以后，孔子返回鲁国，冉求正在帮助季康子推行革新措施。孔子于是对此三人做出了评价。

[2] 果：果断、决断。理雅格、辜鸿铭译为"Yu is a man of decision"，即"有决断力的人"；刘殿爵译为"Yu is resolute"，即"由是坚决的"；韦利译为"You is efficient"，即"很有效率的人"。上述译本相较，刘殿爵的翻译较为忠实《论语》原义。

[3] 达：通达、顺畅。理雅格译为"Ts'ze is a man of intelligence"，即

"有智慧的人";辜鸿铭译为"He is a man of great penetration",即"他是一个很有洞察力的人";刘殿爵译为"Ssu is a man of understanding",即"善解人意的人";韦利译为"He can turn his merits to account",即"他能发挥自己的优点"。"达"此处指"通达事理",辜鸿铭的译本较为准确可靠。

[4] 艺:有才能技艺。理雅格译为"Ch'iu is a man of various ability",即"多才多艺的人";辜鸿铭译为"He is a man of many accomplishments"、刘殿爵译为"Ch'iu is accomplished",即"有很多成就的人";韦利译为"He is versatile",即"他多才多艺"。accomplished 这个词比 versatile 要高一个等级,差不多到了专家的程度,而 versatile 多用来指"能胜任某事"。

【原文】6.9 季氏使闵子骞[1]为费[2]宰。闵子骞曰:"善为我辞焉!如有复我者,则必在汶上[3]矣。"

【译文】季氏派人请闵子骞去做费邑的长官,闵子骞对来请他的人说:"请你好好替我推辞吧!如果再来召我,那我一定逃到汶水那边去了。"

【英译】The chief of the Chi family sent to ask Min Tsze-ch'ien to be governor of Pi. Min Tszech'ien said，"Decline the offer for me politely. If any one come again to me with a second invitation，I shall be obliged to go and live on the banks of the Wan."

【注释】

[1] 闵子(前536—前487),名损,字子骞。春秋时期鲁国人,孔门"十哲"之一。以孝闻名,为"二十四孝"之一。

[2] 费:季氏的封邑,在今山东费县西北一带。

[3] 汶上:汶,水名,即今山东大汶河,当时流经齐、鲁两国之间。在汶上,是说要离开鲁国到齐国去。

【原文】6.10 伯牛[1]有疾,子问之,自牖执其手,曰:"亡之,命矣夫！斯人也有斯疾也！斯人也有斯疾也！"

【译文】伯牛病了，孔子前去探望他，从窗户外面握着他的手说："丧失了这个人，这是命里注定的吧！这样的人竟会得这样的病，这样的人竟会得这样的病！"

【英译】Po-niu being ill，the Master went to ask for him. He took hold of his hand through the window，and said，"It is killing him. It is the appointment of Heaven，alas！That such a man should have such a sickness！That such a man should have such a sickness！"

【注释】

[1] 冉耕（约前544—？），姬姓，冉氏，名耕，字伯牛，鲁国郓城（今山东省菏泽市定陶区冉堌镇）人。孔门"十哲"之一，是孔门四科"德行"科的代表人物之一。

【原文】6.11　子曰："贤哉，回也！一箪[1]食，一瓢饮，在陋巷[2]，人不堪其忧，回也不改其乐。贤哉，回也！"

【译文】孔子说："颜回的品质是多么高尚啊！一箪饭，一瓢水，住在简陋里，别人都忍受不了这种穷困清苦，颜回却没有改变他的乐趣。颜回的品质是多么高尚啊！"

【英译】The Master said，"Admirable indeed was the virtue of Hui！With a single bamboo dish of rice，a single gourd dish of drink，and living in his mean narrow lane，while others could not have endured the distress，he did not allow his joy to be affected by it. Admirable indeed was the virtue of Hui！"

【注释】

[1] 箪：古代盛饭用的竹器。理雅格译为"a single bamboo dish of rice"，即"一份竹制容器的米饭"；辜鸿铭译为"Living on one single meal a day"，即"每天只吃一顿饭"；韦利译为"A handful of rice to eat"，即"吃一

把米饭"。上述译文相较，理雅格的翻译体现了"箪"这一容器的竹制质地，较为精确可靠。

[2] 陋巷：狭小简陋的街巷，此处指颜回的住处。理雅格译为"living in his mean narrow lane"，即"居住在狭窄的巷子里"；辜鸿铭译为"living in the lowest hovels of the city"，即"住在城市最低的破房子里"；韦利译为"living in a mean street"，即"居住在简陋的街道中"。对于"lane"和"street"的区别，"street"是一条大街道，是从一个地方到另一个地方的连接面，贯穿城市之间，街道两旁通常是高楼大厦。"lane"通常比"street"更小或更窄。上述译文相较，理雅格的翻译更为准确。

【原文】 6.12　冉求曰："非不说[1]子之道，力不足也。"子曰："力不足者，中道而废。今女画[2]。"

【译文】 冉求说："我不是不喜欢老师您讲的道，是我的能力不够呀。"孔子说："能力不够是走到半路，走不动而停下来，现在你是自己给自己画了界线不想前进。"

【英译】 Yen Ch'iu said，"It is not that I do not delight in your doctrines，but my strength is insufficient." The Master said，"Those whose strength is insufficient give over in the middle of the way but now you limit yourself."

【注释】

[1] 说：同"悦"。

[2] 画：画定界线，停止前进。理雅格译为"limit yourself"，即"限制自己"；辜鸿铭译为"who only want the necessary strength，show it when they are on the way. But you—you stick at it from the outset altogether"，即"孔子回答说：'那些只需要必要的力量的人，在路上表现出来。但你从一开始就坚持了下来。'"刘殿爵译为"In your case you set the limits beforehand"，即"你事先设定了限制"；韦利译为"but you deliberately draw the line"，即"但

你故意划清界限"。理雅格、刘殿爵将"画"意译为"limit",韦利则直译为"draw the line",此处韦利的翻译更为直接,便于读者理解"画"的含义。

【原文】 6.13 子谓子夏曰:"女为君子儒[1]!无为小人儒[2]!"

【译文】 孔子对子夏说:"你要做君子式的儒者,不要做小人式的儒者。"

【英译】 The Master said to Tsze-hsia,"Do you be a scholar after the style of the superior man,and not after that of the mean man."

【注释】

[1] 君子儒:理雅格译为"The superior man";辜鸿铭译为"a good and wise man";刘殿爵译为"gentleman ju",并在注释中解释"ju":"The original meaning of the words uncertain,but it probably referred to men for whom the qualities of the scholar were more important than those of the warrior. In subsequent ages,ju came to be the name given to the Confucianists."在后来的时代里,"儒"逐渐成为对儒者的称呼;韦利译为"The ru of gentlemen"。刘殿爵、韦利均采用音译来处理"儒",并在注释中解释"儒"的含义,该法较为可取。

[2] 小人儒:理雅格译为"The mean man";辜鸿铭译为"a fool",即"傻瓜";刘殿爵译为"a petty ju";韦利译为"The ru of the common people"。在本章中,孔子提出了"君子儒"和"小人儒"的区别,要求子夏做君子儒,不要做小人儒。"君子儒"是指地位高贵、通晓礼法,具有理想人格的人;"小人儒"则指地位低贱,不通礼仪,品格平庸的人。辜鸿铭译为"fool"、韦利译为"the common people",没有体现出"小人儒"在道德品行上的鄙陋。

【原文】 6.14 子游为武城[1]宰。子曰:"女得人焉耳乎?"曰:"有澹台灭明[2]者,行不由径[3],非公事,未尝至于偃[4]之室也。"

【译文】子游做了武城的长官。孔子说："你在那里得到了人才没有？"子游回答说："有一个叫澹台灭明的人，从来不走邪路，没有公事从不到我屋子里来。"

【英译】Tsze-yu being governor of Wu-ch'ang，The Master said to him，"Have you got good men there？"He answered，"There is Tan-t'ai Miehming，who never in walking takes a short cut，and never comes to my office，excepting on public business."

【注释】

[1] 武城：鲁国的小城邑，在今山东费县境内。

[2] 澹台灭明（前512—？），复姓澹台，名灭明，字子羽，春秋时期鲁国武城（今属山东临沂市平邑县南武城）人，孔门"七十二贤"之一。后来，澹台灭明往南游学到吴地，跟从他学习的有三百多人，他有一套教学管理制度，影响甚大，是当时儒家在南方的一个有影响的学派。

[3] 径：小路，引申为捷径。理雅格、刘殿爵译为"walking takes a short cut"，即"抄近路"；辜鸿铭译为"never act upon expediency"，即"永远不要凭权宜之计行事"；韦利译为"walks on no by paths"，即"在小路上行走"。辜鸿铭采用意译，但《论语》此处"径"指的是"捷径"而非"权宜之计"，应理解为"抄近路""走捷径"，采取投机取巧的方法，辜鸿铭理解为事到临头权衡之下所不得不采用的办法，不够恰当。

[4] 偃：言偃，即子游，这是他自称其名。

【原文】6.15 子曰："孟之反[1]不伐，奔[2]而殿[3]，将入门，策其马，曰：'非敢后也，马不进也。'[4]"

【译文】孔子说："孟之反不喜欢夸耀自己。败退的时候，他留在最后掩护全军。快进城门的时候，他鞭打着自己的马说：'不是我敢于殿后，是马跑得不快。'"

【英译】The Master said，"Mang Chih-fan does not boast of his

merit. Being in the rear on an occasion of flight，when they were about to enter the gate，he whipped up his horse，saying，'It is not that I dare to be last. My horse would not advance.'"

【注释】

[1] 孟之反：名侧，鲁国大夫。

[2] 奔：败走。

[3] 殿：殿后，在全军最后作掩护。

[4] 公元前484年，鲁国与齐国打仗。鲁国右翼军败退的时候，孟之反在最后掩护败退的鲁军。对此，孔子给予了高度评价，宣扬他提出的"功不独居，过不推诿"的学说，认为这是人的美德之一。

【原文】 6.16　子曰："不有祝鮀^[1]之佞，而有宋朝^[2]之美，难乎免于今之世矣。"

【译文】 孔子说："如果没有祝鮀那样的口才，而只有宋朝的美貌，那在今天的社会上处世立足就比较艰难了。"

【英译】 The Master said，"Without the specious speech of the litanist T'o and the beauty of the prince Chao of Sung，it is difficult to escape in the present age."

【注释】

[1] 祝鮀：字子鱼，卫国大夫，有口才，以能言善辩受到卫灵公重用。

[2] 宋朝：宋国的公子朝，以容貌美著称，《左传》中曾记载他因美貌而惹起乱的事情。理雅格、韦利译为"The prince Chao of Sung"，辜鸿铭将"宋朝"译为"That noble lord (the Lord Chesterfield of the time)"，即"那位高贵的勋爵（当时的切斯特菲尔德勋爵）"；刘殿爵以人名形式译为"Sung Chao"。"宋朝"指的是宋国的公子朝，即宋国的一名王子，并非人名即为"宋朝"，因此理雅格、韦利二人的翻译较为准确。

【原文】6.17　子曰："谁能出不由户？何莫由斯道也？"[1]

【译文】孔子说："谁能不经过屋门而走出屋外呢？为什么没有人从我所指出的这条道路行走呢？"

【英译】The Master said，"Who can go out but by the door？How is it that men will not walk according to these ways？"

【注释】

[1] 寓指孔子宣扬的"德治""仁政"在当时不被重视，他的内心感到很不理解，所以发出这样的疑问。

【原文】6.18　子曰："质[1]胜文[2]则野[3]，文胜质则史[4]。文质彬彬[5]，然后君子。"

【译文】孔子说："质朴多于文采，就会流于粗野；文采多于质朴，就流于虚伪、浮夸。只有质朴和文采配合恰当，才是君子。"

【英译】The Master said，"Where the solid qualities are in excess of accomplishments，we have rusticity；where the accomplishments are in excess of the solid qualities，we have the manners of a clerk. When the accomplishments and solid qualities are equally blended，we then have the man of virtue."

【注释】

[1] 质：朴实、自然，无修饰的。理雅格译为"solid qualities"，即"坚毅的品格"；辜鸿铭将"质"理解为人的本质，即"natural qualities"；刘殿爵译为"preponderance of native substance"，即"原生物质的优势"。"质"在这里形容朴实无华、自然无修饰，刘殿爵的翻译较为忠实《论语》原义，或译为"Unpretentious"（形容词"朴实无华的"）较为恰当。

[2] 文：文采，经过修饰的。理雅格译为"accomplishments"，即"才艺"；辜鸿铭译为"the results of education"，即"受教育的结果"；刘殿爵译为"acquired refinement"，即"后天的教养"。辜鸿铭将"人的本质"与"后

天教育"对立，刘殿爵则是将"原生状态"和"后天陶养"对立，上述两种翻译体现了"文"的"经过修饰"义，但没有翻译出"文采"之本义。

[3] 野：此处指粗鲁、鄙野，缺乏文采。理雅格译为"rusticity"，即"乡土气的"；辜鸿铭译为"rude"，即"粗鲁的"；刘殿爵译为"churlishness"，即"粗暴无礼的"。"rude"指（对人）粗鲁无礼的，侧重于（以描述谈吐）粗俗的，下流的；"churlish"则是以缺乏礼仪或不够优雅为特征。《论语》此处更多强调的是行为没有礼节，因此刘殿爵本译为"churlishness"更为恰当。

[4] 史：言词华丽，这里有虚伪、浮夸的意思。理雅格译为"We have the manners of a clerk"；辜鸿铭译为"literati"，即"有文化的人"，没有译出《论语》此处的贬义；刘殿爵、韦利译为"pedantry"，即"迂腐的"。理雅格此处采用比喻，将"史"译为"小职员的行为作风"，这一翻译不够清晰，刘殿爵译为"迂腐的"，则没能体现出"史"的"言辞过分华丽"之义。

[5] 彬彬：指文与质的配合很恰当。理雅格译为"The accomplishments and solid qualities are equally blended"；辜鸿铭译为"The natural qualities and the results of education are properly blended"，即"自然素质和教育成果得到了很好的融合"。

【原文】6.19　子曰："人之生也直，罔[1]之生也幸而免。"

【译文】孔子说："一个人的生存是由于正直，而不正直的人也能生存，那只他侥幸地避免了灾祸。"

【英译】The Master said，"Man is born for uprightness. If a man lose his uprightness，and yet live，his escape from death is the effect of mere good fortune."

【注释】

[1] 罔：诬罔，指不正直的人。

【原文】6.20　子曰："知之^[1]者不如好之者，好之者不如乐之者。"

【译文】孔子说："懂得它的人，不如爱好它的人；爱好它的人，又不如以它为乐的人。"

【英译】The Master said，"They who know the truth are not equal to those who love it，and they who love it are not equal to those who delight in it."

【注释】

[1] 孔子在这里没有具体指懂得什么，"之"表示泛指，包括学问、技艺等。理雅格、刘殿爵、辜鸿铭、韦利等译本此处也是用"It"指代。

【原文】6.21　子曰："中人以上，可以语上^[1]也；中人以下，不可以语上也。"

【译文】孔子说："具有中等以上才智的人，可以给他讲授高深的学问，在中等水平以下的人，不可以给他讲高深的学问。"

【英译】The Master said，"To those whose talents are above mediocrity，the highest subjects may be announced. To those who are below mediocrity，the highest subjects may not be announced."

【注释】

[1] 上：上等的知识，高深的学问。何晏《集解》引王肃说："上，谓上智之所知也。"理雅格译为"the highest subjects"，即"最高的科目"；辜鸿铭译为"high things"，即"崇高的事情"；刘殿爵译为"the best"，即"最好的"；韦利译为"Things higher"，即"更高的事情"。上述译本比较，理雅格、辜鸿铭、韦利采用直译，将"上"译为"high"；但上述译本均未译出"上"指的是"学问""知识"，笔者认为译为"Superior learning"更为恰当。

【原文】6.22　樊迟问知^[1]。子曰："务^[2]民之义^[3]，敬鬼神而

远之，可谓知矣。"问仁。曰："仁者先难而后获^[4]，可谓仁矣。"

【译文】樊迟问孔子怎样才算是智，孔子说："专心致力于倡导老百姓应该遵从的道德，尊敬鬼神但要远离它，就可以说是智了。"樊迟又问怎样才是仁，孔子说："有仁德的人要先受一些劳苦然后收获成功，得到百姓的拥戴，这可以说是仁了。"

【英译】Fan Ch'ih asked what constituted wisdom. The Master said, "To give one's self earnestly to the duties due to men, and, while respecting spiritual beings, to keep aloof from them, may be called wisdom." He asked about perfect virtue. The Master said, "The man of virtue makes the difficulty to be overcome his first business, and success only a subsequent consideration; this may be called perfect virtue."

【注释】

[1] 知：同"智"。理雅格、刘殿爵、韦利译为"wisdom"，辜鸿铭译为"understanding"。"understanding"强调"理解""知道"，"wisdom"则侧重"智慧""才智"。辜鸿铭译本没能译出"知"同"智"的含义，而是把"知"翻译成了"知道""理解"，曲解了《论语》本义。

[2] 务：从事、致力于。

[3] 义：专用力于人道之所宜。理雅格译为"To give one's self earnestly to the duties due to men"，"义"在此处被翻译为"义务"；辜鸿铭译为"To know the essential duties of man living in a society of men"，即"知道生活在人类社会中的人的基本职责"；刘殿爵译为"To work for the things the common people have a right to"，即"为普通人有权得到的东西而工作"，"义"在此处被翻译为"权利"。实际上，中国哲学话语体系中的"义"，其内涵不能简单理解为"义务"或"权利"，作为五常之一的"义"是一种道德，是道德规约下人们"应当"去做的事。此处译为"To devote themselves to promoting the morality that ordinary people should follow"较为恰当

[4] 难：受劳苦。先难而后获：孔安国云："先劳苦而后得功，此所以为仁。"戴望《论语注》云："仁者先勤众事，后乃定贡赋，得民之奉，若尧、禹治水，成汤救旱，皆仁及天下也。"理雅格译为"The man of virtue makes the difficulty to be overcome his first business，and success only a subsequent consideration"，即"首先要克服困难，然后再考虑成功"；辜鸿铭译为"A man who wants to live a moral life must first be conscious within himself of a difficulty and has struggled to overcome the difficulty"，即"首先必须意识到自己有困难，并努力克服困难"；刘殿爵译为"The benevolent man reaps the benefit only after encountering difficulties"，即"仁慈的人只有在遇到困难后才会得到好处"。上述译本相较，辜鸿铭没有翻译出"后获"的意义，理雅格本此处翻译较为恰当。

【原文】6.23　子曰："知者乐水，仁者乐山。知者动，仁者静。知者乐，仁者寿。"[1]

【译文】孔子说："聪明人喜爱水，有仁德者喜爱山；聪明人活动，仁德者沉静。聪明人快乐，有仁德者长寿。"

【英译】The Master said，"The wise find pleasure in water；the virtuous find pleasure in hills. The wise are active；the virtuous are tranquil. The wise are joyful；the virtuous are long-lived."

【注释】

[1] 邢昺《注疏》云："此章初明知、仁之性，次明知、仁之用，三明知、仁之功也。'知者乐水'者，乐，谓爱好。言知者性好运其才知以治世，如水流而不知已止也。'仁者乐山'者，言仁者之性好乐如山之安固，自然不动，而万物生焉。'知者动'者，言知者常务进故动。'仁者静'者，言仁者本无贪欲，故静。'知者乐'者，言知者役用才知，成功得志故欢乐也。'仁者寿'者，言仁者少思寡欲，性常安静，故多寿考也。"

【原文】6.24　子曰："齐一变，至于鲁；鲁一变，至于道[1]。"

【译文】孔子说："齐国一改变，可以达到鲁国的样子，鲁国一改变，就可以达到先王之道了。"

【英译】The Master said, "Ch'i, by one change, would come to the State of Lu. Lu, by one change, would come to a State where true principles predominated."

【注释】

[1] 道：何晏《集解》云："包曰：'言齐、鲁有太公、周公之余化，太公大贤，周公圣人，今其政教虽衰，若有明君兴之，齐可使如鲁，鲁可使如大道行之时。'"朱子《集注》云："孔子之时，齐俗急功利，喜夸诈，乃霸政之余习。鲁则重礼教，崇信义，犹有先王之遗风焉，但人亡政息，不能无废坠尔。道，则先王之道也。言二国之政俗有美恶，故其变而之道有难易。"理雅格译为"True principles"，即"真正有原则"的国家；辜鸿铭译为"perfect government"，即"完美的政府"，该翻译没能体现"道"的含义；刘殿爵、韦利将"道"直译为"The Way"。本章里，孔子提出了"道"的范畴。此处所讲的"道"是治国安邦的最高原则，即"先王之道"。在春秋时期，齐国的经济发展较早，而且实行了一些改革，成为当时最富强的诸侯国家。与齐国相比，鲁国经济的发展比较缓慢，但意识形态和上层建筑保存得比较完备，所以孔子说，齐国改变就达到了鲁国的样子，而鲁国再一改变，就达到了先王之道。此处理雅格的翻译较为忠实孔子本意。

【原文】6.25　子曰："觚[1]不觚，觚哉！觚哉！"

【译文】孔子说："觚不像个觚了，这也算是觚吗？这也算是觚吗？"

【英译】The Master said, "A cornered vessel without corners-a strange cornered vessel! A strange cornered vessel!"

【注释】

[1] 觚：古代盛酒的器具，上圆下方，有棱，容量约有二升。后来觚

被改变了，所以孔子认为觚不像觚。辜鸿铭译为"goblet"，即"高脚杯"；理雅格译为"cornered vessel"，即"有角的容器"，体现出了"觚"的形制是有棱角的；刘殿爵音译为"ku"，并在注释中解释为"a drinking vessel with a regulation capacity"，即"具有固定形制的饮水容器"；韦利译为"horn gourd"，即"角葫芦"。上述译本相较，刘殿爵的处理方式较为恰当。

【原文】6.26　宰我问曰："仁者，虽告之曰，'井有仁焉。'其从之也？"子曰："何为其然也？君子可逝[1]也，不可陷[2]也；可欺也，不可罔[3]也。"

【译文】宰我问道："对于有仁德的人，别人告诉他井里掉下去一位仁人啦，他会跟着下去吗？"孔子说："为什么要这样做呢？君子可以到井边去救，却不可以陷入井中；君子可能被欺骗，但不可以糊涂。"

【英译】Tsai Wo asked, saying, "A benevolent man, though it be told him, 'There is a man in the well' will go in after him, I suppose." Confucius said, "Why should he do so? A superior man may be made to go to the well, but he cannot be made to go down into it. He may be imposed upon, but he cannot be fooled."

【注释】

[1] 逝：往。这里指到井边去看并设法救之。理雅格译为"A superior man may be made to go to the well"；刘殿爵译为"A gentleman can be sent there"，即"被派到现场"；辜鸿铭译为"A good and wise man might be led to hurry to the scene"，即"快速到达现场"。

[2] 陷：陷入井中。

[3] 罔：迷惑。理雅格译为"He may be imposed upon, but he cannot be fooled"，辜鸿铭译为"He could be imposed upon, but not made a fool of"，即"他可能会被欺骗，但不会被愚弄"，两英译本均将"罔"译为"愚弄"；刘殿爵译为"He can be deceived, but cannot be duped"，"罔"被译为"be

duped"，即"被欺骗、被欺诈"。"deceive"突出欺骗、蒙骗一个人，让对方相信一件原本虚假的事情是真实的；"dupe"则暗示受骗的人既无辜也很愚蠢，含贬义。上述译本相较，理雅格的翻译较为恰当。

【原文】6.27　子曰："君子博学于文，约之以礼，亦可以弗畔[1]矣夫！"

【译文】孔子说："君子广泛地学习古代的文化典籍，又以礼来约束自己，也就可以不离经叛道了。"

【英译】The Master said, "The superior man, extensively studying all learning, and keeping himself under the restraint of the rules of propriety, may thus likewise not overstep what is right."

【注释】

[1] 畔：同"叛"，指离经叛道。理雅格译为"may thus likewise not overstep what is right"，即"这样就可以不越界"；辜鸿铭译为"Is not likely to get into a wrong track"，即"不太可能误入歧途"；刘殿爵译为"be relied upon not to turn against what he stood for"，即"（其他人）不会背叛（博学约礼者）的主张"；韦利译为"Is not likely, I think, to go far wrong"，即"不会犯太多错误"。刘殿爵认为，"畔"指的是他人不会背叛君子，而不是君子不会背叛道义，该翻译有误。理雅格、辜鸿铭将"畔"翻译为"越界""误入歧途"，该翻译较为合理。

【原文】6.28　子见南子[1]，子路不说[2]。夫子矢[3]之曰："予所否者，天厌之！天厌之！"

【译文】孔子去见南子，子路不高兴。孔子发誓说："如果我做什么不正当的事，让上天谴责我吧！让上天谴责我吧！"

【英译】The Master having visited Nan-Tsze, Tsze-Lu was displeased, on which the Master swore, saying, "Wherein I have done improperly，may Heaven reject me，may Heaven reject me！"

【注释】

[1] 南子：卫国灵公的夫人，当时实际上左右着卫国政权，有淫乱的行为。

[2] 说：同"悦"。

[3] 矢：同"誓"，发誓。

【原文】 6.29　子曰："中庸[1]之为德也，甚至矣乎！民鲜久矣。"

【译文】 孔子说："中庸作为一种道德，该是最高的了吧！人们缺少这种道德已经很久了。"

【英译】 The Master said，"Perfect is the virtue which is according to the golden mean！Rare for a long time has been its practice among the people."

【注释】

[1] 中庸：孔子提出的道德准则。何晏《集解》云："庸，常也。中和可常行之德。"朱子《集注》云："中者，无过无不及之名也。庸，平常也……程子曰：'不偏之谓中，不易之谓庸。中者天下之正道，庸者天下之定理。自世教衰，民不兴于行，少有此德久矣。'"理雅格译为"The Constant Mean"；辜鸿铭译为"well balanced and kept in perfect equilibrium"，其将"中庸"译为形容词，即"良好的平衡，保持完美的平衡"；刘殿爵译为"supreme indeed"，即"最高的美德"；韦利译为"The moral power of the Middle Use"，即"中间的道德力量"。中庸属于道德行为的评价问题，也是一种德行，而且是最高的德行。不偏不倚谓之中，平常谓庸。中庸就是不偏不倚的平常的道理，使双方保持均衡状态。笔者认为，"中庸之道"译为"golden mean"较为恰当。

【原文】 6.30 子贡曰："如有博施于民而能济众，何如？可谓仁乎？"子曰："何事于仁[1]！必也圣乎！尧舜其犹病诸！夫仁者，己欲立而立人，己欲达而达人[2]。能近取譬[3]，可谓仁之方也已。"

【译文】 子贡说："假若有一个人，他能给老百姓很多好处又能周济大众，怎么样？可以算是仁人了吗？"孔子说："岂止是仁人，简直是圣人了！就连尧、舜尚且难以做到。至于仁人，就是要想自己站得住，也要帮助人家一同站得住；要想自己过得好，也要帮助人家一同过得好。凡事能就近以自己作对比，而推己及人，可以说就是实行仁道的方法了。"

【英译】 Tsze-Kung said，"Suppose the case of a man extensively conferring benefits on the people，and able to assist all，what would you say of him？Might he be called perfectly virtuous？"The Master said，"Why speak only of virtue in connection with him？Must he not have the qualities of a sage？Even Yao and Shun were still solicitous about this. Now the man of perfect virtue，wishing to be established himself，seeks also to establish others；wishing to be enlarged himself，he seeks also to enlarge others. To be able to judge of others by what is nigh in ourselves；-this may be called the art of virtue."

【注释】

[1] 何事于仁：何止是仁。邢昺《注疏》云："言君能博施济众，何止事于仁！谓不啻于仁，必也为圣人乎！"又朱子《集注》："言此何止于仁，必也圣人能之乎！"

[2] 己欲立而立人，己欲达而达人：理雅格译为"Wishing to be established himself，seeks also to establish others；wishing to be enlarged himself，he seeks also to enlarge others"；辜鸿铭译为"A moral man in forming his character forms the character of others；in enlightening himself be enlightens others"，"立"即"形成品格"，"达"即"照亮"；刘殿爵译为"a benevolent

man helps others to take their stand in that he himself wishes to take his stand，and gets others there in that he himself wishes to get there"，"立"被直译为"站立"，"达"被直译为"到达"；韦利译为"you yourself desire rank and standing；then help others to get rank and standing. You want to turn your own merits to account；then help others to turn theirs to account"，"立"被译为"达到地位"，"达"被译为"展示优点"。笔者认为，"立"翻译为"立身"，"达"翻译为"通达"较为恰当。

[3] 能近取譬：能够就自身打比方，即推己及人的意思。理雅格译为"To be able to judge of others by what is nigh in ourselves"，即"能够根据自己的近处来判断别人"；辜鸿铭译为"If one is able to consider how one would see things and act if placed in the position of others"，即"一个人能够考虑，自己如果站在别人的立场上会如何看待事物和采取行动"；刘殿爵译为"The ability to take as analogy what is near at hand"，即"把近在咫尺的事物作为类比的能力"；韦利译为"The ability to take one's own feelings as a guide"，即"以自己的感受为向导的能力"。理雅格翻译出了"近"的意涵，但"判断"一译不够恰当。韦利将"自己的感受"视为行动的指南，但实际上《论语》此处强调"推己及人"，是揣度他人的感受为自己的行为向导。此处辜鸿铭采用意译，还原了"能近取譬"的"推己及人"之义，翻译较为恰当。

述而篇第七

【原文】7.1　子曰：“述而不作^[1]，信而好古，窃比于我老彭^[2]。”

【译文】孔子说：“只阐述而不创作，相信而且喜好古代的文化，我私下把自己比做老彭。”

【英译】The Master said，"A transmitter and not a maker，believing in and loving the ancients，I venture to compare myself with our old P'ang."

【注释】

[1] 述而不作：述，传述。作，创造。

[2] 老彭：一说，人名，殷商时期的大夫，好述古事；一说，指老子和彭祖。郑玄注为两个人，曰：“老，老聃；彭，彭祖。”一说，指老子，王夫之《稗疏》对此有详细考证：“先儒谓老彭为二人。老，老聃；彭，彭铿。乃彭铿他不经见，唯《汉书·艺文志》有《彭祖御女术》，则一淫邪之方士耳。《集注》据《大戴礼》商彭祖、仲傀之教，人谓为殷之贤者。考仲傀即仲虺，莱朱也。老彭在其前，皆成汤时人。而子曰‘我老彭’，亲之之词，必觌面相授受者矣。按老聃亦曰太史儋，聃、儋、彭音盖相近，古人质朴，命名或有音而无字，后人传闻，随以字加之，则老彭即问礼之老子矣。《礼记》称‘吾闻诸老聃’，聃盖多识前言往行以立教者。五千言中称古不一，而曰‘执古之道，御今之有’，则其好古而善述可见矣。特其志意有偏，故庄列之徒得缘饰而为异端。当夫子之时，固未泛滥，以亲相质问，而称道之，又何疑

焉。"理雅格、韦利、刘殿爵直译为"old P'ang",刘殿爵在注释中补充说明"It is not clear who Old P'eng was";辜鸿铭译为"old Worthy Pang"。可见由于学界仍在讨论"老彭"的具体所指,《论语》英译本在处理这一问题时,均采用直译"老彭"的方式。

【原文】7.2　子曰:"默而识[1]之,学而不厌,诲[2]人不倦,何有于我哉[3]?"

【译文】孔子说:"默默地记住(所学的知识),学习不觉得厌烦,教人不知道疲倦,这些事情我做到了哪些呢?"

【英译】The Master said, "The silent treasuring up of knowledge;learning without satiety; and instructing others without being wearied;which one of these things belongs to me?"

【注释】

[1] 识:记住。

[2] 诲:教诲。

[3] 何有于我哉:做到了哪些呢? 理雅格译为"Which one of these things belongs to me",即"哪件东西是我的?""有"被理解为"拥有、占有";刘殿爵译为"For me there is nothing to these things",即"对我来说,这些都不算什么";韦利译为"These at least are merits which I can confidently claim",即"这些至少是我可以自信地宣称的优点";辜鸿铭译为"Which one of these things can I say that I have done",即"我能说我做过哪一件事呢?""有"被翻译为"做过、完成"。上述译本相较,理雅格的翻译较为恰当,体现了孔子的谦逊。

【原文】7.3　子曰:"德之不修,学之不讲,闻义不能徙[1],不善不能改,是吾忧也。"

【译文】孔子说:"对品德不去修养,学问不去讲求,听到义不能去做，有了不善的事不能改正，这些都是我所忧虑的事情。"

【英译】The Master said，"The leaving virtue without proper cultivation；the not thoroughly discussing what is learned；not being able to move towards righteousness of which a knowledge is gained；and not being able to change what is not good：-these are the things which occasion me solicitude."

【注释】

[1] 徙：迁移。此处指靠近义、做到义。理雅格译为"move towards righteousness"，即"靠近正义"；辜鸿铭采用意译，译为"act up to what I believe to be right"，即"实现我认为正确的目标"；刘殿爵译为"Inability, when I am told what is right，to go over to where it is"，即"当别人告诉我什么是正确的时候，我却没有能力走到正确的地方去"，"徙"被译为"走到"；韦利译为"That I have heard of righteous men，but been unable to go to them"，即"我听说有义士，却不能到他们那里去"，其将"义"理解为"义士"，"徙"的意思是"接近义士"。实际上，《论语》此处之"义"并非局限在"义士"，而是包含符合义的一切人事活动。上述译本相较，理雅格、刘殿爵的翻译较为恰当，其中理氏较为契合汉语文本，刘本则较为简明直接。

【原文】7.4　子之燕居[1]，申申如也，夭夭如也[2]。

【译文】孔子闲居在家里的时候，衣冠楚楚，仪态温和舒畅，悠闲自在。

【英译】When the Master was in his leisure hours，his manner was easy，and he looked pleased.

【注释】

[1] 燕居：安居、家居、闲居。理雅格译为"unoccupied with business"，即"不忙于工作"；辜鸿铭译为"In his disengaged hours"，即"在他空闲的时候"；刘殿爵译为"During his leisure moments"；韦利译为"In his

leisure hours", 即"在他的休闲时间"。上述译本相较, 理雅格并未直接译出"燕居"的"闲居在家"之义, 辜鸿铭本"disengaged"有"空闲的、自由的"之义, 刘殿爵、韦利译为"leisure", 则多了"休闲的、安逸的"之义。此处"燕居"不仅强调孔子的"不忙"和"有空", 更强调其居家悠闲舒适的状态, 因此刘殿爵、韦利本更为恰当。

[2] 这句话的理解有多种, 1. 皇侃《义疏》云:"明孔子居处有礼也。燕居者, 退朝而居也。申申者。心和也, 夭夭者, 貌舒也。《品藻》云:'燕居告温温。'注:'告谓教使也。'《诗》云:'温温恭人。'《乡党》云:'居不容。'故当燕居时所以心和而貌舒也。故孙绰曰:'燕居无事, 故云心内夷和外舒畅者也。'《诗》云:'桃之夭夭, 灼灼其华。'即美舒义。"朱子《集注》云:"燕居, 闲暇无事之时。杨氏曰:申申, 其容舒也。夭夭, 其色愉也。"程子曰:"此弟子善形容圣人处也, 为申申字说不尽, 故更着夭夭字。今人燕居之时, 不怠惰放肆, 必太严厉。严厉时着此四字不得, 怠惰放肆时亦着此四字不得, 惟圣人便自有中和之气。"2. 胡绍勋《四书拾义》云:"《汉书·万石君传》:子孙胜冠者在侧, 虽燕必冠, 申申如也。师古注云:'申申, 整饬之貌。'此经记者先言'申申', 后言'夭夭', 犹《乡党》先言'踧踖', 后言'与与'也。"3. 刘宝楠《正义》云:"'申申如'者, 所谓'望之俨然';'夭夭如'者, 所谓'即之也温'。"刘氏之说与胡氏相近。4. 黄式三《论语后案》:"燕, 犹闲也。居, 坐也。《礼·仲尼燕语居》:'子张、子贡、言游侍。子曰:居。'居亦坐言也。今蹲踞字古只用居, 居亦有坐意。详见十七篇。申申如状其躬之直, 夭夭如状其躬之稍俯也。此记圣人徒坐之容, 合伸屈观之而见其得中也。《说文》:'夭, 屈也。'此文上句谓其申, 下句谓其屈。洪筠轩曰:'燕居之时, 其容体可以屈伸如意。'式三以此言坐容。"

【原文】7.5 子曰:"甚矣吾衰也! 久矣吾不复梦见周公[1]!"

【译文】孔子说:"我衰老得很厉害了, 我好久没有梦见周公了。"

【英译】The Master said, "Extreme is my decay. For a long time,

I have not dreamed，as I was wont to do，that I saw The duke of Chau.”

【注释】

[1] 周公：姓姬，名旦，周文王的儿子，武王的弟弟，成王的叔父，鲁国的始祖，是孔子心目中敬服的古代圣人之一。

【原文】 7.6 子曰：“志于道，据于德，依于仁，游于艺[1]。”

【译文】 孔子说：“以道为志向，以德为根据，以仁为凭藉，活动于六艺之中。”

【英译】 The Master said，“Let the will be set on the path of duty. Let every attainment in what is good be firmly grasped. Let perfect virtue be accorded with. Let relaxation and enjoyment be found in the polite arts.”

【注释】

[1] 艺：六艺，即礼、乐、射、御、书、数。理雅格、辜鸿铭译为“The polite arts”，即“礼的艺术”；刘殿爵、韦利译为“arts”。《礼记·学记》曾说：“不兴其艺，不能乐学。故君子之于学也，藏焉，修焉，息焉，游焉。夫然，故安其学而亲其师，乐其及而信其道，是以虽离师辅而不反也。”这个解释阐明了这里所谓的“游于艺”的意思。孔子培养学生，就是以仁、德为纲领，以六艺为基本，使学生能够得到全面均衡的发展。实际上，“艺”在此处不仅仅指艺术活动，而是专指“礼、乐、射、御、书、数”六艺，因此将“艺”译为“The Six Arts”较为恰当。

【原文】 7.7 子曰：“自行束脩[1]以上，吾未尝无诲焉。”

【译文】 孔子说：“只要自愿拿着十条干肉为礼来见我的人，我从来没有不教诲的。”

【英译】 The Master said，“From the man bringing his bundle of dried flesh for my teaching upwards，I have never refused instruction to any one."

【注释】

[1] 束脩：脩，干肉，又叫脯。束脩就是十条干肉。孔子要求他的学生，初次见面时要拿十条干肉作为学费。后来，就把学生送给老师的学费叫作"束脩"。

【原文】7.8　子曰："不愤[1]不启，不悱[2]不发。举一隅不以三隅反，则不复也。"

【译文】孔子说："教导学生，不到他想弄明白而不得的时候，不去开导他；不到他想出来却说不出来的时候，不去启发他。教给他一个方面的东西，他却不能由此而推知其他三个方面的东西，那就不再教他了。"

【英译】The Master said，"I do not open up the truth to one who is not eager to get knowledge，nor help out any one who is not anxious to explain himself. When I have presented one corner of a subject to any one，and he cannot from it learn the other three，I do not repeat my lesson."

【注释】

[1] 愤：苦思冥想而仍然领会不了的样子。理雅格译为"Who is not eager to get knowledge"，"愤"即"急于求知"；刘殿爵译为"Who has not been driven to distraction by trying to understand a difficulty"，即"因为理解困难而发狂"；韦利译为"Who bursts with eagerness"，即"急切的人"，这一翻译没能体现出是因为何种原因而"急切"。上述译本相较，理雅格的翻译较为恰当。

[2] 悱：想说又不能明确说出来的样子。理雅格译为"Who is not anxious to explain himself"，"悱"即"着急去解释自己"，这一翻译没能体

现"悱"所具有的"难以表达自己的想法"的义素；辜鸿铭将该句译为"I also make him find his own illustrations before I give him one of my own"，这一翻译没能体现出"悱"的"想说但难以准确表达"之义；刘殿爵译为"Who has not got into a frenzy trying to put his ideas into words"，即"因为难以用语言表达自己的想法而发狂"；韦利译为"Who bubbles with excitement"，"悱"即为"兴奋"，这一翻译没能体现出是因为何种原因而"兴奋"。上述译本相较，刘殿爵的翻译较为恰当。

【原文】7.9　子食于有丧者之侧，未尝饱也[1]。

【译文】孔子在有丧事的人旁边吃饭，不曾吃饱过。

【英译】When the Master was eating by the side of a mourner, he never ate to the full.

【注释】

[1] 未尝饱也：皇本作"未有尝饱也"。何晏《集解》云："丧者哀戚，饱食于其侧，是无恻隐之心。"邢昺《注疏》云："此章言孔子助丧家执事时，故得有食。饥而废事，非礼也。饱而忘哀，亦非礼。故食而不饱，以丧者哀戚，若饱食于其侧，是无恻怆隐痛之心也。"

【原文】7.10　子于是哭，则不歌[1]。

【译文】孔子在这一天为吊丧而哭泣，就不再唱歌。

【英译】He did not sing on the same day in which he had been weeping.

【注释】

[1] 皇侃《义疏》云："云'子于是日也哭则不歌'者，谓孔子吊丧之日也。吊丧必哭，哭、歌不可同日，故是于吊哭之日不歌。故范宁曰：'是日，即吊赴之日也。礼，歌、哭不同日也，故哭则不歌也。'"又，邢昺《注疏》云："此章言孔子于是日闻丧或吊人而哭，则终是日不歌也。若一日之

中，或哭或歌，是亵渎于礼容，故不为也。《檀弓》曰：'吊于人，是日不乐。'注引此文是也。"此处理雅格、韦利、刘殿爵、辜鸿铭等英译本均未补充说明"哭、歌不可同日"的礼俗，因此对于海外读者而言，难以理解孔子此行背后尊重礼制的深意。此处可在注释中补充说明孔子"哭则不歌"的原因，即"Confucius will cry in mourning, crying and singing are not on the same day, so he does not sing on the day of hanging crying."

【原文】 7.11　子谓颜渊曰："用之则行，舍之则藏[1]，惟我与尔有是夫。"子路曰："子行三军[2]，则谁与？"子曰："暴虎[3]冯河[4]，死而不悔者，吾不与也。必也临事而惧[5]，好谋而成者也。"

【译文】 孔子对颜渊说："用我时，我就去干；不用我，我就隐退，只有我和你才能做到这样吧！"子路问孔子说："老师您如果统帅三军，那么您和谁在一起共事呢？"孔子说："赤手空拳和老虎搏斗，徒步涉水过河，死了都不会后悔的人，我是不会和他在一起共事的。我要找的，一定是遇事小心谨慎，善于谋划而能完成任务的人。"

【英译】 The Master said to Yen Yuan, "When called to office, to undertake its duties; when not so called, to he retired; -it is only I and you who have attained to this." Tsze-lu said, "If you had the conduct of the armies of a great state, whom would you have to act with you?" The Master said, "I would not have him to act with me, who will unarmed attack a tiger, or cross a river without a boat, dying without any regret. My associate must be the man who proceeds to action full of solicitude, who is fond of adjusting his plans, and then carries them into execution."

【注释】

[1] 舍之则藏：舍，舍弃，不用。藏，隐藏。

[2] 三军：是当时大国所有的军队，每军约一万二千五百人。按照规

定，天子有六军，诸侯大国有三军。

[3] 暴虎：空拳赤手与老虎进行搏斗。

[4] 冯河：无船而徒步过河。

[5] 临事而惧：惧，谨慎、警惕，该句形容遇到事情便格外小心谨慎。理雅格将该句译为"proceeds to action full of solicitude"，即"行动中充满关怀"，这一翻译不够恰当。辜鸿铭译为"Who is conscious of the difficulties of any task set before him"，形容一个人"能意识到摆在他面前的任何任务的困难"。刘殿爵译为"When faced with a task，was fearful of failure"，即"面对任务时害怕失败"，其将"惧"理解为"惧怕"，没能凸显"惧"的"小心谨慎"之义。韦利译为"approached difficulties with due caution"，即"以应有的谨慎对待困难"，该翻译较为恰当。孔子在本章提出不与"暴虎冯河，死而无悔"的人在一起去统帅军队。因为在他看来，这种人虽然视死如归，但有勇无谋，是不能成就大事的。"勇"是孔子道德范畴中的一个德目，但勇不是蛮干，而是"临事而惧，好谋而成"的人，这种人智勇兼有，符合"勇"的规定。

【原文】7.12　子曰："富而可求[1]也，虽执鞭之士[2]，吾亦为之。如不可求，从吾所好。"

【译文】孔子说："财富如果可以求得的话，即便是给人执鞭的下等差事，我也愿意去做。如果求它不到，那就还是按我的爱好去做事。"

【英译】The Master said，"If the search for riches is sure to be successful，though I should become a groom with whip in hand to get them，I will do so. As the search may not be successful，I will follow after that which I love."

【注释】

[1] 富而可求：指富贵合于道，可以去求。理雅格译为"If the search for riches is sure to be successful"，即"寻求财富一定会成功"，这一翻译

没能体现出所求必须合乎道义的要求。辜鸿铭译为"If there is a sure way of getting rich",即"可靠的致富方式"。刘殿爵译为"If wealth were a permissible pursuit",即"如果财富是允许被追求的"。韦利译为"If any means of escaping poverty presented itself that did not involve doing wrong",即"如果有任何不涉及做错事且能摆脱贫困的方法",这一翻译体现出追求富贵需要采取合乎道德方式。上述译本相较,韦利的翻译更为恰当。

[2] 执鞭之士:根据《周礼》有两种执鞭之士:一是天子、诸侯出入时,手拿皮鞭开路的人。《周礼·秋官》:"条狼氏掌执鞭以趋辟,王出入,则八人夹道。公则六人,侯伯则四人,子男则二人。"二是在市场入口,手拿皮鞭维护秩序的人,《周礼·司市》:"凡市人,则胥执鞭度守门。"不管哪一种,地位都比较低下。理雅格译为"a groom with whip in hand",即"手中拿着鞭子的马夫";辜鸿铭译为"a groom and keep horses",即"养马的马夫";刘殿爵译为"a guard holding a whip",即"市场外拿着鞭子的守卫",这一翻译从《周礼·司市》说;韦利译为"The gentleman who holds the whip",即"执鞭的绅士",朱子《集注》云:"执鞭,贱者之事。"可见"执鞭之士"地位较为低下,因此韦利将其译为"gentleman"不够恰当。

【原文】 7.13 子之所慎:齐[1],战,疾。

【译文】孔子所谨慎小心对待的是斋戒、战争和疾病三件事。

【英译】 The things in reference to which the Master exercised the greatest caution were-fasting, war, and sickness.

【注释】

[1] 齐:同斋,斋戒。古人在祭祀前要沐浴更衣,不吃荤,不饮酒,不与妻妾同寝,整洁身心,表示虔诚之心。

【原文】 7.14 子在齐闻《韶》[1],三月不知肉味,曰:"不图为乐之至于斯也。"

【译文】孔子在齐国听到了《韶》乐，有很长时间尝不出肉的滋味，他说："想不到《韶》乐的美达到了这样迷人的地步。"

【英译】When the Master was in Ch'i，he heard the Shao，and for three months did not know the taste of flesh. "I did not think'"，he said，"That music could have been made so excellent as this."

【注释】

[1]《韶》：舜时古乐曲名。

【原文】7.15　冉有曰："夫子为[1]卫君[2]乎？"子贡曰："诺；吾将问之。"入，曰："伯夷、叔齐何人也？"曰："古之贤人也。"曰："怨乎？"曰："求仁而得仁，又何怨？"出，曰："夫子不为也。"

【译文】冉有问子贡说："老师会赞同卫国的国君吗？"子贡说："嗯，我去问他。"于是就进去问孔子："伯夷、叔齐是什么样的人呢？"孔子说："古代的贤人。"子贡又问："他们有怨恨吗？"孔子说："他们求仁而得到了仁，为什么又怨恨呢？"子贡出来对冉有说："老师不会赞同卫君。"

【英译】Yen Yu said，"Is our Master for the ruler of Wei？"Tsze-kung said，"Oh！I will ask him."He went in accordingly，and said，"What sort of men were Po-i and Shu-ch'i？""They were ancient worthies，"said the Master. "Did they have any repinings because of their course？"The Master again replied，"They sought to act virtuously，and they did so；what was there for them to repine about？"On this，Tsze-kung went out and said，"Our Master is not for him."

【注释】

[1] 为：这里是赞同的意思。理雅格译为"Is our Master for the ruler of Wei"，即"夫子是魏国的统治者吗？"这一翻译将"为"理解为"作为、担任"；辜鸿铭在翻译中解释了卫出公之典故，并将该句译为"Is the master in

favour of the son，the present ruler"，"为"是"支持、赞成"之意；刘殿爵、韦利译为"Is the Master on the side of the Lord of Wei"，即"夫子是站在卫君那边的吗?""为"被理解为"支持"。相比而言，此处作赞同、支持之义为佳。

[2] 卫君：指卫出公蒯辄，是卫灵公的孙子，太子蒯聩的儿子。蒯聩得罪南子，被卫灵公驱逐出卫国，逃到晋国。卫灵公去世后，立蒯辄为国君。晋国的赵简子打着将蒯聩送回卫国的旗号，借机攻打卫国。卫国举兵反抗，同时将蒯聩拒之国门之外。蒯聩、蒯辄父子争夺王位，蒯辄不让父亲回国，与伯夷、叔齐互相谦让王位形成对比，所以子贡才会用二人之事探问孔子的口风。邢昺《注疏》云："此章记孔子崇仁让也，卫君谓出公辄也。卫灵公逐太子蒯聩，公薨而立孙辄，辄即蒯聩之子也。后晋赵鞅纳蒯聩于戚城，卫石曼姑帅师围之。子而拒父，恶行之甚。时孔子在卫，为辄所宾礼，人疑孔子助辄，孔子以伯夷、叔齐为贤且仁，故知不助卫君明矣。"

【原文】7.16 子曰："饭疏食[1]，饮水，曲肱[2]而枕之，乐亦在其中矣。不义而富且贵，于我如浮云。"

【译文】孔子说："吃粗粮，喝白水，弯着胳膊当枕头，乐趣也就在这中间了。用不正当的手段得来的富贵，对于我来讲就像是天上的浮云一样。"

【英译】The Master said，"With coarse rice to eat，with water to drink，and my bended arm for a pillow；-I have still joy in the midst of these things. Riches and honors acquired by unrighteousness，are to me as a floating cloud."

【注释】

[1] 饭疏食：饭，这里是"吃"的意思，作动词。疏食即粗粮。

[2] 曲肱：肱，胳膊，由肩至肘的部位。曲肱，即弯着胳膊。

【原文】7.17　子曰："加[1]我数年，五十以学《易》[2]，可以无大过矣。"

【译文】孔子说："再给我几年时间，到五十岁学习《易》，我便可以没有大的过错了。"

【英译】The Master said，"If some years were added to my life，I would give fifty to the study of the Yi，and then I might come to be without great faults."

【注释】

[1] 加：通"假"，给予。

[2]《易》：又称《周易》《易经》，是古代占卜用的书，其中的卦辞、爻辞是孔子之前已有的文献，传说孔子为其作传。《鲁论》、定州竹简本"易"作"亦"。元初的《四书辨疑》对作"易"提出了疑问，其文曰："注又言：学《易》则明乎消长吉凶之理、进退存亡之道，故可以无大过。予谓若以此章为孔子七十时所言，假我数年以学《易》，则又期在七十以后。然孔子七十三而卒，直有大过一世矣。只从五十字说，亦有五十年大过，小过则又不论也，何足为圣人乎？孔子天纵生知，不应晚年方始学《易》也。五十、七十义皆不通。又有说学《易》为修《易》，过为《易》书散乱者。复有说学《易》而失之无所不至，孔子忧之，故托以戒人者。皆为曲说。此章之义，本不易知，姑当置之以待后之君子。"钱宾四先生《论语新解》云："然何以读《易》始可以无过，又何以必五十始学《易》？孔子常以《诗》、《书》、礼、乐教，何以独不以《易》教？此等皆当另作详解。今从《鲁论》做亦。"黄怀信《论语汇校集释》云："学，谓学文。此孔子向人道学文的好处，勉人勿以年长而不学也。言即是让他再长几年，到五十岁才开始学文，也可以使终身无有大过。旧不知'易'当为'亦'，而以天命易数为说，穿凿之甚。学《易》岂可以无过？"对于《周易》的书名，理雅格音译为"Yi"；辜鸿铭译为"I-king"，并在脚注中介绍《周易》的背景："This book is now known to foreigners as 'The Book of Changes', one of the so-

called five Classics in the Chinese Bible. It seems，to us，the book is an attempt at a mathematical or exact scientific statement of mental phenomena and moral problems. It might be called，'The Theory of Fluxions'，applied originally to the actions of physical forces in nature，but now，as it stands，to the moral forces and intellectual forces in the world. Sir CHALONER ALABASTER has published the only intelligible papers on this book，which should be consulted by anyone interested in the subject." 刘殿爵将该句译为"五十以学"，即"I may continue to learn at the age of fifty"，该本与韦利本均未翻译出"学"的对象是《易》。辜鸿铭或想译为"I-ching"，该单词是《周易》的英译之一。理雅格译本对《易》的翻译较为恰当，或可译为"The book of change"。

【原文】7.18　子所雅言[1]，《诗》、《书》、执礼，皆雅言也。

【译文】孔子有时讲雅言，读《诗》、读《书》、赞礼时，用的都是雅言。

【英译】The Master's frequent themes of discourse were-the Odes，the History，and the maintenance of the Rules of Propriety. On all these he frequently discoursed.

【注释】

[1] 雅言：朱子释"雅"为常，有误。雅言、正言、正音，即官话、通行的语言。春秋时期各国语言不一，孔子平时谈话用鲁国语言，吟诵《诗》《书》和行礼的时候就用正式的语言。韩李《笔解》认为"言"字误。韩愈云："音作言，字之误也。传写因注云雅言正言，遂误尔。"何晏《集解》引孔说曰："雅言，正言也。"又郑玄注曰："读先王典法，必正言其音，然后义全，故不可有所讳。礼不诵，故言执。"邢昺《注疏》更为详细，其文曰"此章记孔子正言其音，无所讳避之事。雅，正也。子所正言者，《诗》、《书》、《礼》也。此三者，先王典法，临文教学，读之必正言其音，然后义全，故不可有所讳。礼不背文诵，但记其揖让周旋，执而行之，故言

执也。举此三者，则六艺可知。"理雅格、辜鸿铭没有译出"雅言"，而是将该句译为"The Master's frequent themes of discourse"，即"孔子经常谈论的领域"；刘殿爵、韦利将"雅言"译为"The correct pronunciation"，即"正音"。

【原文】7.19　叶公[1]问孔子于子路，子路不对。子曰："女奚不曰，其为人也，发愤忘食[2]，乐以忘忧[3]，不知老之将至云尔。"

【译文】叶公向子路问孔子是什么样的人，子路不答。孔子对子路说："你为什么不这样说：他这个人，发愤用功，连吃饭都忘了，快乐得把一切忧虑都忘了，连自己快要老了都不知道，如此而已。"

【英译】The duke of Sheh asked Tsze-Lu about Confucius，and Tsze-Lu did not answer him. The Master said，"Why did you not say to him，-He is simply a man，who in his eager pursuit of knowledge forgets his food，who in the joy of its attainment forgets his sorrows，and who does not perceive that old age is coming on?"

【注释】

[1] 叶公：叶公姓沈名诸梁，楚国的大夫，封地在叶城（今河南叶县南），僭越称叶公。

[2] 理雅格将"发愤"译为"In his eager pursuit of knowledge"，即"热切地追求知识"；辜鸿铭译为"In the efforts he makes to overcome the difficulty in acquiring knowledge"，即"在求知过程中克服困难"；刘殿爵译为"he works himself into a frenzy over some problem"，"发愤"即"为之疯狂"之意；韦利将"发愤"译为"so intent upon enlightening the eager"，"发"即为"启发他人"，"愤"译为"渴望"。刘殿爵将"愤"译为"frenzy"，该单词作为名词翻译为疯狂、狂乱、狂暴，作为及物动词翻译为使发狂、使狂乱、使狂怒，其情感过分强烈，不符合《论语》本意。上述译本相较，理雅格的翻译更为恰当。

[3] 理雅格、辜鸿铭将"乐"译为"in the joy of its attainment",快乐的原因是"获得了知识"。刘殿爵译为"full of joy",该翻译没能体现出君子之"乐"是由于获得了知识。

【原文】 7.20　子曰:"我非生而知之者,好古,敏[1]以求之者也。"

【译文】 孔子说:"我不是生来就有知识的人,而是爱好古代的东西,勤奋敏捷地去求得知识的人。"

【英译】 The Master said,"I am not one who was born in the possession of knowledge;I am one who is fond of antiquity,and earnest in seeking it there."

【注释】

[1] 敏:敏捷、勤奋。理雅格译为"earnest",即"认真的";辜鸿铭、韦利译为"diligent",即"勤勉的";刘殿爵译为"quick",即"迅敏的"。在孔子的观念当中,"上智"就是"生而知之者",但他却否认自己是生而知之者。他之所以成为学识渊博的人,在于他爱好古代的典章制度和文献图书,而且勤奋刻苦,思维敏捷。由此可见,辜鸿铭、韦利将"敏"译为"勤勉的",更为恰当。

【原文】 7.21　子不语怪,力,乱,神。[1]

【译文】 孔子不谈论怪异、暴力、动乱、鬼神。

【英译】 The subjects on which the Master did not talk,were-extraordinary things,feats of strength,disorder,and spiritual beings.

【注释】

[1] 何晏《集解》引王肃说曰:"怪,怪异也。力,谓若奡荡舟、乌获举千钧之属。乱,谓臣弑君、子弑父。神,谓鬼神之事。或无益于教化,或所不忍言。"朱子《集注》云:"怪异、勇力、悖乱之事,非理之

正，固圣人所不语。鬼神，造化之迹，虽非不正，然非穷理之至，有未易明者，故亦不轻以语人也。"理雅格译为"extraordinary things，feats of strength，disorder，and spiritual beings"，该翻译遵循何晏《集解》之说；辜鸿铭译为"supernatural phenomena；of extraordinary feats of strength；of crime of unnatural depravity of men；or of supernatural beings."刘殿爵的翻译简洁明朗："prodigies，force，disorder and gods"；韦利译为"prodigies，feats of strength，disorders or spirits"，二者均将"怪"译为"神童、天才"，不够恰当。对于"神"的翻译，"God"一词，直译指的是上帝，尤指基督教、天主教、犹太教和伊斯兰教中对宇宙的创造者和主宰者的称呼。如果直接用这个单词的话，首先想到的是欧美所信仰的"上帝"，而不是中国哲学中"神"的范畴；"Spirit"则指与肉体相对的"精神、灵魂"。关于"spirit"与"god"的汉译，可参见刘林海《19世纪中国人关于基督教God/Spirit汉译问题的讨论》一文（《北京师范大学学报》2007年第6期）。

【原文】7.22 子曰："三人行[1]，必有我师焉：择其善者而从之，其不善者而改之。"

【译文】孔子说："三个人一起走路，其中必定有人可以作我的老师。我选择他善的品德向他学习，看到他不善的地方就作为借鉴，改掉自己的缺点。"

【英译】The Master said，"When I walk along with two others，they may serve me as my teachers. I will select their good qualities and follow them，their bad qualities and avoid them."

【注释】

[1] 三人行：这里"三人"不是虚指，三人指三个人，其中一个就是自己。皇本、正平本、定州竹简本、唐石经作"我三人行"。何晏《集解》云："言我三人行，本无贤愚，择善从之，不善改之，故无常师。"邢昺《注疏》云："此章言学无常师也。言我三人行，本无贤愚相悬，但敌体耳，然

彼二人言行，必有一人善，一人不善，我则择其善者而从之，不善者而改之。有善可从，是为师矣，故无常师也。"朱子《集注》云："三人同行，其一我也。彼二人者，一善一恶，则我从其善而改其恶焉，是二人者皆我师也。尹氏曰：'见贤思齐，见不贤而内自省，则善恶皆我之师，进善其有穷乎？'"理雅格译为"I walk along with two others"，即从何晏《集解》说"我三人行"；辜鸿铭译为"Three men meet together"，即"三个人相见"；刘殿爵译为"When walking in the company of two other men"，即"当和另外两个人一起行走的时候"，该翻译从何晏《集解》说"我三人行"；韦利译为"When walking in a party of no more than three"。上述译本均未将"三人"理解为泛指很多人，理雅格、刘殿爵、韦利的翻译中体现出"三人"之中有一人是自己，辜鸿铭本没能体现这一要素。

【原文】7.23　子曰："天生德于予，桓魋[1]其如予何？"

【译文】孔子说："上天把德赋予了我，桓魋能把我怎么样？"

【英译】The Master said, "Heaven produced the virtue that is in me. Hwan T'ui-what can he do to me?"

【注释】

[1] 桓魋：宋国司马向魋，由于是宋桓公的后代，因而又称作桓魋。鲁哀公三年（前492），孔子途经宋国，桓魋派人追杀孔子，孔子的学生催促他赶路，孔子才有这一番话。《史记·孔子世家》："孔子去曹，适宋，与弟子习礼大树下。宋司马桓魋欲杀孔子，拔其树。孔子去，弟子曰：'可以速矣！'孔子曰：'天生德于予，桓魋其如予何？'"皇侃《义疏》云："予，我也。桓魋，宋司马也。凶愚，心恒欲害孔子。孔子故明言语之，使其凶心止也。言天生圣德于我，我与天同体，桓魋虽无道，安能违天而害我乎？故云如予何也。夫凶人亦宜不屡谢，而有时须以道折之。故江熙曰：'小人为恶，以理喻之则愈凶强，晏然待之则更自处，亦尤匡人闻文王之德而兵解也。'"

【原文】7.24　子曰："二三子[1]以我为隐乎？吾无隐乎尔。吾无行而不与二三子者，是丘也。"

【译文】孔子说："学生们，你们以为我对你们有什么隐瞒的吗？我是丝毫没有隐瞒的。我没有什么事不向你们公开的。我孔丘就是这样的人。"

【英译】The Master said，"Do you think，my disciples，that I have any concealments？ I conceal nothing from you. There is nothing which I do that is not shown to you，my disciples；that is my way."

【注释】

[1] 二三子：何晏《集解》引包咸曰："二三子谓诸弟子。圣人知广道深，弟子学之不能及，以为有所隐匿，故解之。"理雅格、辜鸿铭译为"disciples"，即"门徒、信徒、追随者"；刘殿爵、韦利译为"My friends"，即"朋友"之义。

【原文】7.25　子以四教：文[1]、行[2]、忠[3]、信[4]。

【译文】孔子用四种内容教育学生：文献典籍，社会实践的德行，对己对人尽心竭力，与人交际的信实。

【英译】There were four things which the Master taught，letters，ethics，devotion of soul，and truthfulness.

【注释】

[1] 文：文献、古籍等。理雅格译为"letters"，即"文字"；辜鸿铭译为"a knowledge of literature and the arts"，即"有关文学艺术的知识"；刘殿爵、韦利译为"culture"，即"文化"。"文"在《论语》中多指文献典籍，因此此处译为"Documents"或"classics"较为恰当。

[2] 行：指德行，也指社会实践方面的内容。邢昺《注疏》云："此章记孔子行教以此四事为先也。文谓先王之遗文。行谓德行，在心为德，施之为行。中心无隐谓之忠。人言不欺谓之信。此四者有形质，故可举以教

也。"《四书辨疑》与黄怀信《论语汇校集释》认为"行"不当解作"德行"，否则与忠、信重复。皇侃《义疏》引李充言："其典籍辞意谓之文，孝悌恭睦谓之行，为人臣则忠，与朋友交则信，此四者，教之所先也。故以文发其蒙，行以积其德，忠以立其节，信以全其终也。"可见"行"解作"德行"，并不与忠、信重复。理雅格译为"ethics"，即"道德"；辜鸿铭译为"conduct"，即"行为"；刘殿爵译为"moral conduct"，即"道德行为"；韦利译为"conduct of affairs"，即"事务处理"。理氏没有翻译出"行"的"行为"之义，韦利和辜鸿铭则没能译出"道德"之义。上述译本相较，刘殿爵翻译较为恰当。

[3] 忠：尽己之谓忠，对人尽心竭力的意思。理雅格译为"devotion of soul"，即"奉献"；辜鸿铭译为"conscientiousness"，即"尽责"；刘殿爵译为"doing one's best"，即"尽力"；韦利译为"loyalty to superiors"，即"对上级的忠诚"。"devotion"强调"对某人或事的热爱和献身"，道德行为的动机是出于情感上的热爱；"Conscientiousness"则是指尽责性，是细致小心，或按照良心支配自己的行动的人格特质，它在传统上被视为一种道德品质，道德行为的动机是出于责任。韦利译为"loyalty to superiors"，则将"忠"理解成了中国古代君臣伦理中臣事君的"忠心"。上述译本相较，刘殿爵的翻译最为契合《论语》原意。

[4] 信：以实之谓信，诚实的意思。理雅格、辜鸿铭译为"Truthfulness"；刘殿爵译为"being trustworthy in what one says"，即"言语上值得信任"；韦利译为"keeping of promises"，即"遵守诺言"。前三种侧重"诚实"和"值得信任"，韦利本则强调"守信""遵守诺言"。

【原文】7.26 子曰："圣人，吾不得而见之矣；得见君子者，斯可矣。"[1]子曰："善人，吾不得静之矣；得见有恒[2]者，斯可矣。亡而为有，虚而为盈，约而为泰[3]，难乎有恒矣。"

【译文】孔子说："圣人我是不可能看到了，能看到君子，这就可以了。"孔子又说："善人我不可能看到了，能见到始终如一、保持好的品德的人，这也就可以了。没有却装作有，空虚却装作充实，穷困却装作富足，这样的人是难以有恒心保持好的品德的。"

【英译】The Master said，"A sage it is not mine to see；could I see a man of real talent and virtue，that would satisfy me."The Master said，"A good man it is not mine to see；could I see a man possessed of constancy，that would satisfy me. Having not and yet affecting to have，empty and yet affecting to be full，straitened and yet affecting to be at ease：-it is difficult with such characteristics to have constancy."

【注释】

[1] 此处"圣人""君子"皆就君王而言。何晏云："疾世无明君。"邢昺《注疏》云："圣人谓上圣之人，若尧、舜、禹、汤也。君子谓行善无怠之君也。言当时非但无圣人，亦无君子也。"

[2] 恒：恒心。理雅格、刘殿爵译为"constancy"，即"恒心"；辜鸿铭译为"scrupulous"，即"严谨的"；韦利译为"a man of fixed principles"，即"有固定原则的人"。皇侃《义疏》云："善人之称，亦上通圣人，下通一分。而此所言，指贤人以下也。言世道流丧，吾复不得善人也。云'得见有恒者斯可矣'者，有恒，谓虽不能作善，而守常不为恶者也。言尔时非唯无作片善者，亦无直置不为恶者，故亦不得见也。"可见"恒"此处意指"有恒心保持操守"。理雅格、刘殿爵此处直接译为"恒心"，韦利则译出了"有恒者"是坚定自己原则操守的人，辜鸿铭将"恒"翻译为"严谨的"，不够恰当。

[3] 泰：侈泰。此处"约"与"泰"相对，可以理解为俭约、穷困。理雅格将该句译为"straitened and yet affecting to be at ease"，即"拮据却装出安逸"，"泰"即"安逸"；辜鸿铭译为"pretend to be in affluence when they are in actual want"，即"穷困潦倒时却假装很富有"，"泰"即"富裕"；刘殿爵译为"To be comfortable when he is in straitened circumstances"，即"处于

困境中却谎称舒适", "泰"即"舒适"; 韦利译为"Penury pretending to be Affluence", "泰"即"富裕"。"泰"意指物质生活上的富足, 此处从辜鸿铭、韦利说, 译为"affluence"较为恰当。

【原文】7.27　子钓而不纲[1], 戈不射宿[2]。

【译文】孔子用钓竿钓鱼, 而不用有许多鱼钩的大绳钓鱼。只射飞鸟, 不射归巢歇宿的鸟。

【英译】The Master angled, -but did not use a net. He shot, -but not at birds perching.

【注释】

[1] 纲: 大绳。这里作动词用。在水面上拉一根大绳, 在大绳上系许多鱼钩来钓鱼, 叫纲。

[2] 宿: 指归巢歇宿的鸟儿。

【原文】7.28　子曰: "盖有不知而作[1]之者, 我无是也。多闻, 择其善者而从之; 多见而识之; 知之次[2]也。"

【译文】孔子说: "有这样一种人, 可能他什么都不懂, 却在凭空创造, 我却没有这样做过。多听, 选择其中好的来学习; 多看, 然后记在心里, 这是次一等的智慧。"

【英译】The Master said, "There may be those who act without knowing why. I do not do so. Hearing much and selecting what is good and following it; seeing much and keeping it in memory: this is the second style of knowledge."

【注释】

[1] 作: 创作。理雅格译为"act", 即"行动、做事"; 辜鸿铭译为"propound theories", 即"提出理论"; 刘殿爵译为"innovate", 即"创作、创新"; 韦利将该句译为"There may well be those who can do without

knowledge"，没有翻译出"作"的含义。

[2] 知之次：次一等的智慧。理雅格译为"Is the second style of knowledge"，即"次一等的知识"；辜鸿铭译为"next to having a great understanding"，即"仅次于伟大的理解"；刘殿爵译为"This constitutes a lower level of knowledge"，即"这构成了较低水平的知识"；韦利译为"Is the lower of the two kinds of knowledge"，即"两种知识中较低的"。上述译本中，"知"多被翻译为"知识"。实际上，此处孔子主张对自己所不知的东西，应该多闻、多见，努力学习，反对那种本来什么都不懂，却在那里凭空创造的做法，这是一种智慧，译为"wisdom"更为恰当。

【原文】7.29　互乡[1]难与言，童子见，门人惑。子曰："与[2]其进也[3]，不与其退也，唯何甚？人洁己以进，与其洁也，不保其往[4]也。"

【译文】互乡这地方的人难于交谈，但互乡的一个童子却受到了孔子的接见，学生们都感到迷惑不解。孔子说："我肯定他的进步，不是肯定他的倒退。何必做得太过分呢？人家改正了错误以求进步，我们肯定他改正错误，不要抓住他的过去不放。"

【英译】It was difficult to talk profitably and reputably with the people of Hu-hsiang，and a lad of that place having had an interview with the Master，the disciples doubted. The Master said，"I admit people's approach to me without committing myself as to what they may do when they have retired. Why must one be so severe？ If a man purify himself to wait upon me，I receive him so purified，without guaranteeing his past conduct."

【注释】

[1] 互乡：地名，今址不详，传说这个地方的人难以沟通。

[2] 与：赞许。

[3] 与其进也：理雅格将该句译为"I admit people's approach to me"，即"我承认人们对我的态度"，"与"即为"承认"；辜鸿铭译为"I accept his present reformation"，即"我接受他现在的改革"，"与"即为"接受"；刘殿爵译为"Approval of his coming"，即"赞成他的到来"，"与"被译为"赞成"，"进"译为"到来"。此处"与"应解释为"赞成、赞许"，刘殿爵的翻译较为恰当。"进"应被理解为"进取、进步"，即"Applaud his current progress"。

[4] 不保其往：这句话有两种理解：1. 将"往"理解为"去"，即是无法保证他离去后的行为。郑玄注曰："往犹去也。人虚已自洁而来，当与之进，亦何能保其去后之行。"邢昺《注疏》云："往犹去也。言人若虚已自洁而来，当与之进，亦何能保其去后之行。去后之行者，谓往前之行，今已过去。"2. 将"往"理解为"过往"。皇侃《义疏》引顾欢曰："往，谓前日之行也。夫人之为行未必可一，或有始无终，或先迷后得，故教诲之道，洁则与之，往日行，非我所保也。"保：守，死守。理雅格译为"without guaranteeing his past conduct"，即"并不保证他过去的行为"，"保"被译为"保证"，"往"从皇侃说，译为"过往"。辜鸿铭译为"without being able to guarantee that he will not relapes again"，即"无法保证他不会再犯"，"保"被译为"保证"，"往"从郑玄、邢昺说，译为离去后"再犯（错）"。刘殿爵译为"cannot vouch for his past"，即"不能为他的过去担保"。在上述译本中，"保"被译为"保证"，其中"vouch"强调"担保、作证"，用法较为正式；"guarantee"一般指以口头的、协定或合同的形式作为保证，强调口头承诺，含违背许诺，则予以补偿之意。《论语》此处"保"应理解为"死守、抓住不放"，即"Don't hang on to his past"。

【原文】7.30　子曰："仁远乎哉？我欲仁，斯仁至[1]矣。"

【译文】孔子说："仁难道离我们很远吗？只要我想达到仁，仁就来了。"

【英译】The Master said，"Is virtue a thing remote？ I wish to be virtuous，and lo！ virtue is at hand."

【注释】

[1] 斯仁至：戴氏本作"仁斯至"。朱子《集注》云："仁者，心之德，非在外也。放而不求，故有以为远者；反而求之，则即此而在矣，夫岂远哉？程子曰：'为仁由己，欲之则至，何远之有？'"斯：则。理雅格将"仁"译为"virtue"，即"美德"；辜鸿铭译为"moral"，即"道德"；刘殿爵译为"benevolence"，即"仁慈"；韦利译为"Goodness"，即"善良"。Virtue 是指一个人的品质和习惯，是一种积极的态度或良好的行为。英文 moral 源自拉丁文名词 mōs（"行为方式""习惯"）。同样的行为以相同或类似方式完成，就会形成习惯（mores）。习惯被确立后，就具有法则或律法的力量。因此，英文 moral 意义上的"道德"蕴含了"法则或律法"观念。从本章孔子的言论来看，仁是人天生的本性，因此为仁就有赖于自身的努力、道德的自觉，而非仅依靠外在力量，也即"我欲仁，斯仁至矣"。我们认为此处译为"virtue"更为恰当。

【原文】7.31 陈司败[1]问昭公[2]知礼乎，孔子曰："知礼。"孔子退，揖巫马期[3]进之，曰："吾闻君子不党[4]，君子亦党乎？君取于吴，为同姓[5]，谓之吴孟子[6]。君而知礼，孰不知礼？"巫马期以告。子曰："丘也幸，苟有过，人必知之。"

【译文】陈司败问："鲁昭公懂得礼吗？"孔子说："懂得礼。"孔子出来后，陈司败向巫马期作了个揖，请他走近自己，对他说："我听说君子是没有偏私的，难道君子还会包庇别人吗？鲁君在吴国娶了一个同姓的女子为做夫人，是国君的同姓，称她为吴孟子。如果鲁君算是知礼，还有谁不知礼呢？"巫马期把这句话告诉了孔子。孔子说："我真是幸运。如果有错，人家一定给指出来。"

【英译】The minister of crime of Ch'an asked whether the duke

Chao knew propriety, and Confucius said, "He knew propriety." Confucius having retired, the minister bowed to Wu-ma Ch'i to come forward, and said, "I have heard that the superior man is not a partisan. May the superior man be a partisan also? The prince married a daughter of the house of WU, of the same surname with himself, and called her, -The elder Tsze of Wu. If the prince knew propriety, who does not know it?" Wu-ma Ch'i reported these remarks, and The Master said, "I am fortunate! If I have any errors, people are sure to know them."

【注释】

[1] 陈司败：有两种说法，孔颖达认为，司败为官名，陈国大夫；郑玄认为是人名，是齐国大夫。

[2] 昭公：鲁昭公，名裯，或作稠，前541—前510年在位。

[3] 巫马期：姓巫马名施，字子期，孔子的学生，比孔子小三十岁。

[4] 党：偏袒、包庇，帮人隐瞒过失。理雅格译为"partisan"，即"党羽"；辜鸿铭将"不党"译为"Impartial"，即"公正的"；刘殿爵译为"partiality"，韦利译为"partial"，即"偏私"。

[5] 为同姓：鲁国和吴国的国君同姓姬。周礼规定：同姓不婚，昭公娶同姓女，是违礼的行为。

[6] 吴孟子：鲁昭公夫人。春秋时代，国君夫人的称号，一般是她出生的国名加上她的姓，但因她姓姬，故称为吴孟子，而不称吴姬。

【原文】 7.32　子与人歌而善，必使反[1]之，而后和[2]之。

【译文】 孔子与别人一起唱歌，如果唱得好，一定要请他再唱一遍，然后和他一起唱。

【英译】 When the Master was in company with a person who was singing, if he sang well, he would make him repeat the song, while he accompanied it with his own voice.

【注释】

[1] 反：再一次。

[2] 和：应和。

【原文】7.33　子曰："文，莫[1]吾犹人也。躬行君子[2]，则吾未之有得。"

【译文】孔子说："就书本知识来说，大约我和别人差不多，做一个身体力行的君子，那我还没有做到。"

【英译】The Master said，"In letters I am perhaps equal to other men，but the character of the superior man，carrying out in his conduct what he professes，is what I have not yet attained to."

【注释】

[1] 莫：约摸、大概、差不多。

[2] 君子：理雅格译为"The superior man"；辜鸿铭译为"good and wise man"，即"善良而明智的人"；刘殿爵、韦利将"君子"译为"gentleman"，即"绅士"。在各种英译本中对"君子"一词有多种译法，比如"The gentleman""The scholar""The good man""The superior man""Intelligentle man"等。

【原文】7.34　子曰："若圣与仁，则吾岂敢？抑为之不厌，诲人不倦，则可谓云尔已矣。"公西华曰："正唯弟子不能学也。"

【译文】孔子说："如果说到圣与仁，那我如何敢当！不过向圣与仁的方向努力而不感厌烦地做，教诲别人也从不感觉疲倦，就只能这么说而已。"公西华说："这正是我们学不到的。"

【英译】The Master said，"The sage and the man of perfect virtue；-how dare I rank myself with them？It may simply be said of me, that I strive to become such without satiety，and teach others without weariness." Kung-hsi Hwa said，"This is just what we，the disciples，cannot imitate you in."

【原文】7.35   子疾病[1]，子路请祷。子曰："有诸?"子路对曰："有之;《诔》[2]曰：'祷尔于上下神祇[3]。'"子曰："丘之祷久矣[4]。"

【译文】孔子病情严重，子路向鬼神祈祷。孔子说："有这回事吗?"子路说："有的。《诔》文上说：'为你向天地神灵祈祷。'"孔子说："我很早就祈祷过了。"

【英译】The Master being very sick，Tsze-Lu asked leave to pray for him. He said，"May such a thing be done?" Tsze-Lu replied，"It may. In the Eulogies it is said，'Prayer has been made for thee to the spirits of the upper and lower worlds.'" The Master said，"My praying has been for a long time."

【注释】

[1] 疾病：古人称一般的疾病为疾，称重病为病，二字连缀指病重。定州竹简本、《释文》、戴氏本无"病"字。理雅格译为"very sick"、韦利译为"very ill"，强调了疾病的严重程度；刘殿爵译为"illness became grave"，即"疾病变得严重"。上述译本相较，刘殿爵的翻译更为强调古汉语"疾病"二字连缀使用的含义。

[2] 诔：应作"讄"，祈祷文，用于生者的作"讄"，用于死者的作"诔"。《释文》曰："诔，《说文》作'讄'，云：'或作嫘。'"理雅格译为"Eulogies"，即"悼词"；辜鸿铭译为"The Book of Rituals for the Dead"，即"死者仪式之书"；韦利译为"Dirges"，即"挽歌"。上述译本相较，理雅格的翻译较为恰当。

[3] 神祇：古代称天神为神，地神为祇，定州竹简本"祇"作"堤"。

刘殿爵译为"pray ye thus to the gods above and below",即"向天和地的神祈祷";理雅格译为"The spirits of the upper and lower worlds"、韦利译为"The sky-spirits above and the earth-spirits below",即"上界和下界的神灵"。上述英译本均体现出"神"和"祇"的含义不同。

[4] 皇本作"丘之祷之久矣"。邢昺《注疏》云:"此章记孔子不谄求于鬼神也……孔子不许子路,故以此言拒之。若人之履行违忤神明,罹其咎殃则可祷请。孔子素行合于神明,故曰'丘之祷久矣'也。"朱子《集注》云:"悔过迁善,以祈神之佑也。无其理则不必祷,既曰有之,则圣人未尝有过,无善可迁。其素行固已合于神明,故曰:'丘之祷久矣。'又士丧礼,疾病行祷五祀,盖臣子迫切之至情,有不能自已者,初不请于病者而后祷也。故孔子之于子路,不直拒之,而但告以无所事祷之意。"

【原文】7.36 子曰:"奢[1]则不孙[2],俭则固[3]。与其不孙也,宁固。"

【译文】孔子说:"奢侈了就会傲慢,节俭了就会寒酸。与其傲慢,宁可寒酸。"

【英译】The Master said, "Extravagance leads to insubordination, and parsimony to meanness. It is better to be mean than to be insubordinate."

【注释】

[1] 奢:奢侈。理雅格、辜鸿铭、刘殿爵均译为"extravagance",韦利译为"lavishness"。"extravagance"强调"奢侈、挥霍、铺张";"lavishness"则更侧重"浪费、过度"。此处译为"extravagance",强调诸侯国在生活享乐标准和礼仪规模上的奢侈铺张,更为恰当。

[2] 孙:同逊,恭顺。不孙,即为不顺,这里的意思是"越礼"。

[3] 固:简陋、鄙陋。这里是寒酸的意思。理雅格、辜鸿铭、韦利译为"meanness",即"吝啬",刘殿爵则译为"shabbiness",即"破旧"。《论

语》此处在强调仪制节俭带来的简陋寒酸，并非指礼仪简约的诸侯国就是"吝啬的"，因此刘殿爵译为"shabbiness"较为恰当。

【原文】7.37   子曰："君子坦荡荡[1]，小人长戚戚[2]。"[3]

【译文】孔子说："君子心地平坦宽广，小人却经常局促忧愁。"

【英译】The Master said，"The superior man is satisfied and composed；the mean man is always full of distress."

【注释】

[1] 坦荡荡：心胸宽广、开阔、容忍。

[2] 长戚戚：经常忧愁、烦恼的样子。理雅格、辜鸿铭译为"distress"，刘殿爵则译为"anxiety"。"distress"侧重"忧愁困苦"，"anxiety"则强调"焦虑不安"。《论语》此处更强调"小人"心中时常忧愁烦恼，故"戚"译为"distress"更为恰当。

[3] 此句表示君子心胸坦荡，思想坦率，其面容行为自然安定舒畅。而小人欲念丛生，心事满满，其外貌动作就会表现得忐忑不安，心神不宁。鲁金华译为"The superior man"和"The inferior man"强调的是君子和小人地位的差别，刘殿爵、韦利选用的"The gentleman"和"The small man"强调的仍是出身高贵与低贱的差异。周仪译为"a man of virtue"和"a man of meanness"较为接近原意，此句中"君子"和"小人"的主要区别在于个人的德识修养上。

【原文】7.38   子温[1]而厉[2]，威[3]而不猛[4]，恭[5]而安。

【译文】孔子温和而又严厉，有威严而又不凶猛，谦恭而又安详。

【英译】The Master was mild，and yet dignified；majestic，and yet not fierce；respectful，and yet easy.

【注释】

[1] 温：温和的。理雅格译为"mild"，侧重态度的"温和、不严厉"；

辜鸿铭译为"gracious"，侧重对社会地位较低者是"亲切和蔼的"；刘殿爵译为"cordial"，侧重态度的"热情真诚"；韦利译为"affable"，意指孔子为人是"和善可亲、平易近人的"。"温"与"厉"形成对比，主要强调态度的"温和、不严厉"，因此理雅格译为"mild"较为恰当。

[2] 厉：严厉的。理雅格译为"dignified"，强调态度的"端庄、庄严"；辜鸿铭译为"serious"，即"严肃的严谨的"；刘殿爵译为"stern"，即"严厉的、苛刻的"；韦利译为"firm"，即"坚定的"。上述译本相较，刘殿爵的翻译较为恰当。

[3] 威：有威严的。理雅格译为"majestic"，强调"威严的、庄严的"；辜鸿铭、刘殿爵译为"awe-inspiring"，即"令人惊叹敬佩的"；韦利译为"commanding"，强调"指挥的、统帅的"。上述译本相较，理雅格的翻译较为恰当。

[4] 猛：凶猛的。理雅格、刘殿爵译为"fierce"，强调"凶猛、猛烈"；辜鸿铭译为"austere"，即"严峻的"；韦利译为"harsh"，即"严厉严酷的"。上述译本相较，刘殿爵的翻译较为恰当。

[5] 恭：谦恭的。理雅格、刘殿爵译为"respectful"，辜鸿铭、韦利译为"polite"。"polite"强调遵守社会规则；"respectful"则更侧重尊重他人（如尊重长辈）。《论语》此处强调孔子为人的谦恭有礼，译为强调礼貌友好的"courteous"更为恰当。

泰伯篇第八

【原文】8.1　子曰："泰伯[1]，其可谓至德也已矣。三以天下让[2]，民无得而称焉。"

【译文】孔子说："泰伯可以说是品德最高尚的人了，几次把王位让给季历，老百姓都找不到合适的词句来称赞他。"

【英译】The Master said, "T'ai-po may be said to have reached the highest point of virtuous action. Thrice he declined the kingdom, and the people in ignorance of his motives could not express their approbation of his conduct."

【注释】

[1] 泰伯：人名，周朝祖先古公亶父的长子。古公亶父生有三子：泰伯、仲庸、季历。传说古公亶父知道三子季历的儿子姬昌有圣德，想传位给季历，泰伯知道后便与二弟仲雍一起避居到吴。古公亶父死，泰伯不回来奔丧，后来又断发文身，表示终身不返，把君位让给了季历，季历传给姬昌，即周文王。武王时，灭了殷商，统一了天下。这一历史事件在孔子看来，是值得津津乐道的，三让天下的泰伯是道德最高尚的人。只有天下让给贤者、圣者，才有可能得到治理，而让位者则显示出高尚的品格，老百姓对他们是称赞无比的。

[2] 三以天下让：有多种理解：1. 认为泰伯确实礼让了三次。郑玄注云："泰伯，周太王之长子。次子仲雍，次子季历。太王见季历贤，又生文王，有圣人表，故欲立之而未有命。太王疾，太伯因适吴、越采药，太王殁

而不返，季历为丧主，一让也。季历赴之，不来奔丧，二让也。免丧之后，遂断发文身，三让也。三让之美，皆隐蔽不著，故人无得而称焉。"又，皇侃《义疏》引范宁云："有二释，一云：泰伯少弟季历，生子文王昌，昌有望德。泰伯知其必有天下，故欲令传国于季历，以及文王。因太王病，托采药于、越，不反。太王薨而季历立，一让也。季历薨而文王立，二让也。文王薨而武王立，于此遂有天下，是为三让也。又一云：太王病而托采药出，生不事之以礼，一让也。太王薨而不反，使季历主丧，死不葬之以礼，二让也。断发文身，示不可用，使季历住祭礼，不祭之以礼，三让也。"2.认为"三"为虚数，用以表示泰伯礼让态度的坚决，朱子《集注》云："三让，谓固逊也。"这里的"天下"与后世的天下不同，仅就当时的周部落而言，指的是君位、王位。

【原文】8.2　子曰："恭而无礼则劳[1]；慎而无礼则葸[2]；勇而无礼则乱；直而无礼则绞[3]。君子笃[4]于亲，则民兴于仁。故旧不遗，则民不偷[5]。"[6]

【译文】孔子说："只是恭敬而不以礼来指导，就会徒劳无功；只是谨慎而不以礼来指导，就会畏缩拘谨；只是勇猛而不以礼来指导，就会作乱；只是直率而不以礼来指导，就会说话尖刻。在上位的人如果厚待自己的亲族，老百姓当中就会兴起仁的风气；在上位的人不遗弃旧臣子，老百姓就不会对人冷漠无情。"

【英译】The Master said, "Respectfulness, without the rules of propriety, becomes laborious bustle; carefulness, without the rules of propriety, becomes timidity; boldness, without the rules of propriety, becomes insubordination; straightforwardness, without the rules of propriety, becomes rudeness. When those who are in high stations perform well all their duties to their relations, the people are aroused to virtue. When old friends are not neglected by them, the people are preserved from meanness."

【注释】

[1] 劳：辛劳、劳苦。辜鸿铭译为"pedantry"，强调"迂腐的"；理雅格译为"laborious"，即"劳苦的"；刘殿爵译为"wear himself out"，即"筋疲力尽的"；韦利译为"tiresome"，即"令人厌倦的"。上述译本相较，理雅格的翻译更为恰当。

[2] 葸：拘谨、畏惧的样子。理雅格、辜鸿铭、韦利均译为"Timidity"，即"胆怯、胆小"。

[3] 绞：说话尖刻，出口伤人。理雅格译为"rudeness"，即"粗鲁"；辜鸿铭译为"tyrannical"，即"残暴的、专横的"；刘殿爵译为"unrelenting"，即"冷酷无情的"；韦利译为"harshness"，即"严厉"。此处与"直"相对，强调没有礼的约束，直爽则会导向过度的"粗鲁尖刻"，即"rudeness"，理雅格译本较为恰当。

[4] 笃：厚待、真诚。

[5] 偷：淡薄。理雅格译为"meanness"，即"卑劣鄙陋"；辜鸿铭将该句译为"The people will not become grasping in their character"，即"人们不会对自己的性格有把握"，该译文不够准确；刘殿爵将"偷"译为"shirk their obligations"，即"逃避（对他人的）责任"；韦利译为"fickle"，即"反复无常的"。《论语》此处意指上位者不抛弃故旧，则百姓纷纷相仿、不会人情淡薄，"偷"译为"apathy"更为恰当。

[6] 孔子在《礼记·仲尼燕居》中说："夫礼，所以制中也"，礼为求中之器，礼，制中，礼求中，礼，亦为中，亦可以理解为度。"恭""慎""勇""直"等德目不是孤立存在的，必须以"礼"作指导，只有在"礼"的指导下，这些德目的实施才能符合中庸的准则，否则就会出现"劳""葸""乱""绞"，就不可能达到修身养性的目的。

【原文】 8.3 曾子有疾，召门弟子曰："启[1]予足！启予手！《诗》云：'战战兢兢，如临深渊，如履薄冰。'而今而后，吾知免[2]夫！小子[3]！"

【译文】曾子有病，把他的学生召集到身边来，说道："看看我的脚！看看我的手！（看看有没有损伤）《诗经》上说：'小心谨慎呀，好像站在深渊旁边，好像踩在薄冰上面。'从今以后，我知道我的身体是不再会受到损伤了，弟子们！"

【英译】The philosopher Tsang being ill, he cared to him the disciples of his school, and said, "Uncover my feet, uncover my hands. It is said in the Book of Poetry, 'We should be apprehensive and cautious, as if on the brink of a deep gulf, as if treading on thin ice, I and so have I been.' Now and hereafter, I know my escape from all injury to my person. O ye, my little children."

【注释】

[1] 启：开启，曾子让学生掀开被子看自己的手脚。

[2] 免：指身体免于损伤。

[3] 小子：对弟子的称呼。理雅格译为 "my little children"、韦利译为 "my little ones"，即 "我的孩子们"；辜鸿铭、刘殿爵译为 "my young friends"，即 "我的年轻朋友们"。此处 "小子" 是曾子称呼自己的弟子，译为 "my disciples" 更为恰当。

【原文】8.4 曾子有疾，孟敬子[1]问之。曾子言曰："鸟之将死，其鸣也哀；人之将死，其言也善[2]。君子所贵乎道者三：动容貌[3]，斯远暴慢矣；正颜色，斯近信矣[4]；出辞气[5]，斯远鄙倍矣。笾豆之事[6]，则有司存。"

【译文】曾子有病，孟敬子去看望他。曾子对他说："鸟快死了，它的叫声是悲哀的；人快死了，他说的话是善意的。君子所应当重视的道有三个方面：使自己的容貌庄重严肃，这样可以避免粗暴、放肆；使自己的脸色一本正经，这样就接近于诚信；使自己说话的言辞和语气谨慎小心，这样就可以避免粗野和悖理。至于祭祀和礼节仪式，自有主管这些事务的官吏来负责。"

【英译】The philosopher Tsang being ill, Meng Chang went to ask how he was. Tsang said to him, "When a bird is about to die, its notes are mournful; when a man is about to die, his words are good. There are three principles of conduct which the man of high rank should consider specially important: that in his deportment and manner he keep from violence and heedlessness; that in regulating his countenance he keep near to being trusted; and that in his words and tones he keep far from lowness and impropriety. As to such matters as attending to the sacrificial vessels, there are the proper officers for them."

【注释】

[1] 孟敬子：即鲁国大夫孟孙捷。

[2] 其言也善：辜鸿铭将该句译为"his words are true"，"善"被译为"真实的"；理雅格译为"his words are good"，刘殿爵译为"good are the words of a dying man"，其中"善"被译为"好的"；韦利译为"his words are of note"，即"他的话语是值得注意的"。"善""真""好"三者不能混淆："真"是现实生活中的人对于理论和逻辑的把握，是在理论体系的基础上达到主客观的统一；"善""好"是现实生活中的人在有目的性的实践活动中所表现出来的价值取向。《论语》此处的"善"，指的是将死之人其言论在道德上是"善的""好的"，而不仅仅是"真实的"，因此韦利、刘殿爵的翻译更为恰当。

[3] 动容貌：使自己的内心感情表现于面容。

[4] 正颜色，斯近信矣：使自己的脸色庄重严肃，这样就接近于诚信。理雅格译为"In regulating his countenance he keep near to sincerity"，"信"被译为"真诚的"；辜鸿铭将该句译为"In the expression of his countenance, he seeks to inspire confidence"，"信"被译为"自信"；刘殿爵译为"To come

close to being trusted by setting a proper expression"，"信"被译为"值得信任的"；韦利译为"every look that he composes in his face must betoken good faith"，"信"即"诚实、善意、真挚"。在儒家看来，诚信在人际交往和国家管理中具有十分重要的意义：在人际交往中，一个人如果不讲信用，是没法在世上生活的，即"人而无信，不知其也。大车无輗，小车无軏，其何以行之哉？"为政者取信于民、信实无欺，即"道千乘之国，敬事而信，节用而爱民，使民以时。"《论语》中的"信"主要包含"诚实"和"守诺"两个义素，"sincerity"和"good faith"仅体现出"真诚、诚实"之义，"being trusted"（值得被信任的）同时隐含了"这个人是诚实的"和"这个人是重诺的"两个前提。此处刘殿爵的翻译更为恰当。

[5] 出辞气：出言、说话，指注意说话的言辞和口气。

[6] 笾豆之事：笾和豆都是古代祭祀和典礼中的用具。

【原文】8.5 曾子曰："以能问于不能，以多问于寡，有若无，实若虚，犯而不校[1]。昔者吾友[2]，尝从事于斯矣。"

【译文】曾子说："自己有才能却向没有才能的人请教，自己知识多却向知识少的人请教，有学问却像没学问一样，知识很充实却好像很空虚，被人欺侮也不计较。从前我的朋友就这样做过了。"

【英译】The philosopher Tsang said，"Gifted with ability，and yet putting questions to those who were not so；possessed of much，and yet putting questions to those possessed of little；having，as though he had not；full，and yet counting himself as empty；offended against，and yet entering into not to mind；formerly I had a friend who pursued this style of conduct."

【注释】

[1] 校：同较，计较。理雅格译为"altercation"，即"口角、争辩"；刘殿爵译为"not to mind"，即"不在意"；韦利译为"contesting"，强调"争

夺、提出异议"。"犯而不校"此处指"被人侵犯也不在意",刘殿爵的翻译较为恰当。

[2] 吾友:我的朋友。旧注上一般都认为这里指颜渊。刘殿爵在注释中补充"According to tradition，this refers to Yen Hui"，解释了这一问题

【原文】8.6　曾子曰:"可以托六尺之孤[1]，可以寄百里之命[2]，临大节，而不可夺也，君子人与君子人也。"

【译文】曾子说:"可以把年幼的君主托付给他，可以把国家的政权托付给他，面临生死存亡的紧急关头，也不动摇屈服。这样的人是君子吗? 是君子啊!"

【英译】The philosopher Tsang said，"Suppose that there is an individual who can be entrusted with the charge of a young orphan prince，and can be commissioned with authority over a state of a hundred li，and whom no emergency however great can drive from his principles：is such a man a superior man? He is a superior man indeed."

【注释】

[1] 托六尺之孤:孤:死去父亲的小孩叫孤，六尺指 15 岁以下，古人以七尺指成年。托孤，受君主临终前的嘱托辅佐幼君。理雅格、辜鸿铭译为"orphan prince"，即"年幼的孤儿太子";刘殿爵译为"orphan six ch'ih' tall"，即"六尺高的孤儿"，并在注释中补充说明"The ch'ih in Tseng Tzu's time was much shorter than the modem foot"(在曾子的时代，"尺"的长度比现在要短);韦利译为"an orphan not yet fully grown"，即"一个尚未完全长大的孤儿"。本章《论语》"六尺之孤"指的是未成年的新君，刘殿爵、韦利没有译出"六尺之孤"是新任君主的身份，理雅格、辜鸿铭的翻译较为恰当。

[2] 寄百里之命:寄，寄托、委托。百里之命，指掌握国家政权和命运。

【原文】8.7　曾子曰："士不可以不弘毅[1]，任重而道远。仁以为己任，不亦重乎，死而后已，不亦远乎。"

【译文】曾子说："士不可以不弘大刚强而有毅力，因为他责任重大，前程远大。把实现仁作为自己的责任，难道还不重大吗？奋斗终生，到死方休，难道前程还不远大吗？"

【英译】The philosopher Tsang said，"The officer may not be without strength and resoluteness. His burden is heavy and his course is long. Perfect virtue is the burden which he considers it is his to sustain；-is it not heavy？ Only with death does his course stop；-is it not long？"

【注释】

[1] 弘毅："弘毅"即"强毅"，弘，广大。毅，强毅。杨伯峻先生引章太炎《广论语骈枝》曰："《说文》：'弘，弓声也。'后人借'强'焉之，用为'彊'义。此'弘'字即今之'强'字也。《说文》：'毅，有决也。'任重须彊，不彊则力绌；致远须决，不决则志渝。"黄怀信《论语汇校集释》云："弘大与任重不对，'弘'当读为'强'。《说文》'强'从弘声，是弘、强本音同，故可相借。强，谓强壮，指身体言。毅，谓有毅力。此曾子教士子锻炼身体、磨炼意志也。"理雅格译为"The officer may not be without breadth of mind and vigorous endurance"，即"官不可无心胸，不可无耐力"，"弘"被译为"心胸广大"，"毅"被译为"有毅力、有耐力"。辜鸿铭、刘殿爵译为"strength and resoluteness"，"弘"被译为"力量"，"毅"被译为"决心"。韦利译为"broad shouldered and stout of heart"，"弘"即"肩膀宽阔"，"毅"即"内心坚定"。辜鸿铭、刘殿爵同杨伯峻、黄怀信之说，其翻译简明易懂，符合《论语》原义。

【原文】8.8　子曰："兴于《诗》，立于礼，成于乐。"

【译文】孔子说："（人的修养）开始于学《诗》，自立于学礼，完成于学乐。"

【英译】 The Master said，"It is by the Odes that the mind is arou-sed. It is by the Rules of Propriety that the character is established. It is from Music that the finish is received."

【原文】 8.9　子曰："民可使由之，不可使知之。"[1]

【译文】 孔子说："对于老百姓，可以使他们按照我们的想法去做，不能使他们知道为什么要这样做。"

【英译】 The Master said，"The people may be made to follow a path of action，but they may not be made to understand it."

【注释】

[1] 前人多认为这章体现了孔子的愚民思想，如，郑玄注曰："民，冥也，其见人道远。由，从也，言王者设教，务使人从之。若皆知其本末，则愚者或轻而不行。"何晏、皇侃、邢昺理解同，邢昺《注疏》云："此章言圣人之道深远，人不易知也。由，用也。'民可使用之，而不可使知之'者，以百姓能日用而不能知故也。"又戴望《论语注》云："民之言冥，其见人道远。由，从也。王者设教皆于经隐权，故可使民从，不可使民知。老子曰：'国之利器不可以示人。'此之谓也。"亦有人为孔子回护，如朱子《集注》引程子曰："圣人设教，非不欲人家喻而户晓也，然不能使之知，但能使之由之尔。若曰圣人不使民知，则是后世朝四暮三之术也，岂圣人之心乎？"如刘宝楠《正义》云："愚谓上章是夫子教弟子之法，此'民'亦指弟子。"出土文献则为我们提供了新的、更为可靠的解释，郭店楚简《尊德义》篇云："民可使导之，不可使知之。民可导也，而不可强也。"廖名春经过考证，认为此处"知"为"折"的借字，并说："如果按照一般的理解，说民'不可使知之'，那孔子的教学就无从谈起了。因为民'不可使知之'，孔子再怎么'诲人不倦'也没有用。我们只要肯定孔子是一个伟大的教育家，是'有教无类'的，就势必不能接受孔子有民'不可使知之'的说法。把这段话读懂了，就知道孔子这句话非但不是愚民思想，而是非常强烈的民本

思想，即老百姓只能去引导（迪），不能以暴力去强迫、去压服（折）。为什么？因为孔子知道'匹夫不可以夺志'。"（参见廖名春《不要再误读论语了》，《中华读书报》2012 年 12 月 3 日）在《论语》海外译介过程中，理雅格、辜鸿铭、韦利等译者均从《论语》字面义，将该句译为 "not be made to understand it"，即 "不让老百姓知道"，这实是对本章的误解。若廖明春的考证为实，则该句译为 "They cannot be suppressed by violence"（不能暴力镇压老百姓），更为恰当。

【原文】8.10　子曰："好勇疾[1]贫，乱也。人而不仁，疾之已甚，乱也。"

【译文】孔子说："喜好勇敢又厌恶自己穷困，就会犯上作乱。对于不仁德的人厌恶得太过分，也会出乱子。"

【英译】The Master said，"The man who is fond of daring and is dissatisfied with poverty，will proceed to insubordination. So will the man who is not virtuous，when you carry your dislike of him to an extreme."

【注释】

[1] 疾：恨、憎恨。理雅格译为 "dissatisfied"，即 "不满意、不高兴"；辜鸿铭译为 "hate"，即 "厌恶"；刘殿爵译为 "detesting"，即 "憎恨"。detest 与 hate 语义相近但程度不同：detest 的语气较重，表示强烈的恨；hate 次之，厌恶之意。本章《论语》在情感程度上，尚未达到 "极度憎恨自己"，"detesting" 的情感色彩过分强烈，辜鸿铭译为 "hate" 更为恰当。

【原文】8.11　子曰："如有周公之才之美，使骄且吝，其余不足观也已。"

【译文】孔子说："即使有周公那样美好的才能，如果骄傲自大而又吝啬小气，那其他方面也就不值得一看了。"

【英译】The Master said, "Though a man have abilities as admirable as those of The duke of Chau, yet if he be proud and niggardly, those other things are really not worth being looked at."

【原文】8.12　子曰："三年学，不至于穀[1]，不易得也。"

【译文】孔子说："读书三年，还不存有做官的念头，这是难得的。"

【英译】The Master said, "It is not easy to find a man who has learned for three years without coming to be good."

【注释】

[1] 穀：两种解释：1. 解作善。何晏《集解》引孔安国曰："至，善也。言人三岁学，不至于善，不可得言必无也，所以劝人学。"2. 郑玄注解作禄位。朱子《集注》同，其文云："穀，禄也。至，疑当作志。为学之久，而不求禄，如此之人，不易得也。杨氏曰：虽子张之觅犹以干禄为问，况其下者乎？然则三年学而不至于谷，宜不易得也。"理雅格从何晏《集解》说，译为"good"，即"好的、善的"；辜鸿铭译为"improvement"，即"提升、提高"之义；刘殿爵将"穀"译为"salary"、韦利译为"reward"，即"薪水、薪酬"之义，该说更贴近朱子《集注》之说。

【原文】8.13　子曰："笃信好学，守死善道。危邦不人，乱邦不居，天下有道则见，无道则隐。邦有道，贫且贱焉，耻也，邦无道，富且贵焉，耻也。"[1]

【译文】孔子说："坚定信念并努力学习，誓死守卫并完善为人与治国的大道。不进入政局不稳的国家，不居住在动乱的国家。天下有道就出来做官，天下无道就隐居不出。国家有道而自己贫贱，是耻辱；国家无道而自己富贵，也是耻辱。"

【英译】The Master said, "With sincere faith he unites the love of learning; holding firm to death, he is perfecting the excellence of his course." Such an one will not enter a tottering state, nor dwell in a disorganized one. When right principles of government prevail in the kingdom, he will show himself; when they are prostrated, he will keep concealed. "When a country is well governed, poverty and a mean condition are things to be ashamed of. When a country is ill governed, riches and honor are things to be ashamed of."

【注释】

[1] 这是孔子给弟子们传授的入世之道。"天下有道则见，无道则隐"；"用之则行，舍之则藏"，这是孔子为官处世的一条重要原则。此外，他还提出应当把个人的贫贱荣辱与国家的兴衰存亡联系在一起，这才是治理政事的基点。

【原文】 8.14　子曰："不在其位，不谋其政[1]。"

【译文】 孔子说："不在那个职位上，就不考虑那职位上的政务。"

【英译】 The Master said, "He who is not in any particular office has nothing to do with plans for the administration of its duties."

【注释】

[1] 政：政事。理雅格译为"the administration of its duties"，即"行政部门的责任"；刘殿爵译为"matters of government"，即"政府的事情"；辜鸿铭译为"government policy"，即"政府的决策"；韦利译为"State policy"，即"国家的政策"。"administration"的词义核心是"行政分支"，"government"是包含各个统治分支的总的统治机构，因此，"government"与"政府"可以互译，一般用于政府机关，"administration"一般用于行政、管理机关。"government"的范围要比"administration"的用途范围广。"state"即"国家"，是一个政治色彩浓郁的词汇，强调一个国家的政权完整性和独立性。"不在其位，不谋其政"涉及儒家所谓的"名分"问题。不在其位而谋其政，则有僭越之嫌，是违礼之举。这里的"位"指的是国家统

治机构中的职位，不仅仅局限在行政分支中，因此刘殿爵译为"matters of government"更为恰当。

【原文】8.15　子曰："师挚之始[1]，《关雎》之乱[2]，洋洋乎盈耳哉。"

【译文】孔子说："从太师挚演奏的序曲开始，到最后演奏《关雎》的结尾，丰富而优美的音乐在我耳边回荡。"

【英译】The Master said，"When the music master Chih first entered on his office，the finish of the Kwan Tsu was magnificent；-how it filled the ears！"

【注释】

[1] 师挚之始：师挚是鲁国的太师。"始"是乐曲的开端，即序曲。古代奏乐，开端叫"升歌"，一般由太师演奏，师挚是太师，因此称"师挚之始"。

[2]《关雎》之乱："始"是乐曲的开端，"乱"是乐曲的终了。"乱"是合奏乐。此时奏《关雎》乐章，所以叫"《关雎》之乱"。理雅格、刘殿爵、辜鸿铭皆从上述说法；韦利则将该句译为"When Zhi the Chief Musician led the climax of the Ospreysl，what a grand flood of sound filled one's ears！"（当太师挚演奏《奥普雷西》的高潮时，听众的耳朵里充满了巨大的声音），该翻译没能译出"始""乱"之义，不够恰当。

【原文】8.16　子曰："狂[1]而不直，侗[2]而不愿[3]，悾悾[4]而不信，吾不知之矣。"

【译文】孔子说："狂妄而不正直，无知而不谨慎，表面上诚恳而不守信用，我真不知道有的人为什么会是这个样子。"

【英译】The Master said，"Ardent and yet not upright，ignorant and yet not attentive；simple and yet not sincere：-such persons I do not understand."

【注释】

[1] 狂：急躁、急进。理雅格译为"Ardent"，即"热心的"；辜鸿铭译为"high spirit"，即"精神高涨"；刘殿爵译为"reject discipline"，即"拒绝、不服从纪律"；韦利译为"impetuous"，即"急躁冲动的"。《论语》此处含贬义，指过分强烈的急躁情绪，韦利的翻译较为恰当。

[2] 侗：幼稚无知。理雅格译为"stupid"，即"愚蠢的"；辜鸿铭译为"dullness"，即"迟钝的"；刘殿爵译为ignorant，即"无知的"；韦利译为"ingenuous"，即"天真幼稚的"。"stupid"常指人因智力低下而显得愚笨、迟钝的，往往含呆滞木讷之意，意为"愚蠢的、头脑迟钝的"，语气较重。《论语》此处是指人"幼稚、缺乏知识"而非"愚蠢"，因此理雅格译为"stupid"不甚恰当。"ignorant"指一般的无知或指不知道某个具体的事；"ingenuous"则常用于形容孩子般天真坦率的人，不含"无知"之义。"侗"更多形容某人的无知而非直率，刘殿爵译为"ignorant"更为恰当。

[3] 愿：谨慎。皇侃《义疏》云："愿，谨愿也。"朱子《集注》云："愿，谨厚也。"

[4] 悾悾：同空，诚恳的样子。郑玄注曰："悾悾，诚悫也。"又包咸曰："悾悾，悫也，宜可信也。"朱子《集注》则解作"无能"。理雅格译为"simple"、辜鸿铭译为"simplicity"，即"简单"之义；韦利则补充了"简单"形容的对象是"simple minded"，即"头脑简单的"；刘殿爵将"悾悾"译为"devoid of ability"，即"缺乏能力的"，该翻译从朱熹《四书章句集注》之说。此处"悾悾"与"不信"形成对比，译为"诚恳"较恰当。

【原文】 8.17　子曰："学如不及，犹恐失之。"

【译文】 孔子说："学习知识就像追赶不上那样，又会担心丢掉什么。"

【英译】 The Master said,"Learn as if you could not reach your object，and were always fearing also lest you should lose it."

【原文】8.18 子曰："巍巍乎，舜禹之有天下也，而不与[1]焉。"

【译文】孔子说："舜和禹多么崇高啊！贵为天子，富有天下，却好像与自己无关。"

【英译】The Master said，"How majestic was the manner in which Shun and Yu held possession of the empire，as if it were nothing to them！"

【注释】

[1] 不与：有多种理解。1. 指并非自己预求而得。皇侃《义疏》云："舜受尧禅而有天下，禹受舜禅而有天下，此二圣得时有天下，并非身所预求而君自禅之也。"2. 指孔子不得在舜禹之时。皇侃《义疏》云："一曰，孔子叹己不预见舜、禹之时也。若逢其时，则己宜道当用也。"3. 指和自己无关。朱子《集注》云："不与，犹言不相关，言其不以位为乐也。"此处理雅格从朱子说，译为"as if it were nothing to them"，即"好像对自己来说没有什么"。辜鸿铭、韦利更近似皇侃《义疏》之说：辜鸿铭译为"Themselves were unconscious of it"，即"没有意识到这一点"；韦利译为"They remained aloof from it"，即"他们对这件事无动于衷"。刘殿爵将本章译为"How lofty Shun and Yü were in holding aloof from the Empire when they were in possession of it."即"舜和禹在拥有帝国的时候是多么的高尚啊。"该翻译不符合《论语》本章主旨。

【原文】8.19 子曰："大哉，尧之为君也！巍巍乎，唯天为大，唯尧则之。荡荡[1]乎，民无能名[2]焉。巍巍乎其有成功也，焕[3]乎其有文章[4]。"

【译文】孔子说："尧这样的君主真伟大啊！多么崇高啊！只有天

最高大，只有尧才能效法天的高大。他的恩德多么广大，百姓们真不知道该用什么语言来表达对它的称赞。他的功绩多么崇高，他制定的礼乐制度多么光辉啊！"

【英译】The Master said，"Great indeed was Yao as a sovereign！How majestic was he！It is only Heaven that is grand，and only Yao corresponded to it. How vast was his virtue！The people did not know in what language to praise it. How majestic was he in the works which he accomplished！How glorious in the system of rites and music which he instituted！"

【注释】

[1] 荡荡：广大的样子。

[2] 名：形容、称说、称赞。理雅格、韦利根据字面义，将"民无能名"一句译为"The people could find no name for it"，即"人们找不到它的名字"。辜鸿铭将该句译为"The people had no name for such moral greatness"，即"人民没有如此道德伟大的名字"。刘殿爵译为"put a name to his virtues"，即"为美德命名"。此处"名"译为"赞美、称颂"比较恰当，即"The people did not know in what language to praise it"。

[3] 焕：光辉。

[4] 文章：这里指礼法制度。理雅格译为"regulations"（规章制度）；辜鸿铭译为"arts"（艺术）；刘殿爵译为"civilized accomplishments"，即"文明成就"；韦利译为"insignia of his culture"，即"文化的标志"。尧是中国传说时代的圣君。孔子在这里用极美好的语言称赞尧，尤其对他的礼仪制度愈加赞美。《论语》此处"文章"指儒家的礼法制度，译为 the system of rites and music 更为恰当。

【原文】8.20 舜有臣五人[1]，而天下治。武王曰："予有乱臣[2]十人。"孔子曰："才难，不其然乎，唐虞之际[3]，于斯为盛，有妇人焉[4]，九人而已。三分天下有其二[5]，以服事殷。周之德，其可谓至德也已矣。"

【译文】舜有五位贤臣，就能治理好天下。周武王也说过："我有十个辅助我治理国家的大臣。"孔子说："人才难得，难道不是这样吗？唐尧和虞舜之间及周武王这个时期，人才是最盛了。但十个大臣中有一个是妇女，实际上只有九个人而已。周文王得了天下的三分之二，仍然事奉殷朝，周朝的德可以说是最高的了。"

【英译】Shun had five ministers，and the empire was well governed. King Wu said，"I have ten able ministers."Confucius said，"Is not the saying that talents are difficult to find，true？Only when the dynasties of T'ang and Yu met，were they more abundant than in this of Chau，yet there was a woman among them. The able ministers were no more than nine men. King Wan possessed two of the three parts of the empire，and with those he served the dynasty of Yin. The virtue of the house of Chau may be said to have reached the highest point indeed."

【注释】

[1] 舜有臣五人：传说是禹、稷、契、皋陶、伯益等人。

[2] 乱臣：据《说文》："乱，治也。"此处所说的"乱臣"，应为"治国之臣"。理雅格译为"able ministers"，即"有能力的部门长官"；辜鸿铭译为"great Public Servants"，即"伟大的公仆"；刘殿爵译为"capable officials"，即"有能力的官员"。在英语中，minister原本表示牧师（上帝的奴仆）或大臣（国王的奴仆）。后来英国实行君主立宪制，国王的大臣变成了政府的部长，minister则译为"部长"而不再是"大臣"。officials则是指国家政府部门的行政官员、高级职员，指国家的管理人员。英语中"minister"更侧重英国等国家内阁的阁员、部长，政治色彩浓厚，此处译文"officials"更为恰当。

[3] 唐虞之际：传说尧在位的时代叫唐，舜在位的时代叫虞。

[4] 有妇人焉：指武王的乱臣十人中有武王之妻邑姜。

[5] 三分天下有其二：《逸周书·程典篇》说："文王令九州之侯，奉勤于商"。相传当时分九州，文王得六州，是三分之二。

【原文】8.21 子曰："禹，吾无间[1]然矣，菲饮食而致孝乎鬼神，恶衣服而致美乎黻冕[2]，卑宫室而尽力乎沟洫[3]。禹，吾无间然矣。"

【译文】孔子说："对于禹，我没有什么可以挑剔的了；他的饮食很简单而尽力去孝敬鬼神；他平时穿的衣服很简朴，而祭祀时尽量穿得华美，他自己住的宫室很低矮，而致力于修治水利事宜。对于禹，我确实没有什么挑剔的了。"

【英译】The Master said, "I can find no flaw in the character of Yu. He used himself coarse food and drink, but displayed the utmost filial piety towards the spirits. His ordinary garments were poor, but he displayed the utmost elegance in his sacrificial cap and apron. He lived in a low, mean house, but expended all his strength on the ditches and water channels. I can find nothing like a flaw in Yu."

【注释】

[1] 间：一说间隙，作动词，指寻找间隙进行批评、指责。朱子《集注》云："间，罅隙也，谓指其罅隙而非议之也。"一说间厕，插足其间。何晏《集解》引孔疏云："孔子推禹功德之盛美，言己不能复间其间。"邢昺《注疏》云："间谓间厕。"

[2] 黻冕：祭祀时穿戴的礼服和冠帽。

[3] 沟洫：沟渠，指农田水利。朱子《集注》云："沟洫，田间水道，以正疆界、备旱潦者也。"

子罕篇第九

【原文】 9.1　子罕言利与命与仁。[1]

【译文】 孔子很少谈到利益、天命与仁德。

【英译】 The subjects of which the Master seldom spoke were-profitableness，and also the appointments of Heaven，and perfect virtue.

【注释】

[1] 这章只有8个字，但是理解却有多种：1.孔子少言利益、命运和仁。如何晏《集解》："罕者，希也。利者，义之和也。命者，天之命也。仁者，行之盛也。寡能及之，故希言也。"朱子同此。后人对这种说法提出疑问，认为《论语》一书中孔子多次谈到仁、命、利，不能说罕言。《论语》海外译介过程中，理雅格、辜鸿铭、刘殿爵、韦利等译本均从该说。2.程树德认为这里的"言"指自言。程树德《集释》云："窃谓解此章者多未了解'言'字之义。盖'言'者，自言也。记者旁窥已久，知夫子于此三者皆罕自言，非谓以此立教也。说者徒见弟子问答多问仁，遂疑命仁为夫子所常言，实皆非此章之义也。《论语》中如'小人喻于利'、'放于利而行'、'君子畏天命'、'不知命无以为君子'、'我欲仁而仁至'、'当仁不让于师'之类，出于夫子自言者实属无几。大抵言仁稍多，言命次之，言利最少，故以利承罕言之文，而于命、于仁则以两'与'次第之。"杨伯峻《论语译注》认为是孔子鲜少主动谈论利、命和仁，与程氏之说同。3.认为孔子很少以利、命、仁许人。皇侃《义疏》云："利者，天道元亨，利万物者也。与者，言

语许与之也。命，天命，穷通夭寿之目也。仁者，恻隐济众，行之盛者也。弟子记孔子为教化所希言，及所希许与人者也。所以然者，利是元亨利贞之道也，百姓日用而不知，其理玄绝，故孔子希言也。命是人禀天而生，其道难测，又好恶不同，若逆向人说，则伤动人情，故孔子希说与人也。仁是行盛，非中人所能，故亦希说许与人也。"4.释"与"为赞许，句读为"子罕言利，与命与仁"。即孔子很少谈论利，赞许命运和仁德。如史绳祖《学斋占毕》。5.认为孔子少言利益、命运和仁，但少言仁是不轻易许人。杨树达《论语疏证》云："所谓罕言仁者，乃不轻许人以仁之意，与罕言利、命之义似不同。"6.黄怀信《论语汇校集释》认为"言"字下省或脱"其"字，指孔子很少谈论自己的利益、命运和仁德。

【原文】 9.2　达巷党[1]人曰："大哉孔子，博学而无所成名[2]。"子闻之，谓门弟子曰："吾何执？执御乎，执射乎？吾执御矣。"

【译文】 达巷党这个地方有人说："孔子真伟大啊！他学问渊博，可惜没有足以树立名声的专长。"孔子听说了，对他的学生说："我要专长于哪个方面呢？驾车呢？还是射箭呢？我还是驾车吧。"

【英译】 A man of the village of Ta-hsiang said，"Great indeed is the philosopher K'ung！His learning is extensive，and yet he does not render his name famous by any particular thing." The Master heard the observation，and said to his disciples，"What shall I practice？Shall I practice charioteering，or shall I practice archery？I will practice charioteering."

【注释】

[1] 达巷党人：古代五百家为一党，达巷是党名。这是说达巷党这地方的人。

[2] 博学而无所成名：有两种理解：1.认为孔子博学多才，因而不能以某一方面称赞他。皇侃《义疏》云："言大哉孔子，广学道艺，周遍不可

——而称，故云无所成名也，犹如尧德荡荡，民无能名也。"2. 认为孔子博学多才，可惜没有一艺之长以成名。朱子《集注》云："博学无所成名，盖美其学之博而惜其不成一艺之名也。"理雅格译为"he does not render his name famous by any particular thing"，即"不以特别的事情来扬名立万"。辜鸿铭译为"he has not distinguished himself in anything so as to make himself a name"，即"他并没有以任何成就来使自己出名"。韦利译为"But he does nothing to bear out this reputation"，即"但他没有做任何事情来证明这一名声"。上述三家译本，含有"不自夸、不自傲"之意。刘殿爵译为"but has not made a name for himself in any field"，该译文从朱子《集注》之说，认为孔子"学识渊博，但在任何领域都没有出名"。持此说的人认为，孔子表面上伟大，但实际上算不上博学多识，他什么都懂，什么都不精。对此说，我们觉得似乎有求全责备之嫌。

【原文】9.3　子曰："麻冕[1]，礼也。今也纯[2]，俭，吾从众。拜下，礼也。今拜乎上，泰[3]也，虽远众，吾从下。"

【译文】孔子说："用麻布制成的礼帽，符合于礼的规定。现在大家都用黑丝绸制作，这样比过去节省了，我赞成大家的做法。臣见国君，首先要在堂下跪拜，这也是符合于礼的。现在大家都到堂上跪拜，这是骄纵的表现。虽然与大家的做法不一样，我还是主张先在堂下拜。"

【英译】The Master said，"The linen cap is that prescribed by the rules of ceremony，but now a silk one is worn. It is economical，and I follow the common practice. The rules of ceremony prescribe the bowing below the hall，but now the practice is to bow only after ascending it. That is arrogant. I continue to bow below the hall，though I oppose the common practice."

【注释】

[1] 麻冕：麻布制成的礼帽。

[2] 纯：丝绸，黑色的丝。理雅格、辜鸿铭译为"silk"，刘殿爵、韦利译为"black silk"，均为丝绸之义。

[3] 泰：骄纵、傲慢。理雅格译为"arrogant"，即"傲慢自大的"；刘殿爵译为"casual"，即"随意的"；韦利译为"presumptuous"，即"放肆的、专横的"。arrogant 用于贬义，指过高估计自己，以致骄傲自大或傲慢无礼，目中无人。casual 指不太注意场合，仪表等，随意性强。《论语》此处意指堂上跪拜是僭越礼制的，是指为臣者骄纵傲慢、不敬君主，因此理雅格的翻译更为恰当。

【原文】9.4　子绝四：毋意[1]，毋必[2]，毋固[3]，毋我[4]。

【译文】孔子杜绝了四种弊病：不主观揣测，不绝对肯定，不固执己见，不唯我独是。

【英译】There were four things from which the Master was entirely free. He had no foregone conclusions，no expectations to be met，no obstinacy，and no egoism.

【注释】

[1] 意：同臆，猜想、猜疑。理雅格译为"foregone conclusions"，即"预先的结论"。辜鸿铭译为"self-interest"，即"私利"，不够恰当。刘殿爵译为"conjectures"，即"猜测猜想"。韦利译为"Took nothing for granted"，"毋意"即"不认为是理所当然的"。上述译本相较，刘殿爵的翻译更为忠实《论语》原义。

[2] 必：期必，期望必须按照自己希望的那样。理雅格译为"arbitrary predeterminations"，即"武断的预设"；辜鸿铭译为"prepossessions"，即"先入为主的观念"；刘殿爵译为"insist on certainty"，即"坚持确定的事情"；韦利译为"over-positive"，即"过分积极的"。朱子《集注》云："必，期必也。"王夫之《笺解》云："为之而必欲其成，不因时之可否以行止，曰'必'。"若从朱子说，上述译本并未译出"必"的"期必"之义，我们认为

该句译为 "no expectations to be met" 更为恰当。

[3] 固：固执。

[4] 我：私心。理雅格、辜鸿铭译为 "egoism"，即 "利己主义"；刘殿爵、韦利则译为 "egotistical"，即 "任性的、自我本位的"。egoism 侧重利己主义或自我利益，指只顾自己利益而不顾别人利益和集体利益的思想。egotistical 则强调个人自由、个人利益，是一种从个人至上出发，以个人为中心来看待世界、看待社会和人际关系的世界观。由此看来，刘殿爵、韦利译为 "egotistical" 更为契合《论语》"毋我"之意。

【原文】9.5　子畏于匡[1]。曰："文王既没，文不在兹[2]乎。天之章丧斯文也。后死者[3]不得与[4]于斯文也。天之未丧斯文也。匡人其如予何。"

【译文】孔子被匡地的人们围困时，他说："周文王死了以后，周代的礼乐文化不都体现在我的身上吗？上天如果想要消灭这种文化，那我就不可能掌握这种文化了；上天如果不消灭这种文化，那么匡人又能把我怎么样呢？"

【英译】The Master was put in fear in K'wang. He said, "After the death of King Wan，was not the cause of truth lodged here in me? If Heaven had wished to let this cause of truth perish，then I，a future mortal！should not have got such a relation to that cause. While Heaven does not let the cause of truth perish，what can the people of K'wang do to me?"

【注释】

[1] 畏于匡：匡，地名，在今河南省长垣县西南。畏，受到威胁。公元前496年，孔子从卫国到陈国去经过匡地。匡人曾受到鲁国阳虎的掠夺和残杀。孔子的相貌与阳虎相像，匡人误以为孔子就是阳虎，所以将他围困。

[2] 兹：这里，指孔子自己。

[3] 后死者：孔子这里指自己。理雅格译为"future mortal"，即"未来的凡人"，是孔子自称；辜鸿铭译为"a mortal of this late generation"，即"（文王）后来的一代人"，指孔子当时的人民。黄怀信《论语汇校集释》云："后死者，谓己死以后之人……此孔子言死生有命以自慰也。"意思是说，如果上天将要消灭周代的礼乐制度文化，那么孔子就逃不过这次劫难，后来人就无法了解这种文化了。刘殿爵从此说，译为"Those who come after me"，韦利译为"latter-day mortal"，均指孔子后代的人们。

[4] 与：同"举"，理解、掌握。理雅格将该句译为"should not have got such a relation to that cause"，即"不应该和那件事有关系"；辜鸿铭译为"understand"，即"理解"；刘殿爵译为"have"，即"拥有、掌握"；韦利译为"link"，即"联系"在一起。钱穆《论语新解》解作"得知"，黄怀信《论语汇校集释》解作"闻知"。根据上述诠释，辜鸿铭的翻译更为恰当。

【原文】9.6　大宰[1]问于子贡曰："夫子圣者与！何其多能也？"子贡曰："固天纵之将圣，又多能也。"子闻之曰："大宰知我乎？吾少也贱，故多能鄙事[2]。君子多乎哉？不多也！"

【译文】太宰问子贡说："孔夫子是圣人吧？为什么这样多才多艺呢？"子贡说："这本是上天让他成为圣人，而且使他多才多艺。"孔子听到后说："太宰怎么会了解我呢？我因为少年时地位低贱，所以会许多卑贱的技艺。君子会有这么多的技艺吗？不会多的。"

【英译】A high officer asked Tsze-Kung，saying，"May we not say that your Master is a sage？How various is his ability！"Tsze-Kung said，"Certainly Heaven has endowed him unlimitedly. He is about a sage. And，moreover，his ability is various."The Master heard of the conversation and said，"Does the high officer know me？When I was young，my condition was low，and I acquired my ability in many things，but they were mean matters. Must the superior man have such variety of ability? He does not need variety of ability."

【注释】

[1] 太宰：官名，掌握国君宫廷事务。郑玄认为此处指吴国的太宰伯嚭。

[2] 鄙事：卑贱的事情。

【原文】 9.7　牢[1]曰："子云：'吾不试[2]，故艺[3]。'"

【译文】 子牢说："孔子说过：'我年轻时没有去做官，所以学会了许多技艺。'"

【英译】 Lao said, "The Master said, 'Having no official employment, I acquired many arts.'"

【注释】

[1] 牢：郑玄说此人系孔子的学生，但在《史记·仲尼弟子列传》中未见此人。刘殿爵在注释中补充"the identity of the person referred to here is uncertain"，说明"牢"身份的不确定性。

[2] 试：用，被任用。理雅格译为"official employment"，即"官方的职位"；辜鸿铭译为"act in public life"，即"在公共生活中行动"；刘殿爵译为"In office"，即"在位"；韦利译为"been given a chance"，即"被给予机会"。上述译本相较，理雅格、刘殿爵的翻译更为契合《论语》原义。

[3] 艺：理雅格、辜鸿铭译为"art"（艺术）；刘殿爵译为"a jack of all trades"，即"万能的专家"；韦利译为"handy"，形容孔子是"手巧的、有手艺的"。本章与上一章的内容相关联，孔子认为自己的多才多艺是由于年轻时没有去做官，所以掌握了许多谋生技艺。"艺"在这里不仅指艺术或手工艺，而是形容孔子具有在生活和工作中解决实际问题的实践技能。上述译本相较，刘殿爵的翻译更为恰当。

【原文】 9.8　子曰："吾有知乎哉？无知也。有鄙夫问于我，空空如也[1]；我叩[2]其两端[3]而竭[4]焉。”

【译文】孔子说："我有知识吗？其实没有知识。有一个乡下人问我，我对他谈的问题本来一点也不知道。我只是从问题的两端去问，这样对此问题就可以全部搞清楚了。"

【英译】The Master said，"Am I indeed possessed of knowledge? I am not knowing. But if a mean person，who appears quite empty-like，ask anything of me，I set it forth from one end to the other，and exhaust it."

【注释】

[1] 空空如也：指孔子自己心中空空无知。理雅格认为该句是形容"鄙夫"的无知："If a mean person，who appears quite empty-like"；辜鸿铭将该句译为"have no opinion whatever of the subject"，"空空"即"没有任何意见"；刘殿爵译为"my mind was a complete blank"，即"大脑一片空白"；韦利认为该句是形容"鄙夫"的态度诚恳："In all sincerity"。可见在《论语》的海外译介过程中，该句出现至少三种解释。

[2] 叩：叩问、询问。

[3] 两端：两头，指正反、始终、上下方面。

[4] 竭：穷尽、尽力追究。理雅格译为"exhaust"，即"耗尽"；辜鸿铭译为"get to the bottom"，即"深究、彻查"；刘殿爵译为"I got everything out of it"，即"我从中弄明白"。"竭"意指孔子弄清楚问题，而非在"叩两端"中"竭尽全力"。上述译本相较，刘殿爵的翻译更为恰当。

【原文】9.9　子曰："凤鸟[1]不至，河不出图[2]，吾已矣乎！"

【译文】孔子说："凤鸟不来了，黄河中也不出现图画了。我这一生恐怕是完了吧！"

【英译】The Master said，"The Fang bird does not come；the river sends forth no Hetu：-it is all over with me！"

【注释】

[1] 凤鸟：古代传说中的一种神鸟。传说凤鸟在舜和周文王时代都出现过，它的出现象征着"圣王"将要出世。理雅格直接音译为"Fang bird"；刘殿爵、韦利均译为"Phoenix"（凤凰），刘本并在注释中补充："Both the Phoenix and the Chart were auspicious omens. Confucius is here lamenting the hopelessness of putting the Way into practice in the Empire of his day"，表达孔子看到恢复周礼成为泡影的哀叹。

[2] 河不出图：传说在上古伏羲氏时代，黄河中有龙马背负八卦图而出。它的出现也象征着"圣王"将要出世。辜鸿铭将天上的凤凰和地上的《河图》合译为"In heaven or on earth"，并表明孔子此时正处于混乱和无政府状态的时期，难以看到即将开创世界事物的新秩序。理雅格将该句译为"The river sends forth no map"；刘殿爵、韦利则译为"The river gives forth no chart"。chart 指航海地图，也指图表、示意图、曲线图。map 则指标有国家大小、城市、铁路、河流、山脉、海洋等的地图，二者均无法准确描述《河图》。我们认为，《河图》作为专有名词，直接音译为"Hetu"更为恰当。

【原文】 9.10　子见齐衰[1]者、冕衣裳[2]者与瞽者，见之，虽少必作[3]；过之，必趋。

【译文】 孔子遇见穿丧服的人、当官的人和盲人时，虽然他们年轻，孔子也一定要站起来，从他们面前经过时，一定要快步走过。

【英译】 When the Master saw a person in a mourning dress, or any one with the cap and upper and lower garments of full dress，or a blind person，on observing them approaching，though they were younger than himself，he would rise up，and if he had to pass by them，he would do so hastily.

【注释】

[1] 齐衰：丧服，古时用麻布制成。

[2] 冕衣裳者：冕，官帽；衣，上衣；裳，下服，这里统指官服。冕衣裳者指贵族。

[3] 作：站起来，表示敬意。

【原文】9.11 颜渊喟然叹曰："仰之弥高，钻之弥坚，瞻之在前，忽焉在后！夫子循循然善诱人[1]：博我以文，约我以礼，欲罢不能。既竭吾才，如有所立，卓尔[2]；虽欲从之，末由[3]也已！"

【译文】颜渊感叹地说："（对于老师的学问与道德），我抬头仰望，越望越觉得高；我努力钻研，越钻研越觉得不可穷尽。看着它好像在前面，忽然又像在后面。老师善于一步一步地诱导我，用各种典籍来丰富我的知识，又用各种礼节来约束我的言行，使我想停止学习都不可能，直到我用尽了我的全力。好像有一个十分高大的东西立在我前面，虽然我想要追随上去，却没有前进的路径了。"

【英译】Yen Yuan, in admiration of the Master's doctrines, sighed and said, "I looked up to them, and they seemed to become more high; I tried to penetrate them, and they seemed to become more firm; I looked at them before me, and suddenly they seemed to be behind. The Master, by orderly method, skillfully leads men on. He enlarged my mind with learning, and taught me the restraints of propriety. When I wish to give over the study of his doctrines, I cannot do so, and having exerted all my ability, there seems something to stand right up before me; but though I wish to follow and lay hold of it, I really find no way to do so."

【注释】

[1] 循循然善诱人：循循然，有次序地。诱，劝导，引导。

[2] 卓尔：高大、超群的样子。

[3] 末由：末，无、没有。由，途径，路径。这里是没有办法的意思。

理雅格直译为"I really find no way";辜鸿铭、刘殿爵、韦利直译为"I can find no way",即"没有道路"。

【原文】9.12　子疾病,子路使门人为臣[1]。病间[2],曰:"久矣哉,由之行诈也! 无臣而为有臣,吾谁欺? 欺天乎? 且予与其死于臣之手也,无宁死于二三子之手乎! 且予纵不得大葬[3],予死于道路乎?"

【译文】孔子患了重病,子路派了孔子的门人去做孔子的家臣,负责料理后事。后来,孔子的病好了一些,他说:"仲由做这种弄虚作假的事情竟太长久了呀! 我明明没有家臣,却偏偏要装作有家臣,我骗谁呢? 我骗上天吧? 与其在家臣的侍候下死去,我宁可在你们这些学生的侍候下死去,这样不是更好吗? 而且即使我不能以大夫之礼来安葬,难道就会被丢在路边没人埋吗?"

【英译】The Master being very ill, Tsze-Lu wished the disciples to act as ministers to him. During a remission of his illness, he said, "Long has the conduct of Yu been deceitful! By pretending to have ministers when I have them not, whom should I impose upon? Should I impose upon Heaven? Moreover, than that I should die in the hands of ministers, is it not better that I should die in the hands of you, my disciples? And though I may not get a funeral of the scholar-official, shall I die upon the road?"

【注释】

[1] 为臣:臣,指家臣,总管。孔子当时不是大夫,没有家臣,但子路叫门人充当孔子的家臣,准备由此人负责总管安葬孔子之事。

[2] 病间:病情减轻。理雅格译为"remission of his illness",辜鸿铭译为"remission of his sickness",即"病情好转";刘殿爵译为"condition had improved",即"状态有所改善",韦利译为"Coming to himself for a short

while"，即"清醒了一会儿"。

[3] 大葬：指大夫的葬礼。辜鸿铭译为"public funeral"，即"公开的葬礼"；理雅格译为"great burial"，即"盛大的葬礼"；刘殿爵译为"elaborate funeral"，即"精心设计的葬礼"；韦利译为"State Burial"，即"国葬"。burial 指下葬的那一天，强调下葬，是比较普通的葬礼，甚至简单的埋葬；funeral 指整个葬礼，具有一定民俗和宗教色彩。儒家对于葬礼十分重视，尤其重视葬礼的等级规定。对于死去的人，要严格地按照周礼的有关规定加以埋葬。不同等级的人有不同的安葬仪式，违反了这种规定即为僭越礼制。孔子反对学生们按大夫之礼为他办理丧事，是为了恪守周礼的规定。此处"大葬"是指士大夫的葬礼，强调下葬过程要符合士大夫的礼制和仪式，不能僭越，我们认为译为"the funeral of the scholar-official"更为恰当。

【原文】9.13　子贡曰："有美玉于斯，韫椟[1]而藏诸？求善贾[2]而沽[3]诸？"子曰："沽之哉！沽之哉！我待贾者也！"

【译文】子贡说："这里有一块美玉，是把它收藏在柜子里呢？还是找一个识货的商人卖掉呢？"孔子说："卖掉吧，卖掉吧！我正在等着识货的人呢。"

【英译】Tsze-Kung said，"There is a beautiful gem here. Should I lay it up in a case and keep it？or should I seek for a good price and sell it？"The Master said，"Sell it！Sell it！But I would wait for one to offer the price."

【注释】

[1] 韫椟：收藏物件的柜子。理雅格、辜鸿铭译为"case"，刘殿爵、韦利译为"box"。box 的基本意思是"盒、匣、箱"，多指由木板、皮子、纸、铁皮等制成供装东西用的方形器具。case 则泛指所有盒子，用途比较全面。

[2] 善贾：识货的商人。又同"价"，即好的价钱。理雅格、韦利、辜

鸿铭、刘殿爵等译本均将其译为"good price"，即"好的价格"。

[3] 沽：卖出去。

【原文】9.14　子欲居九夷[1]。或曰："陋[2]，如之何？"子曰："君子居之，何陋之有！"

【译文】孔子想要搬到九夷这个地方去居住。有人说："那里非常落后闭塞，不开化，怎么能住呢？"孔子说："有君子居住，就不闭塞落后了。"

【英译】The Master was wishing to go and live among the nine wild tribes of the east. Some one said，"They are uncouth. How can you do such a thing?" The Master said，"If a superior man dwelt among them，what rudeness would there be?"

【注释】

[1] 九夷：中国古代对于东方少数民族的通称。

[2] 陋：鄙野，文化闭塞，不开化。理雅格译为"rude"，即"粗鲁的"；辜鸿铭译为"The want of refinement"，韦利译为"lack of refinement"，即"缺乏精致、不精致的"；刘殿爵译为"uncouth"，即"笨拙的、不开化的"。rude 指某人的言行举止粗鲁无礼，缺乏修养；uncouth 的使用语境更正式，多形容没有文化、不开化。中国古代，中原地区的人把居住在东面的人们称为夷人，认为此地闭塞落后，当地人也愚昧不开化。此处"陋"不仅仅指当地少数民族行为粗野无礼，更形容九夷之人文化闭塞，与中原人相比不够文明。刘殿爵译为"uncouth"更为恰当。

【原文】9.15　子曰："吾自卫反鲁[1]，然后乐正，《雅》《颂》各得其所。"

【译文】孔子说："我从卫国返回到鲁国以后，乐才得到整理，雅乐和颂乐各有适当的安排。"

【英译】The Master said, "I returned from Wei to Lu, and then the music was reformed, and the pieces in the Royal songs and Praise songs all found their proper places."

【注释】

[1] 自卫反鲁：公元前484年（鲁哀公十一年）冬，孔子从卫国返回鲁国，结束了14年游历不定的生活。

【原文】9.16　子曰："出则事公卿，入则事父兄，丧事不敢不勉，不为酒困；何有于我哉！[1]"[2]

【译文】孔子说："在外事奉公卿，在家孝敬父兄，有丧事不敢不尽力去办，不被酒所困，这些事我能做到哪些呢？"

【英译】The Master said, "Abroad, to serve the high ministers and nobles；at home, to serve one's father and elder brothers；in all duties to the dead, not to dare not to exert one's self；and not to be overcome of wine：-which one of these things do I attain to？"

【注释】

[1] 何有于我哉：有多种理解。1. 我做到了哪些呢？ 2. 如果人们都能做到这些，还需要我做什么呢？皆见于皇侃《义疏》："言我何能行此三事，故云'何有于我哉'。又一云：人若能如此，则何复须我，故云'何有于我哉'也。缘人不能，故有我应世耳。"3. 对我来说有什么困难的。刘宝楠《正义》云："'何有'，言不难有也。"理雅格从第一种说法，译为"Which one of these things do I attain to"，即"我能做到哪一件事呢？"辜鸿铭译为"Which one of these things can I say that I have been able to do"，即"在这些事情中，哪一件是我能够做到的呢？"刘殿爵从第三种说法，译为"There is nothing to these at all"，即"这些根本不算什么"。韦利译为"Concerning these things at any rate my mind is quite at rest"，即"关于这些事情，我的心是很平静的"。

[2]"出则事公卿"，是为国尽忠；"入则事父兄"，是为长辈尽孝。邢昺《注疏》云："此章记孔子言忠顺孝悌哀丧慎酒之事也。困，乱也。言出仕朝廷，则尽其忠顺以事公卿也；入居私门，则尽其孝悌以事父兄也；若有丧事则不敢不勉力以从礼也，未尝为酒乱其性也。他人无是行，于我，我独有之，故曰：何有于我哉。"忠与孝是孔子特别强调的两个道德规范。它是对所有人的要求，而孔子本人就是这方面的身体力行者。

【原文】 9.17　子在川上曰："逝者如斯夫！不舍昼夜。"

【译文】 孔子在河边说："消逝的时光就像这河水一样啊，不分昼夜地向前流去。"

【英译】 The Master standing by a stream, said, "The passing time flows forward like this river, day and night."

【原文】 9.18　子曰："吾未见好德[1]如好色[2]者也。"

【译文】 孔子说："我没有见过像好色那样好德的人。"

【英译】 The Master said, "I have not seen one who loves virtue as he loves beauty."

【注释】

[1] 德：理雅格、刘殿爵译为"virtue"，辜鸿铭、韦利译为"moral"。

[2] 色：美色。理雅格、辜鸿铭、刘殿爵译为"beauty"，指女性的美丽容颜。韦利译为"sexual desire"，即"性吸引力"。将"好色"译为"love beauty"更为恰当。

【原文】 9.19　子曰："譬如为山，未成一篑[1]，止，吾止也；譬如平地，虽覆一篑，进，吾往也！"

【译文】 孔子说："譬如用土堆山，只差一筐土就完成了，这时停下来，那是我自己要停下来的；譬如在平地上堆山，虽然只倒下一筐，这时继续前进，那是我自己要坚持前进的。"

【英译】The Master said，"The prosecution of learning may be compared to what may happen in raising a mound. If there want but one basket of earth to complete the work，and I stop，the stopping is my own work. It may be compared to throwing down the earth on the level ground. Though but one basketful is thrown at a time，the advancing with it my own going forward."

【注释】

[1] 篑：土筐。理雅格、辜鸿铭译为"basket"，即"篮子"；刘殿爵、韦利译为"basketful"，即"满满一篮的"。

【原文】9.20　子曰："语之而不惰[1]者，其回也与？"

【译文】孔子说："听我说话而能毫不懈怠的，只有颜回一个人吧！"

【英译】The Master said，"Never flagging when I set forth anything to him；-ah！that is Hui."

【注释】

[1] 惰：懈怠、懒惰。理雅格、刘殿爵译为"flagging"，即"萎靡不振的"，侧重力气、兴趣、热情等正在减退；辜鸿铭译为"tired and inattentive"，即"疲惫且注意力不集中的"。本章《论语》指颜回能认真接受孔子的教诲，并不会倦怠或走神，辜鸿铭的翻译更为恰当。

【原文】9.21　子谓颜渊曰："惜乎！吾见其进也，吾未见其止也！"

【译文】孔子对颜渊说："可惜呀！我只见他不断前进，从来没有看见他停止过。"

【英译】The Master said of Yen Yuan，"Alas！I saw his constant advance. I never saw him stop in his progress."

【原文】9.22 子曰："苗而不秀[1]者，有矣夫！秀而不实者，有矣夫！"

【译文】孔子说："庄稼出了苗而不能吐穗扬花的情况是有的；吐穗扬花而不结果实的情况也有。"

【英译】The Master said，"There are cases in which the blade springs，but the plant does not go on to flower！There are cases where it flowers but fruit is not subsequently produced！"

【注释】

[1] 秀：稻、麦等庄稼吐穗扬花。理雅格译为"go on to flower"，刘殿爵译为"blossom"，韦利、辜鸿铭译为"flower"，均为"开花"之义。

【原文】9.23 子曰："后生可畏，焉知来者之不如今也[1]？四十、五十而无闻焉，斯亦不足畏也已！"

【译文】孔子说："年轻人是值得敬畏的，怎么就知道后一代不如前一代呢？如果到了四五十岁时还默默无闻，那他就没有什么可以敬畏的了。"

【英译】The Master said，"A youth is to be regarded with respect. How do we know that his future will not be equal to our present？If he reach the age of forty or fifty，and has not made himself heard of，then indeed he will not be worth being regarded with respect."

【注释】

[1] 焉知来者之不如今：两种理解：1. 指怎知少年人将来不如我。邢昺《注疏》云："言年少之人，足以积学成德，诚可畏也，安知将来者之道德不如我今日也？"朱子《集注》云："孔子言后生年富力强，足以积学而有待，其势可畏，安知其将来不如我之今日乎？"2. 指怎知少年人将来不如现在。刘宝楠《正义》云："不如今，谓不如今日之可畏也。人少时有聪慧，为人所畏。至年壮老，学力复充，故人常畏服之。曰'焉知'，《论衡·实知篇》

解此文，以为后生难处是也。"理雅格译为"How do we know that his future will not be equal to our present"，即"我们怎么知道他的未来不会等于我们的现在？"辜鸿铭译为"How do we know that their future will not be as good as we are now"，即"我们怎么知道他们的未来不会像我们现在那么好呢？"韦利译为"How do you know that they will not one day be all that you are now"，即"你怎么知道他们有一天不会变成现在的你呢？"上述三家翻译均从第一种理解。刘殿爵译为"How do we know that the generations to come will not be the equal of the present"，即"我们怎么知道子孙后代不会与现在平等呢？"该翻译从第二种理解。我们认为，理雅格等人的翻译更为恰当。

【原文】9.24　子曰："法语之言[1]，能无从乎？改之为贵！巽与之言[2]，能无说乎？绎[3]之为贵！说而不绎，从而不改，吾末如之何也已矣！"

【译文】孔子说："符合礼法的正言规劝，谁能不听从呢？但是只有按它来改正自己的错误，才是可贵的。恭顺赞许的话，谁能听了不高兴呢？但只有认真推究它的真伪是非，才是可贵的。只是高兴而不去分析，只是表示听从而不改正错误，对这样的人，我拿他实在是没有办法了。"

【英译】The Master said, "Can men refuse to assent to the words of strict admonition? But it is reforming the conduct because of them which is valuable. Can men refuse to be pleased with words of gentle advice? But it is unfolding their aim which is valuable. If a man be pleased with these words，but does not unfold their aim，and assents to those，but does not reform his conduct，I can really do nothing with him."

【注释】

[1] 法语之言：法，指礼仪规则。理雅格译为"The words of strict

admonition"，即"严厉的训诫"。辜鸿铭译为"The strict words of the law"，即"严格的法律语言"。刘殿爵译为"exemplary words"，即"训诫性词汇"。strict 偏重于对事情方面的严格严厉、严谨；Exemplary 则来自拉丁语 exemplaris（模式），表示"可作榜样的、楷模的"，亦指受惩罚用来以儆效尤、警戒他人。韦利直接音译为 Fa Yu，并补充说明其指"模范语言"（Model Sayings）。《论语》此处指以礼法规则正言规劝，"法语"是人们行动的规范和楷模。上述译本相较，刘殿爵的翻译更为恰当。

[2] 巽与之言：巽，恭顺，谦逊。与，称许，赞许。这里指恭顺赞许的话。理雅格译为"Words of gentle advice"，即"温柔的忠告"；辜鸿铭译为"parables"，即"比喻、寓言"，该翻译不够恰当；刘殿爵译为"Tactful words"，即"委婉的语言"。gentle 指温柔、亲切、优雅。常含有节制和意味；tactful 则侧重圆滑的、得体的、不得罪人的，含贬义。《论语》此处不是指圆滑的巧言，也不仅仅指言语态度的温柔和善，而是指谦恭与赞美的语言，我们认为该句译为"Courteous language with praise"更为恰当。

[3] 绎：原义为"抽丝"，这里指推究，追求，分析，鉴别。理雅格译为"aim"，即"目标"；辜鸿铭译为"apply the moral to himself"，即"把道理应用到自己身上"；刘殿爵译为"rectify"，即"纠正"；韦利译为"carry them out"，即"执行、落实"。我们认为，此处译为"analysis"（分析）更为恰当。

【原文】9.25　子曰："主忠信。毋友不如己者。过，则勿惮改。"[1]

【译文】孔子说："亲近尽心尽力、讲信用的人，不要结交品德比不上自己的人，有过错不要害怕改正。"

【英译】The Master said, "Hold faithfulness and sincerity as first principles. Have no friends not equal to yourself. When you have faults, do not fear to abandon them."

【注释】

[1] 此章重出，见《学而》篇第8章。

【原文】9.26　子曰："三军可夺帅也，匹夫不可夺志[1]也。"

【译文】孔子说："一国军队，可以夺去它的主帅；但一个男子汉，他的志向是不能强迫改变的。"

【英译】The Master said，"The commander of the forces of a large state may be carried off，but the will of even a common man cannot be taken from him."

【注释】

[1] 志：理雅格译为"Will"，即"意志"；辜鸿铭译为"free will"，即"自由意志"，自由意志是哲学专业概念，理解为意识选择做什么的决定、就是意志的主动性；刘殿爵译为"purpose"，即"目的、目标"；韦利译为"opinion"，即"意见"。"志"即为人的志向、志气。"匹夫不可夺志"，反映出孔子对于"志"的高度重视，甚至将它与三军之帅相比。对于一个人来讲，他有自己的独立人格，任何人都无权侵犯。作为个人，他应维护自己的尊严，不受威胁利诱，始终保持自己的"志向"。我们认为，此处译为"志向"更为恰当，即"ambition"。

【原文】9.27　子曰："衣敝缊袍[1]与衣狐貉[2]者立，而不耻者，其由也与！'不忮不求，何用不臧？'[3]"子路终身诵之。子曰："是道也，何足以臧！"

【译文】孔子说："穿着破旧的丝棉袍子，与穿着狐貉皮袍的人站在一起，但不认为是可耻的，大概只有仲由吧。《诗经》上说：'不嫉妒，不贪求，为什么说不好呢？'"子路听后，便老念着这两句诗。孔子又说："只做到这样，怎么能说够好了呢？"

【英译】The Master said，"Dressed himself in a tattered robe quilted with hemp，yet standing by the side of men dressed in furs，and not ashamed；-ah！it is Yu who is equal to this！"He dislikes none，he covets nothing；what can he do but what is good！"Tsze-Lu kept continually repeating these words of the ode，when The Master said，"Those things are by no means sufficient to constitute perfect excellence."

【注释】

[1] 敝缊袍：敝，坏。缊，旧的丝棉絮。这里指破旧的丝绵袍。

[2] 狐貉：用狐和貉的皮做的裘皮衣服。

[3] 不忮不求，何用不臧：这两句见《诗经·邶风·雄雉》篇。忮，憎恶、嫉妒。臧，善、好。理雅格将"忮"译为"dislike"，即"不喜欢的"；辜鸿铭译为"envy"、刘殿爵译为"envious"，即"嫉妒"；韦利译为"harmed"，即"伤害"。我们认为，辜鸿铭、刘殿爵的翻译更为恰当。

【原文】 9.28　子曰："岁寒，然后知松柏之后凋也。"

【译文】 孔子说："到了寒冷的季节，才知道松柏是最后凋谢的。"

【英译】 The Master said，"When the year becomes cold，then we know how the pine and the cypress are the last to lose their leaves."

【原文】 9.29　子曰："知[1]者不惑[2]，仁者不忧[3]，勇[4]者不惧。"

【译文】 孔子说："聪明人不会迷惑，有仁德的人不会忧愁，勇敢的人不会畏惧。"

【英译】 The Master said，"The wise are free from perplexities；the virtuous from anxiety；and the bold from fear."

【注释】

[1] 知：同智，智慧。理雅格、韦利译为"wise"，刘殿爵译为

"wisdom"，辜鸿铭译为"Intelligence"。wisdom 和 intelligence 这两个单词都可以表示"智力，智慧"的意思，它们之间的区别是：wisdom 用法上较为文雅，也可指明智的言行；intelligence 指的是处理或对付问题或情况的特殊才智，也指运用、展开智慧的能力。intelligence 多指一个人"头脑好，有才智"，而 wisdom 多指一个人有智慧。《论语》此处指一个人是"有智慧的"，译为"wise"或"wisdom"更为恰当。

[2] 惑：迷惑、困惑。理雅格、韦利译为"perplexities"，侧重"困惑、迷惘、难以理解的事物"；辜鸿铭译为"doubts"，指"疑惑、疑问、不确定、不相信"；刘殿爵译为"In two minds"，即在是非判断上摇摆不定。

[3] 忧：忧愁、忧虑。理雅格、辜鸿铭译为"anxiety"，刘殿爵译为"worries"。Anxiety 表示正在发生的事情或者可能发生的事情引发的焦虑和紧张；Worry 则表示一种不开心或者恐慌的情绪，含有惦记意味，有时候还表示瞎操心。《论语》此处强调的是"忧虑"而非"担心"，我们认为该句译为"anxiety"更为恰当。

[4] 勇：勇敢。理雅格译为"bold"，侧重指面对困难或危险时勇往直前，勇于进取的勇敢精神。辜鸿铭、刘殿爵译为"courage"，是正式用词，侧重指在一切情况下都有胆量、无所畏惧，强调基于道德信念，经深思熟虑后所产生的勇敢。韦利译为"brave"，指天生的勇敢，无所畏惧地面对困难与危险，侧重胆识与果断。在儒家传统道德中，智、仁、勇是重要的三个范畴。《礼记·中庸》说："知、仁、勇，三者天下之达德也。"我们认为，此处译为基于道德信念的"courage"更为恰当。

【原文】9.30　子曰："可与共学，未可与适道[1]；可与适道，未可与立[2]；可与立，未可与权[3]。"

【译文】孔子说："可以一起学习的人，未必可以同他一起学到道；可以一起学到道的人，未必可以同他一起坚持守道；可以一起坚持守道的人，未必可以同他一起随机应变。"

【英译】The Master said，"There are some with whom we may study in common，but we shall find them unable to go along with us to principles. Perhaps we may go on with them to principles，but we shall find them unable to get established in those along with us. Or if we may get so established along with them，we shall find them unable to apply the general principles under exceptional circumstances along with us."

【注释】

[1] 适道：适，往。这里是志于道，追求道的意思。理雅格译为"go along with us to principles"，即"共同遵守原则"；刘殿爵译为"In the pursuit of the Way"，即"一起追求道"；韦利译为"join in progress along the Way"，即"加入求道的进程"。"道"是中国古代哲学的基本范畴，道包含天道、人道、地道等。中国哲学中的"道"有以下几层意思：1. 世界的本原（本体），世界由以出发、由以产生的基础；2. 世界的本质或世界之所以然，也即世界面貌（世界的具体现实性）的决定力量；3. 世界形成、产生和发展全部历史的述说，也即对道以自身为本原、以自身为本质的自我产生、自我发展、自我表现、自我完成的全部历史的述说。理雅格、辜鸿铭将"道"译为"原则、准则"，没能完整体现"道"的含义。

[2] 立：坚持道而不变。理雅格译为"established"，即"建立道"；辜鸿铭译为"arrive with you at general principles"，即"一同到达一般原则"；刘殿爵译为"In a common stand"，即"共同立场"；韦利译为"Take one's stand"，即"站在旁边"。《论语》此处"立"，是指共同坚持道义，不轻易改变。我们认为，该句译为"May not be able to uphold the way together"更为恰当。

[3] 权：秤锤。这里引申为权衡轻重。理雅格译为"Weigh"，即"衡量、称重"；辜鸿铭译为"apply the general principles under exceptional circumstances"，即"在特殊情况下应用一般原则"；刘殿爵译为"moral discretion"，即"道德判断"；韦利译为"counsel"，即"商议"。政治哲学上

的"经权"说实际上是中国古代哲学中"常""变"认识在政治理论领域的
具体化。而"常"与"变"又是传统哲学理论体系中一对既能充分体现中国
哲学辩证色彩，又具有最大适应性的范畴，从而构成了中国哲学辩证思维的
最坚实基础。中国传统哲学中的"变""常"认识在强调"常"的同时，本
身就承认"变"的客观存在，承认"权变"的合理性。毕竟，任何事物都存
在着常态和变态的区别，而现实中"变""常"关系的复杂性，也要求人们
必须统筹运用或"变"或"常"的不同方法，以应对不同的情况。也就是
说，在某些特殊情况下必须"从权达变"。由此看来，辜鸿铭将"权"译为
"apply the general principles under exceptional circumstances"较为符合《论语》
原义。

【原文】9.31 "唐棣[1]之华，偏其反而[2]；岂不尔思？室是远
而[3]。"子曰："未之思也，夫何远之有？"

【译文】"唐棣的花朵啊，翩翩地摇摆。我岂能不想念你吗？只是
由于家住的地方太远了。"孔子说："他还是没有真的想念，如果真的想
念，有什么遥远呢？"

【英译】"How the flowers of the aspen-plum flutter and turn！Do
I not think of you？But your house is distant."The Master said，"It is
the want of thought about it. How is it distant？"

【注释】

[1] 唐棣：一种植物，属蔷薇科，落叶灌木。

[2] 偏其反而：形容花摇动的样子。

[3] 室是远而：只是住的地方太远了。

乡党篇第十

【原文】10.1 孔子于乡党，恂恂[1]如也，似不能言者。其在宗庙朝廷，便便[2]言，唯谨尔。朝，与下大夫言，侃侃[3]如也。与上大夫言，訚訚[4]如也。君在，踧踖[5]如也，与与[6]如也。

【译文】孔子在本乡的地方上显得很温和恭敬，像是不会说话的样子。但他在宗庙里、朝廷上，却很善于言辞，只是说得比较谨慎而已。孔子在上朝的时候，同下大夫说话，温和而快乐的样子；同上大夫说话，正直而公正的样子；君主临朝时，他显恭敬而心中不安的样子，但又仪态适中。

【英译】Confucius, in his village, looked simple and sincere, and as if he were not able to speak. When he was in the prince's ancestral temple, or in the court, he spoke minutely on every point, but cautiously. When he was waiting at court, in speaking with the great officers of the lower grade, he spoke freely, but in a straightforward manner; in speaking with those of the higher grade, he did so blandly, but precisely.

【注释】

[1] 恂恂：温和恭顺。理雅格译为"simple and sincere"，即"简单而真诚的"；辜鸿铭译为"shy and diffident"，即"害羞且缺乏自信的"，该翻译含贬义，不够恰当；刘殿爵译为"submissive"，即"顺从的"；韦利译为"simple and unassuming"，即"简单而谦逊的"。本章《论语》意在说明孔子

在乡党之间说话的态度是温和恭顺的，"恭顺"强调态度的谦敬有礼，而非一味服从。我们认为，韦利译为"simple and unassuming"较为恰当。

[2] 便便：辩，善于辞令。理雅格译为"spoke minutely on every point"，即"讲话很详细"；辜鸿铭、韦利译为"spoke readily"，即"轻松地发言"；刘殿爵译为"fluent"，即"流利的"。此处并非形容孔子讲话的详细程度，而是意在说明孔子是能言善辩的，译为"spoke readily"较为恰当。

[3] 侃侃：直言、坦率。辜鸿铭译为"spoke with frankness"，即"坦率地说话"；刘殿爵译为"affable"、韦利译为"friendly and affable"，即"和蔼可亲的"。士大夫地位稍卑，且与孔子同级，因此可以坦率地交谈，辜鸿铭的翻译更为恰当。

[4] 訚訚：正直，和颜悦色而又能直言诤辩。辜鸿铭译为"spoke with self-possession"，即"说话镇定自若"；刘殿爵译为"frank though respectful"，即"坦率而恭敬的"；韦利译为"restrained and formal"，即"正式而克制的"。我们认为，此处刘殿爵译为"frank though respectful"，能更好地体现孔子的儒者气节。

[5] 踧踖：恭敬而不安的样子。理雅格译为"grave"，即"庄严的"；辜鸿铭译为"diffident，awe inspired"，即"羞怯而敬畏"；刘殿爵译为"respectful"，即"举止恭敬的"。理雅格与刘殿爵仅译出了"踧踖"的"恭敬"义素；辜鸿铭的翻译兼顾"恭敬"与"不安"，更为符合《论语》原义。

[6] 与与：威仪适中的样子。理雅格译为"self-possessed"；刘殿爵、辜鸿铭译为"composed"，即"镇定的"；韦利译为"wary"，即"谨慎的"。此处形容孔子见到君王，虽然内心感到紧张局促，但仍能做到威仪适中、镇定自若。我们认为此处译为"composed"更为恰当。

【原文】10.2　君召使摈[1]，色勃如也[2]，足躩[3]如也。揖所与立，左右手，衣前后，襜[4]如也。趋进，翼如也。宾退，必复命，曰：宾不顾矣。

【译文】国君召孔子去接待宾客，孔子脸色立即庄重起来，脚步也快起来，他向和他站在一起的人作揖，手向左或向右作揖，衣服前后摆动，却整齐不乱。快步走的时候，像鸟儿展开双翅一样。宾客走后，必定向君主回报说："客人已经不回头了。"

【英译】When the ruler was present, his manner displayed respectful uneasiness; it was grave, but self-possessed. When the prince called him to employ him in the reception of a visitor, his countenance appeared to change, and his legs to move forward with difficulty. He inclined himself to the other officers among whom he stood, moving his left or right arm, as their position required, but keeping the skirts of his robe before and behind evenly adjusted. He hastened forward, with his arms like the wings of a bird. When the guest had retired, he would report to the prince, "The visitor is not turning round any more."

【注释】

[1] 摈：动词，负责招待国君的官员。

[2] 色勃如也：脸色立即庄重起来。理雅格译为"his countenance appeared to change"，即"脸色发生改变"；辜鸿铭译为"start up with attention"，即"从关注（这件事）开始"；刘殿爵译为"face took on a serious expression"，即"脸上露出严肃的表情"；韦利译为"a look of confusion comes over his face"，即"脸上露出困惑的表情"。本章《论语》形容孔子在接待官员外宾时，脸色仪态是庄重有礼的。上述译本相较，刘殿爵的翻译更为恰当。

[3] 足躩：脚步快的样子。理雅格译为"his legs to move forward with difficulty"，即"他的腿艰难地向前移动"；韦利译为"his legs seem to give beneath his weight"，即"他的腿在体重的重压下似乎要垮掉了"。上述两种翻译均指孔子步伐较慢，不符合《论语》原意。辜鸿铭译为"make

obeisance to receive the command",即"臣服接受命令",没能译出"足躩"的"脚步快"之义。刘殿爵译为"his step became brisk",即"脚步变得轻快"。上述译本相较,刘殿爵的翻译更为恰当。

[4] 襜:整齐。

【原文】10.3 入公门,鞠躬如[1]也,如不容。立不中门,行不履阈[2]。过位,色勃如也,足躩如也,其言似不足者。摄齐[3]升堂,鞠躬如也,屏气似不息者。出,降一等[4],逞颜色,怡怡如也。没阶[5],趋进,翼如也。复其位,踧踖如也。

【译文】孔子走进朝廷的大门,谨慎而恭敬的样子,好像没有他的容身之地。站也不站在门的中间,走也不踩门槛。经过国君的座位时,他脸色立刻庄重起来,脚步也加快起来,说话也好像中气不足一样。提起衣服下摆向堂上走的时候,恭敬谨慎的样子,憋住气好像不呼吸一样。退出来,走下台阶,脸色便舒展开了,怡然自得的样子。走完了台阶,快快地向前走几步,姿态像鸟儿展翅一样。回到自己的位置,是恭敬而不安的样子。

【英译】When he entered the palace gate, he seemed to bend his body, as if it were not sufficient to admit him. When he was standing, he did not occupy the middle of the gateway; when he passed in or out, he did not tread upon the threshold. When he was passing the vacant place of the prince, his countenance appeared to change, and his legs to bend under him, and his words came as if he hardly had breath to utter them. He ascended the reception hall, holding up his robe with both his hands, and his body bent; holding in his breath also, as if he dared not breathe. When he came out from the audience, as soon as he had descended one step, he began to relax his countenance, and had a satisfied look. When he had got the bottom of the steps, he advanced rapidly to his place, with his arms like wings, and on occupying it, his manner still showed respectful uneasiness.

【注释】

[1] 鞠躬如：曲敛身体，谨慎而恭敬的样子。此处各英译本均译为"bend his body"或"bend low his body"。

[2] 履阈：阈，门槛。脚踩门槛。理雅格译为"tread upon the threshold"，辜鸿铭译为"step on the door sill"。Threshold 和 sill 均指"门槛"，sill 偏向于门最下方的部分，threshold 则是 sill 上方的构件，为入口阻挡外力的侵蚀。中国古代门槛高与膝齐，传统住宅的大门口必有门槛，人们进出大门均要跨过门槛，起到缓冲步伐、阻挡外力的作用。我们认为此处译为"threshold"更为恰当。

[3] 摄齐：齐，衣服的下摆。摄，提起。提起衣服的下摆。理雅格译为"holding up his robe"，即"托着长袍"；辜鸿铭译为"holding up the folds of his robes"，即"举起长袍的褶皱"。各家译本对于"摄齐"的翻译差异不大。

[4] 降一等：从台阶上走下一级。

[5] 没阶：走完了台阶。

【原文】 10.4 执圭[1]，鞠躬如也，如不胜，上如揖，下如授，勃如战色[2]。足躩躩[3]如有循。享礼[4]，有容色。私觌[5]，愉愉如也。

【译文】（孔子出使其他诸侯国，）拿着圭，恭敬谨慎，像是举不起来的样子。向上举时好像在作揖，放在下面时好像是给人递东西。脸色庄重得像战栗的样子，步子很小，好像沿着一条直线往前走。在举行赠送礼物的仪式时，显得和颜悦色。和国君举行私下会见的时候，更轻松愉快了。

【英译】 When he was carrying the scepter of his ruler, he seemed to bend his body，as if he were not able to bear its weight. He did not hold it higher than the position of the hands in making a bow，nor lower than their position in giving anything to another. His countenance seemed to change，and look apprehensive，and he walked with slow，measured steps as if they were held by something to the ground. In presenting the presents with which he was charged，he wore a placid appearance. At his private audience，he looked highly pleased.

【注释】

[1] 圭：一种上圆下方的玉器，举行典礼时，不同身份的人拿着不同的圭。出使邻国，大夫拿着圭作为代表君主的凭信。理雅格译为"the scepter of his ruler"，即"统治者的权杖"；辜鸿铭译为"the sceptre of the prince"，即"君王的权杖"；刘殿爵、韦利译为"jade tablet"，即"玉质的碑牌"。此处"圭"是孔子出使别国时用来证明身份的凭信，辜鸿铭将其理解为君王的权柄和象征，较为恰当。

[2] 战色：战，敬畏之意。理雅格译为"apprehensive"，形容面容忧心忡忡；辜鸿铭译为"awe and attention"，形容神情目光充满敬畏和专注；刘殿爵译为"his expression was solemn as though in fear and trembling"，即"他的表情很严肃，好像在害怕和颤抖"；韦利译为"dread"，形容神情恐惧。此处形容孔子在参加外交活动时，脸色庄重如同战栗一般，指孔子对待外交活动十分严肃敬重，并非害怕和恐惧。上述译本相较，刘殿爵译本"his expression was solemn as though in fear and trembling"既体现了严肃与敬意，也译出了"战"的"颤抖"之义，较为恰当。

[3] 蹜蹜：小步走路的样子。理雅格译为"dragged his feet along"，即"拖着两只脚走路"；辜鸿铭译为"walk with slow, measured steps"，即"缓慢而慎重的步伐"；刘殿爵译为"his feet were constrained"，即"他的脚受到束缚"；韦利译为"his feet seem to recoil"，指脚步退缩。上述英译本相较，辜鸿铭的翻译更为恰当。

[4] 享礼：享，献上。指向对方贡献礼物的仪式。使者受到接见后，接着举行献礼仪式。

[5] 觌：音 dí，会见。理雅格、韦利、辜鸿铭、刘殿爵均译为"private audience"，即"私人听众"，没有译出"会见"之义。

【原文】10.5　君子不以绀緅饰[1]，红紫不以为亵服[2]。当暑，袗絺绤，必表而出之[3]。缁衣羔裘[4]，素衣麑裘，黄衣狐裘，亵裘长，短右袂[5]。必有寝衣，长一身有半。狐貉之厚以居[6]。去丧，无所不佩。非帷裳[7]，必杀之。羔裘玄冠，不以吊[8]。吉月[9]，必朝服而朝。

【译文】君子不用深青透红或黑中透红的布镶边，不用红色或紫色的布做平常在家穿的衣服。夏天穿粗的或细的葛布单衣，但一定要套在内衣外面。黑色的羔羊皮袍，配黑色的罩衣。白色的鹿皮袍，配白色的罩衣。黄色的狐皮袍，配黄色的罩衣。平常在家穿的皮袍做得长一些，右边的袖子短一些。睡觉一定要有睡衣，要有一身半长。用狐貉的厚毛皮做坐垫。丧服期满，脱下丧服后，便佩戴上各种各样的装饰品。如果不是礼服，一定要加以剪裁。不穿着黑色的羔羊皮袍和戴着黑色的帽子去吊丧。每月初一，一定要穿着礼服去朝拜君主。

【英译】The superior man did not use a deep purple, or a puce color, in the ornaments of his dress. Even in his undress, he did not wear anything of a red or reddish color. In warm weather, he had a single garment either of coarse or fine texture, but he wore it displayed over an inner garment. Over lamb's fur he wore a garment of black; over fawn's fur one of white; and over fox's fur one of yellow. The fur robe of his undress was long, with the right sleeve short. He required his sleeping dress to be half as long again as his body. When staying at home, he used thick furs of the fox or the badger. When he put off mourning，he wore all the appendages of the girdle. His undergarment，except when it was required to be of the curtain shape，was made of silk cut narrow above and wide below. He did not wear lamb's fur or a black cap on a visit of condolence. On the first day of the month he put on his court robes，and presented himself at court.

【注释】

[1] 不以绀緅饰：绀，深青透红，斋戒时服装的颜色。緅，黑中透红，丧服的颜色。这里是说，不以深青透红或黑中透红的颜色布给平常穿的衣服镶上边作饰物。

[2] 红紫不以为亵服：亵服，平时在家里穿的衣服。古人认为，红紫不是正色，便服不宜用红紫色。

[3] 必表而出之：把麻布单衣穿在外面，里面还要衬有内衣。

[4] 羔裘：羔皮衣。古代的羔裘都是黑羊皮，毛皮向外。

[5] 短右袂：袂，袖子。右袖短一点，是为了便于做事。

[6] 狐貉之厚以居：狐貉之厚，厚毛的狐貉皮。居，坐。

[7] 帷裳：上朝和祭祀时穿的礼服，用整幅布制作，不加以裁剪，折叠缝上。

[8] 不以吊：不用于丧事。

[9] 吉月：有多种解释。1. 朔日，即每月初一，一般这天要举行朝会；2. "吉"为"告"之误。俞樾《群经平议》云："每月之末，有司以月朔告于君，是曰告月。"3. 正月。程树德《集释》云："所谓吉月者，谓正月也。从前解吉月为月朔，断无致仕官每月月朔朝君之礼，毛西河驳之是也。即曰孔子仕鲁时事，而鲁自文公四不视朔，至定哀间，此礼之废已久，夫子犹必每月月朔朝服而朝，亦与事理不合。今人虽致仕官，元旦尚可随班朝贺，古犹是也。"理雅格、辜鸿铭译为"On the first day of the month"，即"每月的第一天"；刘殿爵译为"On New Year's Day"，即元旦；韦利译为"At the Announcement of the New Moon"，即"在宣布新月的时候"，该译文以朔望

月作为确定历月的基础，指夏历的第一天（朔日）。

【原文】 10.6 齐[1]，必有明衣[2]，布。齐，必变食[3]，居必迁坐。

【译文】 斋戒沐浴的时候，一定要有浴衣，用布做的。斋戒的时候，一定要改变平常的饮食，居住也一定搬移地方。

【英译】 When fasting，he thought it necessary to have his clothes brightly clean and made of linen cloth. When fasting，he thought it necessary to change his food，and also to change the place where he commonly sat in the apartment.

【注释】

[1] 齐：同斋，斋戒之意。刘殿爵译为"in periods of purification"，即"在净化期间"；《说文解字》记载："斋，戒洁也。"斋最初的本意是指洁净和禁戒，刘殿爵将"斋戒"理解为"净化"也是这个原因。理雅格、辜鸿铭译为"fast"，即"斋戒、禁食"；韦利译为"When preparing himself for sacrifice"，即"准备祭祀期间"。《礼记·郊特牲》记载："故君子三日齐，必见其所祭者。"即君子穿着黑色的衣冠，连续斋戒三天，就能看到他所祭祀的对象。斋戒原意是指人们在进行祭祀或者某种重大活动之前，所进行的沐浴更衣、禁酒禁荤的一系列准备活动，以此表示对所祭祀的天地、神灵、祖先的尊崇和虔诚。可见，斋戒与祭祀是流程当中的两个不同环节，因此韦利将"斋戒"译为"祭祀"不够恰当。

[2] 明衣：斋前沐浴后穿的浴衣。

[3] 变食：改变平常的饮食。指不饮酒，不吃葱、蒜等有刺激味的东西。

【原文】 10.7 食不厌精，脍不厌细。食饐[1]而餲[2]，鱼馁而肉败，不食。色恶不食，臭恶不食。失饪不食，不时不食。割不正[3]不食。不得其酱不食。肉虽多，不使胜食气。惟酒无量，不及乱[4]。沽酒，市脯，不食。不撤姜食，不多食。祭于公，不宿肉[5]。祭肉不出三日，出三日，不食之矣。食不语，寝不言。虽疏食、菜羹、瓜祭[6]，必齐如也。

【译文】粮食不嫌舂得精，鱼和肉不嫌切得细。粮食陈旧和变味了，鱼和肉腐烂了，都不吃。食物的颜色变了，不吃。气味变了，不吃。烹调不当，不吃。不时新的东西，不吃。肉切得不方正，不吃。佐料放得不适当，不吃。席上的肉虽多，但吃的量不超过米面的量。只有酒没有限制，但不喝醉。从市上买来的肉干和酒，不吃。每餐必须有姜，但也不多吃。孔子参加国君祭祀典礼时分到的肉，不能留到第二天。祭祀用过的肉不超过三天。超过三天，就不吃了。吃饭的时候不说话，睡觉的时候也不说话。即使是粗米饭蔬菜汤，吃饭前也要把它们取出一些来祭祖，而且表情要像斋戒时那样严肃恭敬。

【英译】He did not eat rice which had been injured by heat or damp and turned sour，nor fish or flesh which was gone. He did not eat what was discolored，or what was of a bad flavor，nor anything which was ill-cooked，or was not in season. He did not eat meat which was not cut properly，nor what was served without its proper sauce. Though there might be a large quantity of meat，he would not allow what he took to exceed the due proportion for the rice. It was only in wine that he laid down no limit for himself，but he did not allow himself to be confused by it. He did not partake of wine and dried meat bought in the market. He was never without ginger when he ate. He did not eat much. When he had been assisting at the prince's sacrifice，he did not keep the flesh which he received overnight. The flesh of his family sacrifice he did not keep overthree days. If kept over three days，people could not eat it. When eating，he did not converse. When in bed，he did not speak.

Although his food might be coarse rice and vegetable soup，he would offer a little of it in sacrifice with a grave，respectful air.

【注释】

[1] 饐：陈旧。食物放置时间长了。

[2] 餲：食物腐烂变味。

[3] 割不正：肉切得不方正。朱子云："割肉不方正者不食，造次不离于正也。汉陆续之母，切肉未尝不方，断葱以寸为度，盖其质美，与此暗合也。"邢昺《注疏》云："谓折解牲体，脊胁臂、臑之属，礼有正数，若解割不得其正，则不食也。"理雅格译为"meat which was not cut properly"、辜鸿铭译为"meat not properly cut"，即"没有切好的肉"；刘殿爵译为"food that was not properly prepared"，即"没有恰当准备的食物"；韦利译为"He must not eat what has been crookedly cut"，即"他不吃切得弯曲的肉"。韦利此说更接近朱熹《四书章句集注》之解。

[4] 不及乱：乱，指酒醉。不到酒醉时。

[5] 不宿肉：不使肉过夜。古代大夫参加国君祭祀以后，可以得到国君赐的祭肉。但祭祀活动一般要持续二三天，所以这些肉就已经不新鲜，不能再过夜了。超过三天，就不能再过夜了。

[6] 瓜祭：古人在吃饭前，把席上各种食品分出少许，放在食具之间祭祖。

【原文】 10.8　席不正，不坐。

【译文】 席子放得不端正，不坐。

【英译】 If his mat was not straight，he did not sit on it.

【原文】 10.9　乡人饮酒[1]，杖者[2]出，斯出矣。乡人傩[3]，朝服而立于阼阶[4]。

【译文】 行乡饮酒的礼仪结束后，要等老年人先出去，然后自己才出去。乡里人举行迎神驱鬼的宗教仪式时，孔子总是穿着朝服站在东边的台阶上。

【英译】When the villagers were drinking together，upon those who carried staffs going out，he also went out immediately after. When the villagers were going through their ceremonies to drive away pestilential influences，he put on his court robes and stood on the eastern steps.

【注释】

[1] 乡人饮酒：指举行乡饮酒礼。理雅格译为"The villagers were drinking together"，即"乡里一起饮酒"；辜鸿铭译为"a public dinner in his native place"，即"家乡的公共晚宴"；刘殿爵译为"drinking at a village gathering"，即"在乡村聚会上喝酒"。乡饮酒礼是周代流行的宴饮风俗，主要目的是为了向国家推荐贤者，由乡大夫作主人设宴。后演为地方官设宴招待应举之士，此宴为"乡饮酒"。古代诸侯之乡有乡学，学制为三年。学成者作为人才推荐给诸侯。为此，每过三年的正月，乡大夫都要作为主人举行乡饮酒礼，招待乡学中的贤能之士和德高望重者。可见周代的乡饮酒礼不仅是简单的乡村饮酒聚会，其目的在于序长幼，别贵贱，以一种普及性的道德实践活动，成就孝弟、尊贤、敬长养老的道德风尚，达到德治教化的目的。我们认为，此处应译为"Community Dringking Ceremony"，强调"乡人饮酒"是一种以道德教化为目的的礼乐仪式。

[2] 杖者：拿拐杖的人，指老年人。理雅格译为"Who carried staffs"，即那些"拿着棍子的人"；辜鸿铭译为"old people"，即"老人"；刘殿爵译为"Those carrying walking sticks"，即"拿着拐杖的人"。此处辜鸿铭的翻译更为恰当。

[3] 傩：古代迎神驱鬼的宗教仪式。理雅格译为"Through their ceremonies to drive away pestilential influences"，即"举办驱逐瘟疫的仪式"；辜鸿铭译为"Purification Festival"，即"净化的节日"；刘殿爵译为

"exorcizing evil spirits"、韦利译为"Expulsion Ritel",即"驱魔仪式"。傩又称跳傩、傩舞、傩戏,是中国最古老的一种祭神跳鬼、驱瘟避疫、表示安庆的娱神舞蹈。我们认为,此处理雅格译为"驱逐瘟疫",或刘殿爵等译为"驱逐仪式",较为恰当。

[4] 阼阶:阼,东面的台阶。主人立在大堂东面的台阶,在这里欢迎客人。理雅格、刘殿爵、韦利译为"eastern steps";辜鸿铭译为"on the left-hand side of the house",即"站在房子的左边"。

【原文】 10.10　问人于他邦。再拜而送之[1]。康子馈药,拜而受之。曰:"丘未达,不敢尝。"

【译文】 孔子托人向在其他诸侯国的朋友问候送礼,向受托者拜两次送行。季康子给孔子赠送药品,孔子拜谢之后接受了,说:"我对药性不了解,不敢尝。"

【英译】 When he was sending complimentary inquiries to any one in another state, he bowed twice as he escorted the messenger away. Chi K'ang having sent him a present of physic, he bowed and received it, saying, "I do not know it. I dare not taste it."

【注释】

[1] 再拜而送之:在送别客人时,两次拜别。

【原文】 10.11　厩焚,子退朝,曰:"伤人乎?"不问马。

【译文】 马棚失火烧掉了。孔子退朝回来,说:"伤人了吗?"不问马的情况怎么样。

【英译】 The stable being burned down, when he was at court, on his return he said, "Has any man been hurt?" He did not ask about the horses.

【原文】10.12 君赐食，必正席先尝之。君赐腥，必熟而荐之。君赐生，必畜之。侍食于君，君祭，先饭[1]。

【译文】国君赐给熟食，孔子一定摆正座席先尝一尝。国君赐给生肉，一定煮熟了，先给祖宗上供。国君赐给活物，一定要饲养起来。同国君一道吃饭，在国君举行饭前祭礼的时候，一定要先尝一尝。

【英译】When the he would adjust his mat，first taste it，and then give it away to others. When the prince sent him a gift of undressed meat，he would have it cooked，and offer it to the spirits of his ancestors. When the prince sent him a gift of a living animal，he would keep it alive. When he was in attendance on the prince and joining in the entertainment，the prince only sacrificed. He first tasted everything.

【注释】

[1] 古代君主吃饭前，要有人先尝一尝。孔子对国君十分尊重。他在与国君吃饭时，都主动尝一下，表明他对礼的敬重。

【原文】10.13 疾，君视之，东首[1]，加朝服，拖绅[2]。君命召，不俟驾行矣。

【译文】孔子病了，国君来探视，他便头朝东躺着，身上盖上朝服，拖着大带子。国君召见孔子，他不等车马驾好就先步行走去了。

【英译】When he was ill and the prince came to visit him，he had his head to the east，made his court robes be spread over him，and drew his girdle across them. When the prince's order called him，without waiting for his carriage to be yoked，he went at once.

【注释】

[1] 东首：头朝东。

[2] 绅：束在腰间的大带子。理雅格、辜鸿铭译为"drew his girdle"，即"系紧腰带"；刘殿爵译为"grand sash trailing over the side of the bed"，即

"宽大的腰带拖在床边";韦利译为"his sash drawn across the bed",即"腰带系在床上"。Girdle 是束缚、封闭的服饰(束胸衣),应该穿在里层;sash 则指正式服装或官员服装上的腰带、彩带、肩带等。此处指孔子朝服上的腰带,译为"sash"更为恰当。

【原文】 10.14　入太庙,每事问。[1]

【译文】 孔子进入太庙助祭,每件事都询问。

【英译】 When he entered the ancestral temple of the state, he asked about everything.

【注释】

[1] 此章重出,参见《八佾》篇第 15 章。

【原文】 10.15　朋友死,无所归。曰:"于我殡[1]。"朋友之馈,虽车马,非祭肉,不拜。

【译文】 孔子的朋友死了,没有亲属负责敛埋,孔子说:"丧事由我来办吧。"朋友馈赠物品,即使是车马,只要不是祭肉,孔子在接受时是不行礼的。

【英译】 When any of his friends died, if he had no relations offices, he would say, "I will bury him." When a friend sent him a present, though it might be a carriage and horses, he did not bow. The only present for which he bowed was that of the flesh of sacrifice.

【注释】

[1] 殡:停放灵柩和埋葬都可以叫殡,这里是泛指丧葬事务。韦利、刘殿爵译为"funeral",即"举办丧礼";理雅格、辜鸿铭则译为"bury",即"埋葬"。《论语》此处"殡"不仅包含"埋葬"这一环节,而是囊括一切丧葬事宜,因此译为"举办葬礼"更为恰当。

【原文】10.16 寝不尸，居不容[1]。见齐衰[2]者，虽狎[3]必变。见冕者与瞽者，虽亵必以貌。凶服者式[4]之。式负版者[5]。有盛馔[6]，必变色而作。迅雷，风烈，必变。

【译文】孔子睡觉不像死尸一样挺着，平日家居也不像作客或接待客人时那样庄重严肃。看见穿丧服的人，即使是关系很亲密的，也一定要把态度变得严肃起来。看见当官的和盲人，即使是常在一起的，也一定要有礼貌。在乘车时遇见穿丧服的人，便俯伏在车前横木上（以示同情）。遇见背负国家图籍的人，也这样做（以示敬意）。如果有丰盛的筵席，就神色一变，并站起来致谢。遇见迅雷大风，一定要改变神色（以示对上天的敬畏）。

【英译】In bed，he did not lie like a corpse. At home，he did not put on any formal deportment. When he saw any one in a mourning dress，though it might be an acquaintance，he would change countenance；when he saw any one wearing the cap of full dress，or a blind person，though he might be in his undress，he would salute him in a ceremonious manner. To any person in mourning he bowed forward to the crossbar of his carriage；he bowed in the same way to any one bearing the tables of population. When he was at an entertainment where there was an abundance of provisions set before him，he would change countenance and rise up. On a sudden clap of thunder，or a violent wind，he would change countenance.

【注释】

[1] 容：容仪。

[2] 齐衰：指丧服。

[3] 狎：亲近。

[4] 式：同轼，古代车辆前部的横木。这里作动词用。遇见地位高的人或其他人时，驭手身子向前微俯，伏在横木上，以示尊敬或者同情。

[5] 负版者：背负国家图籍的人。当时无纸，用木板来书写，故称"版"。理雅格译为"The tables of population"，即"人口表"；辜鸿铭译为"The mortality returns of the population"，即"人口的死亡率"；刘殿爵译为"official documents"，即"官方文件"；韦利译为"planks"，即"木板"。对于"版"的理解，理雅格的翻译较为恰当。

[6] 馔：饮食。盛馔，盛大的宴席。

【原文】 10.17　升车，必正立，执绥[1]。车中，不内顾，不疾言[2]，不亲指[3]。

【译文】 上车时，一定先直立站好，然后拉着扶手带上车。在车上，不回头，不高声说话，不用自己的手指指点点。

【英译】 When he was about to mount his carriage，he would stand straight，holding the cord. When he was in the carriage，he did not turn his head quite round，he did not shout，he did not point with his hands.

【注释】

[1] 绥：上车时扶手用的索带。

[2] 疾言：大声说话。理雅格译为"talk hastily"，即"匆忙地讲话"；辜鸿铭译为"talk fast"，即"快速地讲话"；刘殿爵译为"叫喊"（shout）；韦利译为"speak rapidly"，即"语速很快"。《论语》此处指高声讲话，刘殿爵的翻译更为恰当。

[3] 不亲指：不用自己的手指划。

【原文】 10.18　色斯举矣。翔而后集[1]。曰："山梁雌雉[2]，时哉！时哉！"[3]子路共之，三嗅而作[4]。

【译文】 孔子在山谷中行走，看见一群野鸡，孔子神色动了一下，野鸡飞翔了一阵落在树上。孔子说："这些山梁上的母野鸡，得其时呀！

得其时呀！"子路向它们拱拱手，野鸡便拍了三次翅膀，飞走了。

【英译】 Seeing the countenance，it instantly rises. It flies round，and by and by settles. The Master said，"There is the hen-pheasant on the hill bridge. At its season！ At its season！"Tsze-lu made a motion to it. Thrice it smelt him and then rose.

【注释】

[1] 翔而后集：飞翔一阵，然后落到树上。鸟群停在树上叫"集"。

[2] 山梁雌雉：聚集在山梁上的野母鸡。

[3] 时哉时哉：得其时呀！得其时呀！指野鸡时运好，能自由飞翔，自由落下。理雅格译为"At its season"，即"在它的季节"；辜鸿铭译为"You know the times"；刘殿爵译为"how timely her action is"，即"她的行动是多么及时啊"；韦利译为"Knows how to bide its time"，即"知道如何等待时机"。此处孔子有感而发，他感到自己却不得其时、东奔西走，没有获得普遍响应，而山谷里的野鸡能够自由飞翔降落。孔子羡慕山中野鸡恰当地把握了它的时运，此处韦利的翻译更为恰当。

[4] 三嗅而作：嗅应为"狊"字之误。理雅格将"嗅"译为"smelt"，即"闻"；辜鸿铭将该句译为"conned it over three times"，即"骗了三次"；刘殿爵译为"flapping its wings three times"，即"拍了三次翅膀"；韦利译为"sniffed three times"，即"闻了三次"。狊，形容鸟张开两翅。上述译本相较，刘殿爵的翻译更为恰当。

先进篇第十一

【原文】11.1 子曰："先进[1]于礼乐，野人[2]也；后进于礼乐，君子也。如用之，则吾从先进。"

【译文】孔子说："先学习礼乐而后再做官的人，是原来没有爵禄的平民；先当了官然后再学习礼乐的人，是君子。如果要先用人才，那我主张选用先学习礼乐的人。"

【英译】The Master said,"The men of former times in the matters of ceremonies and music were rustics，it is said，while the men of these latter times，in ceremonies and music，are accomplished gentlemen. If I have occasion to use those things，I follow the men of former times."

【注释】

[1] 先进、后进：两词的理解有很多种。1. 先学礼乐后当官和先当官后学礼乐。孔安国云："先进、后进，谓仕先后辈也。"2. 皇侃《义疏》云："先进、后进者，谓先、后辈人也。先辈谓五帝以上也，后辈谓三王以还也。"3. 先进指殷之前，后进指周以后。江永《群经补义》："意指殷以前为野人，周以后为君子。"4. 朱子云："犹言前辈、后辈。"5. 释"进"为"学"，先进、后进指孔子学生中的前后辈。刘宝楠《正义》云："郑注云：'先进、后进，谓学也。野人，粗略也。'郑此注文不备，莫由知其义。愚谓此篇皆说弟子言行，先进、后进，即指弟子。《大戴礼记·卫将军文子篇》：'吾闻夫子之施教也，先以《诗》。'卢辩注引此文，则'先进、后进'，皆

谓弟子受夫子所施之教，进学于此也。"钱宾四先生批驳前述二、三、四的说法，采用刘氏之说。6. 释"进"为"行"。黄怀信《论语汇校集释》批驳前述诸说，并提出新说："愚谓'进'当训'行'，今所谓进行。先进于礼乐，言进在礼乐之先，即凡事不待礼乐而进行。后进于礼乐，言进在礼乐之后，即凡事皆先礼乐而后进行。野，国野之野。野人，农夫也。君子，贵族也。用，用其'进'事之法也。从先进，从不待礼乐而行事之法也。见孔子注重实干。"理雅格将"先进"与"后进"译为"The men of former times"与"The men of these latter times"，该译文从朱子之说，指前辈、后辈。辜鸿铭译为"Men of the last generation"与"men of the present generation"，即"上一代的人"与"当代人"，该翻译更贴近江永《群经补义》之说。刘殿爵译为"The disciples who were the first to come to me"与"Who came to me afterwards"，即"第一个来找我的门徒"和"随后来找我的门徒"，该译文更贴近刘宝楠《论语正义》之说。韦利将该句译为"Only common people wait till they are advanced in ritual and music [before taking office]. A gentleman can afford to get up his ritual and music later on"，即"只有乡下人才会等到他们礼乐有所进步才会做官，君子可以先做官再学习礼乐。"该翻译从孔安国之说。

[2] 野人：野指城郊之外的乡村地区，野人即指乡下人。理雅格、刘殿爵译为"rustics"，即"乡下人"；韦利译为"common people"，即"普通人"。下文的君子指贵族。朱子《集注》云："野人，谓郊外之民。君子，谓贤士大夫也。"此处各英译本均译为"gentlemen"。

【原文】11.2　子曰："从我于陈、蔡[1]者，皆不及门[2]也。"

【译文】孔子说："曾跟随我从陈国到蔡地去的学生，现在都不在我身边受教了。"

【英译】The Master said，"Of those who were with me in Ch'an and Ts'ai，there are none to be found to enter my door."

【注释】

[1] 陈、蔡：均为国名。

[2] 不及门：门，这里指受教的场所。不及门，是说不在跟前受教。公元前489年，孔子和他的学生从陈国到蔡地去。途中，他们被陈国的人们所包围，绝粮7天，许多学生饿得不能行走。当时跟随他的学生有子路、子贡、颜渊等人。公元前484年，孔子回鲁国以后，子路、子贡等先后离开了他，颜回也死了。所以，孔子时常想念他们。这句话反映了孔子这种心情。

【原文】 11.3　德行：颜渊、闵子骞、冉伯牛、仲弓；言语：宰我、子贡；政事：冉有、季路；文学：子游、子夏。

【译文】 德行好的有：颜渊、闵子骞、冉伯牛、仲弓。善于辞令的有：宰我、子贡。擅长政事的有：冉有、季路。通晓文献知识的有：子游、子夏。

【英译】 Distinguished for their virtuous principles and practice，there were Yen Yuan，Min Tsze-ch'ien，Zan Po-niu，and Chung-kung；for their ability in speech，Tsai Wo and Tsze-Kung；for their administrative talents，Zan Yu and Chi Lu；for their literary acquirements，Tsze-yu and Tsze-hsia.

【原文】 11.4　子曰："回也，非助我者也！于吾言，无所不说[1]。"

【译文】 孔子说："颜回不是对我有所帮助的人，他对我说的话没有不心悦诚服的。"

【英译】 The Master said，"Hui gives me no assistance. There is nothing that I say in which he does not delight."

【注释】

[1] 说：同"悦"，愉快、高兴、心悦诚服。辜鸿铭译为"satisfied"，

即"满意的"；理雅格译为"delight"，即"高兴的"；刘殿爵译为"pleased"，即"愉快的"；韦利译为"accepted"，即"接受"。delighted形容高兴的、欣喜的，指人对事物感到喜欢，主语常是人，更有一层"乐意"的意思。pleased指一些微小的事物引起的愉悦感，还可以用来说明事物，表示"令人愉快的"或"舒适的"等。此处"悦"不仅指情感上的愉悦，还包含颜回对孔子的敬佩之情。我们认为，理解为"心悦诚服"更为恰当。

【原文】11.5 子曰："孝哉闵子骞，人不间[1]于其父母昆[2]弟之言。"

【译文】孔子说："闵子骞真是孝顺呀！别人对于他的父母兄弟称赞他的话并没有什么异议。"

【英译】The Master said, "Filial indeed is Min Tsze-ch'ien! Other people say nothing of him different from the report of his parents and brothers."

【注释】

[1] 间：非难、批评、挑剔。

[2] 昆：哥哥，兄长。

【原文】11.6 南容三复白圭[1]，孔子以其兄之子妻之。

【译文】南容反复诵读"白圭之玷，尚可磨也；斯言不玷，不可为也"的诗句。孔子把侄女嫁给了他。

【英译】Nan Yung was frequently repeating the lines about a white scepter stone. Confucius gave him the daughter of his elder brother to wife.

【注释】

[1] 白圭：白圭指《诗经·大雅·抑之》的诗句："白圭之玷，尚可磨也，斯兰之玷，不可为也。"意思是白玉上的污点还可以磨掉，我们言论

中有毛病，就无法挽回了。这是告诫人们要谨慎自己的言语。理雅格译为"White scepter stone"；辜鸿铭将《诗经》整句译出，即"A fleck on the stone may be ground away，A word misspoken will remain always"；刘殿爵将"白圭"译为"white jade sceptre"，并在注释中补充说明《诗经》的典故。我们认为，此处刘殿爵的翻译策略更为恰当。

【原文】11.7　季康子问："弟子孰为好学？"孔子对曰："有颜回者好学，不幸短命死矣！今也则亡。"

【译文】季康子问孔子："你的学生中谁是好学的？"孔子回答说："有一个叫颜回的学生很好学，不幸短命死了。现在再也没有像他那样的了。"

【英译】Chi K'ang asked which of the disciples loved to learn. Confucius replied to him，"There was Yen Hui；he loved to learn. Unfortunately his appointed time was short，and he died. Now there is no one who loves to learn，as he did."

【原文】11.8　颜渊死，颜路[1]请子之车以为之椁[2]。子曰："才不才，亦各言其子也。鲤[3]也死，有棺而无椁；吾不徒行，以为之椁，以吾从大夫之后[4]，不可徒行也。"

【译文】颜渊死了，他的父亲颜路请求孔子卖掉车子，给颜渊买个外椁。孔子说："不管有才能或者没有才能，但总是自己的儿子。孔鲤死的时候，也是有棺无椁。我没有卖掉自己的车子步行而给他买椁。因为我还跟随在大夫之后，是不可以步行的。"

【英译】When Yen Yuan died，Yen Lu begged the carriage of the Master to sell and get an outer shell for his son's coffin. The Master said，"Every one calls his son his son，whether he has talents or has not talents. There was Li；when he died，he had a coffin but no outer coffin. I would not walk on foot to get a shell for him，because，having followed in the rear of the great officers，it was not proper that I should walk on foot."

【注释】

[1] 颜路：颜无繇，字路，颜渊的父亲，也是孔子的学生，生于公元前 545 年。

[2] 椁：古人所用棺材，内为棺，外为椁。理雅格译为"outer shell"、辜鸿铭译为"outer case"，即棺外的外壳；韦利译为"enclosure"，即"外壳"；刘殿爵译为"outer coffin"。此处译为 outer coffin 较为恰当。

[3] 鲤：孔子的儿子，字伯鲁，死时 50 岁，孔子 70 岁。

[4] 从大夫之后：跟随在大夫们的后面，意即当过大夫。孔子在鲁国曾任司寇，是大夫一级的官员。

【原文】 11.9　颜渊死，子曰："噫！天丧予！天丧予！"

【译文】 颜渊死了，孔子说："唉！是老天爷真要我的命呀！是老天爷真要我的命呀！"

【英译】 When Yen Yuan died，The Master said，"Alas！ Heaven is destroying me！ Heaven is destroying me！"

【原文】 11.10　颜渊死，子哭之恸[1]。从者曰："子恸矣！"曰："有恸乎！非夫人之为恸而谁为！"

【译文】 颜渊死了，孔子哭得极其悲痛。跟随孔子的人说："您悲痛过度了！"孔子说："是太悲伤过度了吗？我不为这个人悲伤过度，又为谁呢？"

【英译】 When Yen Yuan died，the Master bewailed him exceedingly，and the disciples who were with him said，"Master，your grief is excessive！" "Is it excessive？" said he. "If I am not to mourn bitterly for this man，for whom should I mourn？"

【注释】

[1] 恸：哀伤过度，过于悲痛。理雅格译为"grief is excessive"、辜鸿铭译为"grieve exceedingly"，即"过分悲伤"；刘殿爵译为"undue sorrow"，即"不正当的悲伤"；韦利译为"wailing without restraint"，即"毫无节制地哭泣"。grief 和 sorrow 都是悲伤之义，但是 grief 的悲伤程度要远远大于 sorrow，sorrow 是伤心，而 grief 是悲痛。此处理雅格、辜鸿铭的翻译体现出孔子面对颜回早逝的过度哀痛，更为恰当。

【原文】11.11　颜渊死，门人欲厚葬[1]之，子曰："不可。"门人厚葬之。子曰："回也，视予犹父也，予不得视犹子也[2]。非我也，夫二三子也。"

【译文】颜渊死了，孔子的学生们想要隆重地安葬他。孔子说："不能这样做。"学生们仍然隆重地安葬了他。孔子说："颜回把我当父亲一样看待，我却不能把他当亲生儿子一样看待。这不是我的过错，是那些学生们干的呀。"

【英译】When Yen Yuan died，the disciples wished to give him a great funeral，and The Master said，"You may not do so." The disciples did bury him in great style. The Master said，"Hui behaved towards me as his father. I have not been able to treat him as my son. The fault is not mine；it belongs to you，O disciples."

【注释】

[1] 厚葬：隆重地安葬。理雅格、辜鸿铭译为"great funeral"，刘殿爵译为"lavish burial"，韦利译为"grand burial"。funeral 表示葬礼仪式，burial 强调埋葬过程。《论语》中"葬"多指完整的一套丧葬仪式，含有对礼乐制度的敬重。此处理雅格、辜鸿铭的翻译更为恰当。

[2] 予不得视犹子也：我不能把他当亲生儿子一样看待。孔子遵从礼

的规范，即使是在厚葬颜渊的问题上仍是如此。

【原文】11.12 季路问事鬼神。子曰："未能事人，焉能事鬼[1]？""敢问死？"曰："未知生，焉知死？"

【译文】季路问怎样去事奉鬼神。孔子说："没能事奉好人，怎么能事奉鬼呢？"季路说："请问死是怎么回事？"孔子回答说："还不知道活着的道理，怎么能知道死呢？"

【英译】Chi Lu asked about serving the spirits of the dead. The Master said，"While you are not able to serve men，how can you serve their spirits？"Chi Lu added，"I venture to ask about death？"He was answered，"While you do not know life，how can you know about death？"

【注释】

[1] 鬼：韦利译为"ghosts"，即鬼魂；理雅格、辜鸿铭、韦利译为"spirits"，指灵魂，强调人的精神素质，也指神仙、精灵等。此处"鬼"不仅指已逝亡魂，更包含国人传统敬天法祖的祖先信仰。我们认为，此处译为含义更为丰富的"spirits"较为恰当。

【原文】11.13 闵子侍侧，訚訚[1]如也；子路，行行[2]如也；冉有、子贡，侃侃[3]如也。子乐。"若由也，不得其死然。"[4]

【译文】闵子骞侍立在孔子身旁，一派和悦而温顺的样子；子路是一副刚强的样子；冉有、子贡是坦然的样子。孔子高兴起来，但又说："像仲由这样，恐怕会天年不保！"

【英译】The disciple Min was standing by his side，looking bland and precise；Tsze-Lu，looking bold and soldierly；Zan Yu and Tsze-Kung，with a free and straightforward manner. The Master was pleased. He said，"Yu，there！-he will not die a natural death."

【注释】

[1] 訚訚：温和而快乐的样子。理雅格译为"bland and precise"，即"简洁而精确"；辜鸿铭译为"calm and self-possessed"，即"冷静而沉着"；刘殿爵译为"respectful and upright"，即"恭敬而正直"；韦利译为"polite restraint"，即"有礼且自制"。此处应理解为"和颜悦色"，我们认为译为"Looks mild and cheerful"较为恰当。

[2] 行行：刚强的样子。理雅格译为"bold and soldierly"，即"勇敢而英武"；辜鸿铭译为"upright and soldier-like"，即"正直、像军人一样"；刘殿爵译为"unbending"，即"不屈服的"；韦利译为"impatient energy"，即"有活力但焦躁"。朱子引尹氏曰："子路刚强，有不得其死之理，故因以戒之。其后子路卒死于卫孔悝之难。"子路在孔子门徒中以勇毅刚强著称，孔子在下文也嗟叹子路过于刚强恐怕天命不保。此处译为"刚强"（fortitude）或从刘殿爵译为"不屈服的"（unbending）较为恰当。

[3] 侃侃：说话理直气壮。

[4] 看到每个弟子都表现出最本然的状态，孔子感叹子路的性格恐怕是不得善终的。因为子路的性格过于刚直，所有的喜怒哀乐都表露在自己的行为上，任何人都可以看得出来。后面发生的事情果不其然，子路在卫国的暴乱中身亡。

【原文】11.14　鲁人为长府[1]。闵子骞曰："仍旧贯[2]，如之何？何必改作！"子曰："夫人不言，言必有中。"

【译文】鲁国翻修长府的国库。闵子骞道："照老样子下去，怎么样？何必改建呢？"孔子道："这个人平日不大开口，一开口就说到要害上。"

【英译】Some parties in Lu were going to take down and rebuild the Long Treasury. Min Tsze-ch'ien said, "Suppose it were to be repaired after its old style; -why must it be altered and made anew?" The Master said, "This man seldom speaks; when he does, he is sure to hit the point."

【注释】

[1] 为长府：为，这里是改建的意思。藏财货、兵器等的仓库叫"府"，长府是鲁国的国库名。理雅格、韦利译为"The Long Treasury"、刘殿爵译为"Treasury"，即"国库"之义。辜鸿铭译为"State-house"，即"州议会"。上述译本相较，理雅格等人的翻译较为恰当。

[2] 仍旧贯：贯：事，例。沿袭老样子。

【原文】 11.15 子曰："由之瑟，奚为于丘之门[1]？"门人不敬子路。子曰："由也升堂矣！未入于室[2]也！"

【译文】 孔子说："仲由弹瑟，为什么在我这里弹呢？"孔子的学生们因此都不尊敬子路。孔子便说："仲由嘛，他在学习上已经达到升堂的程度了，只是还没有入室罢了。"

【英译】 The Master said, "What has the lute of Yu to do in my door?" The other disciples began not to respect Tszelu. The Master said, "Yu has ascended to the hall, though he has not yet passed into the inner apartments."

【注释】

[1] 奚为于丘之门：奚，为什么。为，弹。为什么在我这里弹呢？

[2] 升堂入室：堂是正厅，室是内室，用以形容学习程度的深浅。理雅格、刘殿爵将"堂"与"室"分别译为"The hall"和"The inner apartments"；韦利译为"The guest-hall"和"The inner apartments"；辜鸿铭译为"The gate"和"house"，即"大门"和"房子"。上述译本相较，辜鸿铭的翻译不够恰当。

【原文】 11.16 子贡问："师与商[1]也孰贤？"子曰："师也过，

商也不及。"曰："然则师愈与?"子曰："过犹不及^[2]。"

【译文】子贡问孔子："子张和子夏二人谁更好一些呢?"孔子回答说："子张太过,子夏不足。"子贡说："那么是子张好一些吗?"孔子说："太过和不足是一样的。"

【英译】Tsze-Kung asked which of the two，Shih or Shang，was the superior. The Master said，"Shih goes beyond the due mean，and Shang does not come up to it.""Then，"said Tsze-Kung，"The superiority is with Shih，I suppose." The Master said，"To go beyond is as wrong as to fall short."

【注释】

[1] 师与商:师,颛孙师,即子张。商,卜商,即子夏。

[2] 过犹不及:既然子张做得过分、子夏做得不足,两人都不好,孔子对此二人的评价为"过犹不及"。理雅格译为"To go beyond is as wrong as to fall short"，即"过分和不足一样是错误的";辜鸿铭译为"To go beyond the mark is just as bad as not to come up to it"，即"超越目标和不达到目标一样糟糕";刘殿爵译为"There is little to choose between overshooting the mark and falling short"，即"在超越目标和没有达到目标之间没有什么选择"。实际上,《论语》此处并未提及"目标",译出则画蛇添足。韦利译为"To go too far is as bad as not to go far enough"，即"走得太远和走得不够糟糕",以行走路途长短来比喻行为是否合宜。"过犹不及"即中庸思想的具体说明。《中庸》:"道之不行也,我知之矣。知者过之,愚者不及也。道之不明也,我知之矣。贤者过之,不肖者不及也。""执其两端,用其中于民,其斯以为舜乎?"舜于两端取其中,既非过,也非不及,以中道教化百姓,所以为大圣。

【原文】11.17 季氏富于周公^[1],而求也为之聚敛而附益^[2]之。子曰："非吾徒也,小子鸣鼓而攻之可也。"

【译文】季氏比周朝的公侯还要富有，而冉求还帮他搜刮，来增加他的钱财。孔子说："他不是我的学生了，你们可以大张旗鼓地去攻击他。"

【英译】The head of the Chi family was richer than The duke of Chau had been，and yet Ch'iu collected his imposts for him，and increased his wealth. The Master said，"He is no disciple of mine. My little children，beat the drum and assail him."

【注释】

[1] 鲁国的三家曾于公元前562年将公室，即鲁国国君直辖的土地和附属于土地上的人口瓜分，季氏分得三分之一。公元前537年，三家第二次瓜分公室，季氏分得四分之二。由于季氏推行了新的政治和经济措施，所以很快富了起来。孔子的学生冉求帮助季氏积敛钱财，搜刮人民，所以孔子很生气，表示不承认冉求是自己的学生，而且让其他学生打着鼓去声讨冉求。

[2] 益：增加。理雅格、辜鸿铭译为"increase"，刘殿爵、韦利译为"add"。add多指增加、加添、补充，强调"把……加入"；increase侧重某物数量的增长、增多、增加。此处形容季氏的财富日益增多，译为"increase"更为恰当。

【原文】11.18 柴[1]也愚[2]，参也鲁，师也辟[3]，由也喭[4]。子曰："回也其庶[5]乎，屡空[6]。赐不受命而货殖焉，亿[7]则屡中。"

【译文】高柴愚直，曾参迟钝，颛孙师偏激，仲由鲁莽。孔子说："颜回的学问道德接近于完善了吧，可是他常常贫困。端木赐不安于命运的安排，囤积投机，猜测行情，竟每每猜中。"

【英译】Ch'ai is simple. Shan is dull. Shih is specious. Yu is coarse. The Master said，"There is Hui！He has nearly attained to perfect virtue. He is often in want. "Ts'ze does not acquiesce in the appointments of Heaven，and his goods are increased by him. Yet his judgments are often correct."

【注释】

[1] 柴：高柴，字子羔，孔子学生。

[2] 愚：理雅格、辜鸿铭译为"simple"，即"简单的"；刘殿爵、韦利译为"stupid"，即"愚笨的"。

[3] 辟：偏邪，偏激。理雅格、辜鸿铭译为"specious"，即"似是而非的"；韦利译为"Too formal"，即"过分正式"；刘殿爵译为"one-sided"，即"片面的"。这里我们认为刘殿爵的翻译更为恰当。

[4] 喭：鲁莽，粗鲁，刚猛。理雅格、辜鸿铭译为"coarse"，即"粗鲁的"；韦利译为"Too free and easy"，即"过分自由轻松的"；刘殿爵译为"forthright"，即"直率的"。coarse 指缺乏教养、言谈粗俗、举止粗野，而《论语》此处强调子路做事鲁莽，译为"rash"更为恰当。

[5] 庶：庶几，相近。这里指颜渊的学问道德接近于完善。

[6] 空：贫困、匮乏。

[7] 亿：同"臆"，猜测、估计。理雅格、辜鸿铭译为"judgments"，即"判断"；刘殿爵译为"conjectures"，即"猜测"；韦利译为"calculations"，即"计算"，引申为"规划、筹谋"。此处并非指有根据的"判断"和"计算"，而是指"猜测""猜度"，刘殿爵的翻译更为恰当。

【原文】 11.19 子张问善人[1]之道。子曰："不践迹[2]，亦不入于室[3]！"子曰："论笃是与[4]，君子者乎？色庄者乎？"

【译文】 子张问做善人的方法。孔子说："如果不沿着前人的脚印走，其学问和修养就不到家。"孔子说："听到别人议论笃实诚恳，就表示赞许，还应看他是真君子呢？还是伪装庄重的人呢？"

【英译】 Tsze-Chang asked what were the characteristics of the good man. The Master said，"He does not tread in the footsteps of others，but moreover，he does not enter the chamber of the sage." The Master said, "If, because a man's discourse appears solid and sincere, we allow him to be a good man, is he really a superior man? or is his gravity only in appearance?"

【注释】

[1] 善人：辜鸿铭译为"honest man"，即"诚实的人"；理雅格、刘殿爵、韦利译为"good man"，即"好人"。

[2] 践迹：迹，脚印。踩着前人的脚印走。

[3] 入于室：比喻学问和修养达到了精深地步。理雅格译为"enter the chamber of the sage"，即"进入圣人的房间"；刘殿爵、韦利译为"entrance into the inner room"，即"升堂入室"。"升堂入室"本义是先进门，次升堂，后入室，后比喻学习所达到的境地有程度深浅的差别，多用以赞扬人在学问或技能方面有高深的造诣。

[4] 论笃是与：论，言论。笃，诚恳。与，赞许。辜鸿铭译为"Men now are earnest in what they profess"，即"现在的人对他们所宣称的都是认真的"。理雅格译为"We allow him to be a good man"，即"我们承认他是个好人"。刘殿爵译为"simply sides with tenacious opinions"，形容一个人"固执于某一方面的观点"。韦利译为"his conversation is sound one may grant"，即"他的言论是健全的（人们对此赞誉）"。《论语》此处意为"对说话笃实诚恳的人表示赞许"，我们认为韦利的翻译更为恰当。

【原文】 11.20 子路问："闻斯行诸？"子曰："有父兄在，如之何其闻斯行之！"冉有问："闻斯行诸？"子曰："闻斯行之！"公西华曰："由也问闻斯行，子曰：'有父兄在'；求也问闻斯行诸，子曰：'闻斯行之'。赤也惑，敢问？"子曰："求也退，故进之；由也兼人[1]，故退之。"

【译文】 子路问："听到了就行动起来吗？"孔子说："有父兄在，怎么能听到就行动起来呢？"冉有问："听到了就行动起来吗？"孔子说：

"听到了就行动起来。"公西华说:"仲由问'听到了就行动起来吗?'你回答说'有父兄健在'。冉求问'听到了就行动起来吗?'你回答'听到了就行动起来'。我被弄糊涂了,敢再问个明白。"孔子说:"冉求总是退缩,所以我鼓励他;仲由好勇过人,所以我约束他。"

【英译】Tsze-Lu asked whether he should immediately carry into practice what he heard. The Master said, "There are your father and elder brothers to be consulted; -why should you act on that principle of immediately carrying into practice what you hear?" Zan Yu asked the same, whether he should immediately carry into practice what he heard, and the Master answered, "Immediately carry into practice what you hear." Kung-hsi Hwa said, "Yu asked whether he should carry immediately into practice what he heard, and you said, 'There are your father and elder brothers to be consulted.' Ch'iu asked whether he should immediately carry into practice what he heard, and you said, 'Carry it immediately into practice.' I, Ch'ih, am perplexed, and venture to ask you for an explanation." The Master said, "Ch'iu is retiring and slow; therefore I urged him forward. Yu has more than his own share of energy; therefore I kept him back."

【注释】

[1] 兼人:好勇过人。理雅格译为"has more than his own share of energy",即"拥有比自己更多的能量";辜鸿铭译为"too froward",即"过分顽固的";刘殿爵译为"Yu has the drive of two men",即"有两个人的干劲";韦利译为"fanatical about Goodness",即"对道德很狂热"。"兼"为"倍"之意,指一人做两人事,形容人鲁莽好勇。本章是孔子把中庸思想贯穿于教育实践中的一个具体事例。在这里,他要自己的学生不要退缩,也不要冒进,要进退适中。此处刘殿爵译出了"兼"的"倍"之义,但没能补充出该词的引申义。我们认为,此处译为"Yu is reckless and brave"较为恰当。

【原文】11.21　子畏于匡，颜渊后。子曰："吾以女为死矣！"曰："子在，回何敢死！"

【译文】孔子在匡地受到围困，颜渊最后才逃出来。孔子说："我以为你已经死了呢。"颜渊说："夫子还活着，我怎么敢死呢？"

【英译】The Master was put in fear in K'wang and Yen Yuan fell behind. The Master, on his rejoining him, said, "I thought you had died." Hui replied, "While you were alive, how should I presume to die?"

【原文】11.22　季子然[1]问："仲由、冉求，可谓大臣[2]与？"子曰："吾以子为异之问，曾由与求之问？所谓大臣者，以道事君，不可则止；今由与求也，可谓具臣[3]矣。"曰："然则从之者与？"子曰："弑父与君[4]，亦不从也。"

【译文】季子然问："仲由和冉求可以算是大臣吗？"孔子说："我以为你是问别人，原来是问由和求呀。所谓大臣是能够以仁义之道来事奉君主，如果这样不行，宁肯辞职不干。现在由和求这两个人，只能算是充数的臣子罢了。"季子然说："那么他们会一切都跟着季氏干吗？"孔子说："杀父亲、杀君主的事，他们也不会跟着干的。"

【英译】Chi Tsze-zan asked whether Chung Yu and Zan Ch'iu could be called great ministers. The Master said, "I thought you would ask about some extraordinary individuals, and you only ask about Yu and Ch'iu! What is called a great minister, is one who serves his prince according to what is right, and when he finds he cannot do so, retires. Now, as to Yu and Ch'iu, they may be called ordinary ministers." Tsze-zan said, "Then they will always follow their chief, win they?" The Master said, "In an act of parricide or regicide, they would not follow him."

【注释】

[1] 季子然：鲁国季氏的同族人。

[2] 大臣：理雅格、刘殿爵、韦利译为"great minister"，即"伟大的大臣"；辜鸿铭译为"statesmen"，即"政治家"。

[3] 具臣：普通的臣子。辜鸿铭译为"states-functionaries"，即"国家官员"；理雅格译为"ordinary ministers"，即"普通的大臣"；韦利译为"stop-gap ministers"，即"临时的大臣"。我们认为，此处理雅格译为"great minister"和"ordinary ministers"形成对比，较为恰当。

[4] 理雅格、刘殿爵译为"patricide or regicide"，即"弑君罪；弑君者"之义。弑是指古代臣子杀死君主，子女杀死父母等卑幼杀死尊长的大不敬行为，patricide or regicide 很好地翻译出了其内涵。

【原文】 11.23 子路使子羔为费宰。子曰："贼[1]夫人之子[2]！"子路曰："有民人焉，有社稷[3]焉，何必读书，然后为学？"子曰："是故恶夫佞者。"

【译文】 子路让子羔去作费地的长官。孔子说："这简直是害人子弟。"子路说："那个地方有老百姓，有社稷，难道一定要读书才算学习吗？"孔子说："所以我讨厌那种花言巧语狡辩的人。"

【英译】 Tsze-Lu got Tsze-kao appointed governor of Pi. The Master said, "You are injuring a man's son." Tsze-Lu said, "There are, there, common people and officers; there are the altars of the spirits of the land and grain. Why must one read books before he can be considered to have learned?" The Master said, "It is on this account that I hate your glib-tongued people."

【注释】

[1] 贼：害。

[2] 夫人之子：指子羔。孔子认为他没有经过很好的学习就去从政，

这会害了他自己。

[3] 社稷：社，土地神。稷，谷神。理雅格译为"The altars of the spirits of the land and grain"，即"供奉土地和谷物的神灵的祭坛"；刘殿爵译为"questions of the interests of the country"，即"关于国家利益的问题"；刘殿爵译为"The altars to the gods of earth and grain"，即"大地和谷物之神的祭坛"；韦利译为"The Holy Ground"，即"圣地"。这里"社稷"指祭祀土地神和谷神的地方，即社稷坛。古代国都及各地都设立社稷坛，分别由国君和地方长官主祭，故社稷成为国家政权的象征。我们认为，此处理雅格和刘殿爵的翻译较为恰当。

【原文】11.24　子路、曾皙[1]、冉有、公西华侍坐。子曰："以吾一日长乎尔，毋吾以也。居则曰：'不吾知也!'如或知尔，则何以哉?"子路率尔[2]而对曰："千乘之国，摄[3]乎大国之间，加之以师旅，因之以饥馑，由也为之，比及三年，可使有勇，且知方也[4]。"夫子哂之。"求，尔何如?"对曰："方六七十[5]，如五六十，求也为之，比及三年，可使足民。如其礼乐，以俟君子。""赤，尔何如?"对曰："非曰能之，愿学焉。宗庙之事，如会同，端章甫[6]，愿为小相焉。""点，尔何如?"鼓瑟希，铿尔，舍瑟而作，对曰："异乎三子者之撰。"子曰："何伤乎? 亦各言其志也。"曰："莫春者，春服既成，冠者[7]五六人，童子六七人，浴乎沂[8]，风乎舞雩[9]，咏而归。"夫子喟然叹曰："吾与点也!"三子者出，曾皙后。曾皙曰："夫三子者之言何如?"子曰："亦各言其志也已矣。"曰："夫子何哂由也?"曰："为国以礼。其言不让，是故哂之。""唯求则非邦也与?""安见方六七十如五六十而非邦也者?""唯赤则非邦也与?""宗庙会同，非诸侯而何? 赤也为之小，孰能为之大?"

【译文】子路、曾皙、冉有、公西华四个人陪孔子坐着。孔子说：

"我年龄比你们大一些，不要因为我年长而不敢说。你们平时总说：'没有人了解我呀！'假如有人了解你们，那你们要怎样去做呢？"子路赶忙回答："一个拥有一千辆兵车的国家，夹在大国中间，常常受到别的国家侵犯，加上国内又闹饥荒，让我去治理，只要三年，就可以使人们勇敢善战，而且懂得礼仪。"孔子听了，微微一笑。孔子又问："冉求，你怎么样呢？"冉求答道："国土有六七十里或五六十里见方的国家，让我去治理，三年以后，就可以使百姓饱暖。至于这个国家的礼乐教化，就要等君子来施行了。"孔子又问："公西赤，你怎么样？"公西赤答道："我不敢说能做到，而是愿意学习。在宗庙祭祀的活动中，或者在同别国的盟会中，我愿意穿着礼服，戴着礼帽，做一个小小的赞礼人。"孔子又问："曾点，你怎么样呢？"这时曾点弹瑟的声音逐渐放慢，接着"铿"的一声，离开瑟站起来，回答说："我想的和他们三位说的不一样。"孔子说："那有什么关系呢？也就是各人讲自己的志向而已。"曾晳说："暮春三月，已经穿上了春天的衣服，我和五六位成年人，六七个少年，去沂河里洗洗澡，在舞雩台上吹吹风，一路唱着歌走回来。"孔子长叹一声说："我是赞成曾晳的想法的。"子路、冉有、公西华三个人都出去了，曾晳后走。他问孔子说："他们三人的话怎么样？"孔子说："也就是各自谈谈自己的志向罢了。"曾晳说："夫子为什么要笑仲由呢？"孔子说："治理国家要讲礼让，可是他说话一点也不谦让，所以我笑他。"曾晳又问："那么是不是冉求讲的不是治理国家呢？"孔子说："哪里见得六七十里或五六十里见方的地方就不是国家呢？"曾晳又问："公西赤讲的不是治理国家吗？"孔子说："宗庙祭祀和诸侯会盟，这不是诸侯的事又是什么？像赤这样的人，如果只能做一个小相，那谁又能做大相呢？"

【英译】 Tsze-Lu, Tsang Hsi, Zan Yu, and Kunghsi Hwa were sitting by the Master. He said to them, "Though I am a day or so older than you, do not think of that. From day to day you are saying, 'We are not known.' If some ruler were to know you, what would you like to do?" Tsze-Lu hastily and lightly replied, "Suppose the case of a state of ten thousand chariots; let it be straitened between other large cities; let it be suffering from invading armies; and to this let there be added a famine in corn and in all vegetables: -if I were intrusted with the government of it, in three years' time I could make the people to be bold, and to recognize the rules of righteous conduct." The Master smiled at him. Turning to Yen Yu, he said, "Ch'iu, what are your wishes?" Ch'iu replied, "Suppose a state of sixty or seventy li square, or one of fifty or sixty, and let me have the government of it; -in three years' time, I could make plenty to abound among the people. As to teaching them the principles of propriety, and music, I must wait for the rise of a superior man to do that." "What are your wishes, Ch'ih," said the Master next to Kung-hsi Hwa. Ch'ih replied, "I do not say that my ability extends to these things, but I should wish to learn them. At the services of the ancestral temple, and at the audiences of the princes with the sovereign, I should like, dressed in the dark square-made robe and the black linen cap, to act as a small assistant." Last of all, the Master asked Tsang Hsi, "Tien, what are your wishes?" Tien, pausing as he was playing on his lute, while it was yet twanging, laid the instrument aside, and "My wishes," he said, "are different from the cherished purposes of these three gentlemen." "What harm is there in that?" said the Master; "do you also, as well as they, speak out your wishes." Tien then said, "In this, the last month of spring, with the dress of the season all complete, along with five or six young men who have assumed the cap, and six or seven boys, I would wash in the I, enjoy the breeze among the rain altars, and return home singing." The Master heaved a sigh and said，"I give my approval to Tien." The three others having gone out，Tsang Hsi remained behind，and said，"What do you think of the words of these three friends?" The Master replied，"They simply told each one his wishes." Hsi pursued，"Master，why did you smile at Yu?" He was answered，"The management of a state demands the rules of propriety. His words were not humble；therefore I smiled at him." Hsi again said，"But was it not a state which Ch'iu proposed for himself?" The reply was，"Yes；did you ever see a territory of sixty or seventy li or one of fifty or sixty，which was not a state?" Once more，Hsi inquired，"And was it not a state which Ch'ih proposed for himself?" The Master again replied，"Yes；who but princes have to do with ancestral temples，and with audiences but the sovereign? If Ch'ih were to be a small assistant in these services，who could be a great one?"

【注释】

[1] 曾皙：名点，字子皙，曾参的父亲，也是孔子的学生。

[2] 率尔：轻率、急切。

[3] 摄：迫于、夹于。

[4] 可使有勇，且知方也：理雅格译为"I could make the people to be bold，and to recognize the rules of righteous conduct"，即"使人民勇敢起来，认识到正直行为的准则"；辜鸿铭译为"make the people brave and，moreover，know their duty"，即"人们很勇敢，而且还知道自己的责任"；刘殿爵译为"give the people courage and a sense of direction"，即"给人民勇气和方向感"；韦利译为"endow the people with courage and teach them in what direction right conduct lies"，即"赋予人民勇气，教导他们正确的行为方向"。上述译本相较，韦利的翻译更为恰当。

[5] 方六七十：纵横各六七十里。

[6] 端章甫：端，古代礼服的名称。章甫，古代礼帽的名称。

[7] 冠者：成年人。古代子弟到 20 岁时行冠礼，表示已经成年。

[8] 浴乎沂：沂，水名，发源于山东南部，流经江苏北部入海。在水边洗头面手足。浴：有多种解释：1.沐浴。何晏《集解》引包咸云："欲得冠者五六人，童子六七人，浴乎沂水之上，风凉于舞雩之下，歌咏先王之道，而归夫子之门。"2.被除。朱子《集注》云："浴，盥濯也，今上已被除是也。沂，水名，在鲁城南，地志以为有温泉焉，理或然也。"3.雩祭。王充《论衡·明篇》云："鲁设雩祭于沂水之上。'暮'者，晚也。'春'，谓四月也。'春服既成'，谓四月之服成也。'冠者'，'童户'，雩祭乐人也。'浴乎沂'，涉沂水也，像龙之从水中出也。'风乎舞雩'，'风'，歌也，'咏而馈'，咏歌馈祭，歌咏而祭也。说《论》之家，以为'浴'者，浴沂水中也，'风'，干身也。周之四月，正岁二月也，尚寒，安得浴而风干身。由此言之，涉水不浴，雩祭审也。"4.浴为"沿"之误。韩李《笔解》云："浴当为沿字之误。"今人李伯勋对此有详细考证，赞同韩李《笔解》之说。（参见李伯勋《"浴乎沂，风乎舞雩"考释》，《兰州大学学报》（社会科学版）1991 年第 2 期）

[9] 舞雩：雩，地名，原是祭天求雨的地方，在今山东曲阜。

颜渊篇第十二

【原文】12.1　颜渊问仁。子曰："克己复礼[1]，为仁。一日克己复礼，天下归仁焉。为仁由己，而由仁乎哉?"颜渊曰："请问其目[2]?"子曰："非礼勿视，非礼勿听，非礼勿言，非礼勿动。"颜渊曰："回虽不敏，请事[3]斯语矣!"

【译文】颜渊问怎样做才是仁。孔子说："克制自己，一切都照着礼的要求去做，这就是仁。一旦这样做了，天下的人都会称许你是仁人。实行仁德，完全在于自己，难道还在于别人吗?"颜渊说："请问实行仁的条目。"孔子说："不合于礼的不要看，不合于礼的不要听，不合于礼的不要说，不合于礼的不要做。"颜渊说："我虽然迟钝，也要照您的这些话去做。"

【英译】Yen yuan asked about perfect virtue. The Master said, "To subdue one's self and return to propriety, is perfect virtue. If a man can for one day subdue himself and return to propriety, an under heaven will ascribe perfect virtue to him. Is the practice of perfect virtue from a man himself, or is it from others?" Yen yuan said, "I beg to ask the steps of that process." The master replied, "look not at what is contrary to propriety; listen not to what is contrary to propriety; speak not what is contrary to propriety; make no movement which is contrary to propriety." Yen yuan then said, "Though I am deficient in intelligence and vigor, I will make it my business to practice this lesson."

【注释】

[1] 克己复礼：克己，克制自己。复礼，使自己的言行符合于礼的要求。理雅格译为"subdue himself and return to propriety"，即"克制自己并回归礼仪"，理氏本将"复"译为"回归"，不太恰当。辜鸿铭将该句译为"Renounce yourself and conform to the ideal of decency and good sense"，即"放弃你自己，符合体面和明智的理想"。辜鸿铭从宗教的角度，解释为何将"克己"译为"放弃自己"："D'ALEMBERT remarked that the ancient Stoic Diogenes would be the greatest man in antiquity in Europe，if he only had 'decency.' The first part is the self-renunciaiton（Entsagen）of GOETHE：'Stirb und werde Denn so lang du das nicht hast，Bist du nur ein trüber Gast Auf der dunklen Erde.' The second part is the imperious ideal of Art（礼）-of the Greeks and Italians，which in itself，as GOFTHE says，is religion."我们认为，此处"克"并不能理解为"放弃、抛弃"义，儒家不会提出这么消极的主张。刘殿爵译为"To return to the observance of the rites through overcoming the self"，即"通过克服自我来恢复仪式"，此处"克己"是实现"复礼"的条件，二者之间是逻辑递进关系。韦利译为"submit to ritual"，"复礼"即"顺服礼制仪式"。"克己复礼为仁"，礼以仁为基础，以仁来维护，仁是内在的，礼是外在的，二者紧密结合。这里实际上包括两个方面的内容，一是克己，二是复礼。此处译为"克制自己，符合礼的要求"（Restrain yourself and behave in accordance with etiquette）较为恰当。

[2] 目：具体的条目。目和纲相对。

[3] 事：从事，照着去做。

【原文】 12.2 仲弓问仁。子曰："出门如见大宾；使民如承大祭[1]；己所不欲，勿施于人；在邦无怨，在家无怨[2]。"仲弓曰："雍虽不敏，请事斯语矣！"

【译文】 仲弓问怎样做才是仁。孔子说："出门办事如同去接待贵宾，使唤百姓如同去进行重大的祭祀，（都要认真严肃。）自己不愿意要的，不要强加于别人；做到在诸侯的朝廷上没人怨恨自己，在卿大夫的封地里也没人怨恨自己。"仲弓说："我虽然迟钝，也要照您的话去做。"

【英译】Chung-kung asked about perfect virtue. The Master said, "It is，when you go abroad，to behave to every one as if you were receiving a great guest；to employ the people as if you were assisting at a great sacrifice；not to do to others as you would not wish done to yourself；to have no murmuring against you in the country，and none in the family." Chung-kung said，"Though I am deficient in intelligence and vigor，I will make it my business to practice this lesson."

【注释】

[1] 出门如见大宾，使民如承大祭：邢昺《注疏》云："此言为仁之道，莫尚乎敬也。大宾，公侯之宾也。大祭，禘郊之属也。人之出门，失在倨傲，故戒之出门如见公侯之宾。使民失于骄易，故戒之如承奉郊之祭。"出门办事和役使百姓，都要像迎接贵宾和进行大祭时那样恭敬严肃。理雅格将"大宾"译为"great guest"、刘殿爵、韦利译为"important guest"，即"尊贵重要的客人"；辜鸿铭译为"Emperor"，即"皇帝"，该本注意到了"大宾"在中国古代语境中指代公侯等王爵，而不仅仅是普通的宾客。

[2] 在邦无怨，在家无怨：邦，诸侯统治的国家。家，卿大夫统治的封地。理雅格译为"To have no murmuring against you in the country，and none in the family"，"邦""家"即"国"和"家庭"。辜鸿铭译为"In your public life in the State as well as in your private life in your family，give no one a just cause of complaint against you"，即"在你的公共生活中，在你的私人生活中，在你的家庭中，不要给任何人一个抱怨你的正当理由"，此处"邦"被译为"State"。刘殿爵译为"In this way you will be free from ill will whether in a state or in a noble family"，即"无论是在一个国家，还是在一个高贵的家庭，你都将免于恶意"，理雅格将"家"译为"贵族家庭"，注意到了《论

语》此处"家"意指卿大夫统治之处。country 表示地理概念，侧重"疆土"，即一个国家的整个区域；state 则侧重"政权"，即独立的国家，也可指其政府。此处"邦"指诸侯统治的国家，"在邦无怨"强调在政治生活中没有遭受怨恨，侧重"政权、政府"。上述译本相较，刘殿爵的翻译更为恰当。

【原文】12.3　司马牛[1]问仁。子曰："仁者，其言也讱[2]。"曰："斯言也讱，其谓之仁矣乎？"子曰："为之难，言之得无讱乎？"

【译文】司马牛问怎样做才是仁。孔子说："仁人说话是慎重的。"司马牛说："说话慎重，这就叫作仁了吗？"孔子说："做起来很困难，说起来能不慎重吗？"

【英译】Sze-ma niu asked about perfect virtue. The Master said，"The man of perfect virtue is cautious and slow in his speech.""Cautious and slow in his speech！" said niu；"Is this what is meant by perfect virtue？" The Master said，"When a man feels the difficulty of doing, can he be other than cautious and slow in speaking？"

【注释】

[1] 司马耕，一名犁，子姓，向氏，字子牛，向罗之子，司马桓魋之弟，孔子"七十二贤"之一。公元前481年，因桓魋专权，司马牛交出封邑，离开宋国到齐国。桓魋出奔齐国，司马牛又到吴国，赵简子、陈成子召他，司马牛没有去，逃到鲁国，拜孔子为师，并声称桓魋不是他的哥哥，后来在鲁国城门外去世。

[2] 讱：话难说出口。这里引申为说话谨慎。理雅格译为"cautious and slow in his speech"，形容说话"谨慎而缓慢"；辜鸿铭译为"one who is sparing of his words"，即"寡言少语的人"；刘殿爵译为"loath to speak"，即"不愿意说话"；韦利译为"chary of speech"，即"言语谨慎"。cautious 指对某事加以戒心，特别指对做某事成败与否的担忧，害怕伤害自己和他人，也用来指做某事前深思熟虑，做好计划再予以实施，以避免失败或使危险降

到最低程度。chary 特别强调行为上持谨慎或小心翼翼的态度。"訒"引申为说话谨慎，强调行为态度上的谨慎小心，而非做事抱有戒心，韦利译为"chary of speech"较为恰当。

【原文】12.4　司马牛问君子。子曰："君子不忧不惧。"曰："不忧不惧，斯谓之君子矣乎？"子曰："内省不疚，夫何忧何惧？"

【译文】司马牛问怎样做一个君子。孔子说："君子不忧愁，不恐惧。"司马牛说："不忧愁，不恐惧，这样就可以叫作君子了吗？"孔子说："自己问心无愧，那还有什么忧愁和恐惧呢？"

【英译】Sze-ma niu asked about the superior man. The Master said, "The superior man has neither anxiety nor fear." "Being without anxiety or fear！" said niu；"does this constitute what we call the superior man?" The Master said, "When internal examination discovers nothing wrong，what is there to be anxious about，what is there to fear?"

【原文】12.5　司马牛忧曰："人皆有兄弟，我独亡[1]！"子夏曰："商闻之矣：'死生有命，富贵在天'。君子敬而无失，与人恭而有礼；四海之内，皆兄弟也。君子何患乎无兄弟也？"

【译文】司马牛忧愁地说："别人都有兄弟，唯独我没有。"子夏说："我听说过：'死生听之命运，富贵由天安排。'君子只要对待所做的事情严肃认真，不出差错，对人恭敬而合乎于礼的规定，那么，天下人就都是自己的兄弟了。君子何愁没有兄弟呢？"

【英译】Sze-ma niu, full of anxiety, said, "other men all have their brothers, I only have not." Tsze-hsia said to him, "There is the following saying which I have heard-'death and life have their determined appointment；riches and honors depend upon heaven.' Let the superior men never fail reverentially to order his own conduct, and let him be respectful to others and observant of propriety：then all within the four seas will bee his brothers. What has the superior man to do with being distressed because he has no brothers?"

【注释】

[1] 亡：同"无"。

【原文】 12.6　子张问明。子曰："浸润之谮[1]，肤受之愬[2]，不行焉，可谓明也已矣。浸润之谮，肤受之愬，不行焉，可谓远[3]也已矣。"

【译文】 子张问怎样做才算是明智的。孔子说："点滴而来、日积月累的谗言和肌肤所受、急迫切身的诬告，在你那里都行不通，那你可以算是明智的了。暗中挑拨的坏话和直接的诽谤，在你那里都行不通，那你可以算是有远见的了。"

【英译】 Tsze-Chang asked what constituted intelligence. The Master said，"he with whom neither slander that gradually soaks into the mind，nor statements that startle like a wound in the flesh，are successful may be called intelligent indeed. Yea，he with whom neither soaking slander，nor startling statements，are successful，may be called farseeing."

【注释】

[1] 浸润之谮：谮，谗言。这是说像水那样一点一滴地渗进来的谗言，不易觉察。理雅格译为"slander that gradually soaks into the mind"，即"渗入人心的诽谤"；辜鸿铭译为"resist long-continued attempts of others to insinuate prejudice into him"，即"长期抵制他人的偏见"；刘殿爵译为"slanders which are assiduously repeated"，即"反复重复的诽谤"。理雅格的翻译体现出"浸润"之意，更为恰当。

[2] 肤受之愬：愬，诬告。这是说像皮肤感觉到疼痛那样的诬告，即

直接的诽谤。理雅格译为"statements that startle like a wound in the flesh"，即"像身体产生伤口那样疼痛的谗言"；辜鸿铭译为"one who cannot be influenced by a sudden appeal to his own personal safety"，即"能够不受出于个人安全考虑的突然呼吁的影响"；刘殿爵译为"by complaints for which he feels a direct sympathy"，即那些"直接的抱怨"。理雅格采用直译，译出了伤口的疼痛感，较为恰当。

[3] 远：明之至，明智的最高境界。理雅格译为"farseeing"、刘殿爵译为"far-sight"，即"有远见的"；辜鸿铭译为"really superior man"，即"真正卓越的"；韦利译为"aloof"，即"冷漠"，该翻译或因译者将"远"理解为"疏远、难以接近"之义。我们认为，此处刘殿爵、理雅格的翻译更为准确。

【原文】 12.7 子贡问政。子曰："足食，足兵，民信[1]之矣。"子贡曰："必不得已而去，于斯三者何先？"曰："去兵。"子贡曰："必不得已而去，于斯二者何先？"曰："去食，自古皆有死，民无信不立。"

【译文】 子贡问怎样治理国家。孔子说，"粮食充足，军备充足，老百姓信任统治者。"子贡说："如果不得不去掉一项，那么在三项中先去掉哪一项呢？"孔子说："去掉军备。"子贡说："如果不得不再去掉一项，那么这两项中去掉哪一项呢？"孔子说："去掉粮食。自古以来人总是要死的，如果老百姓对统治者不信任，那么国家就不能存在了。"

【英译】 Tsze-Kung asked about government. The Master said, "The requisites of government are that there be sufficiency of food, sufficiency of military equipment, and the common people will have trust in their ruler." Tsze-Kung said, "If it cannot be helped, and one of these must be dispensed with, which of the three should be foregone first?" "The military equipment," said the master. Tsze-Kung again asked，"If it cannot be helped，and one of the remaining two must be dispensed with，which of them should be foregone？" The master answered，"part with the food. From of old，death has been the lot of an men；but if the people have no faith in their rulers，there is no standing for the state."

【注释】

[1] 信：信任。理雅格、辜鸿铭译为 "The confidence of the people in their ruler"，韦利译为 "The confidence of the common people"，即百姓对统治者的 "信心"。刘殿爵译为 "The common people will have trust in you"，即普通人对统治者的 "信任"。trust 通常是指对别人的人品、能力的信任；confidence 是指自信。本章里孔子回答了子贡问政中所连续提出的三个问题。孔子认为，治理一个国家，应当具备三个起码条件：食、兵、信。但这三者当中，信是最重要的。这体现了儒学的人学思想。只有兵和食，而百姓对统治者不信任，那这样的国家也就不能存在下去了。《论语》此处是指百姓对统治者的信任，译为 "trust" 更为恰当。

【原文】 12.8　棘子成[1]曰："君子质而已矣，何以文为？"子贡曰："惜乎，夫子之说君子也，驷不及舌[2]！文犹质也，质犹文也；虎豹之鞟[3]，犹犬羊之鞟。"

【译文】 棘子成说："君子只要具有好的品质就行了，要那些表面的仪式干什么呢？"子贡说："真遗憾啊，夫子您是这样谈论君子的。一言既出，驷马难追。本质就像文采，文采就像本质，都是同等重要的。去掉了毛的虎、豹皮，就如同去掉了毛的犬、羊皮一样。"

【英译】 Chi Tsze-ch'ang said，"In a superior man it is only the substantial qualities which are wanted；why should we seek for ornamental accomplishments？" Tsze-Kung said，"alas！ your words，sir，show you to be a superior man，but four horses cannot overtake the tongue. ornament is as substance；substance is as ornament. The hide of a tiger or a leopard stripped of its hair，is like the hide of a dog or a goat stripped of its hair."

【注释】

[1] 棘子成：卫国大夫。古代大夫都可以被尊称为夫子，所以子贡这样称呼他。

[2] 驷不及舌：指话一说出口，就收不回来了。驷，拉一辆车的四匹马。理雅格直译为"four horses cannot overtake the tongue"，即"四匹马也赶不上您的舌头"。辜鸿铭译为"What you would say is true；but，stated in that way，it is impossible for men not to misunderstand your meaning"，即"你说的是对的，但是人们不可能不误解你的意思"，这种翻译并不符合孔子原意。刘殿爵译为"a team of horses cannot catch up with one's tongue"，并在注释中补充说明"In other words，words once spoken cannot be recalled"，即"说出的话无法挽回"。刘殿爵的翻译既保留了古汉语俚语的语言特色，又向海外读者介绍了该句的深层含义，更便于读者理解。

[3] 鞟：去掉毛的皮，即革。理雅格译为"stripped of its hair"，即"剥去毛发"；辜鸿铭译为"skin"，"鞟"即"皮肤"；刘殿爵译为"pelt"，即"毛皮"。"鞟"即没有毛的皮，刘殿爵译为"pelt"（带毛的皮）不够恰当。我们认为，此处可直接译为"leather"，即"革"。

【原文】 12.9 哀公问于有若曰："年饥，用不足，如之何？"有若对曰："盍彻[1]乎！"曰："二[2]，吾犹不足；如之何其彻也？"对曰："百姓足，君孰不足？百姓不足，君孰与足？"

【译文】 鲁哀公问有若说："遭了饥荒，国家用度困难，怎么办？"有若回答说："为什么不实行彻法，只抽十分之一的田税呢？"哀公说："现在抽十分之二，我还不够，怎么能实行彻法呢？"有若说："如果百姓的用度够，您怎么会不够呢？如果百姓的用度不够，您怎么又会够呢?"

【英译】The duke Ai inquired of Yu zo，saying，"The year is one of scarcity，and there turns for expenditure are not sufficient；what is to be done?" Yu zo replied to him，"Why not simply tithe the people?" "With two tenths，" said the duke，"I find it not enough；-how could I do with that system of one tenth?" Yu zo answered，"If the people have plenty，their prince will not be left to want alone. If the people are in want，their prince cannot enjoy plenty alone."

【注释】

[1] 彻，西周奴隶主国家的一种田税制度。旧注曰:"什一而税谓之彻。"理雅格译为"Why not simply tithe the people"、辜鸿铭译为"Why not tithe (take one-tenth) the people"，即向百姓征收十分之一的税；刘殿爵译为"What about taxing the people one part in ten"，即"征收十分之一"。上述译本无甚差别。

[2] 二：抽取十分之二的税。辜鸿铭译为"With two-thirds"，即"三分之二"的税率；刘殿爵译为"Tax them two parts in ten"、韦利译为"With two-tenths"，即"十分之二"。这一章反映了儒家学派的经济思想，其核心是"富民"思想。鲁国所征的田税是十分之二的税率，即使如此，国家的财政仍然是十分紧张的。这里，有若的观点是，削减田税的税率，改行"彻税"即什一税率，使百姓减轻经济负担。只要百姓富足了，国家就不可能贫穷。反之，如果对百姓征收过甚，这种短期行为必将使民不聊生，国家经济也就随之衰退了。这种以"富民"为核心的经济思想有其值得借鉴的价值。

【原文】12.10 子张问崇德[1]、辨惑[2]。子曰:"主忠信，徙义[3]，崇德也。爱之欲其生，恶之欲其死；既欲其生又欲其死，是惑也!'诚不以富，亦祇以异。'[4]"

【译文】子张问怎样提高道德修养水平和辨别是非迷惑的能力。孔子说："以忠信为主,使自己的思想合于义,这就是提高道德修养水平了。爱一个人,就希望他活下去,厌恶起来就恨不得他立刻死去,既要他活,又要他死,这就是迷惑。正如《诗》所说的:'即使不是嫌贫爱富,也是喜新厌旧。'"

【英译】Tsze-chang having asked how virtue was to be exalted, and delusions to be discovered, the Master said, "Hold faithfulness and sincerity as first principles, and be moving continually to what is right, -this is the way to exalt one's virtue. You love a man and wish him to live; you hate him and wish him to die. Having wished him to live, you also wish him to die. This is a case of delusion.' It may not be on account of her being rich, yet you come to make a difference.'"

【注释】

[1] 崇德:提高道德修养的水平。理雅格译为"how virtue was to be exalted",即"美德如何被推崇";辜鸿铭译为"raise the moral sentiment",即"提高道德情操";刘殿爵译为"The exaltation of virtue",即"培养美德";韦利译为"piling up moral force",即"积聚道德力量"。上述译本相较,刘殿爵的翻译更为恰当。

[2] 惑:迷惑,不分是非。理雅格、辜鸿铭译为"delusions",即"错觉、谬见";刘殿爵译为"perplexities",即"困惑";韦利译为"deciding when in two minds",即"在犹豫中做决定"。此处"惑"指迷惑、困惑,而非产生的错觉,刘殿爵的翻译更为恰当。

[3] 徙义:徙,迁移。看到"义"就改变意念而跟从,向义靠扰。理雅格译为"moving continually to what is right",即"朝着正确的方向前进";辜鸿铭译为"Act up to what is right",即"采取正确行动";韦利译为"migrating to places where right prevails",即"移居到正义盛行的地方"。包咸注曰:"徙义,见义则徙意而从之。"一说,"徙"为"从"字之误。俞樾《群经平议》云:"所主者必忠信,所从者必义,是谓崇德……包氏以'徙

义'为徙意从之，其说迂曲，殆非也。'徙'当为'从'。《述而篇》'闻义不能徙'，阮氏《校勘记》曰：'高丽本作从。'是其证矣。"可见"徙"是"跟从"之义，刘殿爵的翻译较为恰当。

[4] 诚不以富，亦祇以异：这是《诗经·小雅·我行其野》篇的最后两句。此诗表现了一个被遗弃的女子对其丈夫喜新厌旧的愤怒情绪。邢昺云："言此行诚不足以致富，适足以为异耳。取此诗之异义，以非人之惑也。"朱熹注："旧说：夫子引之，以明欲其生死者不能使之生死。如此诗所言，不足以致富而适足以取异也。程子曰：'此错简，当在第十六篇齐景公有马千驷之上。因此下文亦有齐景公字而误也。'杨氏曰：'堂堂乎张也，难与并为仁矣。则非诚善补过不蔽于私者，故告之如此。'"孔子在这里引此句，较为费解。

【原文】12.11　齐景公[1]问政于孔子。孔子对曰："君君，臣臣，父父，子子。"公曰："善哉！信如君不君，臣不臣，父不父，子不子，虽有粟，吾得而食诸？"

【译文】齐景公问孔子如何治理国家。孔子说："做君主的要像君的样子，做臣子的要像臣的样子，做父亲的要像父亲的样子，做儿子的要像儿子的样子。"齐景公说："讲得好呀！如果君不像君，臣不像臣，父不像父，子不像子，虽然有粮食，我能吃得上吗？"

【英译】The duke Ching，of Ch'i，asked Confucius about government. Confucius replied，"There is government，when the prince is prince，and the minister is minister；when the father is father，and the son is son.""good！"said the duke；"If，indeed，the prince be not prince，the not minister，the father not father，and the son not son，although I have my revenue，can I enjoy it？"

【注释】

[1] 齐景公：名杵臼，齐国国君，公元前547—前490年在位。

【原文】12.12　子曰："片言[1]可以折狱[2]者，其由也与[3]！"子路无宿诺[4]。

【译文】孔子说："只听了单方面的供词就可以判决案件的，大概只有仲由吧。"子路说话没有不算数的时候。

【英译】The Master said，"ah！it is Yu，who could with half a word settle litigations！"Tsze-Lu never slept over a promise.

【注释】

[1]　片言：又叫"单辞"，诉讼双方中一方的证词。朱熹认为是子路的话："片言，半言。折，断也。子路忠信明决，故言出而人信服之，不待其辞之毕也。"理雅格、韦利从朱子说，译为"half a word"；辜鸿铭译为"half a sentence"，即"半句话"；刘殿爵将该处理解为"诉讼某方的证词"，译为"on the evidence of only one party"，即"只有一方证据"。仲由可以以"片言"而"折狱"，这是为什么？历来有这样几种解释。一说子路明决，凭单方面的陈述就可以作出判断；二说子路为人忠信，人们都十分信服他，所以有了纠纷都在他面前不讲假话，所以凭一面之词就可以明辨是非；三说子路忠信，他所说的话决无虚假，所以只听其中一面之词，就可以断定案件。但无论哪种解释，都可以证明子路在刑狱方面是卓有才干的。

[2]　折狱：断案。《释文》曰："《鲁》读'折'为'制'，今从《古》。"理雅格译为"settle litigations"、辜鸿铭译为"settle a dispute"，即"解决争端"。

[3]　其由也与：两种理解，一种认为子路忠信，人们信服他，所以可以三言两语断案，如上引朱子之言。一种认为是子路明断，凭单方证人的证词就可以断案。孔安国云："片犹偏也。听讼必须两辞以定是非，偏信一言以折狱者，唯子路可。"邢昺曰："故知听讼必须两辞方定是非。偏信一言，则是非难决。唯子路才性明辨，能听偏言决断狱讼，故云唯子路可。"

[4]　宿诺：两种理解：1.宿犹预，宿诺指预先的承诺。何晏《集解》云："宿，犹预也。子路笃信，恐临时多故，故不预诺。"2.宿为留的意思，

宿诺指拖延的承诺。朱子云："宿，留也，犹宿怨之宿。急于践言，不留其诺也。记者因夫子之言而记此，以见子路之所以取信于人者，由其养之有素也。"理雅格、辜鸿铭、韦利译为"slept over a promise"，即"拖延兑现承诺"；刘殿爵译为"put off the fulfillment of a promise to the next day"，即"把承诺的履行推迟到第二天"。上述译本均从朱熹之说，译为"拖延兑现的承诺"。

【原文】12.13　子曰："听讼[1]，吾犹人也。必也，使无讼乎！"

【译文】孔子说："审理诉讼案件，我同别人也是一样的。重要的是必须使诉讼的案件根本不发生！"

【英译】The Master said, "In hearing lawsuits, I am like any other body. What is necessary, however, is to cause the people to have no litigations."

【注释】

[1] 听讼：讼，诉讼。审理诉讼案件。理雅格、刘殿爵译为"litigation"，即"诉讼、案件"；辜鸿铭译为"court"，即"法院、法庭"；韦利译为"civil suit"，即"民事诉讼"。litigation 主要强调是通过法院的诉讼程序解决问题，而不是通过调解或和解等非诉讼方式解决纠纷；suit 是 lawsuit 的简略形式，主要用于指民事诉讼。《论语》中诉讼案件多指民事诉讼，"无讼"体现了孔子的仁民主张，此处译为"suit"或"lawsuit"更为恰当。

【原文】12.14　子张问政。子曰："居之无倦；行之以忠[1]。"

【译文】子张问如何治理政事。孔子说："居于官位不懈怠，执行君令要忠实。"

【原文】Tsze-Chang asked about government. The Master said,

"The art of governing is to keep its affairs before the mind without weariness，and to practice them with undeviating consistency."

【注释】

[1] 忠：理雅格译为 "undeviating consistency"，形容事君 "坚定不移、持之以恒"；辜鸿铭译为 "conscientiousness"，指为臣者具备 "责任心"；刘殿爵译为 "do your best"，即事君时 "竭尽全力"；韦利译为 "loyally"，形容臣子对待君王是 "忠诚的"。

【原文】 12.15　子曰："博学于文，约之以礼，亦可以弗畔矣夫。"[1]

【译文】 孔子说："广泛地学习文献，用礼仪约束自己，就可以不离经叛道了。"

【英译】 The Master said，"By extensively studying all learning, and keeping himself under the restraint of the rules of propriety，one may thus likewise not err from what is right."

【注释】

[1] 本章重出，见《雍也》篇第 27 章。

【原文】 12.16　子曰："君子成人之美[1]，不成人之恶；小人反是。"

【译文】 孔子说："君子成全别人的好事，而不助长别人的恶处。小人则与此相反。"

【英译】 The Master said，"The superior man seeks to perfect the admirable qualities of men，and does not seek to perfect their bad qualities. the mean man does the opposite of this."

【注释】

[1] 成人之美：成全别人的好事，帮助别人实现愿望。理雅格译为

"seeks to perfect the admirable qualities of men"，即"力求完善人的优点"；辜鸿铭译为"encourages men to develop the good qualities in their nature"，即"鼓励人们发展他们本性中的好品质"。理雅格、辜鸿铭的翻译体现出儒家对教化的重视。刘殿爵译为"helps others to effect what is good"，即"帮助他人产生好的效果"。"成人之美，不成人之恶"贯穿了儒家一贯的思想主张，即"己欲立而立人，己欲达而达人""己所不欲，勿施于人"的忠恕之道。此处"成人之美"应理解为"成全别人的美事"，刘殿爵的翻译更为恰当。

【原文】12.17　季康子问政于孔子，孔子对曰："政者，正[1]也，子帅以正，孰敢不正？"

【译文】季康子问孔子如何治理国家。孔子回答说："政就是正的意思。你本人带头走正路，那么还有谁敢不走正道呢？"

【英译】Chi k'ang asked Confucius about government. Confucius replied，"To govern means to rectify. If you lead on the people with correctness，who will dare not to be correct？"

【注释】

[1] 正：端正、走正路。理雅格、刘殿爵译为"correct"，即"正确的"；辜鸿铭译为"order"，即"秩序"；韦利译为"straightening"，即"矫正"。刘殿爵从字源角度，补充说明了"政"与"正"的同源："Besides being homophones, the two words in Chinese are cognate, thus showing that the concept of 'government' Was felt to be related to that of 'being correct'."（除了同音外，这两个词在汉语中是同源的，这表明"政府"的概念被认为与"正确"的概念有关）上述译本相较，刘殿爵的翻译更为翔实可靠。

【原文】12.18　季康子患盗，问于孔子。孔子对曰："苟子之不欲，虽赏之不窃。"[1]

【译文】季康子担忧盗窃，问孔子怎么办。孔子回答说："假如你自己不贪图财利，即使奖励偷窃，也没有人偷盗。"

【英译】 Chi k'ang，distressed about the number of thieves in the state，inquired of Confucius how to do away with them. Confucius said，"If you，sir，were not covetous，although you should reward them to do it，they would not steal."

【注释】

[1] 孔子谈论为官从政之道，即为政者要正人先正己的道理。他希望当政者以自己的德行感染百姓，这就表明了他主张政治道德化的倾向。具体到治理社会问题时也是如此。他没有让季康子用严刑峻法去制裁盗窃犯罪，而是主张用德治去教化百姓，以使人免于犯罪。

【原文】 12.19　季康子问政于孔子曰："如杀无道[1]，以就有道，何如？"孔子对曰："子为政，焉用杀？子欲善而民善矣。君子之德风，人小之德草，草上之风，必偃。"

【译文】 季康子问孔子如何治理政事，说："如果杀掉无道的人来成全有道的人，怎么样？"孔子说："你治理政事，哪里用得着杀戮的手段呢？你只要想行善，老百姓也会跟着行善。在位者的品德好比风，在下的人的品德好比草，风吹到草上，草就必定跟着倒。"

【英译】 Chi k'ang asked Confucius about government，saying，"What do you say to kill the unprincipled for the good of the principled？" Confucius replied，"sir，in carrying on your government，why should you use killing at all？ Let your evinced desires be for what is good，and the people will be good. The relation between superiors and inferiors is like that between the wind and the grass. The grass must bend，when the wind blows across it."

【注释】

[1] 无道：指无道的人。下文"有道"指有道的人。理雅格译为

"unprincipled"，"道"即为"原则"；辜鸿铭译为"wicked"和"good"，即"恶人"与"好人"；刘殿爵将"无道"译为"do not follow the way"，即"不走这条路的人"；韦利直接翻译为"have not the way"。"无道"指不行正道的坏人或暴君，孔子反对杀人，主张"德政"。在上位的人只要善理政事，百姓就不会犯上作乱。这里讲的人治，是有仁德者的所为。那些暴虐的统治者滥行无道，必然会引起百姓的反对。上述理雅格、辜鸿铭等译本更为明白晓畅。

【原文】 12.20　子张问士："何如斯可谓之达[1]矣?"子曰："何哉? 尔所谓达者!"子张对曰："在邦必闻[2]，在家必闻。"子曰："是闻也，非达也。夫达也者：质直而好义，察言而观色，虑以下人[3]；在邦必达，在家必达。夫闻也者：色取仁而行违，居之不疑；在邦必闻，在家必闻。"

【译文】 子张问："士怎样才可以叫作通达?"孔子说："你说的通达是什么意思?"子张答道："在国君的朝廷里必定有名望，在大夫的封地里也必定有名声。"孔子说："这只是虚假的名声，不是通达。所谓达，那是要品质正直，遵从礼义，善于揣摩别人的话语，对察别人的脸色，经常想着谦恭待人。这样的人，就可以在国君的朝廷和大夫的封地里通达。至于有虚假名声的人，只是外表上装出仁的样子，而行动上却正是违背了仁，自己还以仁人自居不惭愧。但他无论在国君的朝廷里和大夫的封地里都必定会有名声。"

【英译】 Tsze-Chang asked, "What must the officer be, who may be said to be distinguished?" The Master said, "What is it you call being distinguished?" Tsze-Chang replied, "It is to be heard of through the state, to be heard of throughout his clan." The Master said, "That is notoriety, not distinction." "Now the man of distinction is solid and straightforward, and loves righteousness. He examines people's words，and looks at their countenances. He is anxious to humble himself to others. Such a man will be distinguished in the country；he will be distinguished in his clan. as to the man of notoriety，he assumes the appearance of virtue，but his actions are opposed to it，and he rests in this character without any doubts about himself. Such a man will be heard of in the country；he will be heard of in the clan."

【注释】

[1] 达：通达，显达。理雅格、辜鸿铭译为 "distinction"；刘殿爵译为 "getting through"，即 "通达的"；韦利译为 "influential"，即 "有影响力的"。上述译本相较，刘殿爵的翻译更为恰当。

[2] 闻：有名望。理雅格、辜鸿铭译为 "notoriety"，即 "名声"；刘殿爵译为 "being known"，即 "被知道的"；韦利译为 "famous"，即 "著名的"。本章中孔子提出了一对相互对立的名词，即 "闻" 与 "达"。"闻" 是虚假的名声，并不是显达；而 "达" 则要求士大夫必须从内心深处具备仁、义、礼的德性，注重自身的道德修养，而不仅是追求虚名。这里同样讲的是名实相符，表里如一的问题。

[3] 下人：下，动词。对人谦恭有礼。理雅格译为 "humble himself to others"，即 "对待别人很谦逊"；辜鸿铭译为 "Reflection makes him humble in his estimate of himself as compared with other men"，即 "反思使他在与他人相比时显得谦逊"，该翻译不合《论语》原意；刘殿爵译为 "always mindful of being modest"，即 "永远保持谦虚"；韦利译为 "deferring to others"，即 "顺从他人"。此处 "下人" 形容对人谦恭有礼，理雅格的翻译更为恰当。

【原文】 12.21 樊迟从游于舞雩之下，曰："敢问崇德、修慝[1]、辨惑。"子曰："善哉问！先事后得[2]，非崇德与？攻其恶，无攻人之恶，非修慝与？一朝之忿[3]，忘其身，以及其亲，非惑与？"

【译文】 樊迟陪着孔子在舞雩台下散步，说："请问怎样提高品德修养？怎样改正自己的邪念？怎样辨别迷惑？"孔子说："问得好！先努力致力于事，然后才有所收获，不就是提高品德了吗？批判自己的坏处，不去批判别人的坏处，检讨自己的邪念了吗？由于一时的气愤，就忘记了自身的安危，以至于牵连自己的亲人，这不就是迷惑吗？"

【英译】 Fan Ch'ih rambling with the master under the trees about the rain altars，said，"I venture to ask how to exalt virtue，to correct cherished evil，and to discover delusions." The Master said，"Truly a good question！If doing what is to be done be made the first business，and success a secondary consideration：-is not this the way to exalt virtue？To assail one's own wickedness and not assail that of others；-is not this the way to correct cherished evil？For a morning's anger to disregard one's own life，and involve that of his parents；-is not this a case of delusion？"

【注释】

[1] 修慝：慝，邪恶的念头。修，改正。理雅格译为"correct cherished evil"，即"纠正恶念"；辜鸿铭译为"To discover the secret vices"，即"去发现秘密的恶习"；刘殿爵译为"The reformation of the depraved"，即"对堕落者的改造"；韦利译为"repairing shortcomings"，即"修复缺点"。这里是指改正邪恶的念头，并非纠正人的缺点，理雅格译为"correct cherished evil"较为恰当。

[2] 先事后得：先致力于事，把利禄放在后面。

[3] 忿：忿怒，气愤。

【原文】 12.22 樊迟问仁。子曰："爱人。"问知。子曰："知人。"樊迟未达。子曰："举直错诸枉[1]，能使枉者直。"樊迟退，见子夏曰："乡[2]也吾见于夫子而问知，子曰'举直错诸枉，能使枉者直'，何谓也？"子夏曰："富哉言乎！舜有天下，选于众，举皋陶[3]，不仁者远矣。汤有天下，选于众，举伊尹[4]，不仁者远矣。"

【译文】樊迟问什么是仁。孔子说："爱人。"樊迟问什么是智，孔子说："了解人。"樊迟还不明白。孔子说："选拔正直的人，罢黜邪恶的人，这样就能使邪者归正。"樊迟退出来，见到子夏说："刚才我见到老师，问他什么是智，他说'选拔正直的人，罢黜邪恶的人，这样就能使邪者归正'，这是什么意思？"子夏说："这话说得多么深刻呀！舜有天下，在众人中挑选人才，把皋陶选拔出来，不仁的人就被疏远了。汤有了天下，在众人中挑选人才，把伊尹选拔出来，不仁的人就被疏远了。"

【英译】Fan Ch'ih asked about benevolence. The Master said, "It is to love all men." He asked about knowledge. The Master said, "It is to know all men." Fan Ch'ih did not immediately understand these answers. The Master said, "employ the upright and put aside all the crooked; in this way the crooked can be made to be upright." Fan Ch'ih retired, and, seeing Tsze-hsia, he said to him, "a little while ago, I had an interview with our master, and asked him about knowledge. He said, 'employ the upright, and put aside all the crooked; -in this way, the crooked will be made to be upright.' what did he mean?" Tsze-hsia said, "Truly rich is his saying! Shun, being in possession of the kingdom, selected from among all the people, and employed kai-yao-on which all who were devoid of virtue disappeared. T'ang, being in possession of the kingdom, selected from among all the people, and employed I yin-and an who were devoid of virtue disappeared."

【注释】

[1] 举直错诸枉：错，同"措"，放置。诸，这是"之于"二字的合

音。枉，不正直，邪恶。意为选拔直者，罢黜枉者。理雅格译为"employ the upright and put aside all the crooked"，即"任用正直的人，舍弃一切弯曲的人"。辜鸿铭译为"Upbold the cause of the just，and put down every cause that is unjust in such a way"，即"为正义的事业鼓足勇气，放下一切不公正的事业"，该翻译将"直"理解为"正义的事"而非"正直的人"。刘殿爵采用直译，将该句译为"Raise the straight and set them over the crooked"，即"把直的举起来，放在弯的上面"，该句并未译出孔子此喻的内涵。韦利同样采用直译，译为"By raising the straight and putting them on top of the crooked"。孔子在各处对仁的解释都有内在的联系。他所说的爱人，包含有古代的人文主义精神，把仁作为他全部学说的对象和中心。关于智，孔子认为是要了解人，选拔贤才，罢黜邪才。但在历史上，许多贤能之才不但没有被选拔反而受到压抑，而一些奸佞之人却平步青云，这说明真正做到智并不容易。结合本章主旨我们认为，孔子此处意在称赞那些能够选贤举能的贤明君主，"直"指的是正直的贤人，而非正义的事情。上述译本相较，理雅格的翻译避免了直译谚语带来的误解，更为明白恰当。

[2] 乡：同"向"，过去。

[3] 皋陶：传说中舜时掌握刑法的大臣。

[4] 伊尹：汤的宰相，曾辅助汤灭夏兴商。

【原文】 12.23 子贡问友[1]。子曰："忠告而善道之，不可则止，毋自辱焉。"

【译文】 子贡问怎样对待朋友。孔子说："忠诚地劝告他，恰当地引导他，如果不听也就罢了，不要自取其辱。"

【英译】 Tsze-Kung asked about friendship. The Master said，"Faithfully admonish your friend，and skillfully lead him on. If you find him impracticable，stop. Do not disgrace yourself."

【注释】

[1] 在人伦关系中，"朋友"是最松弛的一种。朋友之间讲求一个"信"字，这是维系双方关系的纽带。对待朋友的错误，要开诚布公地劝导他，推心置腹地讲明利害关系，但他坚持不听，也就作罢。如果别人不听，你一再劝告，就会自取其辱。这是交友的一个基本准则。所以清末志士谭嗣同就认为朋友一伦最值得称赞，他甚至主张用朋友一伦改造其他四伦。孔子这里所讲的是对别人作为主体的一种承认和尊重。

【原文】 12.24 曾子曰："君子以文会友，以友辅仁[1]。"

【译文】 曾子说："君子以文章学问来结交朋友，依靠朋友帮助自己培养仁德。"

【英译】 The philosopher Tsang said, "The superior man on grounds of culture meets with his friends, and by friendship helps his virtue."

【注释】

[1] 仁：曾子继承了孔子的思想，主张以文章学问作为结交朋友的手段，以互相帮助培养仁德作为结交朋友的目的。理雅格译为"virtue"，泛指一切美德；辜鸿铭译为"live a moral life"，即友情能使人过上"道德生活"；刘殿爵译为"benevolence"，指"仁慈、仁爱"；韦利译为"Goodness"，即"善良"。goodness 侧重固有的仁爱，慷慨等高尚的美德。morality 强调符合道德标准的行为或用道德准则衡量某事，尤注重男女间的道德品行。virtue 是一般用词，强调人的优点，以及有意识去做善事的高尚美德。"仁"在儒家推崇的诸德中具有特殊的地位，高于诸德并统摄、涵盖诸德，仁作为至德，是指所有美德都是因为仁才能称得上是美德，仁是一切美德的价值根源，只有指向仁的品质才是美德。此处"仁"不仅指人的慈爱善良，更包含人之为人的一切美德，理雅格译为"virtue"较为恰当。

子路篇第十三

【原文】13.1 子路问政。子曰："先之劳之[1]。"请益。曰："无倦[2]。"

【译文】子路问怎样管理政事。孔子说："做在老百姓之前，使老百姓勤劳。"子路请求多讲一点。孔子说："不要懈怠。"

【英译】Tsze-Lu asked about government. The Master said，"Go before the people with your example，and be laborious in their affairs." He requested further instruction，and was answered，"Be not slack in these things."

【注释】

[1] 先之劳之：先，引导、先导、以身作则。之，指老百姓。自己以身作则，辛勤劳作。理雅格译为"go before the people with your example，and be laborious in their affairs"，即"走在百姓面前，为他们的事尽心尽力"。辜鸿铭译为"Go before the people with your example，show them your exertion"，即"带着你的榜样走在人民面前；向他们展示你的努力"，《论语》此处"劳"指的是统治者为了百姓的事辛勤劳作，而非向百姓刻意展现自己的努力。刘殿爵译为"Before working the people hard first set an example yourself"，即"在努力工作之前，人们要先树立榜样"。《论语》此处"先"指的是"以身作则"，刘殿爵此译不够恰当。韦利译为"Lead them；encourage them"，即"引导他们、鼓励他们"，此处将"劳"译为"鼓励"，不够恰当。我们认为，此处理雅格的译文更为切合《论语》原意。

[2] 无倦：不厌倦，不松懈。

【原文】13.2　仲弓为季氏宰，问政。子曰："先有司[1]，赦小过，举贤才。"曰："焉知贤才而举之？"曰："举尔所不知，人其舍诸！"

【译文】仲弓做了季氏的家臣，问怎样管理政事。孔子说："先责成手下负责具体事务的官吏，让他们各负其责，赦免他们的小过错，选拔贤才来任职。"仲弓又问："怎样知道是贤才而把他们选拔出来呢？"孔子说："选拔你所知道的，至于你不知道的贤才，别人难道还会埋没他们吗？"

【英译】Chung-Kung，being chief minister to the head of the chi family，asked about government. The Master said，"Employ first the services of your various officers，pardon small faults，and raise to office men of virtue and talents." Chung-Kung said，"How shall I know the men of virtue and talent，so that I may raise them to office？" He was answered，"Raise to office those whom you know. As to those whom you do not know，will others neglect them？"

【注释】

[1] 有司：古代负责具体事务的官吏。

【原文】13.3　子路曰："卫君[1]待子而为政，子将奚先？"子曰："必也正名[2]乎！"子路曰："有是哉？子之迂也！奚其正？"子曰："野哉，由也！君子于其所不知，盖阙如也。名不正则言不顺，言不顺则事不成，事不成则礼乐不兴，礼乐不兴则刑罚不中，刑罚不中则民无所措手足[3]。故君子名之必可言也，言之必可行也。君子于其言，无所苟而已矣！"

【译文】子路对孔子说："卫国国君要您去治理国家，您打算先从哪些事情做起呢？"孔子说："首先必须正名分。"子路说："有这样做的吗？您想得太不合时宜了。这名怎么正呢？"孔子说："仲由，真粗野啊。君子对于他所不知道的事情，总是采取存疑的态度。名分不正，说起话来就不顺当合理，说话不顺当合理，事情就办不成。事情办不成，礼乐也就不能兴盛。礼乐不能兴盛，刑罚的执行就不会得当。刑罚不得当，百姓就不知怎么办好。所以，君子一定要定下一个名分，必须能够说得明白，说出来一定能够行得通。君子对于自己的言行，是从不马马虎虎对待的。"

【英译】Tsze-Lu said，"The ruler of wei has been waiting for you，in order with you to administer the government. What will you consider the first thing to be done?" The master replied，"What is necessary is to rectify names." "so！ indeed！" said Tsze-Lu. "you are wide of the mark！ why must there be such rectification?" The Master said，"how uncultivated you are yu！ a superior man，in regard to what he does not know，shows a cautious reserve. If names be not correct，language is not in accordance with the truth of things. If language be not in accordance with the truth of things，affairs cannot be carried on to success. When affairs cannot be carried on to success，proprieties and music do not flourish. When proprieties and music do not flourish，punishments will not be properly awarded. When punishments are not properly awarded，the people do not know how to move hand or foot. Therefore a superior man considers it necessary that the names he uses maybe spoken appropriately and also that what he speaks may be carried out appropriately. What the superior man requires is just that in his words there may be nothing incorrect."

【注释】

[1] 卫君：指卫出公蒯辄，是卫灵公的孙子，太子蒯聩的儿子。蒯聩

得罪南子，被卫灵公驱逐出卫国，逃到晋国。卫灵公去世后，蒯辄继位为国君。晋国的赵简子打着将蒯聩送回卫国的旗号，借机攻打卫国。卫国举兵反抗，同时将蒯聩拒之国门之外。

[2] 正名：辨正名称、名分，使名实相符。朱子云："是时出公不父其父而祢其祖，名实紊矣，故孔子以正名为先。谢氏曰：正名虽为卫君而言，然为政之道，皆当以此为先。"理雅格、刘殿爵译为"rectify names"，即"纠正名份"；辜鸿铭译为"defining the names of things"，即"定义事物的名称"；韦利译为"correct language"，即"纠正语言"。"正名"是孔子"礼"的思想的组成部分。正名的具体内容就是"君君、臣臣、父父、子子"，只有"名正"才可以做到"言顺"。蒯辄与父亲争夺王位，且不让父亲回国，破坏了父子名分，因此孔子主张拨乱反正，纠正错误名分。我们认为，此处刘殿爵、理雅格的翻译更为恰当。

[3] 措手足：定州竹简本、诸唐写本、唐石经、戴氏本"措"作"错"，即放置手足之意。这句话表达了孔子正名的原因。《论语注疏》云："此孔子更陈正名之理也。夫事以顺成，名由言举。名若不正则言不顺，言不顺则政事不成。政事不成，则君不安于上，风不移于下，是礼乐不兴行也。礼乐不行，则有淫刑滥罚，故不中也。刑罚枉滥，民则蹐地局天，动罹刑网，故无所错其手足也。"理雅格译为"move hand or foot"，即"移动手和脚"；辜鸿铭采取意译，将该句理解为"The people will be at a loss to know what to do"（人民将会手足无措）；刘殿爵、韦利直译为"put hand and foot"，即"放置手和脚"。

【原文】13.4　樊迟请学稼[1]，子曰："吾不如老农。"请学为圃[2]，曰："吾不如老圃。"樊迟出，子曰："小人哉，樊须也！上好礼，则民莫敢不敬；上好义，则民莫敢不服；上好信，则民莫敢不用情[3]。夫如是，则四方之民，襁负其子而至矣；焉用稼！"

【译文】樊迟向孔子请教如何种庄稼。孔子说："我不如老农。"樊

迟又请教如何种菜。孔子说："我不如老菜农。"樊迟退出以后，孔子
说："樊迟真是小人。在上位者只要重视礼，老百姓就不敢不敬畏；在上
位者只要重视义，老百姓就不敢不服从；在上位的人只要重视信，老百
姓就不敢不用真心实情来对待你。要是做到这样，四面八方的老百姓就
会背着自己的小孩来投奔，哪里用得着自己去种庄稼呢？"

【英译】Fan Ch'ih requested to be taught husbandry. The Master
said, "I am not so good for that as an old husbandman." He requested
also to be taught gardening, and was answered, "I am not so good for
that as an old gardener." Fan Ch'ih having gone out, The Master said,
"A small man, indeed, is fan hsu! If a superior man loves propriety,
the people will not dare not to be reverent. If he loves righteousness,
the people will not dare not to submit to his example. If he loves good
faith, the people will not dare not to be sincere. Now, when these
things obtain, the people from all quarters will come to him, bearing
their children on their backs; What need has he of a knowledge of
husbandry?"

【注释】

[1] 稼：种植庄稼。

[2] 圃：菜地，引申为种菜。

[3] 用情：情，情实。以真心实情来对待。理雅格译为"sincere"，即
"真诚的"；辜鸿铭译为"never fail in honesty"，指人民"永远不会失去诚
信"；刘殿爵译为"show their true colours"，即"展示自己的真面目"；韦利
译为"depart from the facts"，指人民没有"远离事实"的。此处"用情"指
民众能够真心对待统治者，译为"sincere"较为恰当。

【原文】 13.5　子曰："诵《诗》三百，授之以政，不达[1]；使
于四方，不能专对[2]。虽多，亦奚以为？"

【译文】孔子说："把《诗》三百篇背得很熟，让他处理政务，却不会办事；让他当外交使节，不能独立地交涉.背得很多，又有什么用呢?"

【英译】The Master said, "Though a man may be able to recite the three hundred odes, yet if, when in trusted with a governmental charge, he knows not how to act, or if, when sent to any quarter on a mission, he cannot give his replies unassisted, notwithstanding the extent of his learning, of what practical use is it?"

【注释】

[1] 达：通达。这里是会运用的意思。理雅格将该句译为"he knows not how to act"，"达"即"处事"，即面对事情能够合理应对。辜鸿铭将该句译为"can do nothing"，即"不能做任何事"，也是形容人缺乏具体的实践智慧。刘殿爵译为"fails when given administrative responsibilities"，即面对"行政责任"时"失败了"。韦利译为"he cannot turn his merits to account"，形容一个人在工作中"无法说明自己的功绩"。孔子教学生诵《诗》，不单纯是为了经典文献的学习，更是为了把《诗》的思想运用到指导政治活动之中。"达"形容的是那些能够学以致用，具有实践智慧的儒者，此处理雅格的翻译较为恰当，韦利则违背了《论语》原意。

[2] 专对：独立对答。

【原文】13.6　子曰："其身正[1]，不令而行；其身不正，虽令不从。"

【译文】孔子说："自身正了，即使不发布命令，老百姓也会去做；自身不正，即使发布命令，老百姓也不会服从。"

【英译】The Master said, "When a prince's personal conduct is upright, his government is effective without the issuing of orders. If his personal conduct is not upright, he may issue orders, but they will not be followed."

【注释】

[1] 正：形容在上位者自身言行端正。理雅格、刘殿爵译为"correct"，形容统治者自身的行为是"正确的"；辜鸿铭译为"In order"，形容统治者行为是"合秩序的"；韦利译为"upright"，即"正直的"。理雅格、刘殿爵、辜鸿铭等译本均强调统治者行为的合宜，韦利则是强调统治者自身品格的正直。从儒家的视角看，孔子应更主张统治者具有正直的品格，具有仁义的美德，在此基础上自然会具有合宜的行为。因此我们认为，此处韦利的翻译更为恰当。

【原文】 13.7 子曰："鲁、卫之政，兄弟也。"[1]

【译文】 孔子说："鲁和卫两国的政事，就像兄弟一样相差不远。"

【英译】 The Master said，"The governments of Lu and Wei are brothers."

【注释】

[1] 鲁国是周公旦的封地，卫国是康叔的封地，周公旦和康叔是兄弟，当时两国的政治情况有些相似。所以孔子说，鲁国的国事和卫国的国事，就像兄弟一样。

【原文】 13.8 子谓卫公子荆[1]："善居室[2]。始有，曰：'苟合矣。'少有，曰：'苟完矣。'富有，曰：'苟美矣。'"

【译文】 孔子谈到卫国的公子荆时说："他把家里的经济管理得很好。刚开始有一点，他说：'差不多也就够了。'稍为多一点时，他说：'差不多就算完备了。'更多一点时，他说：'差不多算是完美了'。"

【英译】 The Master said of Ching，a scion of the ducal family of Wei，that he ordered the economy of his home well. When he began to have means，he said，"Ha！here is a collection！" When they were a little increased，he said，"Ha！ This is complete！" When he had become rich，he said，"Ha！ This is admirable！"

【注释】

[1] 卫公子荆：卫国大夫，字南楚，卫献公的儿子。

[2] 善居室：善于管理经济，居家过日子。理雅格译为"knew the economy of a family well"，即"了解一个家庭的经济状况"；辜鸿铭译为"ordered the economy of his home"，即"管理家庭经济"；刘殿爵译为"showed a laudable attitude towards a house as a place to live in"，其将"善"译为"赞赏、夸奖"；韦利译为"dwell in his house"，形容一个人安居在自己家中。结合上下文看，此处"善居室"是形容一个人擅长管理自己的家务，"善"即"善于、擅长"之义，辜鸿铭的翻译更为恰当。

【原文】13.9　子适卫，冉有仆[1]。子曰："庶[2]矣哉！"冉有曰："既庶矣，又何加焉？"曰："富之。"曰："既富矣，又何加焉？"曰："教之[3]。"

【译文】孔子到卫国去，冉有为他驾车。孔子说："人口真多呀！"冉有说："人口已经够多了，还要再做什么呢？"孔子说："使他们富起来。"冉有说："富了以后又还要做些什么？"孔子说："对他们进行教化。"

【英译】When the master went to Wei，Zan Yu acted as driver of his carriage. The master observed，"How numerous are the people！" yu said，"Since they are thus numerous，what more shall be done for them？" Enrich them，was the reply. "And when they have been enriched，what more shall be done？" The Master said，"Educate them."

【注释】

[1] 仆：驾车。理雅格译为"acted as driver of his carriage"，即"充当

他的车夫";辜鸿铭译为"driving the carriage for him"、刘殿爵译为"drove for him",即为他驾车。

[2] 庶:众多,这里指人口众多。

[3] 教:教育、教化。理雅格译为"teach",辜鸿铭译为"educate",刘殿爵译为"train",韦利译为"instruct"。teach 和 educate 都有"教育、教授"的意思,teach 用在教育、学术和日常生活场景中的时候,它的意思是"教书,教授";educate 比 teach 更正式,常用于学术场景当中,我们还可以在谈论和道德教育等相关的话题中使用它。train 所强调的目的常常是为达到特定目标所执行的严格而重点明确的任务。instruct 侧重系统化、注重过程的教授,同时也有"指令、命令"的含义。在本章里,孔子提出"富民"和"教民"的思想,而且是"先富后教","教"在这里侧重文章和道德品行的教化引导,译为"educate"更为恰当。

【原文】13.10 子曰:"苟有用我者,期月[1]而已可也,三年有成。"

【译文】孔子说:"如果有人用我治理国家,一年便可以搞出个样子,三年就一定会有成效。"

【英译】The Master said, "If there were any of the princes who would employ me, in the course of twelve months, I should have done something considerable. In three years, the government would be perfected."

【注释】

[1] 期月:一整年。理雅格译为"twelve months",即十二个月;其余各家译本均译为"In a year"或"in one year",即一年。

【原文】13.11 子曰:"'善人为邦百年,亦可以胜残[1]去杀[2]矣。'诚哉是言也!"

【译文】孔子说："善人治理国家，经过一百年，也就可以消除残暴，废除刑罚杀戮了。这话真对呀！"

【英译】The Master said，"'If good men were to govern a country in succession for a hundred years，they would be able to get the better of cruelty，and do away with killing.' True indeed is this saying！"

【注释】

[1] 胜残：克服残暴，使残暴的人不再作恶。理雅格译为"Transform the violently bad"，即"改造坏的人"；辜鸿铭译为"make deeds of violence impossible"，即"使暴力行为不可能"；刘殿爵译为"get the better of cruelty"，即"战胜残酷"。"胜"这里指"克服、战胜"，而非"改造"。我们认为，此处刘殿爵的翻译更为恰当。

[2] 去杀：去除杀戮，不用刑杀。理雅格、辜鸿铭译为"dispense with capital punishments"，即"取消死刑"；刘殿爵译为"do away with killing"，即"消除杀戮"。此处"杀"不仅指代死刑，而是泛指一些杀戮伤害有关的行为，刘殿爵译为"killing"更为恰当。

【原文】13.12 子曰："如有王者，必世而后仁。"

【译文】孔子说："如果有王者兴起，也一定要三十年才能实现仁政。"

【英译】The Master said，"If a truly royal ruler were to arise，it would stir require a generation，and then virtue would prevail."

【原文】13.13 子曰："苟正其身矣，于从政乎何有？不能正其身，如正人何？"

【译文】孔子说："如果端正了自身的行为，管理政事还有什么困难呢？如果不能端正自身的行为，怎能使别人端正呢？"

【英译】The Master said，"If a minister make his own conduct

correct, what difficulty will he have in assisting in government? If he cannot rectify himself, what has he to do with rectifying others?"

【原文】 13.14 冉子退朝[1]，子曰："何晏[2]也?"对曰："有政[3]。"子曰："其事[4]也！如有政，虽不吾以，吾其与闻之！"

【译文】 冉求退朝回来，孔子说："为什么回来得这么晚呀?"冉求说："有政事。"孔子说："只是一般的事务吧？如果有政事，虽然国君不用我了，我也会知道的。"

【英译】 The disciple Zan returning from the court, The Master said to him, "How are you so late?" He replied, "We had government affairs." The Master said, "It must have been private business. If there had been government affairs, though I am not now in office, I should have been consulted about it."

【注释】

[1] 退朝：1. 从鲁君之朝回来。周生烈云："谓罢朝于鲁君。" 2. 从季氏议事的地方回来。朱子云："冉有时为季氏宰。朝，季氏之私朝也。"邢昺《注疏》详辨二说云："周氏以为，夫子云'虽不吾以，吾其与闻'，皆论若朝之事，故云罢朝于鲁君。郑玄以冉有臣于季氏，故以朝为季氏之朝。《少仪》云：'朝廷曰退。'谓于朝廷之中，若欲散还，则称曰退。以近君为进，还私远君为退朝。此退朝谓罢朝也。案昭二十五年《左传》曰：为政事、庸力、行务以从四时。杜预曰：'在君为政，在臣为事。'杜意据此文，时冉子仕于季氏，称季氏有政，孔子谓之为事，是在君为政，在臣为事也。何晏以为，仲尼称孝友是亦为政，明其政、事通言，但随事大小异其名耳，故不同郑、杜之说，而取周，马之言，以朝为鲁君之朝，以事为君之凡行常事也。"

[2] 晏：晚、迟。

[3] 政：国政。理雅格译为"government business"，即"政府事务"；辜鸿铭译为"State affairs"，刘殿爵、韦利译为"affairs of state"，即"国家

事务"。business 通常指较重要或较难而又必须承担的事情,也可指商事;affair 含义较广,侧重指已发生或必须去做的任何事情或事务。复数形式多指重大或较复杂的事务。"国政"指国家大事,译为"affairs"较为恰当。

[4] 事:季氏家事。理雅格译为"family affairs",即"家事";刘殿爵译为"routine matters",即"例行公事";韦利译为"private business",即私人事务。与 business 和 affairs 相比,matter 所表示的"事情"在含义上比较模糊,通常指客观存在的或有待处理的问题。季氏家事是季氏的私人事务,韦利译为"private business"较为恰当。

【原文】13.15　定公问:"一言而可以兴邦,有诸?"孔子对曰:"言不可以若是其几也。人之言曰:'为君难,为臣不易。'如知为君之难也,不几乎一言而兴邦乎?"曰:"一言而丧邦,有诸?"孔子对曰:"言不可以若是其几也。人之言曰:'予无乐乎为君,唯其言而莫予违也。'如其善而莫之违也,不亦善乎?如不善而莫之违也,不几乎一言而丧邦乎?"

【译文】鲁定公问:"一句话就可以使国家兴盛,有这样的话吗?"孔子答道:"不可能有这样的话,但有近乎这样的话。有人说:'做君难,做臣不易。'如果知道了做君的难,这不近乎一句话可以使国家兴盛吗?"鲁定公又问:"一句话可以亡国,有这样的话吗?"孔子回答说:"不可能有这样的话,但有近乎这样的话。有人说过:'我做君主并没有什么可高兴的,我所高兴的只在于我所说的话没有人敢于违抗。'如果说得对而没有人违抗,不也好吗?如果说得不对而没有人违抗,那不就近乎一句话可以亡国吗?"

【英译】The duke Ting asked whether there was a single sentence which could make a country prosperous. Confucius replied, "Such an effect cannot be expected from one sentence. There is a saying, however, which people have 'to be a prince is difficult; to be a minister is not easy.' If a ruler knows this, -the difficulty of being a prince, may there not be expected from this one sentence the prosperity of his country?" The duke then said, "Is there a single sentence which can ruin a country?" Confucius replied, "Such an effect as that cannot be expected from one sentence. There is, however, the saying which people have 'I have no pleasure in being a prince, but only in that no one can offer any opposition to what I say!' If a ruler's words be good, is it not also good that no one oppose them? But if they are not good, and no one opposes them, may there not be expected from this one sentence the ruin of his country?"

【原文】13.16 叶公问政。子曰:"近者说[1],远者来。"

【译文】叶公问孔子怎样管理政事。孔子说:"使近处的人高兴,使远处的人来归附。"

【英译】The duke of Sheh asked about government. The Master said, "Good government obtains when those who are near are made happy, and those who are far off are attracted."

【注释】

[1] 说:同"悦",愉悦、高兴。理雅格、辜鸿铭译为"happy",即"高兴";刘殿爵译为"pleased",即"愉悦的";韦利译为"approve",即"满意、赞成"。happy 是指广义的快乐,可以用于任何用法中;pleased 指一些微小的事物引起的愉悦感,也指某人对某事物非常满意。皇侃《论语义疏》解释为:"言为政之道,若能使近民欢悦,则远人来至也。""说"在这里指情感上的快乐愉悦,并未体现民众对国家政策的满意感,译为 happy 即可。

【原文】13.17 子夏为莒父[1]宰,问政。子曰:"无欲速,无见小利[2]。欲速则不达，见小利则大事不成。"

【译文】 子夏做莒父的总管，问孔子怎样办理政事。孔子说："不要求快，不要贪求小利。求快反而达不到目的，贪求小利就做不成大事。"

【英译】 Tsze-Hsia being governor of Chu-Fu，asked about government. The Master said，"Do not be desirous to have things done quickly；do not look at small advantages. Desire to have things done quickly prevents their being done thoroughly. Looking at small gains prevents great affairs from being accomplished."

【注释】

[1] 莒父：莒，鲁国城邑，在今山东省莒县境内。

[2] 小利：微小的利益。理雅格译为 "small advantages"，辜鸿铭译为 "petty advantages"，即 "小的好处"；刘殿爵译为 "petty gains"，即 "微小的收获"；韦利译为 "minor considerations"，即 "微小的注意事项"。petty 作形容词，指琐碎的问题、细节等。small 作形容词指尺寸或数量小的，也指工作、问题、错误等不重要的或影响不大的。minor 则强调次要的、不重要的。此处 "小利" 指微小的、不重要的利益，译为 "small" 更为恰当。gain 指获得的物质利益，也暗示不损坏他人利益而得的无形好处。advantage 则侧重因某方面占优势或利用某机会以及对方弱点而获得利益与好处。此处 "利" 指的是物质利益，译为 gains 更为恰当。

【原文】 13.18　叶公语孔子曰："吾党[1]有直躬[2]者：其父攘羊[3]而子证[4]之。"孔子曰："吾党之直者异于是：父为子隐[5]，子为父隐，直在其中矣。"

【译文】 叶公告诉孔子说："我的家乡有个正直的人，他的父亲偷了人家的羊，他告发了父亲。"孔子说："我家乡的正直的人和你讲的正直人不一样：父亲为儿子隐瞒，儿子为父亲隐瞒，正直就在其中了。"

【英译】The duke of Sheh informed Confucius，saying，"Among us here there are those who may be styled upright in their conduct. If their father has stolen a sheep，they will bear witness to the fact." Confucius said，"Among us，in our part of the country，those who are upright are different from this. The father conceals the misconduct of the son，and the son conceals the misconduct of the father. Uprightness is to be found in this."

【注释】

[1] 党：乡党，古代以五百户为一党。

[2] 直躬者：正直的人。刘殿爵、理雅格、辜鸿铭、韦利等人均译为"Upright"。

[3] 攘羊：偷羊。

[4] 证：告发。

[5] 隐：隐瞒。理雅格译为"conceals the misconduct"，即"隐瞒不正当行为"；辜鸿铭译为"silent concerning the misdeed"，即"对罪行保持沉默"；刘殿爵译为"cover up"，即"掩饰"；韦利将该句译为"A father will screen his son"，即"父亲要屏蔽儿子"，该译文不够恰当。孔子认为"父为子隐，子为父隐"就是具有了"直"的品格，"隐"即"隐瞒、隐藏"，理雅格的翻译更为恰当。

【原文】13.19 樊迟问仁。子曰："居处恭[1]，执事敬[2]，与人忠[3]；虽之夷狄，不可弃也。"

【译文】樊迟问怎样才是仁。孔子说："平日容貌端正庄严，办事严肃认真，待人忠心诚意。如此即使到了夷狄之地，也不可背弃。"

【英译】Fan Ch'ih asked about perfect virtue. The Master said，"It is，in retirement，to be sedately courteous；in the management of business，to be Solemn and respectful；in intercourse with others， to be strictly sincere. Though a man goes among rude，uncultivated tribes，these qualities may not be neglected."

【注释】

[1] 恭：谦恭。理雅格译为"sedately grave"，即"沉着庄重"；辜鸿铭译为"serious"，即"严肃的"；刘殿爵译为"hold yourself in a respectful attitude"，即"保持尊敬的态度"；韦利译为"courteous"，即"有礼貌的"。"恭"多指人肃敬、谦逊有礼貌，刘殿爵的翻译更侧重"敬"的意涵，相较之下韦利的译本更为恰当。

[2] 敬：认真。理雅格译为"reverently attentive"，即"虔诚专注"；辜鸿铭译为"earnest"，即"认真、诚挚的"；刘殿爵译为"reverent"，即"虔诚的"；韦利译为"diligent"，即"勤奋的"。在表示敬重有礼貌的意思上，敬和恭是同义词，文献中常对举。"居处恭，执事敬"对举，"恭"侧重于外貌的谦逊有礼，"敬"侧重于内心的严肃敬重。我们认为，此处译为"Solemn and respectful"更为恰当。

[3] 这里孔子对"仁"的解释，是以"恭""敬""忠"三个德目为基本内涵。在家恭敬有礼，就是要符合孝悌的道德要求；办事严肃谨慎，就是要符合"礼"的要求；待人忠厚诚实显示出仁德的本色。

【原文】 13.20　子贡问曰："何如斯可谓之士[1]矣？"子曰："行已有耻，使于四方，不辱君命，可谓士矣。"曰："敢问其次。"曰："宗族称孝焉，乡党称弟焉。"曰"敢问其次。"曰："言必信，行必果[2]，硁硁[3]然小人哉！抑亦可以为次矣。"曰："今之从政者何如？"子曰："噫！斗筲之人[4]，何足算也？"

【译文】 子贡问道："怎样才可以叫作士？"孔子说："自己在做事时有知耻之心，出使外国各方，能够完成君主交付的使命，可以叫作士。"子贡说："请问次一等的呢？"孔子说："宗族中的人称赞他孝顺父母，乡党们称他尊敬兄长。"子贡又问："请问再次一等的呢？"孔子说：

"说到一定做到，做事一定坚持到底，不问是非地固执己见，那是小人啊。但也可以说是再次一等的士了。"子贡说："现在的执政者，您看怎么样？"孔子说："唉！这些器量狭小的人，哪里能数得上呢？"

【英译】Tsze-Kung asked，saying，"What qualities must a man possess to entitle him to be called an officer？" The Master said，"He who in his conduct of himself maintains a sense of shame，and when sent to any quarter will not disgrace his prince's commission，deserves to be called an officer." Tsze-Kung pursued，"I venture to ask who may be placed in the next lower rank？" And he was told，"He whom the circle of his relatives pronounce to be filial，whom his fellow villagers and neighbors pronounce to be fraternal." Again the disciple asked，"I venture to ask about the class still next in order." The Master said，"They are determined to be sincere in what they say，and must speak credibly and act decisively. They are obstinate little men. yet perhaps they may make the next class." Tsze-Kung finally inquired，"Of what sort are those of the present day，who engage in government？" The Master said，"Pooh！ They are so many pecks and hampers，not worth being taken into account."

【注释】

[1] 士：士在周代贵族中位于最低层。此后，士成为古代社会知识分子的通称。

[2] 果：果断、坚决。理雅格、辜鸿铭译为"carry out what they do"，并未译出"行为果断"之意。我们认为，该句译为"You must speak credibly and act decisively"较为恰当。

[3] 硁硁：象声词，敲击石头的声音，像石块那样坚硬，形容固执的人。理雅格译为"obstinate"，即"固执的"；辜鸿铭、刘殿爵译为"stubborn"，即"固执的"；韦利译为"humblest"，即"最卑微的"。stubborn

指有倔强的性格，看问题有自己的主见，不轻易被他人说服，可以是褒义或贬义；obstinate 指不顾他人的忠告、劝说、反对或抗议固执己见，不改变自己的看法或做法，通常是贬义。《论语》此处形容人固执己见、不听劝告，采用 obstinate 更为恰当。

[4] 斗筲之人：筲，竹器，容一斗二升。比喻器量狭小的人。理雅格译为"They are so many pecks and hampers"，该句直译了"斗筲"，并未译出"气量狭小"之引申义。辜鸿铭译为"red-taped bureaucrats"，即"繁文缛节的官僚"，并在注释中解释为"The Chinese expression for 'red tape' Is 'pecks and hampers', from the fact that rhe duty of mere routine officers inanrient times was to weigh and measure the grain and other produce collected from the people."（中国对"繁文缛节"的意思是"斗和筲"，因为当时日常官员的职责是称重和测量从人民那里收集的农产品）刘殿爵意译为"limited capacity"，"斗筲"即形容人能力有限。辜鸿铭的翻译更为翔实，但其将"斗筲"误解为"繁文缛节"，不够恰当。

【原文】13.21　子曰："不得中行[1]而与之，必也狂狷[2]乎？狂者进取，狷者有所不为也。"

【译文】孔子说："我找不到奉行中庸之道的人和他交往，只能与狂者、狷者相交往了。狂者敢作敢为，狷者行为谨慎。"

【英译】The Master said, "Since I cannot get men pursuing the due medium, to whom I might communicate my instructions, and I must find the ardent and the cautiously-decided. the ardent will advance and lay hold of truth; the cautiously-decided will keep themselves from what is wrong."

【注释】

[1] 中行：行为合乎中庸。辜鸿铭译为"equitable and reasonable men"，即"公平和理性的人"；辜鸿铭译为"moderate men"，形容那些情感上"温

和"的人；韦利译为"Who steer a middle course"，即"走中间路线的人"，形容行为上不偏不倚、合乎中道。此处将"中行"译为"Follow the golden mean"（奉行中庸之道）更为恰当。

[2] 狂狷：狂，指志气大、激进却不能完全做到的人；狷，指行为谨慎。《孟子·尽心下》解释狂狷说："'何以谓之狂也？'曰：其志嘐嘐然，曰：'古之人，古之人，夷考其行而不掩焉者也。狂者又不可得，欲得不屑不洁之士而与之，是狷也。'""狂"与"狷"是两种对立的品质。一是流于冒进，进取，敢作敢为；一是流于退缩，不敢作为。理雅格译为"The ardent and the cautiously-decided"，即"热情和谨慎的人"，其中"狂"是"热情"，"狷"被译为"谨慎的"。刘殿爵译为"undisciplined and the over-scrupulous"，即"没有纪律和过于谨慎的人"，"狷"被译为"过分谨慎"。辜鸿铭译为"men of enthusiastic or even fanatical character"，即"性格热情甚至狂热的人"，此处"狷"更进一步，指情绪更加狂热。韦利译为"impetuous and hasty"，即"浮躁的和草率的"，"狷"即为"草率的"。可见在"狷"的解释上，理雅格、刘殿爵持相同观点，辜鸿铭与韦利观点相近。孔子认为，中行就是不偏不狂，也不偏于狷。人的气质、作风、德行都不偏于任何一个方面，对立的双方应互相牵制，互相补充，这样，才符合中庸的思想。

【原文】13.22 子曰："南人有言曰：'人而无恒，不可以作巫医[1]。'善夫！'不恒其德，或承之羞。'[2]"子曰："不占[3]而已矣。"

【译文】孔子说："南方人有句话说：'人如果做事没有恒心，就不能当巫医。'这句话说得真好啊！"《易经·恒卦》的爻辞说：'人不能长久地保存自己的德行，免不了要遭受耻辱。'"孔子说："这句话是说，没有恒心的人用不着去占卦了。"

【英译】The Master said，"The people of the south have a saying a man without constancy cannot be either a wizard or a doctor good！Inconstant in his virtue，he will be visited with disgrace."The Master said，"This arises simply from not attending to the prognostication."

【注释】

[1] 巫医：用卜筮为人治病的人。

[2] 不恒其德，或承之羞：此二句引自《易经·恒卦·爻辞》。本章中孔子讲了两层意思：一是人必须有恒心，这样才能成就事业。二是人必须恒久保持德行，否则就可能遭受耻辱。

[3] 占：占卜。

【原文】 13.23　子曰："君子和而不同；小人同而不和。"[1]

【译文】 孔子说："君子讲求和谐而不同流合污，小人只求完全一致而不讲求协调。"

【英译】 The Master said，"The superior man is affable，but not adulatory；the mean man is adulatory， but not affable."

【注释】

[1] 有两种理解：1."和"指心和、不相争，"同"指志向同。何晏《集解》云："君子心和，然其所见各异，故曰不同。小人所嗜好者同，然各争利，故曰不和。"又，皇侃《义疏》云："云'君子和而不同'者，和谓心不争也。不同，谓立志各异也。君子之人千万，千万其心和如一，而所习立之志业不同也。云'小人同而不和'者，小人为恶如一，故云同也；好斗争，故云不和也。"2."和"指心和、没有不一致的心思，"同"指阿党。朱子《集注》云："和者，无乖戾之心。同者，有阿比之意。尹氏曰：'君子尚义，故有不同。小人尚利，安得而和?'"理雅格将"和"译为"affable"，即"和善的"，将"同"译为"adulatory"，即"诌媚的"。辜鸿铭译为"A wise man is sociable，but not familiar. A fool is familiar but not sociable"，其中"和"译为"善于交际的"，"同"译为"亲切的"。刘殿爵译为"The gentleman agrees with others without being an echo. The small man echoes without being in agreement."，"和"译为"同意别人的意见"，"同"译

为"附和别人的意见"。韦利译为"The true gentleman is conciliatory but not accommodating. Common people are accommodating but not conciliatory","和"译为"conciliatory",即"和解的","同"译为"accommodating",即"乐于助人的"。"和而不同"是孔子思想体系中的重要组成部分。"君子和而不同，小人同而不和。"君子可以与他周围的人保持和谐融洽的关系，但他对待任何事情都必须经过自己大脑的独立思考，从来不愿人云亦云，盲目附和；但小人则没有自己独立的见解，只求与别人完全一致，而不讲求原则，但他却与别人不能保持融洽友好的关系。这是在处事为人方面。我们认为，上述译本相较，刘殿爵的翻译更为恰当。

【原文】13.24　子贡问曰："乡人皆好之，何如？"子曰："未可也。""乡人皆恶之，何如？"子曰："未可也。不如乡人之善者好之，其不善者恶之。"

【译文】子贡问孔子说："全乡人都喜欢、赞扬他，这个人怎么样？"孔子说："这还不能肯定。"子贡又问孔子说："全乡人都厌恶、憎恨他，这个人怎么样？"孔子说："这也是不能肯定的。最好的人是全乡的好人都喜欢他，全乡的坏人都厌恶他。"

【英译】Tsze-Kung asked，saying，"What do you say of a man who is loved by all the people of his neighborhood?" The master replied，"We may not for that accord our approval of him." "And what do you say of him who is hated by all the people of his neighborhood?" The Master said，"We may not for that conclude that he is bad. It is better than either of these cases that the good in the neighborhood love him，and the bad hate him."

【原文】13.25　子曰："君子易事[1]而难说[2]也。说之不以道，不说也；及其使人也，器之[3]。小人难事而易说也。说之虽不以道，说也；及其使人也，求备焉。"

【译文】 孔子说："为君子办事很容易，但很难取得他的欢喜。不按正道去讨他的喜欢，他是不会喜欢的。但是，当他用人的时候，总是量才而用人。为小人办事很难，但要取得他的欢喜则是很容易的。不按正道去讨他的喜欢，也会得到他的喜欢。但等到他用人的时候，却是百般挑剔，求全责备。"

【英译】 The Master said，"The superior man is easy to serve and difficult to please. If you try to please him in any way which is not accordant with right，he will not be pleased. But in his employment of men，he uses them according to their capacity. The mean man is difficult to serve，and easy to please. If you try to please him，though it is in a way which is not accordant with right，he may be pleased. But in his employment of men，he wishes them to be equal to everything."

【注释】

[1] 易事：易于与人相处共事。英译本多译为"easy to serve"，即"容易伺候"。

[2] 难说：难以取得他的欢喜。英译本多译为"difficult to please"，即"难以取悦"。这一章里，孔子又提出了君子与小人之间的另一个区别。这一点也是十分重要的。作为君子，他并不对人百般挑剔，而且也不轻易表明自己的喜好，但在选用人才的时候，往往能够量才而用，不会求全责备。但小人就不同了。在现实社会中，君子并不多见，而此类小人则屡见不鲜。

[3] 器之：量才使用他。理雅格译为"uses them according to their capacity"，即"根据能力使用他们"；辜鸿铭译为"takes into consideration their capacity"，即"考虑他们的能力"；刘殿爵译为"the limits of their capacity"，即"在他们的能力范围内"；韦利译为"expects of them what they are capable of performing"，即"期望他们的能力"。上述译本相较，理雅格的翻译更为明白晓畅。

【原文】13.26　子曰："君子泰[1]而不骄[2]；小人骄而不泰。"

【译文】孔子说："君子安静坦然而不傲慢无礼，小人傲慢无礼而不安静坦然。"

【英译】The Master said，"The superior man has a dignified ease without haughty. The mean man has haughty without a dignified ease."

【注释】

[1] 泰：安静坦然的样子。理雅格译为 "has a dignified ease"，即 "从容安逸的"；辜鸿铭、韦利译为 "dignified"，即 "端庄的、有尊严的"；刘殿爵译为 "at ease"，即 "自在的"。此处 "泰" 强调君子处事的从容不迫、端正有礼，译为 "dignified" 更能体现君子的气节。

[2] 骄：傲慢无礼的样子。理雅格译为 "pride"、辜鸿铭译为 "proud"，即 "骄傲的"；刘殿爵译为 "arrogant"，即 "傲慢的"；韦利译为 "haughty"，即 "高傲自大的"。proud 含义广，普通用词，褒义指自豪和荣耀以及强烈的自尊；贬义则指傲慢、自以为是或自鸣得意。arrogant 用于贬义，指过高估计自己，以致骄傲自大或傲慢无礼、目中无人。haughty 较正式用词，多用于贬义，指对身份或地位比自己低的人采取冷淡、轻视或鄙互的态度。此处 "骄" 更强调对地位低下者的鄙视冷漠，译为 "haughty" 较为恰当。

【原文】13.27　子曰："刚、毅、木、讷，近仁。"

【译文】孔子说："刚强、果敢、朴实、谨慎，这四种品德接近于仁。"

【英译】The Master said，"The firm, the enduring, the simple, and the modest are near to virtue."

【原文】13.28　子路问曰："何如斯可谓之士矣？"子曰："切切偲偲[1]，怡怡[2]如也，可谓士矣。朋友切切偲偲，兄弟怡怡。"

【译文】子路问孔子道："怎样才可以称为士呢？"孔子说："互助

督促勉励，相处和和气气，可以算是士了。朋友之间互相督促勉励，兄弟之间相处和和气气。"

【英译】Tsze-Lu asked，saying，"What qualities must a man possess to entitle him to be called a scholar?" The Master said，"He must be thus，-earnest，urgent，and bland：-among his friends，earnest and urgent；among his brethren，bland."

【注释】

[1] 切切偲偲：勉励、督促、诚恳的样子。理雅格译为"earnest and urgent"，即"认真、迫切的"；辜鸿铭译为"sympathetic and obliging"，即"富有同情心和乐于助人的"；刘殿爵译为"earnest and keen"，即"认真而敏锐的"；韦利译为"critical and exacting"，即"严谨而苛刻的"。《论语》此处强调君子对待友人的忠诚劝勉之意，理雅格、刘殿爵的翻译更为恰当。

[2] 怡怡：和气、亲切、顺从的样子。理雅格译为"bland"，形容态度是"平淡温和的"；辜鸿铭译为"affectionate"，形容对亲人是"充满深情的"；刘殿爵译为"genial"，即"和蔼的"；韦利译为"indulgent"，即"过分宽容的"。《论语》本章主要强调君子对兄弟的亲爱和悌顺，"indulgent"侧重"放纵的"，含贬义；"genial"强调君子对兄弟态度和蔼恭顺，较为恰当。

【原文】13.29　子曰："善人教民七年，亦可以即戎矣。"

【译文】孔子说："善人教练百姓达七年之久，也就可以叫他们去当兵打仗了。"

【英译】The Master said，"Let a good man teach the people seven years，and they may then likewise be employed in war."

【原文】13.30　子曰："以不教民[1]战，是谓弃[2]之。"

【译文】孔子说："用未曾受过训练的百姓去作战，这等于抛弃他们。"

【英译】The Master said, "To lead an untrained people to war, is to throw them away."

【注释】

[1] 不教民：指未曾受过训练的百姓。理雅格译为"uninstructed people"，即"未经教导的人"；刘殿爵译为"untrained"，即"未经训练的"。结合上下文意，这里译为"训练"更为恰当。

[2] 弃：抛弃。辜鸿铭、韦利译为"betray"，即"背叛"；理雅格、刘殿爵译为"throw"，即"丢下、抛弃"。"抛弃"一般用于上对下；"背叛"一般用于下对上，此处译为"throw"更为恰当。

宪问篇第十四

【原文】 14.1　宪[1]问耻。子曰："邦有道，谷[2]，邦无道，谷；耻也。""克[3]、伐[4]、怨、欲，不行焉，可以为仁矣？"子曰："可以为难矣，仁则吾不知也。"

【译文】 原宪问孔子什么是可耻。孔子说："国家有道，做官拿俸禄；国家无道，还做官拿俸禄，这就是可耻。"原宪又问："好胜、自夸、怨恨、贪欲都没有的人，可以算做到仁了吧？"孔子说："这可以说是很难得的，但至于是不是做到了仁，那我就不知道了。"

【英译】 Hsien asked what was shameful. The Master said，"When good government prevails in a state，to be thinking only of salary；and，when bad government prevails，to be thinking，in the same way，only of salary；this is shameful.""When the love of competitive heart，boasting，resentments，and covetousness are repressed，this may be deemed perfect virtue." The Master said，"This may be regarded as the achievement of what is difficult. But I do not know that it is to be deemed perfect virtue."

【注释】

[1] 原宪（前515—?），字子思，春秋末年宋国商丘人，孔门"七十二贤"之一。原宪出身贫寒，个性狷介，一生安贫乐道，不肯与世俗合流。孔子为鲁司寇时，曾做过孔子的家宰，孔子给他九百斛的俸禄，他推辞不要。孔子死后，原宪遂隐居卫国草泽中，茅屋瓦牖，粗茶淡饭，生活极为清苦。

[2] 谷：这里指做官者的俸禄。理雅格、刘殿爵译为"salary"，即"薪水"，侧重非体力劳动者所得的工资、薪水；辜鸿铭译为"pay"，即"报酬"，指工作所得到的酬金；韦利译为"rewards"，一般指额外的"奖励""福利"等。"谷"指的是士大夫的俸禄，译为"salary"更为恰当。

[3] 克：好胜。理雅格译为"superiority"，即"优越感"；辜鸿铭译为"ambition"，即"野心"；刘殿爵译为"Standing firm against the temptation to press one's advantage"，即"坚决反对压制自己的利益"，"克"被理解为"克制""抑制"。孔子认为"君子无所争"，《论语》此处意在强调君子不应争强好胜，"克"译为"competitive"更为恰当。

[4] 伐：夸耀、自夸。理雅格译为"boasting"，即"自夸"，该词偏中性，除了表示"吹嘘"以外，也可以表示正面的"引以自豪"的含义；辜鸿铭译为"vanity"，即"虚荣心"；刘殿爵译为"brag about oneself"，即"吹嘘自己"，其夸耀和吹嘘意味强于 boast，到了过分夸大。此处"伐"意为过分地自夸，译为贬义鲜明的"brag about oneself"更为恰当。

【原文】14.2　子曰："士而怀居[1]，不足以为士矣！"

【译文】孔子说："士如果留恋家庭的安逸生活，就不配做士了。"

【英译】The Master said，"The scholar who cherishes the love of comfort is not fit to be deemed a scholar."

【注释】

[1] 怀居：怀，思念，留恋。居，家居。指留恋家居的安逸生活。

【原文】14.3　子曰："邦有道，危[1]言危行；邦无道，危行言孙[2]。"

【译文】孔子说："国家有道，要正言正行；国家无道，还要正直，但说话要随和谨慎。"

【原文】The Master said，"When good government prevails in a state，language may be lofty and bold，and actions the same. When bad government prevails，the actions may be lofty and bold，but the language may be with some reserve."

【注释】

[1] 危：直，正直。理雅格、辜鸿铭译为"lofty and bold"，即"勇敢豪迈的"；刘殿爵将"危"理解为"危险"，此处译为"perilous high-mindedness"，即"危险的高尚品格"。此处"危"形容士君子的气节正直、勇毅不屈，译为"upright and courageous"（正直勇敢的）更为恰当。

[2] 孙：同"逊"，形容言语谨慎。理雅格、辜鸿铭均译为"reserve"，形容在国政不清明时，士的言谈应当是"含蓄、有所保留的"；刘殿爵译为"self-effacing diffidence"，即"低调内向的"；韦利译为"conciliatory"，形容言语态度是"安抚的、调和的"。此处孔子劝告自己的学生，当国家无道时，应注意言谈谨慎以避免祸端。

【原文】14.4 子曰："有德者，必有言；有言者，不必有德。仁者，必有勇；勇者，不必有仁。"[1]

【译文】孔子说："有美德的人一定有名言，有名言的人不一定有美德。仁人一定勇敢，勇敢的人都不一定有仁德。"

【英译】The Master said，"The virtuous will be sure to speak correctly，but those whose speech is good may not always be virtuous. Men of virtuous are sure to be bold，but those who are bold may not always be men of principle."

【注释】

[1] 本条解释了言论与道德、勇敢与仁德之间的关系。孔子认为勇敢只是仁德的一个方面，人除了有勇以外，还要修养其他各种美德，从而成为有德之人。理雅格将"仁"译为"principle"，"仁者"即为能够恪守道德准

则的人，这一翻译沿着规范伦理学的进路，将"德"视为是规范和原则，忽视了儒家"仁德"的博大内涵；辜鸿铭将"仁"译为"moral character"，即"道德品质"；刘殿爵将"仁"译为"benevolence"，突出了"仁者"慈爱、能爱人的特点；韦利将仁者译为"a good man"，即"一个好人"，该翻译情感色彩稍显单薄，不足以体现儒家"仁者"的高尚修养。我们认为，此处译为"virtue character"较为恰当。

【原文】 14.5　南宫适[1]问于孔子曰："羿[2]善射，奡[3]荡舟[4]，俱不得其死然。禹稷[5]躬稼而有天下。"夫子不答。南宫适出。子曰："君子哉若人！尚德哉若人！"

【译文】 南宫适问孔子："羿善于射箭，奡善于水战，最后都不得好死。禹和稷都亲自种植庄稼，却得到了天下。"孔子没有回答，南宫适出去后，孔子说："这个人真是个君子呀！这个人真重德。"

【英译】 Nan-Kung Kwo, submitting an inquiry to Confucius, said, "I was skillful at archery, and ao could move a boat along upon the land, but neither of them died a natural death. Yu and Chi personally wrought at the toils of husbandry, and they became possessors of the kingdom." The master made no reply；but when Nan-Kung Kwo went out, he said, "A superior man indeed is this! An esteemer of virtue indeed is this!"

【注释】

[1] 南宫适：适，同"括"，即南容。

[2] 羿：传说中夏代有穷国的国君，善于射箭，曾夺夏太康的王位，后被其臣寒浞所杀。

[3] 奡：传说中寒浞的儿子，后来为夏少康所杀。

[4] 荡舟：用手推船。传说中奡力大，善于水战。

[5] 禹稷：禹，夏朝的开国之君，善于治水，注重发展农业。稷，传

说是周朝的祖先，又为谷神，教民种植庄稼。南宫适以禹和稷为有德之君，认为其凭借德行而顺承天命民心、获得正当的统治地位。后代儒家发展了这一思想，提出"恃德者昌，恃力者亡"的主张，要求统治者以德治天下，而不要以武力得天下。

【原文】14.6　子曰："君子而不仁[1]者有矣夫？未有小人而仁者也！"

【译文】孔子说："君子中没有仁德的人是有的，而小人中有仁德的人是没有的。"

【英译】The Master said，"Superior men，and yet not always virtuous，there have been，alas！But there never has been a mean man，and，at the same time，virtuous."

【注释】

[1] 仁：仁德。此处理雅格并未译为"benevolent"（仁慈的），而是译为"virtuous"，即"德行高尚的、品行端正的"。辜鸿铭译为"a moral character"，指有道德品质的人。辜鸿铭译为"benevolent"，"仁"即为"仁慈的、慈善的"。韦利译为"goodness"，形容一个人是"善良的"。

【原文】14.7　子曰："爱之，能勿劳乎？忠焉，能勿诲乎？"

【译文】孔子说："爱他，能不为他操劳吗？忠于他，能不对他劝告吗？"

【英译】The Master said，"Can there be love which does not lead to strictness with its object？Can there be loyalty which does not lead to the instruction of its object？"

【原文】14.8　子曰："为命[1]，裨谌[2]草创之，世叔[3]讨论之，行人[4]子羽[5]修饰之，东里[6]子产润色之。"

【译文】孔子说："郑国发表的公文，都是由裨谌起草的，世叔提出意见，外交官子羽加以修饰，由子产作最后修改润色。"

【英译】The Master said，"In preparing the governmental notifications，P'i Shan first made the rough draft；Shi-Shu examined and discussed its contents；Tsze-Yu，the manager of foreign intercourse，then polished the style；and，finally，Tsze-Ch'an of Tung-Li gave it the proper elegance and finish."

【注释】

[1] 命：指国家的政令。

[2] 裨谌：人名，郑国的大夫。

[3] 世叔：即子太叔，名游吉，郑国的大夫。子产死后，继子产为郑国宰相。

[4] 行人：官名，掌管朝觐聘问，即外交事务。

[5] 子羽：郑国大夫公孙挥的字。

[6] 东里：地名，郑国大夫子产居住的地方。

【原文】14.9　或问子产。子曰："惠人也。"问子西[1]。曰："彼哉彼哉！"问管仲。曰："人也，夺伯氏骈邑[2]三百，饭疏食，没齿[3]无怨言。"

【译文】有人问子产是个怎样的人。孔子说："是个有恩惠于人的人。"又问子西。孔子说："他呀！他呀！"又问管仲。孔子说："他是个有才干的人，他把伯氏骈邑的三百家夺走，使伯氏终生吃粗茶淡饭，直到老死也没有怨言。"

【英译】Some one asked about Tsze-ch'an. The Master said，"He was a kind man." He asked about Tsze-hsi. The Master said，"That man！That man！" He asked about Kwan Chung. "For him，" said the Master，"The city of pien，with three hundred families，was taken from the chief of the po family，who did not utter a murmuring word，though，to the end of his life，he had only coarse rice to eat."

【注释】

[1] 子西：这里的子西指楚国的令尹，名申。

[2] 伯氏：齐国的大夫。骈邑：地名，伯氏的采邑。

[3] 没齿：死。

【原文】 14.10　子曰："贫而无怨，难；富而无骄，易。"

【译文】 孔子说："贫穷而能够没有怨恨是很难做到的，富裕而不骄傲是容易做到的。"

【英译】 The Master said，"To be poor without murmuring is difficult. To be rich without being proud is easy."

【原文】 14.11　子曰："孟公绰[1]为赵、魏老[2]则优，不可以为滕、薛[3]大夫。"

【译文】 孔子说："孟公绰做晋国越氏、魏氏的家臣，是才力有余的，但不能做滕、薛这样小国的大夫。"

【英译】 The Master said，"Mang Kung-ch'o is more than fit to be chief officer in the families of Chao and Wei，but he is not fit to be great officer to either of the states Tang or Hsieh."

【注释】

[1] 孟公绰：鲁国大夫，属于孟孙氏家族。

[2] 老：这里指古代大夫的家臣。理雅格译为"chief officer in the families"，即"家臣"；辜鸿铭译为"As an officer in the retinue of a great noble"，即"贵族的随从"；刘殿爵译为"steward"，即"管家"；韦利译为"comptroller"，即"审计员"。上述译本相较，刘殿爵、理雅格的翻译更符合中国古代"家臣"的职能。

[3] 滕薛：滕，诸侯国家，在今山东滕州。薛，诸侯国家，在今山东滕州东南一带。

【原文】14.12 子路问成人[1]。子曰："若臧武仲[2]之知，公绰之不欲，卞庄子[3]之勇，冉求之艺，文之以礼乐；亦可以为成人矣！"曰："今之成人者，何必然？见利思义，见危授命，久要[4]不忘平生之言；亦可以为成人矣！"

【译文】子路问怎样做才是一个完美的人。孔子说："如果具有臧武仲的智慧，孟公绰的克制，卞庄子的勇敢，冉求那样多才多艺，再用礼乐加以修饰，也就可以算是一个完人了。"孔子又说："现在的完人何必一定要这样呢？见到财利想到义的要求，遇到危险肯付出生命，长久处于穷困还不忘平日的诺言，这样也可以成为一位完美的人。"

【英译】Tsze-Lu asked what constituted a complete man. The Master said, "Suppose a man with the knowledge of Tsang Wu-chung, the freedom from covetousness of Kung-ch'o, the bravery of Chwang of Pien, and the varied talents of Zan ch'iu; add to these the accomplishments of the rules of propriety and music; -such a one might be reckoned a complete man." He then added, "But what is the necessity for a complete man of the present day to have all these things? The man, who in the view of gain, thinks of righteousness; who in the view of danger is prepared to give up his life; and who does not forget an old agreement however far back it extends: -such a man maybe reckoned a complete man."

【注释】

[1] 成人：人格完备的完人。理雅格、刘殿爵直译为"complete man"，即"完整的人""完备的人"；辜鸿铭译为"perfect character"，即"完美人格"；韦利译为"the perfect man"，即"完美的人"。上述译本相较，辜鸿铭

的翻译更为明白晓畅。

[2] 臧武仲：鲁国大夫臧孙纥。

[3] 卞庄子：鲁国卞邑大夫。

[4] 久要：长久处于穷困中。理雅格译为"Who does not forget an old agreement however far back it extends"，"久要"被译为"无论追溯到多远"。刘殿爵译为"In straitened circumstances"，即"在窘迫的环境中"。辜鸿铭则译为"under long-continued trying circumstances"，即"长期艰难的环境中"。理雅格将"要"理解为"约定、约言"，"久要"则指很久之前的约定；其余译本则将"要"理解为"穷困"之意。上述译本相较，刘殿爵的翻译更为恰当。

【原文】14.13　子问公叔文子[1]于公明贾[2]，曰："信乎？夫子[3]不言不笑不取乎？"公明贾对曰："以告者过也！夫子时然后言，人不厌其言；乐然后笑，人不厌其笑；义然后取，人不厌其取。"子曰："其然！岂其然乎？"

【译文】孔子向公明贾问到公叔文子，说："先生他不说、不笑、不取钱财，是真的吗？"公明贾回答道："这是告诉你话的那个人的过错。先生他到该说时才说，因此别人不厌恶他说话；快乐时才笑，因此别人不厌恶他笑；合于礼要求的财利他才取，因此别人不厌恶他取。"孔子说："原来这样，难道真是这样吗？"

【英译】The Master asked Kung-Ming Chia about Kung-Shu wan, saying, "Is it true that your Master speaks not, laughs not, and takes not?" Kung-Ming Chia replied, "This has arisen from the reporters going beyond the truth. My Master speaks when it is the time to speak, and so men do not get tired of his speaking. He laughs when there is occasion to be joyful, and so men do not get tired of his laughing. He takes when it is consistent with righteousness to do so, and so men do not get tired of his taking." The Master said，"So！but is it so with him？"

【注释】

[1] 公叔文子：卫国大夫公孙拔，卫献公之子。谥号"文"。

[2] 公明贾：姓公明字贾。卫国人。

[3] 夫子：文中指公叔文子。

【原文】 14.14 子曰："臧武仲以防求为后于鲁，虽曰不要君[1]，吾不信也。"

【译文】 孔子说："臧武仲凭借防邑请求立其子弟嗣为鲁国卿大夫，虽然有人说他不是要挟君主，我不相信。"

【英译】 The Master said，"Tsang Wu-chung，keeping possession of fang，asked of The duke of lu to appoint a successor to him in his family. Although it may be said that he was not using force with his sovereign，I believe he was."

【注释】

[1] 臧武仲因得罪孟孙氏逃离鲁国，后来回到防邑，向鲁君要求，以立臧氏之后为卿大夫作为条件，自己离开防邑。"不要君"一句，理雅格译为"using force with his sovereign"，即"向自己的君主使用武力"；辜鸿铭译为"use intimidation with the prince"，"intimidation"即"恐吓、恫吓、威胁"之意，该句意为"向君主进行恐吓"；刘殿爵译为"exerting pressure on his lord"，即"向自己的君主施加压力"。本章《论语》认为，臧武仲以自己的封地为据点要挟君主，是犯上作乱的不义行为。

【原文】 14.15 子曰："晋文公[1]谲[2]而不正；齐桓公[3]正而不谲。"

【译文】 孔子说："晋文公诡诈而不正派，齐桓公正派而不诡诈。"

【英译】The Master said，"The duke Wan of Tsin was crafty and not upright. The duke Hwan of Ch'i was upright and not crafty."

【注释】

[1] 晋文公：姓姬名重耳，公元前 636—前 628 年在位。

[2] 谲：欺诈，玩弄手段。孔子主张"礼乐征伐自天子出"，对时人的违礼行为一概加以指责。晋文公称霸后召见周天子，这对孔子来说是不可接受的，所以他说晋文公诡诈。齐桓公打着"尊王"的旗号称霸，孔子认为他的做法符合于礼的规定。理雅格、辜鸿铭、刘殿爵均译为"crafty"，即"狡猾的"；韦利译为"rise to an emergency"，即"陷入紧急情况"。我们认为，此处直接译为"crafty"较为恰当。

[3] 齐桓公：姓姜名小白，公元前 685—前 643 年在位。

【原文】14.16 子路曰："桓公杀公子纠[1]，召忽[2]死之，管仲不死。"曰："未仁乎！"子曰："桓公九合诸侯[3]，不以兵车[4]，管仲之力也。如其仁[5]！如其仁！"

【译文】子路说："齐桓公杀了公子纠，召忽自杀以殉，但管仲却没有自杀。管仲不能算是仁人吧？"孔子说："桓公多次召集各诸侯国的盟会，不用武力，都是管仲的力量啊。这就是他的仁德，这就是他的仁德。"

【英译】Tsze-Lu said，"The duke Hwan caused his brother Chiu to be killed，when Shaohu died，with his master，but Kwan Chung did not die. may not I say that he was wanting in virtue?" The Master said，"The duke Hwan assembled all the princes together，and that not with weapons of war and chariots：-it was all through the influence of Kwanchung. Whose beneficence was like his? Whose beneficence was like his?"

【注释】

[1] 公子纠：齐桓公的哥哥。齐桓公与他争位，杀掉了他。

[2] 召忽：管仲和召忽都是公子纠的家臣。公子纠被杀后，召忽自杀，管仲归服于齐桓公，并当上了齐国的宰相。

[3] 九合诸侯：指齐桓公多次召集诸侯盟会。

[4] 不以兵车：即不用武力。

[5] 如其仁：这就是他的仁德。理雅格译为"beneficence"，即"慈善"；辜鸿铭译为"moral character"，"仁"被视为一种"道德品质"；刘殿爵译为"benevolence"，即"仁慈"；韦利译为"Goodness"，即"善良、美德"。孔子认为，管仲不依靠武力，帮助齐桓公召集诸侯会盟，这是"仁"的行为，是值得称赞的。

【原文】14.17　子贡曰："管仲非仁者与？桓公杀公子纠，不能死，又相之。"子曰："管仲相桓公，霸诸侯，一匡天下，民到于今受其赐。微管仲，吾其被发左衽[1]矣。岂若匹夫匹妇之为谅[2]也，自经于沟渎而莫之知也。"

【译文】子贡问："管仲不能算是仁人了吧？桓公杀了公子纠，他不能为公子纠殉死，反而做了齐桓公的宰相。"孔子说："管仲辅佐桓公，称霸诸侯，匡正了天下，老百姓到了今天还享受到他的好处。如果没有管仲，恐怕我们也要披散着头发，衣襟向左敞开。他哪能像普通百姓那样恪守小节，自杀在小山沟里而谁也不知道。"

【英译】Tsze-Kung said, "Kwan Chung, I apprehend was wanting in virtue. When the duke Hwan caused his brother Chiu to be killed, Kwan Chung was not able to die with him. Moreover, he became prime minister to Hwan." The Master said, "Kwan Chung acted as prime minister to the duke Hwan made him leader of all the princes, and united and rectified the whole kingdom. Down to the present day, the people enjoy the gifts which he conferred. But for Kwanchung，we should now be wearing our hair unbound，and the lappets of our coats buttoning on the left side. Will you require from him the small fidelity of common men and common women，who would commit suicide in a stream or ditch，no one knowing anything about them?"

【注释】

[1] 被发左衽：被，同"披"。衽，衣襟。"被发左衽"是当时的夷狄之俗。理雅格将该句直译为"wearing our hair unbound，and the lappets of our coats buttoning on the left side"，即"把头发解开，外套的襟扣在左边"。刘殿爵、韦利同样采用直译，即"wearing our hair down and folding our robes to the left"。辜鸿铭意译为"be living like savages"，即"像野人一样生活"。

[2] 谅：遵守信用，这里指恪守小节。孔子认为面对管仲的功绩，我们不必像匹夫匹妇一般，对他的小节进行苛刻评价。

【原文】 14.18 公叔文子之臣大夫僎[1]与文子同升诸公[2]。子闻之，曰："可以为文矣。"

【译文】公叔文子的家臣僎和文子一同做了卫国的大夫。孔子知道了这件事以后说："他死后可以给他'文'的谥号了。"

【英译】 The great officer，Hsien，who had been family minister to Kung-shu Wan，ascended to the prince's court in company with Wan. The Master，having heard of it，said，"He deserved to be considered Wan（the accomplished）."

【注释】

[1] 僎：人名，公叔文子的家臣。

[2] 升诸公：僎由家臣升为大夫，与公叔文子同位。

【原文】 14.19 子言卫灵公之无道[1]也，康子曰："夫如是，奚而不丧?"孔子曰:"仲叔圉[2]治宾客,祝鮀治宗庙,王孙贾治军旅,夫如是,奚其丧?"

【译文】 孔子讲到卫灵公的无道,季康子说:"既然如此,为什么他没有败亡呢?"孔子说:"因为他有仲叔圉接待宾客,祝鮀管理宗庙祭祀,王孙贾统率军队,像这样,怎么会败亡呢?"

【英译】 The Master was speaking about the unprincipled course of the duke Ling of Weil when Ch'i K'ang said, "Since he is of such a character, how is it he does not lose his state?" Confucius said, "The Chung-Shu Yu has the superintendence of his guests and of strangers; the litanist, T'o, has the management of his ancestral temple; and Wang-Sun Chia has the direction of the army and forces: with such officers as these, how should he lose his state?"

【注释】

[1] 无道:理雅格将政治上的"无道"译为"the unprincipled course",即"无原则的路线"。辜鸿铭统治者的"无道"译为"the scandalous life",形容君主过着荒淫无道的生活。刘殿爵译为"total lack of moral principle",形容统治者是"完全缺乏道德原则的"。韦利译为"no follower of the true way","无道"之人即"不是正道的追随者"。

[2] 仲叔圉:孔文子。其与祝鮀、王孙贾都是卫国的大夫。

【原文】 14.20 子曰:"其言之不怍[1],则为之也难!"

【译文】 孔子说:"说话如果大言不惭,那么实现这些话就是很困难的了。"

【英译】 The Master said, "He who speaks without modesty will find it difficult to make his words good."

【注释】

[1] 怍:惭愧、谦虚。理雅格译为"without modesty",即"缺乏谦

虚的"；辜鸿铭译为"not bashful"，即"不害羞的"；韦利译为"too ready to speak of it"，形容一个人过分夸耀自己，沉溺在言语炫耀而忽略了行动。

【原文】14.21　陈成子[1]弑简公[2]。孔子沐浴而朝，告于哀公曰："陈恒弑其君，请讨之。"公曰："告夫三子[3]。"孔子曰："以吾从大夫之后[4]，不敢不告也。君曰'告夫三子'者。"之三子告，不可。孔子曰："以吾从大夫之后，不敢不告也。"

【译文】陈成子杀了齐简公。孔子斋戒沐浴以后，随即上朝去见鲁哀公，报告说："陈恒把他的君主杀了，请你出兵讨伐他。"哀公说："你去报告那三位大夫吧。"孔子退朝后说："因为我曾经做过大夫，所以不敢不来报告，君主却说'你去告诉那三位大夫吧'！"孔子去向那三位大夫报告，但三位大夫不愿派兵讨伐，孔子又说："因为我曾经做过大夫，所以不敢不来报告呀！"

【英译】Chan Ch'ang murdered the duke Chien of Ch'i. Confucius bathed, went to court and informed the duke Ai, saying, "Chan Hang has slain his sovereign. I beg that you will undertake to punish him." The duke said, "Inform the chiefs of the three families of it." Confucius retired, and said, "Following in the rear of the great officers, I did not dare not to represent such a matter, and my prince says, 'Inform the chiefs of the three families of it'." He went to the chiefs, and informed them, but they would not act. Confucius then said, "Following in the rear of the great officers, I did not dare not to represent such a matter."

【注释】

[1] 陈成子：即陈恒，齐国大夫，又叫田成子。他以大斗借出，小斗收进的方法受到百姓拥护。公元前481年，他杀死齐简公，夺取了政权。

[2] 简公：齐简公，姓姜名壬。

[3] 三子：指季孙、孟孙、叔孙三家。

[4] 从大夫之后：孔子曾任过大夫职，但此时已经去官家居，所以说从大夫之后。理雅格译为"following in the rear of the great officers"，即"跟随在重要官员身后"。韦利译为"As I rank next to the Great Officers"，即"我排在重要官员旁边"。上述翻译均未能体现出孔子去官家居之意。辜鸿铭译为"As I have the honour to sit in the State council of the country"，即"就像我有幸成为这个国家的管理机构的一员"。刘殿爵译为"I take my place after the Counsellors"，即"我接替辅臣们的位置"，实际《论语》此处意为孔子曾任大夫，但现在已经卸任，并非指孔子接替了大夫们的官职。我们认为，此处译为"我曾经担任过大夫一职"（I used to be a scholar-official）较为恰当。

【原文】14.22　子路问事君。子曰："勿欺也，而犯[1]之。"

【译文】子路问怎样事奉君主。孔子说："不能欺骗他，但可以犯颜直谏。"

【英译】Tsze-Lu asked how a ruler should be served. The Master said，"Do not impose on him，and，moreover，withstand him to his face."

【注释】

[1] 犯：这里形容为臣者对君主的直言进谏。理雅格、辜鸿铭译为"withstand him to his face"，即"当面反抗"。刘殿爵以该句句读为"勿欺也而犯之"，译为"Do not stand up to him while，all the time，you have been dishonest with him."，即"你一直对他不诚实，就不要反抗他"，意指只有以诚对待君主的人，才可以去直言进谏、提出与君主相左的观点。韦利译为"Never oppose him by subterfuges"，即"不要用诡计欺骗君主"，认为可以用合道义的方式向君主进行劝谏，但是不能欺罔君主。上述译本相较，理雅格的翻译更为恰当。

【原文】 14.23　子曰："君子上达[1]，小人下达[2]。"

【译文】 孔子说："君子长进向上，小人沉沦向下。"

【英译】 The Master said，"The progress of the superior man is upwards；the progress of the mean man is downwards."

【注释】

[1] 上达：理雅格、辜鸿铭译为"upwards"，刘殿爵译为"up above"，直译为"向上的"。

[2] 下达：理雅格、辜鸿铭译为"downward"，刘殿爵译为"down below"，直译为"向下的"。

【原文】 14.24　子曰："古之学者为己；今之学者为人[1]。"

【译文】 孔子说："古代的人学习是为了提高自己，而现在的人学习是为了给别人看。"

【英译】 The Master said，"In ancient times，men learned with a view to their own improvement. Nowadays，men learn with a view to the approbation of others."

【注释】

[1] 为人：理雅格译为"with a view to the approbation of others"，即"为了得到别人的认可"；辜鸿铭、刘殿爵、韦利译为"impress others"，学习是为了"让人印象深刻"。此处意在批评今人学习是为了获得他人的认可、赞扬，译为"approbation"更为恰当。

【原文】 14.25　蘧伯玉[1]使人于孔子。孔子与之坐，而问焉。曰："夫子何为？"对曰："夫子欲寡其过而未能也。"使者出。子曰："使乎！使乎！"[2]

【译文】 蘧伯玉派使者去拜访孔子。孔子让使者坐下，然后问道："先生最近在做什么？"使者回答说："先生想要减少自己的错误，但未能做到。"使者走了以后，孔子说："好一位使者啊，好一位使者啊！"

【英译】Chu Po-Yu sent a messenger with friendly inquiries to Confucius. Confucius sat with him，and questioned him. "What，"said he！"Is your master engaged in?" The messenger replied，"My master is anxious to make his faults few，but he has not yet succeeded." He then went out，and The Master said，"A messenger indeed！A messenger indeed！"

【注释】

[1] 蘧伯玉：蘧，人名，卫国的大夫，又名瑗，孔子到卫国时曾住在他的家里。

[2] 一般认为孔子这话是夸赞使者。朱子《集注》云："使者之言愈自卑约，而其主之贤益彰，亦可谓深知君子之心，而善于辞令者矣。故夫子再言使乎以重美之。"今人黄怀信《论语汇校集释》则认为是孔子表达对使者的不满："使者云'夫子欲寡其过而未能也'，明有非议其主之嫌，故孔子不以其为使，而以为是'非之'，言这还算是使者吗？重言之，不满之甚也。"

【原文】14.26　子曰："不在其位[1]，不谋其政。"[2] 曾子曰："君子思不出其位。"

【译文】孔子说："不在那个职位，就不要考虑那个职位上的事情。"曾子说："君子考虑问题，从来不超出自己的职位范围。"

【英译】The Master said，"He who is not in any particular office has nothing to do with plans for the administration of its duties." The philosopher Tsang said，"The superior man，in his thoughts，does not go out of his position."

【注释】

[1] 位：职分、职位。理雅格译为"particular office"，即"特定的职务"；刘殿爵、辜鸿铭译为"office"，即"工作、办公室"；韦利译为"holds

no rank in a State"，形容那些"在国家中没有地位的人"。上述译本相较，理雅格的翻译较为恰当。

[2] 此句重出，又见《泰伯》第 14 章。

【原文】14.27　子曰："君子耻其言而过其行。[1]"

【译文】孔子说："君子认为说得多而做得少是可耻的。"

【英译】The Master said，"the superior man is modest in his speech，but exceeds in his actions."

【注释】

[1] 理雅格将该句译为 "The superior man is modest in his speech，but exceeds in his actions"，即"君子言语谦虚，行为超群"，"耻"被译为"谦虚"。辜鸿铭译为 "A wise man is ashamed to say. Confucius remarked，much；he prefers to do more." 即"智者羞于启齿，他更愿意做更多的事情"，"耻"被译为"羞耻、耻于"。刘殿爵译为 "The gentleman is ashamed when the words he utters outstrip his deeds." 即"君子若言多行少，则为耻。"韦利译为："A gentleman is ashamed to let his words outrun his deeds"，即"君子耻于言过其实"。理雅格将"耻"译为"谦虚"，不够恰当。

【原文】14.28　子曰："君子道者三，我无能焉：仁者不忧；知者不惑；勇者不惧。"子贡曰："夫子自道也！"

【译文】孔子说："君子之道有三个方面，我都未能做到：仁德的人不忧愁，聪明的人不迷惑，勇敢的人不畏惧。"子贡说："这正是老师的自我表述啊！"

【英译】The Master said，"The way of the superior man is threefold，but I am not equal to it. virtuous，he is free from anxieties；wise，he is free from perplexities；bold，he is free from fear." Tsze-Kung said，"Master，that is what you yourself say."

【原文】14.29　子贡方人[1]。子曰："赐也，贤乎哉？[2]夫我则不暇！"

【译文】子贡评论别人的短处。孔子说："赐啊，你真的就那么贤良吗？我可没有闲工夫去评论别人。"

【英译】Tsze-Kung was in the habit of comparing men together. The Master said，"Tsze must have reached a high pitch of excellence！Now，I have not leisure for this."

【注释】

[1] 方人：评论、诽谤别人。理雅格译为"comparing men together"，指子贡喜欢"比较他人"；辜鸿铭译为"criticizing men and making comparisons"，形容子贡喜欢"批评别人和进行比较"；刘殿爵译为"grading people"，即"给人分级"；韦利译为"criticizing other people"，指子贡喜欢批评别人。"方"强调比较与评论，并非是"批评"之义，"criticize"语气较重，理雅格、刘殿爵的翻译更为恰当。

[2] 赐也贤乎哉：疑问语气，批评子贡不贤。

【原文】14.30　子曰："不患人之不己知，患其不能[1]也。"

【译文】孔子说："不忧虑别人不知道自己，只担心自己没有本事。"

【英译】The Master said，"I will not be concerned at men's not knowing me；I will be concerned at my own want of ability."

【注释】

[1] 不能：没有能力。理雅格、刘殿爵、辜鸿铭将"能"翻译为"ability"，即"才能、能力"；韦利则将"不能"译为"incapacities"，即"没有能力的"。ability 的含义较广，主要指人具有从事体力或脑力劳动的能力，并且暗含能够干好的意味。其复数形式表示"才能，专门技能"。capacities 主要指完成某项工作的能力，也可以是非人的能力（如机器工作的效率等）；abilities 主要指个人的能力。上述译本相较，我们认为理雅格等人的翻译更

为恰当。

【原文】14.31　子曰："不逆[1]诈，不亿[2]不信。抑亦先觉者，是贤[3]乎？"

【译文】孔子说："不预先怀疑别人欺诈，也不猜测别人不诚实，然而能事先觉察别人的欺诈和不诚实，这就是贤人了吗？"

【英译】The Master said，"He who does not anticipate attempts to deceive him，nor think beforehand of his not being believed，and yet apprehends these things readily when they occur；is he not a man of superior worth？"

【注释】

[1] 逆：迎，预先猜测。理雅格、辜鸿铭、刘殿爵均译为"anticipate"，即"预测、预判"；韦利译为"count beforehand upon"，即"预先估计"。两种翻译并无明显差异。

[2] 亿：同"臆"，猜测的意思。

[3] 贤：贤人。韦利译为"true sage"，形容现实中拥有非凡智慧的贤者，即"真正的圣人"；理雅格、辜鸿铭、刘殿爵译为"a man of superior"，即"行为高尚的人"。

【原文】14.32　微生亩[1]谓孔子曰："丘何为是栖栖[2]者与？无乃为佞乎？"孔子曰："非敢为佞也，疾固[3]也。"

【译文】微生亩对孔子说："孔丘，你为什么这样四处奔波游说呢？你不就是要显示自己的口才和花言巧语吗？"孔子说："我不是敢于花言巧语，只是痛恨世道固陋。"

【英译】Wei-Shang Mau said to Confucius，"Ch'iu，how is it that you keep roosting about？Is it not that you are an insinuating talker？" Confucius said，"I do not dare to play the part of such a talker，but I hate obstinacy."

【注释】

[1] 微生亩：鲁国人，姓微生，名亩。

[2] 栖栖：忙碌不安、不安定的样子。理雅格译为"keep roosting"、韦利译为"going round perching"，均是采用直译，形容孔子"一直在栖息"。辜鸿铭译为"rambling"，形容孔子的状态是"散漫的"。刘殿爵译为"restless"，即"不安的"。此处形容孔子内心是栖栖惶惶、不安定的，刘殿爵的翻译更为恰当。

[3] 疾固：疾，恨。固，固陋。辜鸿铭将"固"译为"narrow-minded bigotry"，即"狭隘的偏执"。理雅格、韦利将"固"译为"obstinacy"，即"固执的"。刘殿爵将"固"译为"Inflexibility"，即"不灵活的、固执的"。obstinacy 更侧重性格脾气的顽固、倔强；inflexibility 则侧重不知变通。上述英译本均将"固"理解为"顽固"，指孔子痛恨那些冥顽不灵的人。

【原文】 14.33　子曰："骥[1]不称其力，称其德也。"

【译文】 孔子说："千里马值得称赞的不是它的气力，而是称赞它的品德。"

【英译】 The Master said，"A horse is called a Ch'i，not because of its strength，but because of its other good qualities."

【注释】

[1] 骥：千里马。古代称善跑的马为骥。

【原文】 14.34　或曰："以德[1]报怨，何如？"子曰："何以报德？以直[2]报怨，以德报德。"

【译文】 有人说："用恩德来报答怨恨怎么样？"孔子说："用什么来报答恩德呢？应该是用正直来报答怨恨，用恩德来报答恩德。"

【英译】 Some one said，"What do you say concerning the principle

that injury should be recompensed with kindness?" The Master said，
"With what then will you recompense kindness?" "Recompense injury
with justice，and recompense kindness with kindness."

【注释】

[1] 德：恩德。理雅格、辜鸿铭译为"kindness"，即"善良"；刘殿爵
译为"good turn"，即"恩惠、善良的行为"；韦利译为"inner power"，即
"内在的力量"。

[2] 直：正直。理雅格、辜鸿铭译为"justice"，刘殿爵译为
"straightness"，韦利译为"upright"，均为"正直"之意。justice 更强调"公
平的、公正的"，多指司法上的正义；straightness 强调"笔直"；upright 则强
调人的品格是"正直的、诚实的"。三者相较，我们认为该词译为"upright"
更为恰当。

【原文】 14.35　子曰："莫我知也夫！"子贡曰："何为其莫知
子也？"子曰："不怨天，不尤[1]人。下学而上达，知我者其天乎！"

【译文】 孔子说："没有人了解我啊！"子贡说："怎么能说没有人
了解您呢？"孔子说："我不埋怨天，也不责备人，下学人事而上达天
命，了解我的只有天吧！"

【英译】 The Master said，"Alas！There is no one that knows me."
Tsze-Kung said，"What do you mean by thus saying-that no one knows
you?" The master replied，"I do not murmur against heaven. I do not
blame against men. My studies lay low，and my penetration rises high.
But there is heaven；that knows me！"

【注释】

[1] 尤：责怪、怨恨。理雅格译为"grumble"，即"抱怨"；辜鸿铭
译为"complain"，即"抱怨"；刘殿爵、韦利译为"blame"，即"责怪"。
complain 意为"抱怨""诉苦""发牢骚"，指向他人诉说心中对某事、某人

的不满；grumble 则强调一边发脾气一边诉说受到的不公正的对待，也可指自言自语、唠唠叨叨地埋怨；blame 更侧重"责怪""归咎于"等含义。综合上述译本，我们认为此处译为"不把错误归咎于（blame）他人"更为恰当。

【原文】 14.36　公伯寮[1]愬[2]子路于季孙。子服景伯[3]以告，曰："夫子固有惑志于公伯寮，吾力犹能肆诸市朝[4]。"子曰："道之将行也与，命也；道之将废也与，命也。公伯寮其如命何！"

【译文】 公伯寮向季孙告发子路。子服景伯把这件事告诉孔子，并且说："季孙氏已经被公伯寮迷惑了，我的能力可把公伯寮杀了，把他陈尸于市。"孔子说："道能够得到推行，是天命决定的；道不能得到推行，也是天命决定的。公伯寮能把天命怎么样呢？"

【英译】 the Kung-Po Liao, having slandered Tsze-Lu to Chi-Sun, Tsze-fu Ching-po informed Confucius of it, saying, "Our Master is certainly being led astray by the Kung-Po Liao, but I have still power enough left to cut liao off, and expose his corpse in the market and in the court." The Master said, "If my principles are to advance, it is so ordered. If they are to fall to the ground, it is so ordered. What can the Kung-Po Liao do where such ordering is concerned?"

【注释】

[1] 公伯寮：姓公伯名寮，字子周，孔子的学生，曾任季氏的家臣。

[2] 愬：同"诉"，告发。

[3] 子服景伯：鲁国大夫，姓子服名伯，景是他的谥号。

[4] 肆诸市朝：古时处死罪人后陈尸示众。理雅格译为"expose his corpse in the market and in the court"，即"把他的尸体暴露在市场和法庭上"。辜鸿铭译为"expose his carcass on the market-place"，刘殿爵、韦利译为"have his carcass exposed in the market place"，即"让他的尸体暴露在市场上"。上述翻译并无明显差异。

【原文】 14.37 子曰："贤者辟[1]世，其次辟地，其次辟色，其次辟言。"子曰："作者七人[2]矣！"

【译文】 孔子说："贤人逃避动荡的社会而隐居，次一等的逃避到另外一个地方去，再次一点的避免别人难看的脸色，再次一点的回避别人难听的话。"孔子又说："这样做的已经有七个人了。"

【英译】 The Master said, "Some men of worth retire from the world. Some retire from particular states. Some retire because of disrespectful looks. Some retire because of contradictory language." The Master said, "Those who have done this are seven men."

【注释】

[1] 辟：同"避"，逃避。理雅格、辜鸿铭译为"retire from"，即"退出"之义；韦利译为"Withdraw"，即"撤回"；刘殿爵译为"shun"，即故意"躲避、避开"。上述译本相较，刘殿爵的翻译更为恰当。

[2] 七人：即伯夷、叔齐、虞仲、夷逸、朱张、柳下惠、少连。

【原文】 14.38 子路宿于石门[1]。晨门[2]曰："奚自？"子路曰："自孔氏。"曰："是知其不可而为之者与？"

【译文】 子路夜里住在石门，看门的人问："从哪里来？"子路说："从孔子那里来。"看门的人说："是那个明知做不到却还要去做的人吗？"

【英译】 Tsze-Lu happening to pass the night in Shih-man, the gatekeeper said to him, "Whom do you come from?" Tsze-Lu said, "From Mr. K'ung." "It is he, -is it not?" -said the other, "Who knows the impracticable nature of the times and yet will be doing in them."

【注释】

[1] 石门：地名。鲁国都城的外门。

[2] 晨门：早上看守城门的人。

【原文】 14.39 子击磬于卫，有荷蒉[1]而过孔氏之门者，曰：
"有心哉，击磬乎！"既而曰："鄙哉！硁硁[2]乎！莫己知也，斯己
而已矣。深则厉[3]，浅则揭[4]。"子曰："果哉！末之难[5]矣。"

【译文】 孔子在卫国，一次正在敲击磬，有一位背扛草筐的人从门
前走过说："这个敲磬是有深意的呀！"一会儿又说："声音硁硁的，真
可鄙呀，（它好像在说）没有人了解自己，就只做自己而已。好像涉水
一样，水深就穿着衣服趟过去，水浅就撩起衣服趟过去。"孔子说："好
坚决，没有什么可以责问他了。"

【英译】 The Master was playing, one day, on a musical stone in
Weil when a man carrying a straw basket passed door of the house
where Confucius was, and said, "His heart is full who so beats the
musical stone." A little while after, he added, "How contemptible
is the one-ideaed obstinacy those sounds display! When one is taken
no notice of, he has simply at once to give over his wish for public
employment. 'Deep water must be crossed with the clothes on; shallow
water may be crossed with the clothes held up.'" The Master said, "How
determined is he in his purpose! But this is not difficult!"

【注释】

[1] 荷蒉：荷，肩扛。蒉，草筐，肩背着草筐。理雅格译为"carrying
a straw basket"，辜鸿铭、刘殿爵、韦利译为"carrying a basket"。

[2] 硁硁：击磬的声音。

[3] 深则厉：穿着衣服涉水过河。

[4] 浅则揭：提起衣襟涉水过河。出自《诗经·卫风·匏有苦叶》。

[5] 难：责问、驳难。理雅格、辜鸿铭将该句译为"This is not
difficult"，即"这并不难"；刘殿爵译为"There can be no argument"，即"这

没什么可与他争辩的了";韦利译为"That is indeed an easy way out",即"这确实是一个简单的出路"。钱穆《论语新解》注为:"言此荷蒉者果决于忘世,亦无以难之。"该解将"难"解释为"驳难、发难",较为恰当。理雅格、辜鸿铭、韦利均将"难"理解为"困难",相较之下刘殿爵的翻译更为契合《论语》原义。

【原文】14.40　子张曰:"《书》云:'高宗[1]谅阴[2],三年不言。'何谓也?"子曰:"何必高宗?古之人皆然。君薨[3],百官总己以听于冢宰[4]三年。"

【译文】子张说:"《尚书》上说,'高宗守丧,三年不谈政事。'这是什么意思?"孔子说:"不仅是高宗,古人都是这样。国君死了,朝廷百官都各管自己的职事,听命于冢宰三年。"

【英译】Tsze-Chang said, "What is meant when the shu says that Kao-Tsung, while observing the usual imperial mourning, was for three years without speaking?" The Master said, "Why must kao-tsung be referred to as an example of this? The ancients all did so. When the sovereign died, the officers all attended to their several duties, taking instructions from the prime minister for three years."

【注释】

[1] 高宗:商王武宗。

[2] 谅阴:古时天子守丧之称。理雅格、辜鸿铭译为"observing the usual imperial mourning",即"按照惯例进行皇家哀悼"。刘殿爵译为"confined himself to his mourning hut",即"把自己关在房间里哀悼"。"谅阴"是一种皇家行为,上述译本相较,理雅格、辜鸿铭体现出了进行"谅阴"的主体是天子,该翻译较为恰当。

[3] 薨:周代时诸侯死称"薨"。理雅格、辜鸿铭译为"The sovereign died",即"国君死后";刘殿爵译为"The ruler died",即"统治者死后";

韦利译为"a prince died",即"王子死后"。sovereign 意为"君主、元首",ruler 意为"统治者";但本章"薨"意为周代时的诸侯,译为"vassal"(附庸国)或"dukes or princes under an emperor"(天子统治下的爵位)更为恰当。

[4] 冢宰:官名,相当于后世的宰相。理雅格、刘殿爵、韦利译为"The prime minister",即"首相、主要大臣";辜鸿铭译为"The Chief Minister",即"首席部长"。

【原文】 14.41 子曰:"上好礼[1],则民易使也。"

【译文】孔子说:"在上位的人喜好礼,那么百姓就容易指挥了。"

【英译】 The Master said,"When rulers love to observe the rules of propriety,the people respond readily to the calls on them for service."

【注释】

[1] 礼:理雅格译为"observe the rules of propriety",即"遵守礼仪规则";辜鸿铭将"好礼"译为"encourage education and good manners",即"鼓励教育和礼貌";刘殿爵译为"are given to the observance of the rites",即"被要求遵守礼仪";韦利则译为"The ruler loves ritual",即"统治者喜欢仪式"。上述译本相较,propriety 更强调礼节、行为规范,rites 则侧重宗教式的仪式、典礼,good manners 则形容人很有礼貌。

【原文】 14.42 子路问君子。子曰:"修己以敬[1]。"曰:"如斯而已乎?"曰:"修己以安人。"曰:"如斯而已乎?"曰:"修己以安百姓。修己以安百姓,尧舜其犹病诸?"

【译文】子路问什么叫君子。孔子说:"修养自己,保持严肃恭敬的态度。"子路说:"这样就够了吗?"孔子说:"修养自己,使周围的人们安乐。"子路说:"这样就够了吗?"孔子说:"修养自己,使所有百姓都安乐。修养自己使所有百姓都安乐，尧舜还怕难以做到呢！"

【英译】Tsze-Lu asked what constituted the superior man. The Master said, "The cultivation of himself in reverential carefulness." "And is this all?" said Tsze-Lu. "He cultivates himself so as to give rest to others," was the reply. "And is this all?" again asked Tsze-Lu. The Master said, "He cultivates himself so as to give rest to all the people. He cultivates himself so as to give rest to all the people; even Yao and Shun were still solicitous about this."

【注释】

[1] 修己以敬：修养自己，保持严肃恭敬的态度。理雅格译为"reverential carefulness"，即"虔诚的细心"；刘殿爵译为"Thereby achieves reverence"（从而获得崇敬），"敬"即"崇敬"之义；韦利译为"be diligent in his tasks"（勤奋工作），"敬"即"做事勤奋"之义。"敬"是中国哲学中的重要概念，其含义丰富，不能简单译为"做事勤奋""细心"等。

【原文】14.43　原壤[1]夷俟[2]。子曰："幼而不孙弟[3]，长而无述焉，老而不死，是为贼。"以杖叩其胫。

【译文】原壤又开双腿坐着等待孔子。孔子骂他说："年幼的时候，你不恭顺友爱，长大了又没有什么可说的成就，老而不死，真是害人精。"说着，用手杖敲他的小腿。

【英译】Yuan Zang was squatting on his heels, and so waited the approach of the Master, who said to him, "To be neither modest nor deferential when young; in manhood, doing nothing worthy of being handed down; and living on to old age: this is to be a pest." With this he hit him on the shank with his staff.

【注释】

[1] 原壤：鲁国人，孔子的旧友。他母亲死了，他还大声歌唱，孔子

认为这是大逆不道。

[2] 夷俟：夷，双腿分开而坐。俟，等待。

[3] 孙弟：同逊悌。理雅格译为 "In youth not humble as befits a junior"，即 "年轻的时候不应当低三下四"，该译本将 "孙弟" 译为含贬义的 "低三下四、过分谦卑"。辜鸿铭译为 "A wilful man and a bad citizen in your youth"，即 "你年轻时是个任性的人和坏公民"，该译本将 "不孙弟" 译为 "任性无德"，"孙弟" 则是一种好的品质。刘殿爵译为 "To be neither modest nor deferential when young"，即 "年轻时既不谦虚也不恭敬"，该译本采取直译方法，"孙" 即 "谦逊"，"弟" 即 "恭敬"。韦利译为 "Those who when young show no respect"，形容 "那些年轻时不尊重别人的人"，"孙弟" 用以形容一个人能尊重他人。上述译本相较，刘殿爵的翻译更为恰当。

【原文】 14.44 阙党[1]童子将命[2]。或问之曰："益者与？"子曰："吾见其居于位[3]也，见其与先生并行也；非求益者也，欲速成者也。"

【译文】 阙里的一个童子，来向孔子传话。有人问孔子："这是个求上进的孩子吗？"孔子说："我看见他坐在成年人的位子上，又见他和长辈并肩而行，他不是要求上进的人，只是个急于求成的人。"

【英译】 A youth of the village of Ch'ueh was employed by Confucius to carry the messages between him and his visitors. Some one asked about him, saying, "I suppose he has made great progress." The Master said, "I observe that he is fond of occupying the seat of a full-grown man; I observe that he walks shoulder to shoulder with his elders. He is not one who is seeking to make progress in learning. He wishes quickly to become a man."

【注释】

[1] 阙党：即阙里，孔子家住的地方。

[2] 将命：在宾主之间传言。理雅格译为"carry the messages between him and his visitors"，即"在主宾之间传递消息"。辜鸿铭则译为"answer the door and introduce visitors"，即"开门并介绍宾客"。韦利译为"come with messages"，指这个童子"带着信息来（拜访孔子）"。上述译本相较，理雅格的翻译更为恰当。

[3] 居于位：童子与长者同坐。

卫灵公篇第十五

【原文】15.1　卫灵公问陈^[1]于孔子。孔子对曰："俎豆^[2]之事，则尝闻之矣；军旅之事，未之学也。"明日遂行。

【译文】卫灵公向孔子问军队列阵之法。孔子回答说："祭祀礼仪方面的事情，我还听说过；用兵打仗的事，从来没有学过。"第二天，孔子便离开了卫国。

【英译】The duke Ling of Wei asked Confucius about tactics. Confucius replied，"I have heard all about sacrificial vessels，but I have not learned military matters." On this，he took his departure the next day.

【注释】

[1] 陈：同"阵"，军队作战时，布列的阵势。理雅格译为"tactics"、辜鸿铭译为"military tactics"，即"战术、兵法"；刘殿爵译为"military formations"，即"军阵、军事方队"；韦利译为"The marshalling of troops"，即"军队的集结情况"。此处"陈"通"阵"，指军队的排布、阵法等，刘殿爵与韦利的翻译更为恰当。

[2] 俎豆：古代盛食物的器皿，被用作祭祀时的礼器。理雅格、刘殿爵译为"sacrificial vessels"，即"祭器"；韦利译为"ritual vessels"，即"礼器"。辜鸿铭意译为"art"，意指孔子熟悉"礼制、艺术"而不熟悉军武之事。上述译本相较，前两种翻译更为恰当。

【原文】15.2 在陈绝粮。从者病，莫能兴。子路愠见曰："君子亦有穷乎?"子曰:"君子固穷[1]，小人斯滥矣。"

【译文】孔子一行在陈国断了粮食，随从的人都饿病了。子路很不高兴地来见孔子，说:"君子也有穷得毫无办法的时候吗?"孔子说:"君子虽然穷困，但还是坚持着；小人一遇穷困就无所不为了。"

【英译】When he was in Chan，their provisions were exhausted，and his followers became so in that they were unable to rise. Tsze-Lu，with evident dissatisfaction，said，"Has the superior man likewise to endure in this way?" The Master said，"It comes as no surprise to the gentleman to find himself in extreme straits，but the mean man，when he is in want，gives way to unbridled license."

【注释】

[1] 固穷:固守穷困、安守穷困。理雅格译为"endure want"，"固穷"即"遏制自己的欲望"，理雅格将"穷"理解为物质上的贫乏，因此"固穷"即为遏制欲望。刘殿爵将该句译为"It comes as no surprise to the gentleman to find himself in extreme straits"，即"对君子来说发现自己处于极端困境并不奇怪"，"固穷"即在极端境遇中能保持稳重应对。韦利译为"A gentleman can withstand hardships"，即"君子能忍受困境"，"固"被译为"忍受"而非"安守"。上述译本相较，刘殿爵的翻译更为契合《论语》原义。

【原文】15.3 子曰:"赐也，女以予为多学而识之者与?"对曰:"然，非与?"曰:"非也! 予一以贯之。"

【译文】孔子说:"赐啊! 你以为我是学习得多了才一一记住的吗?"子贡答道:"是啊，难道不是这样吗?"孔子说:"不是的。我是用一个根本的东西把它们贯穿起来的。"

【英译】The Master said，"Ts'ze，you think，I suppose，that I am one who learns many things and keeps them in memory?" Tsze-Kung replied，"Yes，but perhaps it is not so?" "No，" was the answer；"I seek a unity all pervading."

【原文】15.4　子曰："由，知德^[1]者鲜矣！"

【译文】孔子说："由啊，懂得德的人太少了。"

【英译】The Master said，"Yu I those who know virtue are few."

【注释】

[1] 德：此处理雅格、刘殿爵译为 virtue，即美德；辜鸿铭、韦利译为 moral，即道德。

【原文】15.5　子曰："无为而治^[1]者，其舜也与！夫何为哉？恭己正南面而已矣。"

【译文】孔子说："能够无所作为而治理天下的人，大概只有舜吧？他做了些什么呢？只是庄严端正地坐在朝廷的王位上罢了。"

【英译】The Master said，"May not Shun be instanced as achieving order without taking any action? What did he do? He did nothing but gravely and reverently occupy his royal seat."

【注释】

[1] 无为而治："无为而治"是道家所主张的治国方略，孔子以舜为例赞赏无为而治，说明儒家以三代的德政礼治为理想。理雅格译为"having governed efficiently without exertion"，形容舜"毫不费力地有效管理"。辜鸿铭译为"The principle of no-government"，"无为而治"即"无政府主义"，该翻译不够恰当。刘殿爵译为"achieved order without taking any action"，即"不采取任何行动而维持秩序"。韦利译为"ruled by inactivity"，形容舜在管理国家中"不够活跃"。上述译本相较，刘殿爵的翻译更为恰当。

【原文】15.6　子张问行。子曰："言忠信，行笃敬，虽蛮貊^[1]

之邦，行矣。言不忠信，行不笃敬，虽州里[2]，行乎哉？立则见其参于前也，在舆则见其倚于衡[3]也，夫然后行。"子张书诸绅。

【译文】 子张问如何才能使自己到处都能行得通。孔子说："说话要忠信，行事要笃敬，即使到了蛮貊地区，也可以行得通。说话不忠信，行事不笃敬，就是在本乡本土，能行得通吗？站着就仿佛看到'忠信笃敬'这几个字显现在面前，坐车就好像看到这几个字刻在车辕前的横木上，这样才能使自己到处行得通。"子张把这些话写在腰间的大带上。

【英译】 Tsze-Chang asked how a man should conduct himself, so as to be everywhere appreciated. The Master said, "Let his words be sincere and truthful and his actions honorable and careful；-such conduct may be practiced among the rude tribes of the south or the north. If his words are not sincere and truthful and his actions not honorable and careful will he，with such conduct，is appreciated，even in his neighborhood？When he is standing，let him see those two things，as it were，fronting him. When he is in a carriage，let him see them attached to the yoke. Then may he subsequently carry them into practice." Tsze-Chang wrote these counsels on the end of his sash.

【注释】

[1] 蛮貊：古人对少数民族的贬称，蛮在南，貊在北方。理雅格译为"The rude tribes of the south or the north"，即"南方和北方的蛮荒部落"；辜鸿铭译为"barbarous countries"，即"野蛮的国家"；刘殿爵译为"The lands of the barbarians"，即"在野蛮人的土地上"。rude 强调"粗鲁的、狂暴的"，barbarous 则侧重"野蛮残暴的"，专指只有原始或未开化的人才会有的残忍行为，更为恰当。

[2] 州里：五家为邻，五邻为里。五党为州，二千五百家。州里指近处。

[3] 衡：车辕前面的横木。理雅格、韦利译为"yoke"，即"轭"，指驾车时套在牲口脖子上的曲木。辜鸿铭译为"on the head of your horse"，即"驾车的马的头"。刘殿爵译为"handle-bar"，即"车把手"之义。上述译本相较，将"衡"译为"yoke"更为恰当。

【原文】15.7　子曰："直哉史鱼[1]！邦有道，如矢[2]；邦无道，如矢。君子哉蘧伯玉！邦有道，则仕；邦无道，则可卷而怀之。"

【译文】孔子说："史鱼真是正直啊！国家有道，他的言行像箭一样直；国家无道，他的言行也像箭一样直。蘧伯玉也真是一位君子啊！国家有道就出来做官，国家无道就辞退官职，把自己的主张收藏在心里。"

【英译】The Master said, "Truly straightforward was the historiographer Yu. When good government prevailed in his state, he was like an arrow. When bad government prevailed, he was like an arrow. A superior man indeed is Chu Po-Yu! When good government prevails in his state, he is to be found in office. When bad government prevails, he can roll his principles up, and keep them in his breast."

【注释】

[1] 史鱼：卫国大夫，名鲋，字子鱼，他多次向卫灵公推荐蘧伯玉。

[2] 如矢：矢，箭，形容其直。

【原文】15.8　子曰："可与言而不与之言，失人；不可与言而与之言，失言。知者不失人，亦不失言。"

【译文】孔子说："可以同他谈的话，却不同他谈，这就是失掉了朋友；不可以同他谈的话，却同他谈，这就是说错了话。有智慧的人既不失去朋友，又不说错话。"

【英译】The Master said, "When a man may be spoken with, not

to speak to him is to err in reference to the man. When a man may not be spoken with，to speak to him is to err in reference to our words. The wise err neither in regard to their man nor to their words."

【原文】 15.9 子曰："志士仁人[1]，无求生以害仁，有杀身以成仁。"

【译文】 孔子说："志士仁人，没有贪生怕死而损害仁的，只有牺牲自己的性命来成全仁的。"

【英译】 The Master said，"The determined scholar and the man of virtue will not seek to live at the expense of injuring their virtue. They will even sacrifice their lives to preserve their virtue complete."

【注释】

[1] 志士仁人：理雅格译为"The determined scholar and the man of virtue"，即"有决心的学者和有美德的人"。辜鸿铭译为"A gentleman of spirit or a man of moral character"，即"一个有精神的绅士或一个有道德品质的人"。刘殿爵译为"Gentlemen of purpose and men of benevolence"，即"有目标的绅士和仁慈的人"。韦利译为"The knight who has truly the heart of a knight nor the man of good stock who has the qualities that belong to good stock"，即"一个真正拥有骑士之心的骑士，或者一个拥有优秀品质的人"。上述译本相较，理雅格的翻译更为契合《论语》原义。

【原文】 15.10 子贡问为仁。子曰："工欲善其事，必先利其器。居是邦也，事其大夫之贤者，友其士之仁者。"[1]

【译文】 子贡问怎样实行仁德。孔子说："做工的人想把活儿做好，必须首先使他的工具锋利。住在这个国家，就要事奉大夫中的那些贤者，与士人中的仁者交朋友。"

【英译】 Tsze-Kung asked about the practice of virtue. The Master said，"The mechanic，who wishes to do his work well，must first sharpen his tools. When you are living in any state，take service with the most worthy among its great officers，and make friends of the most virtuous among its scholars."

【注释】

[1] 理雅格将"大夫"译为"great officers"，即"伟大的官员"；"士"译为"scholars"，即"学者、读书人"。辜鸿铭将"大夫"译为"nobles and nrinisters"，即"贵族"；"士"译为"gentlemen"，即"绅士"。刘殿爵将"大夫"译为"The most distinguished Counsellors"，即"最杰出的顾问"；"士"译为"gentlemen"，即"绅士"。

【原文】 15.11 颜渊问为邦。子曰："行夏之时[1]，乘殷之辂[2]。服周之冕。乐则韶舞[3]。放[4]郑声，远佞人，郑声[5]淫，佞人殆。"

【译文】 颜渊问怎样治理国家。孔子说："用夏代的历法，乘殷代的车子，戴周代的礼帽，奏《韶》乐，禁绝郑国的乐曲，疏远能言善辩的人，郑国的乐曲浮靡不正派，佞人太危险。"

【英译】 Yen yuan asked how the government of a country should be administered. The Master said，"Follow the seasons of Hsia. Ride in the state carriage of Yin. Wear the ceremonial cap of Chau. Let the music be the Shao with its pantomimes. Banish the songs of Chang，and keep far from specious talkers. The songs of Chang are licentious；specious talkers are dangerous."

【注释】

[1] 夏之时：夏代的历法，便于农业生产，又称阴历、农历等。它与黄帝历、颛顼历、殷历、周历、鲁历合称古六历。理雅格、韦利译为"seasons of Hsia"，即"夏的季节"，不够恰当。辜鸿铭、刘殿爵译为"The

calendar of the Hsia dynasty"，即"夏代的历法"，该译文较为恰当。

[2] 殷之辂：辂，天子所乘的车。殷代的车是木制成，比较朴实。

[3] 韶舞：是舜时的舞乐，孔子认为是尽善尽美的。

[4] 放：禁绝、排斥、抛弃的意思。

[5] 郑声：郑国的乐曲，孔子认为是淫声。

【原文】15.12　子曰："人无远虑，必有近忧[1]。"

【译文】孔子说："人没有长远的考虑，一定会有眼前的忧患。"

【英译】The Master said，"If a man take no thought about what is distant，he will find sorrow near at hand."

【注释】

[1] 近忧：理雅格解释为"sorrow near at hand"，即"近在眼前的悲伤"。辜鸿铭译为"he will be sorry before to-day is out"，形容一个没有深谋远虑的人会在"今天结束前懊悔"。刘殿爵、韦利译为"by worries close at hand"，即"近在眼前的担忧"。上述译本相较，刘殿爵、韦利的翻译更为恰当。

【原文】15.13　子曰："已矣乎！吾未见好德如好色者也！"

【译文】孔子说："完了，我从来没有见像好色那样好德的人。"

【英译】The Master said，"It is all over！I have not seen one who loves virtue as he loves beauty."

【原文】15.14　子曰："臧文仲，其窃位[1]者与？知柳下惠[2]之贤，而不与立也。"

【译文】孔子说："臧文仲是一个做官不管事的人吧！他明知道柳下惠是个贤人，却不举荐他一起做官。"

【英译】The Master said，"Was not Tsang Wan like one who had

stolen his situation? He knew the virtue and the talents of Hui of Liu-Hsia, and yet did not procure that he should stand with him in court."

【注释】

[1] 窃位：身居官位而不称职。理雅格直译为"stolen his situation"，即"窃走了他的官位"；辜鸿铭译为"stolen his position"，即"偷走了他的位置"；刘殿爵译为"does not deserve his position"，形容臧文仲是一个"不配身居现在的官位"的人，该翻译较为恰当。

[2] 柳下惠：春秋中期鲁国大夫，姓展名获，又名禽，他受封的地名是柳下，惠是他的私谥，所以，人称其为柳下惠。

【原文】 15.15 子曰："躬自厚而薄责于人，则远怨矣！"

【译文】 孔子说："多责备自己而少责备别人，那就可以避免别人的怨恨了。"

【英译】 The Master said, "He who requires much from himself and little from others, will keep himself from being the object of resentment."

【原文】 15.16 子曰："不曰'如之何，如之何'[1]者，吾末如之何也已矣？"

【译文】 孔子说："从来遇事不说'怎么办，怎么办'的人，我对他也不知怎么办才好。"

【英译】 The Master said, "When a man is not in the habit of saying 'What shall I think of this? What shall I think of this?' I can indeed do nothing with him!"

【注释】

[1] 如之何：怎么办。理雅格译为"What shall I think of this?"即"我该怎么想呢？"辜鸿铭译为"What is the right thing to do?"即"什么是正确

的做法呢？"刘殿爵译为"What am I to do?"即"我该怎么办呢？"上述译本相较，刘殿爵的翻译更为恰当。

【原文】15.17　子曰："群居终日，言不及义，好行小慧[1]，难矣哉！"

【译文】孔子说："同大家整天在一块，所说的话都达不到义的标准，专好卖弄小聪明，这种人真难教导。"

【英译】The Master said, "When a number of people are together, for a whole day, without their conversation turning on righteousness, and when they are fond of carrying out the suggestions of a small shrewdness；theirs is indeed a hard case."

【注释】

[1] 小慧：小聪明。理雅格译为"small shrewdness"，即"小机灵"；辜鸿铭译为"small wit and smart sayings"，即"小机智和聪明的说法"；刘殿爵译为"petty cleverness"，即"小机灵"；韦利译为"petty acts of clemency"，即"微不足道的仁慈行为"。shrewdness 侧重形容人是"精明的、有城府的"，cleverness 形容人聪明机灵、反应快、学习好，偏重智商层面的解读，smart 倾向于包涵了智商、反应、动作、行为，策略等综合层面的考评。《论语》此处微含贬义，译为 shrewdness 更为恰当。

【原文】15.18　子曰："君子义[1]以为质，礼[2]以行之，孙[3]以出之，信[4]以成之。君子哉！"

【译文】孔子说："君子以义作为根本，用礼加以推行，用谦逊的语言来表达，用忠诚的态度来完成，这就是君子了。"

【英译】The Master said, "The superior man in everything considers righteousness to be essential. He performs it according to the rules of propriety. He brings it forth in modesty. He completes it with sincerity.

This is indeed a superior man."

【注释】

[1] 义：理雅格译为"righteousness"，即"正义"；辜鸿铭译为"makes Right"，即"做正确的事"；刘殿爵将"义"译为"morality"，义即道德；韦利译为"right"，即"义"。

[2] 礼：理雅格译为"The rules of propriety"，即"礼仪规则"；辜鸿铭将"礼以行之"译为"he carries it out with judgment and good sense"，形容一个人在做事时"有判断力和理智"；刘殿爵将"礼"译为"rites"，即"礼节、仪式"；韦利译为"ritual"，即"仪式"。

[3] 孙：理雅格译为"humility"，即"谦逊"；辜鸿铭、韦利译为"modesty"，即"谦虚"。Humility 更侧重人的性格是"谦逊的、谦卑的"，modesty 则侧重对自己的技能的评价，在自我评价中的态度是"谦虚的"。我们认为，此处译为 modesty 更为恰当。

[4] 信：理雅格、辜鸿铭译为"sincerity"，即"真诚"；刘殿爵译为"Trustworthy"，信即"值得信任"；韦利译为"faithful"，即"忠实的"。

【原文】 15.19　子曰："君子病无能焉，不病人之不己知也。"

【译文】 孔子说："君子只怕自己没有才能，不怕别人不知道自己。"

【英译】 The Master said，"The superior man is distressed by his want of ability. He is not distressed by men's not knowing him."

【原文】 15.20　子曰："君子疾没世而名不称焉。"

【译文】 孔子说："君子担心死后他的名字不为人们所称颂。"

【英译】 The Master said，"The superior man dislikes the thought of his name not being mentioned after his death."

【原文】 15.21　子曰："君子求诸己；小人求诸人。"

【译文】孔子说："君子求之于自己，小人求之于别人。"

【英译】The Master said，"What the superior man seeks，is in himself. What the mean man seeks is in others."

【原文】15.22　子曰："君子矜[1]而不争，群而不党。"

【译文】孔子说："君子庄重而不与别人争执，合群而不结党营私。"

【英译】The Master said，"The superior man is dignified，but does not wrangle. He is sociable，but not a partisan."

【注释】

[1] 矜：庄重的意思。理雅格译为"dignified"，即"庄重的、有尊严的"；辜鸿铭、韦利译为"proud"，即"骄傲的"；刘殿爵译为"superiority"，"矜"形容君子"意识到自己的优越性"。此处"矜"为"矜庄"之义，理雅格的翻译更为恰当。

【原文】15.23　子曰："君子不以言举人，不以人废言。"

【译文】孔子说："君子不凭一个人说的话来举荐他，也不因为一个人不好而不采纳他的好话。"

【英译】The Master said，"The superior man does not promote a man simply on account of his words，nor does he put aside good words because of the man."

【原文】15.24　子贡问曰："有一言而可以终身行之者乎？"子曰："其恕[1]乎！己所不欲，勿施于人。"

【译文】子贡问孔子问道："有没有一个字可以终身奉行的呢？"孔子回答说："那就是恕吧！自己不愿意的，不要强加给别人。"

【英译】Tsze-Kung asked，saying，"Is there one word which may serve as a rule of practice for all one's life？" The Master said，"Is not shu such a word? What you do not want done to yourself, do not do to others."

【注释】

[1] 恕：理雅格译为"reciprocity"，即"互惠的"；辜鸿铭译为"charity"，即"仁慈、宽厚"。辜鸿铭音译为"shu"，并在注释中解释为"I.e., using oneself as a measure in gauging the wishes of others. Cf. IV.15 and VI.30. It is interesting to note that in V.12 when Tzu-kung remarked that if he did not wish others to impose on him neither did he wish to impose on others, Confucius' comment was that this was be-yond his ability."（用自己来衡量别人的愿望。参见 4.15 和 6.30。有趣的是当子贡说，如果他不希望别人强加于他，他也不希望强加于别人，孔子的评论是，这超出了他的能力）韦利译为"consideration"，即"思考、考虑"。"忠恕之道"是孔子"仁学"思想体系的重要组成部分，也是儒家伦理思想的精髓，意思是己欲利而利人，己欲达而达人。此处我们认为，辜鸿铭的处理方式更为巧妙。

【原文】15.25 子曰："吾之于人也，谁毁谁誉？如有所誉者，其有所试矣。斯民也，三代之所以直道而行[1]也。"

【译文】孔子说："我对于别人，诋毁过谁？赞美过谁？如有所赞美的，必须是曾经考验过他的。夏商周三代的人都是这样做的，所以三代能直道而行。"

【英译】The Master said, "In my dealings with men, whose evil do I blame, whose goodness do I praise, beyond what is proper? If I do sometimes exceed in praise, there must be ground for it in my examination of the individual. This people supplied the ground why the three dynasties pursued the path of straightforwardness."

【注释】

[1] 直道而行：理雅格译为"pursued the path of straightforwardness"，

即"追求直捷的道路"。刘殿爵译为"kept to the straight path"，即"保持直道而行"。韦利译为"followed the straight way"，即"顺着直道走"。

【原文】15.26　子曰："吾犹及史之阙文[1]也。有马者借人乘之[2]，今亡矣夫！"

【译文】孔子说："我还能够看到史书存疑的地方。有马的人（自己不会训练），先给别人使用，这种精神，今天没有了吧？"

【英译】The Master said，"Even in my early days，a historiographer would leave blank in his text，and he who had a horse would lend him to another to ride. Now，alas！ There are no such things."

【注释】

[1] 阙文：史官记史，遇到有疑问的地方便缺而不记，这叫作阙文。

[2] 此句意思不好理解。邢昺《注疏》云："此章疾时人多穿凿也。子曰：'吾犹及史之阙文也'者，史是掌书之官也。文，字也。古之良史，于书字有疑则阙之，以待能者，不敢穿凿。孔子言我尚及见此古史阙疑之文。'有马者借人乘之'者，此举喻也。喻己有马不能调良，当借人乘习之也。'今亡矣夫'者，亡，无也。孔子自谓及见其人如此，阙疑至今，则无有矣。言此者，以俗多穿凿。"一说为衍文。《汉书·艺文志》曰："古者书必同文，不知则阙，问诸故老。至于衰世，是非无正，人用其私。故孔子曰：'吾犹及史之阙文也，今亡矣夫。'盖伤其浸不正。"据此，叶梦得《石林燕语》疑此句为衍文。又顾炎武《日知录》引《汉书·艺文志》之语曰："是知穿凿之弊自汉已然，故有行赂改兰台漆书，以合其私者矣。"

【原文】15.27　子曰："巧言乱德。小不忍，则乱大谋。"

【译文】孔子说："花言巧语会败坏人的德行。小事情不忍耐，就会败坏大事情。"

【英译】The Master said，"Specious words confound virtue. Want

of forbearance in small matters confounds great plans."

【原文】15.28　子曰："众恶之，必察[1]焉；众好之，必察焉。"

【译文】孔子说："大家都厌恶他，我必须考察一下；大家都喜欢他，我也一定要考察一下。"

【英译】The Master said，"When the multitude hate a man，it is necessary to examine into the case. When the multitude like a man，it is necessary to examine into the case."

【注释】

[1] 察：考察、审查。理雅格译为 "examine"，即 "考察、审核"；辜鸿铭译为 "find out"，即 "发现、查明"；刘殿爵译为 "Be sure to go carefully into the case of the man"，即 "一定要仔细调查这个人的情况"；韦利译为 "enquiry"，即 "询问、盘询"。此处理解为 "考察、审查" 更契合孔子本意，理雅格与刘殿爵本更为精确。

【原文】15.29　子曰："人能弘道[1]，非道弘人。"

【译文】孔子说："人能够使道发扬光大，不是道使人的才能扩大。"

【英译】The Master said，"A man can enlarge tao which he follows；but tao do not enlarge the man."

【注释】

[1] 道：理雅格、辜鸿铭将 "道" 译为 "principles"，即 "原则、准则"；刘殿爵、韦利译为 "The way"，即 "道路" 之义。儒家之 "道" 并非客观的行为准则，译为 principle 不够恰当。

【原文】15.30　子曰："过而不改，是谓过矣！"

【译文】孔子说："有了过错而不改正，这才真叫错了。"

【英译】The Master said，"To have faults and not to reform them,

this，indeed，should be pronounced having faults."

【原文】 15.31 子曰："吾尝终日不食，终夜不寝，以思，无益，不如学也。"

【译文】 孔子说："我曾经整天不吃饭，彻夜不睡觉，去思考，结果没有什么好处，还不如去学习为好。"

【英译】 The Master said，"I have been the whole day without eating，and the whole night without sleeping：occupied with thinking. It was of no use. Better plan is to learn."

【原文】 15.32 子曰："君子谋道不谋食。耕也，馁[1]在其中矣；学也，禄[2]在其中矣。君子忧[3]道不忧贫。"

【译文】 孔子说："君子只谋求行道，不谋求衣食。耕田，也常要饿肚子；学习，可以得到俸禄。君子只担心道不能行，不担心贫穷。"

【英译】 The Master said，"The object of the superior man is truth. Food is not his object. There is plowing；even in that there is sometimes want. So with learning；emolument may be found in it. The superior man is worry lest he should not get truth；he is not worry about lest poverty should come upon him."

【注释】

[1] 馁：饥饿。

[2] 禄：做官的俸禄。

[3] 忧：理雅格、辜鸿铭、韦利译为"anxious"，即"焦虑的、渴望的"；刘殿爵译为"worries about"，即"担忧、忧虑"。此处"忧"侧重担心而非焦虑，译为"worry about"更为明白晓畅。

【原文】 15.33 子曰："知及之，仁不能守之，虽得之，必失之。知及之，仁能守之，不庄以涖[1]之，则民不敬。知及之，仁能守之，庄以涖之，动之不以礼，未善也。"

【译文】孔子说："凭借聪明才智足以得到它，但仁德不能保持它，即使得到，也一定会丧失。凭借聪明才智足以得到它，仁德可以保持它，不用严肃态度来治理百姓，那么百姓就会不敬。凭借聪明才智足以得到它，仁德可以保持它，能用严肃态度来治理百姓，但动员百姓时不照礼的要求，那也是不完善的。"

【英译】The Master said, "When a man's knowledge is sufficient to attain, and his virtue is not sufficient to enable him to hold, whatever he may have gained, he will lose again. When his knowledge is sufficient to attain, and he has virtue enough to hold fast, if he cannot dignity wherewith to approach the common people, the people will not respect him. When his knowledge is sufficient to attain, and he has virtue enough to hold fast；When he governs also with dignity, yet if he try to move the people contrary to the rules of propriety：full excellence is not reached."

【注释】

[1] 涖：临，到的意思。理雅格译为"govern"，即"管理、统治"；刘殿爵译为"rule over them with dignity"，即"有尊严地统治他们"，刘殿爵与理雅格均将"涖"解释为"统治、管理"。辜鸿铭译为"set themselves seriously"，形容统治者用认真的态度对待百姓；韦利将该句译为"dignity wherewith to approach the common people"，即"用尊重的方式来接近普通人"。上述译本相较，韦利的翻译较为准确。

【原文】15.34　子曰："君子不可小知[1]，而可大受[2]也；小人不可大受，而可小知也。"

【译文】孔子说："君子不能让他们做那些小事，但可以让他们承担重大的使命。小人不能让他们承担重大的使命，但可以让他们做那些小事。"

【英译】The Master said, "The superior man cannot be known in little matters; but he may be in trusted with great concerns. The small man may not be in trusted with great concerns, but he may be known in little matters."

【注释】

[1] 小知：知，作为的意思，做小事情。理雅格将该句译为"cannot be known in little matters"，形容君子"不能因为小的事情为人所知"。辜鸿铭译为"show his quality in small affairs"，形容君子不在小事上展示自己的才能。刘殿爵将该句译为"be valued on the strength of small matters"，形容君子不因为小事的力量而为人所重视。韦利将该句译为"It is wrong for a gentleman to have knowledge of menial matters"，该文认为君子认识到，做卑微的事情是错误的；此处"小知"是指微小、不重要的事情，并非指卑微、下贱的工作，韦利译为 menial matters 不够恰当。

[2] 大受：受，责任，使命的意思，承担大任。理雅格、辜鸿铭将该句译为"be in trusted with great concerns"，指君子能"在重要事情上被委以重任"。刘殿爵译为"be given great responsibilities"，指君子可以被给予重要的任务。韦利译为"be entrusted with great responsibilities"，形容君子应当"承担重要的责任"。

【原文】15.35　子曰："民之于仁也，甚于水火。水火，吾见蹈而死[1]者矣，未见蹈仁而死者也。"

【译文】孔子说："百姓们对于仁的需要，比对于水的需要更迫切。我只见过人跳到水火中而死的，却没有见过实行仁而死的。"

【英译】The Master said, "Virtue is more to man than either water or fire. I have seen men die from treading on water and fire, but I have never seen a man die from treading the course of virtue."

【注释】

[1] 蹈而死：因某事而死。本章劝谏人向仁。朱子《集注》云："民之于水火，所赖以生，不可一日无。其于仁也亦然。但水火外物，而仁在己。无水火，不过害人之身，而不仁则失其心。是仁有甚于水火，而尤不可以一日无也。况水火或有时而杀人，仁则未尝杀人，亦何惮而不为哉？"理雅格直译为"die from treading"、韦利译为"treading upon"，即"踩在……路上而死"；辜鸿铭译为"die from falling into……"，指"陷入某事而死"；刘殿爵译为"die by stepping on"，指人"因踩在……道路上而死"。理雅格、刘殿爵等人多采直译之法，"蹈"即"踩、践履"之义。

【原文】 15.36　子曰："当仁，不让于师。"

【译文】 孔子说："面对仁德，就是老师，也不同他谦让。"

【英译】 The Master said, "Let every man consider virtue as what devolves on himself. He may not yield the performance of it even to his teacher."

【原文】 15.37　子曰："君子贞[1]而不谅[2]。"

【译文】 孔子说："君子固守正道，而不拘泥于小信。"

【英译】 The Master said, "The superior man is correctly firm, and not firm merely."

【注释】

[1] 贞：正。理雅格译为"correctly firm"，即"正确的坚定"；辜鸿铭译为"faithful"，形容君子是"忠实可信的"；刘殿爵译为"steadfast"，形容君子是"坚定的"。

[2] 谅：信，守信用。理雅格译为"firm merely"，形容"仅仅是坚守（而非正确地坚守）"。辜鸿铭译为"merely constant"，形容君子不应当"仅

仅是恒定守常的"。firm 强调坚固、稳固，constant 则侧重不变的、恒常的。刘殿爵将"谅"译为"inflexible"，即"不灵活的"。上述译本相较，理雅格、辜鸿铭将"谅"理解为坚守，而非秉持道义的坚守，刘殿爵则以"谅"为"不知变通的"。上述译本相较，理雅格、辜鸿铭的翻译更为贴近"谅"的"小信"之义。

【原文】 15.38　子曰："事君敬其事而后其食[1]。"

【译文】 孔子说："事奉君主，要认真办事而把领取俸禄的事放在后面。"

【英译】 The Master said, "A minister, in serving his prince, reverently discharges his duties, and makes his emolument a secondary consideration."

【注释】

[1] 食：食禄，俸禄。

【原文】 15.39　子曰："有教无类[1]。"

【译文】 孔子说："人人都可以接受教育，没有类别区分。"

【英译】 The Master said, "In teaching there should be no distinction of classes."

【注释】

[1] 类：类别，这里可以理解为区分类别。具体类别为何，有多种理解：一种以身份贵贱的区别，如邢昺《注疏》云："此章言教人之法也。类谓种类。言人所在见教，无有贵贱种类也。"一种以人性善恶区别，如朱子《集注》云："人性皆善，而其类有善恶之殊者，气习之染也。故君子有教，则人皆可以复于善，而不当复论其类之恶矣。"

【原文】 15.40　子曰："道不同，不相为谋。"

【译文】孔子说："主张不同，不互相商议。"

【英译】The Master said，"Those whose courses are different cannot lay plans for one another."

【原文】15.41　子曰："辞，达而已矣！"

【译文】孔子说："言辞只要能表达意思就行了。"

【英译】The Master said，"In language it is simply required that it convey the meaning."

【原文】15.42　师冕[1]见。及阶，子曰："阶也！"及席，子曰："席也！"皆坐，子告之曰："某在斯！某在斯！"师冕出，子张问曰："与师言之道与?"子曰："然，固相[2]师之道也。"

【译文】乐师冕来见孔子，走到台阶沿，孔子说："这儿是台阶。"走到座席旁，孔子说："这是座席。"等大家都坐下来，孔子告诉他："某某在这里，某某在这里。"师冕走了以后，子张就问孔子："这就是与乐师谈话的方式吗?"孔子说："这就是帮助乐师的方式。"

【英译】The music master，Mien，having called upon him，when they came to the steps，the Master said，"Here are the steps." When they came to the mat for the guest to sit upon，he said，"Here is the mat." When all were seated，the master informed him，saying，"So and so is here；so and so is here." The music master，Mien，having gone out，Tsze-Chang asked，saying. "Is it the rule to tell those things to the music master?" The Master said，"Yes. This is certainly the rule for those who lead the blind."

【注释】

[1] 师冕：乐师，这位乐师的名字是冕。古代乐官一般用瞎子充当。

[2] 相：帮助。理雅格将该句译为"This is certainly the rule for those

who lead the blind",即"这当然是引导盲人的规则","相"即"引导、引领"。辜鸿铭译为"That is certainly the way to behave to blind people",即"这当然是对待盲人的方式","相"即"对待"之义。刘殿爵译为"assist a musician"、韦利译为"help a Music master","相"即"帮助"之义。刘殿爵与韦利译本相较,assist 表示协助某人做某事,尤指在体力上或具体事务上帮助和扶持,强调的则是在提供帮助时,所给的帮助只能起从属作用;help 的使用场景则更通俗,强调主动应别人所需要地帮助。由此可见,此处将"相"译为"help"更为恰当。

季氏篇第十六

【原文】16.1 季氏将伐颛臾[1]。冉有、子路见于孔子，曰："季氏将有事[2]于颛臾。"孔子曰："求，无乃尔是过与？夫颛臾，昔者先王以为东蒙主[3]，且在邦域之中矣，是社稷之臣也，何以伐为？"冉有曰："夫子欲之；吾二臣者，皆不欲也。"孔子曰："求！周任[4]有言曰：'陈力就列[5]，不能者止。'危而不持，颠而不扶，则将焉用彼相[6]矣？且尔言过矣！虎兕[7]出于柙[8]，龟玉毁于椟中，是谁之过与？"冉有曰："今夫颛臾，固而近于费；今不取，后世必为子孙忧。"孔子曰："求！君子疾夫舍曰'欲之'而必为之辞。丘也，闻有国有家者不患寡而患不均，不患贫而患不安；盖均无贫，和无寡，安无倾。夫如是，故远人不服，则修文德以来之。既来之，则安之。今由与求也，相夫子，远人不服而不能来也，邦分崩离析，而不能守也，而谋动干戈于邦内，吾恐季孙之忧，不在颛臾，而在萧墙[9]之内也！"

【译文】季氏将要讨伐颛臾。冉有、子路去见孔子说："季氏快要攻打颛臾了。"孔子说："冉求，这不就是你的过错吗？颛臾从前是周天子让它主持东蒙的祭祀的，而且已经在鲁国的疆域之内，是国家的臣属，为什么要讨伐它呢？"冉有说："季孙大夫想去攻打，我们两个人都不愿意。"孔子说："冉求，周任有句话说：'尽自己的力量去负担你的职务，实在做不好就辞职。'有了危险不去扶助，跌倒了不去搀扶，那还用辅助的人干什么呢？而且你说的话错了。老虎、犀牛从笼子里跑出来，龟甲、玉器在匣子里毁坏了，这是谁的过错呢？"冉有说："现在颛臾城墙坚固，而且离费邑很近。现在不把它夺取过来，将来一定会成为子孙的忧患。"孔子说："冉求，君子痛恨那种不肯实说自己想要那样做而又一定要找出理由来为之辩解的做法。我听说，诸侯和大夫不怕贫穷，而怕财富不均；不怕人口少，而怕不安定。财富均衡了，也就没有所谓贫穷；大家和睦了，就不会感到人少；安定了，也就没有倾覆的危险了。因为这样，所以如果远方的人还不归服，就用仁、义、礼、乐招徕他们；已经来了，就让他们安心住下去。现在，仲由和冉求你们两个人辅助季氏，远方的人不归服，而不能招徕他们；国内民心离散，你们不能保全，反而策划在国内使用武力。我只怕季孙的忧患不在颛臾，而是在自己的内部呢！"

【英译】The head of the Chi family was going to attack Chwan-Yu. Zan Yu and Chi-lu had an interview with Confucius, and said, "Our chief, Chil is going to commence operations against Chwan-Yu." Confucius said, "Ch'iu, is it not you who are in fault here? Now, in regard to Chwan-Yu, long ago, a former king appointed its ruler to preside over the sacrifices to the eastern mang; moreover, it is in the midst of the territory of our state; and its ruler is a minister in direct connection with the sovereign: what has your chief to do with attacking it?" Zan Yu said, "Our master wishes the thing; neither of us two ministers wishes it." Confucius said, "Ch'iu, there are the words of Chau Zan, 'When he can put forth his ability, he takes his place in the ranks of office; when he finds himself unable to do so, he retires from it.' How can he be used as a guide to a blind man, who does not support him when tottering, nor raise him up when fallen? And further, you speak wrongly. When a tiger or rhinoceros escapes from his cage; when a tortoise or piece of jade is injured in its repository:

whose is the fault?" Zan Yu said, "But at present, Chwan-Yu is strong and near to Pi; if our chief do not now take it, it will hereafter be a sorrow to his descendants." Confucius said. "Ch'iu, the superior man hates those declining to say 'I want such and such a thing,' and framing explanations for their conduct. I have heard that rulers of states and chiefs of families are not troubled lest their people should be few, but are troubled lest they should not keep their several places; that they are not troubled with fears of poverty, but are troubled with fears of a want of contented repose among the people in their several places. For when the people keep their several places, there will be no poverty; when harmony prevails, there will be no scarcity of people; and when there is such a contented repose, there will be no rebellious upsetting. So it is. Therefore, if remoter people are not submissive, all the influences of civil culture and virtue are to be cultivated to attract them to be so; and when they have been so attracted, they must be made contented and tranquil. Now, here are you, Yu and Ch'iu, assisting your chief. Remoter people are not submissive, and, with your help, he cannot attract them to him. In his own territory there are divisions and downfalls, leavings and separations, and, with your help, he cannot preserve it. And yet he is planning these hostile movements within the state. I am afraid that the sorrow of the Chi-Sun family will not be on account of Chwan-Yu, but will be found within the screen of their own court."

【注释】

[1] 颛臾：鲁国的附属国，在今山东省费县西。

[2] 有事：指有军事行动，用兵作战。理雅格译为"going to commence operations against"、刘殿爵译为"Take action against"，均指季氏将对颛臾

"有所行动"。辜鸿铭此处译为"preparing to commence hostilities against a small principality",即季氏"准备对一个小公国开战"。

[3] 东蒙主：东蒙，蒙山。主，主持祭祀的人。

[4] 周任：人名，周代史官。

[5] 陈力就列：陈力，发挥能力，按才力担任适当的职务。理雅格将这句话译为"When he can put forth his ability, he takes his place in the ranks of office",即"能施展才能，就能在官位上谋得一席之地"。辜鸿铭则是从战争的角度，译为"Let those who can stand the fight fall into the ranks",即"让那些经得起战斗的人加入队伍"。刘殿爵译为"displaying your strength you join the ranks",即"加入队伍，展示你的力量"

[6] 相：搀扶盲人的人叫相，这里是辅助的意思。理雅格、辜鸿铭均译为"as a guide to a blind man",即"给盲人领路"。刘殿爵将"相"译为"assistant",指协助盲人的人。

[7] 兕：雌性犀牛。

[8] 柙：用以关押野兽的木笼。

[9] 萧墙：照壁屏风。此处指宫廷之内。理雅格直译为"The screen of their own court",即"宫廷屏风";辜鸿铭、刘殿爵将其译为"宫墙",即"The walls of your master's own palace";韦利译为"The screen wall of his own gate",即"大门旁边的影壁"。

【原文】16.2 孔子曰："天下有道，则礼乐征伐[1]自天子出；天下无道，则礼乐征伐自诸侯出。自诸侯出，盖十世希不失矣；自大夫出，五世希不失矣；陪臣执国命，三世希不失矣。天下有道，则政不在大夫。天下有道，则庶人不议。"

【译文】孔子说："天下有道的时候，制作礼乐和出兵打仗都由天子作主决定；天下无道的时候，制作礼乐和出兵打仗，由诸侯作主决定。由诸侯作主决定，大概经过十代很少有不败亡的；由大夫决定，经过五代很少有不败亡的。天下有道，国家政权就不会落在大夫手中。天下有道，老百姓也就不会议论国家政治了。"

【英译】Confucius said，"When good government prevails in the empire，ceremonies，music，and punitive military expeditions proceed from the son of heaven. When bad government prevails in the empire，ceremonies，music，and punitive military expeditions proceed from the princes. When these things proceed from the princes，as a rule，the cases will be few in which they do not lose their power in ten generations. When they proceed from the great officers of the princes，as a rule，the case will be few in which they do not lose their power in five generations. When the subsidiary ministers of the great officers hold in their grasp the orders of the state，as a rule the cases will be few in which they do not lose their power in three generations. When right principles prevail in the kingdom，government will not be in the hands of the great officers. "When right principles prevail in the kingdom，there will be no discussions among the common people."

【注释】

[1] 礼乐征伐：指制礼作乐与征伐作战。理雅格将其译为"good government prevails in the empire，ceremonies，music，and punitive military expeditions"，即"良好的政治、仪式、音乐、惩罚性的军事远征"。辜鸿铭译为"religion，education，and declaration of war"，即"宗教、教育、战争"。刘殿爵、韦利译为"the rites and music and punitive expeditions"，即"仪式、音乐和惩罚性的远征"，该本翻译较为恰当。

【原文】16.3 孔子曰："禄之去公室，五世[1]矣；政逮于大夫，四世[2]矣；故夫三桓[3]之子孙微矣。"

【译文】孔子说："鲁国失去国家政权已经有五代了，政权落在大夫之手已经四代了，所以三桓的子孙也衰微了。"

【英译】Confucius said，"The revenue of the state has left the ducal house now for five generations. The government has been in the hands of the great officers for four generations. On this account，the descendants of the three Hwan are much reduced."

【注释】

[1] 五世：指鲁国宣公、成公、襄公、昭公、定公五世。

[2] 四世：指季孙氏文子、武子、平子、桓子四世。

[3] 三桓：鲁国伸孙、叔孙、季孙都出于鲁桓公，所以叫三桓。

【原文】16.4　孔子曰："益者三友，损者三友；友直，友谅[1]，友多闻，益矣。友便辟[2]，友善柔[3]，友便佞[4]，损矣。"

【译文】孔子说："有益的交友有三种，有害的交友有三种。同正直的人交友，同诚信的人交友，同见闻广博的人交友，这是有益的。同惯于走邪道的人交朋友，同善于阿谀奉承的人交朋友，同惯于花言巧语的人交朋友，这是有害的。"

【英译】Confucius said，"There are three friendships which are advantageous，and three which are injurious. Friendship with the upright；friendship with the trustworthy；and friendship with the man of much observation：these are advantageous. Friendship with the man of specious airs；friendship with the insinuatingly soft；and friendship with the glib-tongued：these are injurious."

【注释】

[1] 谅：诚信。理雅格译为"sincere"，即"真诚"；辜鸿铭译为"faithful"，即"忠诚的"；刘殿爵译为"trustworthy"，形容那些"值得信赖"的益友；韦利译为"true-to-death"，形容那些"至死不渝"的友情。"谅"即诚实守信，可引申为"值得信赖"，刘殿爵之译较为恰当。

[2] 便辟：惯于走邪道。理雅格将该句译为"friendship with the man of specious airs"，即"与装腔作势的人交朋友"；辜鸿铭译为"plausible"，形容那些"似是而非"的朋友；刘殿爵译为"ingratiatiating in action"，形容行为谄媚的损友；韦利译为"obsequious"，形容损友是"奉承的、顺从的"。

[3] 善柔：善于和颜悦色骗人。理雅格译为"The insinuatingly soft"，形容有的损友带有"谄媚的温柔"；辜鸿铭译为"insinuating manners"，形容损友"行为谄媚"。刘殿爵译为"Who are good at accommodating their principles"，形容那些"善于适应自己原则"的损友。"善柔"形容损友的行为是谄媚附和的，此处辜鸿铭与理雅格的翻译更为恰当。

[4] 便佞：惯于花言巧语。理雅格、辜鸿铭译为"glib-tongued"，即"巧舌如簧的"；刘殿爵将"善柔"与"便佞"译为"the pleasant in appearance and the plausible in speech"，形容一个人"外表赏心悦目，言语似是而非"；韦利译为"Who are clever at talk"，形容损友是擅长讲话、巧言令色的。

【原文】16.5　孔子曰："益者三乐，损者三乐。乐节礼乐[1]，乐道人之善，乐多贤友，益矣。乐骄乐[2]，乐佚[3]游，乐宴乐[4]，损矣。"

【译文】孔子说："有益的喜好有三种，有害的喜好有三种。以得到礼乐的调节为快乐，以称道别人的好处为快乐，以有许多贤德之友为快乐，这是有益的。喜好骄傲，喜欢闲游，喜欢宴饮享乐，这就是有害的。"

【英译】Confucius said, "There are three things men find enjoyment in which are advantageous, and three things they find enjoyment in which are injurious. To find enjoyment in the correct regulation of the rites and music；to find enjoyment in speaking of the goodness of others；to find enjoyment in having many worthy friends：-these are advantageous. To find enjoyment in extravagant pleasures；to find enjoyment in idleness and sauntering; to find enjoyment in the pleasures of feasting: these are injurious."

【注释】

[1] 节礼乐：孔子主张用礼乐来节制人。理雅格译为 "discriminating study of ceremonies and music"，即 "仪式和音乐的辨别性研究"。辜鸿铭译为 "The study and criticism of the polite arts"，即 "对礼乐的研究和批评"。刘殿爵译为 "take pleasure in the correct regulation of the rites and music"，即 "在正确的礼乐规范中感到快乐"，该翻译较为恰当。

[2] 骄乐：骄纵不知节制的乐。理雅格译为 "extravagant pleasures"，即 "奢侈的享乐"；辜鸿铭译为 "pleasure in dissipation"，即 "放荡的乐趣"；刘殿爵译为 "showing off"，"骄乐" 即形容人是 "骄傲、爱炫耀的"。此处形容骄傲放纵、不加以自我约束的取乐，理雅格的翻译更为恰当。

[3] 佚：同 "逸"。理雅格将其译为 "idleness and sauntering"，即 "闲散、闲逛"；辜鸿铭译为 "extravagance"，形容人处在 "过分的奢侈" 之中；刘殿爵译为 "In a dissolute life"，即 "在放荡的生活中"。"逸" 形容人游荡无度，上述译本相较，理雅格的翻译更为具体，刘殿爵则是将 "游荡无度" 引申为生活放纵、无所事事。

[4] 晏乐：沉溺于宴饮取乐。理雅格译为 "The pleasures of feasting"，即 "盛宴中的乐趣"。辜鸿铭将 "晏乐" 译为 "in mere conviviality"，即 "只是在欢宴中"，conviviality 有 "宴乐、宴饮交际" 之义。刘殿爵译为 "in food and drink is to lose"，意指 "在吃吃喝喝中失去自我" 是有害的快乐。

【原文】 16.6 孔子曰："侍于君子有三愆[1]：言未及之而言，谓之躁；言及之而不言，谓之隐；未见颜色而言，谓之瞽[2]。"

【译文】 孔子说："侍奉在君子旁边陪他说话，要注意避免犯三种过失：还没有问到你的时候就说话，这是急躁；已经问到你的时候你却不说，这叫隐瞒；不看君子的脸色而贸然说话；这是瞎子。"

【英译】Confucius said, "There are three errors to which they who stand in the presence of a man of virtue and station are liable. They may speak when it does not come to them to speak; this is called rashness. They may not speak when it comes to them to speak; this is called concealment. They may speak without looking at the countenance of their superior; -this is called blindness."

【注释】

[1] 愆：过失。

[2] 瞽：盲人。

【原文】16.7　孔子曰："君子有三戒；少之时，血气未定，戒之在色；及其壮也，血气方刚，戒之在斗；及其老也，血气既衰，戒之在得[1]。"

【译文】孔子说："君子有三种事情应引以为戒：年少的时候，血气还不成熟，要戒除对女色的迷恋；等到身体成熟了，血气方刚，要戒除与人争斗；等到老年，血气已经衰弱了，要戒除贪得无厌。"

【英译】Confucius said, "There are three things which the superior man guards against. In youth, when the physical powers are not yet settled, he guards against lust. When he is strong and the physical powers are full of vigor, he guards against quarrelsomeness. When he is old, and the animal powers are decayed, he guards against covetousness."

【注释】

[1] 得：贪得无厌。理雅格译为"covetousness"，形容人应该戒除自己的"贪婪"之心；韦利译为"avarice"，即"贪财、贪婪"；辜鸿铭译为"greed"，同样为"贪婪"之义。刘殿爵译为"acquisitiveness"，指人到老年要戒除自己的"占有欲"。Greed 最常用于描述物产等其他财产，avarice

则只与财富（金钱）有关。指人的安羡、贪婪之心。我们认为，此处译为avarice 较为恰当。

【原文】16.8　孔子曰："君子有三畏[1]：畏天命，畏大人[2]，畏圣人之言。小人不知天命而不畏也，狎大人，侮圣人之言。"

【译文】孔子说："君子有三件敬畏的事情：敬畏天命，敬畏地位高贵的人，敬畏圣人的话。小人不懂得天命，因而不敬畏，不尊重地位高贵的人，轻侮圣人之言。"

【英译】Confucius said，"There are three things of which the superior man stands inawe. He stands in awe of the ordinances of heaven. He stands in awe of great men. He stands in awe of the words of sages. The mean man does not know the ordinances of heaven，and consequently does not stand in awe of them. He is disrespectful to great men. He makes sport of the words of sages."

【注释】

[1] 畏：敬畏。理雅格、刘殿爵译为"in awe of"，即"尊敬、敬畏"；韦利译为"fears"，即"害怕、畏惧"。《论语》此处之"畏"指的是对某事保持敬畏，译为 awe 更为恰当。

[2] 大人：这里指品格高尚、地位高贵的人。理雅格、刘殿爵、韦利译为"great men"，即"伟大的人"；辜鸿铭译为"persons in authority"，指那些"有权威的人"。儒家所言之"大人"侧重人格的伟大高尚，并不仅是权势地位的崇高，因此译为 great men 较为恰当。

【原文】16.9　孔子曰："生而知之者，上也；学而知之者，次也；困而学之，又其次也。困而不学，民斯为下矣！"

【译文】孔子说："生来就知道的人，是上等人；经过学习以后才知道的，是次一等的人；遇到困难再去学习的，是又次一等的人；遇到困难还不学习的人，这种人就是下等的人了。"

【英译】Confucius said，"Those who are born with the possession of knowledge are the highest class of men. Those who learn，and so readily get possession of knowledge，are the next. Those who are dull and stupid，and yet compass the learning，are another class next to these. As to those who are dull and stupid and yet do not learn；-they are the lowest of the people."

【原文】16.10　孔子曰："君子有九思：视思明，听思聪，色思温，貌思恭，言思忠，事思敬[1]，疑思问，忿思难，见得思义[2]。"

【译文】孔子说："君子有九种要思考的事：看的时候，要思考看清与否；听的时候，要思考是否听清楚；自己的脸色，要思考是否温和，容貌要思考是否谦恭；言谈的时候，要思考是否忠诚；办事时，要思考是否谨慎严肃；遇到疑问，要思考是否应该向别人询问；忿怒时，要思考是否有后患；获取财利时，要思考是否合乎义。"

【英译】Confucius said，"The superior man has nine things which are subjects with him of thoughtful consideration. In regard to the use of his eyes，he is anxious to see clearly. In regard to the use of his ears，he is anxious to hear distinctly. In regard to his countenance，he is anxious that it should be benign. In regard to his demeanor，he is anxious that it should be respectful. In regard to his speech，he is anxious that it should be sincere. In regard to his doing of business，he is anxious that it should be reverently careful. In regard to what he doubts about，he is anxious to question others. When he is angry，he thinks of the difficulties his anger may involve him in. When he sees gain to begot，he thinks of righteousness."

【注释】

[1] 敬：理雅格、刘殿爵、韦利译为"respectful"，即"尊重"；辜鸿铭译为"serious"，形容做事时要思考是否"严肃认真"。孔子曾言："居处恭，执事敬，与人忠。"做事时的"敬"，是指态度和行为严肃认真，译为 serious 更为恰当。

[2] 义：理雅格译为"righteousness"，即"正义、正直"；辜鸿铭、刘殿爵译为"What is right"，指君子在获得财富时要考虑"什么是正确的"；韦利译为"be consonant with the Right"，即"与正确行为保持一致"。

【原文】 16.11　子曰："见善如不及，见不善如探汤[1]。吾见其人矣，吾闻其语矣。隐居以求其志，行义以达其道。吾闻其语矣，未见其人也。"

【译文】 孔子说："看到善良的行为，就担心达不到，看到不善良的行动，就好像把手伸到开水中一样赶快避开。我见到过这样的人，也听到过这样的话。以隐居避世来保全自己的志向，依照义来贯彻自己的主张。我听到过这种话，却没有见到过这样的人。"

【英译】 Confucius said，"Contemplating well，and pursuing it，as if they could not reach it；contemplating evil！And shrinking from it，as they would from thrusting the hand into boiling water：I have seen such men，as I have heard such words. Living in retirement to study their aims，and practicing righteousness to carry out their principles：I have heard these words，but I have not seen such men."

【注释】

[1] 探汤：把手伸到开水中，"见不善如探汤"形容心中规避不善行为的迫切感就如同躲避沸水一般。

【原文】 16.12　"齐景公有马千驷，死之日，民无德而称焉；

伯夷、叔齐饿于首阳之下，民到于今称之。其斯之谓与?”

【译文】齐景公有马四千匹，死的时候，百姓们觉得他没有什么德行可以称颂。伯夷、叔齐饿死在首阳山下，百姓们到现在还在称颂他们。说的就是这个意思吧。

【英译】"The duke Ching of Ch'i had a thousand teams，each of four horses，but on the day of his death，the people did not praise him for a single virtue. Po-I and Shu-Ch'i died of hunger at the foot of the Shau-Yang mountains，and the people，down to the present time，praise them. Is not that saying illustrated by this?"

【原文】16.13 陈亢[1]问于伯鱼曰:"子亦有异闻[2]乎?"对曰:"未也。尝独立，鲤趋而过庭。曰:'学《诗》乎?'对曰:'未也'。'不学《诗》，无以言。'鲤退而学《诗》。他日又独立，鲤趋而过庭。曰:'学礼乎?'对曰:'未也'。'不学礼，无以立。'鲤退而学礼。闻斯二者。"陈亢退而喜曰:"问一得三。闻诗，闻礼，又闻君子之远[3]其子也。"

【译文】陈亢问伯鱼:"你在老师那里听到过什么特别的教诲吗?"伯鱼回答说:"没有呀。有一次他独自站在堂上，我快步从庭中走过，他说:'学《诗》了吗?'我回答说:'没有。'他说:'不学《诗》，就不懂得怎么说话。'我回去就学《诗》。又有一天，他又独自站在堂上，我快步从庭中走过，他说:'学礼了吗?'我回答说:'没有。'他说:'不学礼就不懂得怎样立身。'我回去就学礼。我就听到过这两件事。"陈亢回去高兴地说:"我提一个问题，得到三方面的收获，听了关于《诗》的道理，听了关于礼的道理，又听了君子不偏爱自己儿子的道理。"

【英译】Ch'an K'ang asked Po-Yu，saying，"Have you heard any lessons from your father different from what we have all heard?" Po-Yu replied，"No. He was standing alone once，when I passed below the hall with hasty steps，and said to me，'have you learned the odes?' On my replying 'not yet,' he added，'If you do not learn the odes，you will not be fit to converse with.' I retired and studied the odes. Another day，he was in the same way standing alone，when I passed by below the hall with hasty steps，and said to me，'Have you learned the rules of propriety?' On my replying 'not yet,' he added，'If you do not learn the rules of propriety，your character cannot be established.' I then retired，and learned the rules of propriety. I have heard only these two things from him." Ch'ang K'ang retired，and，quite delighted，said，"I asked one thing，and I have got three things. I have heard about the odes. I have heard about the rules of propriety. I have also heard that the superior man maintains a distant reserve towards his son."

【注释】

[1] 陈亢：即陈子禽。

[2] 异闻：这里指不同于对其他学生所讲的内容。

[3] 远：不亲近，不偏爱。理雅格将该句译为"the superior man maintains a distant reserve towards his son"，刘殿爵将该句译为"a gentleman keeps his distance from his son"，均形容"圣人对他的儿子保持着距离感"。辜鸿铭译为"a wise and good man does not treat even his own son with familiarity"，即"一个聪明而善良的人，甚至对自己的儿子也不会过于亲昵"。上述译本相较，辜鸿铭的翻译更为恰当。

【原文】16.14　邦君子之妻，君称之曰"夫人"，夫人自称"小童"；邦人称之曰"君夫人"，称诸异邦曰"寡小君"；异邦人称之，亦曰"君夫人"。[1]

【译文】国君的妻子，国君称她为夫人，夫人自称为小童；国人称她为君夫人，但对外国人则称她为寡小君，外国人也称她为君夫人。

【英译】The wife of the prince of a state is called by him Fu Zan. She calls herself Hsiao T'ung. The people of the state call her Chun Fu Zan, and, to the people of other states, they call her K'wa Hsiao Chun. The people of other states also call her Chun Fu Zan.

【注释】

[1] 这套称号是周礼的内容之一。这是为了维护等级名分制度，以达到"名正言顺"的目的。对于上述名号，理雅格均采取音译，将其译为"Hsiao t'ung""chun fu zan"等。辜鸿铭采用意译方法，将上述名号分别译为"Madame""Sire""Our good little princess"。刘殿爵译为"lady""little boy""The lady of the lord"等。对于本章的含义，刘殿爵在注释中补充说明："This is probably a ritual text which was copied into the blank space at the end of this scroll, and has nothing to do with the rest of the book." 其认为本章为一段礼乐仪式的具体文本，被抄写在卷轴末尾的空白处，与书的其余部分没有任何关系。

阳货篇第十七

【原文】17.1　阳货[1]欲见孔子，孔子不见，归孔子豚[2]。孔子时其亡[3]也，而往拜之。遇诸涂[4]。谓孔子曰："来！予与尔言。"曰："怀其宝而迷其邦[5]，可谓仁乎？"曰："不可。""好从事而亟失时，可谓知乎？"曰："不可。""日月逝矣！岁不我与[6]！"孔子曰："诺，吾将仕矣！"

【译文】阳货想见孔子，孔子不见，他便赠送给孔子一只熟小猪，想要孔子去拜见他。孔子打听到阳货不在家时，往阳货家拜谢，却在半路上遇见了。阳货对孔子说："来，我有话要跟你说。"（孔子走过去）阳货说："把自己的本领藏起来而听任国家迷乱，这可以叫作仁吗？"孔子回答说："不可以。"阳货说："喜欢参与政事而又屡次错过机会，这可以说是智吗？"孔子回答说："不可以。"阳货说："时间一天天过去了，年岁是不等人的。"孔子说："好吧，我打算做官了。"

【英译】Yang Ho wished to see Confucius, but Confucius would not go to see him. On this, he sent a present of a pig to Confucius, who, having chosen a time when how as not at home went to pay his respects for the gift. He met him, however, on the way. Ho said to Confucius, "Come, let me speak with you." He then asked, "Can he be called benevolent who keeps his jewel in his bosom, and leaves his country to confusion?" Confucius replied, "No." "Can he be called wise, who is anxious to be engaged in public employment, and yet is constantly losing the opportunity of being so?" Confucius again said, "No." "The days and months are passing away; the years do not wait for us." Confucius said, "Right; I will go into office."

【注释】

[1] 阳货：又叫阳虎，季氏的家臣。

[2] 归孔子豚：归，赠送。豚，小猪。

[3] 时其亡：等他外出的时候。理雅格译为"having chosen a time when how as not at home"；辜鸿铭译为"When the officer was not at home"，即"等他不在家的时候"；刘殿爵译为"Went to pay his respects during his absence"，即"在他不在的时候去致谢"；韦利译为"choosing a time when he knew Yang Huo would not be at home"，即"选择了一个阳虎不在家的时间"。

[4] 遇诸涂：涂，同"途"，道路。在路上遇到了他。

[5] 迷其邦：听任国家迷乱。理雅格译为"leaves his country to confusion"，即"让自己的国家陷入混乱"；辜鸿铭译为"leaves his country to go astray"，形容人"让自己的国家误入歧途"，"迷"是指人的迷失；刘殿爵译为"allows the state to go astray"，形容人"让自己的国家走上邪路"；韦利译为"lets his country continue to go astray"，即"让他的国家走入歧途"。上述译本相较，confusion 侧重强调国家局面的政治混乱，go astray 则强调走错路、误入歧途。"迷"这里为使动用法，意为"使自己的国家迷失"，即迷路、走上邪路。

[6] 与：等待的意思。

【原文】 17.2　子曰："性相近也，习[1]相远也。"

【译文】 孔子说："人的本性是相近的，由于习染不同才相互有了差别。"

【英译】 The Master said, "By nature, men are nearly alike; by practice, they get to be wide apart."

【注释】

[1] 习：理雅格、辜鸿铭、韦利将"习"译为"practice"，即"练习、习染"；刘殿爵译为"behaviour that is constantly repeated"，指后天那些"不断重复的行为"。我们认为，这里"习"更多指后天的行为习惯、习染，译为 practice 较为恰当。

【原文】 17.3　子曰："唯上知[1]与下愚[2]，不移。"

【译文】 孔子说："只有上等的智者与下等的愚者是改变不了的。"

【英译】 The Master said，"There are only the wise of the highest class，and people of the grossest dullness，who cannot be changed."

【注释】

[1] 上知：理雅格译为"the wise of the highest class"、韦利译为"the very wisest"，形容那些"最具智慧的人"；辜鸿铭译为"men of the highest understanding"，"上知"即指那些理解能力最高的人；刘殿爵译为"the most intelligent"，即"最聪明的"。intelligent 指在理解新的、抽象东西或处理解决问题时，智力超过一般常人。wise 侧重不是一般的聪明伶俐，而是有远见，有智慧，能明智地处理问题。可指某人的头脑灵活或做某事的正确性，意味着具有广博知识和丰富的经验。《论语》此处不仅指理解能力的"聪明"，而是形容人有远见、有智慧，译为 wise 更为恰当。

[2] 下愚：理雅格译为"the stupid of the lowest class"，指"最底层的愚昧之人"；辜鸿铭译为"men of the grossest dullness"，指那些最为鲁钝的人；刘殿爵译为"the most stupid"、韦利译为"the very stupidest"，均为"最愚钝的"。我们认为，此处译为 men of the grossest dullness 较为恰当。

【原文】 17.4　子之武城[1]，闻弦歌[2]之声，夫子莞尔而笑曰："割鸡焉用牛刀?"子游对曰："昔者，偃也闻诸夫子曰：'君子学道则爱人，小人学道则易使也。'"子曰："二三子! 偃之言是也，前言戏之耳^[3]！"

【译文】孔子到武城，听见弹琴唱歌的声音。孔子微笑着说："杀鸡何必用宰牛的刀呢？"子游回答说："以前我听先生说过，'君子学习了礼乐就能爱人，小人学习了礼乐就容易指使。'"孔子说："学生们，言偃的话是对的，我刚才说的话，只是开个玩笑而已。"

【英译】The Master，having come to Wu-Ch'ang，heard there the sound of stringed instruments and singing. Well pleased and smiling，he said，"Why use an ox knife to kill a fowl?"Tsze-yu replied，"Formerly，master，I heard you say，-'When the man of high station is well instructed，he loves men；when the man of low station is well instructed，he is easily ruled.'"The Master said，"My disciples，yen's words are right. What I said was only in sport."

【注释】

[1] 武城：鲁国的一个小城，当时子游是武城宰。

[2] 弦歌：弦，指琴瑟。以琴瑟伴奏歌唱。

[3] 前言戏之耳："之"指子游，这句话有褒奖子游的意思。朱子《集注》云："嘉子游之笃信，又以解门人之惑也。治有大小，而其治之必用礼乐，则其为道一也。但众人多不能用，而子游独行之。故夫子骤闻深喜之，因反其言以戏之。而子游以正对，故复是其言，而自实其戏也。"

【原文】17.5　公山弗扰^[1]以费畔，召，子欲往。子路不说，曰："末之也已^[2]，何必公山民之之也？"子曰："夫召我者，而岂徒^[3]哉？如有用我者，吾其为东周乎！^[4]"

【译文】公山弗扰据费邑反叛，来召孔子，孔子准备前去。子路不高兴地说："没有地方去就算了，为什么一定要去公山弗扰那里呢？"孔子说："他来召我，难道只是一句空话吗？如果有人用我，我就要在东方复兴周礼，建设一个东方的西周。"

【英译】Kung-Shan Fu-Zao，when he was holding Pi，and in an attitude of rebellion，invited the master to visit him，who was rather inclined to go. Tsze-Lu was displeased. And said，"Indeed，you cannot go！Why must you think of going to see Kung-Shan？"The Master said，"Can it be without some reason that he has invited me？If any one employs me，may I not make an eastern Chau？"

【注释】

[1] 公山弗扰：人名，又称公山不狃，字子洩，季氏的家臣。

[2] 末之也已：末，无。之，到、往。末之，无处去。已，止，算了。

[3] 徒：徒然，空无所据。

[4] 吾其为东周乎：为东周，建造一个东方的周王朝，在东方复兴周礼。两种理解皆见于皇侃《义疏》："云如有云云者，若必不空，然而用我时则我当为兴周道也。路在东，周在西，云东周者，欲于鲁而兴周道，故云吾其为东周也。一云：周室东迁洛阳，故曰东周。王弼曰：言如能用我者，不择地而兴周室道也。"朱子同第一说："为东周，言兴周道于东方。程子曰：'圣人以天下无不可有为之人，亦无不可改过之人，故欲往。然而终不往者，知其必不能改故也。'"

【原文】17.6　子张问仁于孔子。孔子曰："能行五者于天下，为仁矣。""请问之？"曰："恭、宽、信、敏、惠。恭[1]则不侮，宽[2]则得众，信[3]则人任焉，敏[4]则有功，惠[5]则足以使人。"

【译文】子张向孔子问仁。孔子说："能够处处实行五种品德，就是仁人了。"子张说："请问哪五种？"孔子说："庄重、宽厚、诚实、勤敏、慈惠。庄重就不致遭受侮辱，宽厚就会得到众人的拥护，诚信就能得到别人的任用，勤敏就会提高工作效率，慈惠就能够役使他人。"

【英译】Tsze-Chang asked Confucius about perfect virtue. Confucius said，"To be able to practice five things everywhere under heaven constitutes perfect virtue." He begged to ask what they were, and was told, "Respectful, tolerant of soul, trustful, earnestness, and benevolence. If you are respectful, you will not be treated with disrespect. If you are tolerant, you will win all. If you are trustworthy, people will repose trust in you. If you are earnest, you will accomplish much. If you are benevolent, this will enable you to employ the services of others."

【注释】

[1] 恭：恭敬持重。理雅格译为"grave"，即"严肃的"；辜鸿铭译为"earnest"，形容仁人是"认真的"；刘殿爵译为"respectful"，形容仁者是有礼有节的。此处刘殿爵的翻译更为恰当。

[2] 宽：宽厚容众。理雅格译为"generous"，即"慷慨大方的"；辜鸿铭译为"considerate to others"，"宽"即"为他人着想"；刘殿爵译为"tolerant"，即"宽容的"，该译文较为恰当。

[3] 信：诚实有信。理雅格译为"sincere"，即"真诚的"；辜鸿铭、刘殿爵译为"trustworthy"，即"值得信赖的"，该翻译较为恰当。

[4] 敏：敏慧。理雅格译为"earnest"，形容做事认真会让人取得功绩；辜鸿铭译为"diligent"，"敏"即做事"勤奋努力"；刘殿爵将"敏"理解为"机敏、迅速"，译为"quick"。此处理雅格的翻译较为恰当。

[5] 惠：慈惠、对他人有恩惠。理雅格译为"kind"，即"善良可亲"的；辜鸿铭、刘殿爵译为"generous"形容仁者是"慷慨大方的"。"惠"形容仁者对他人的仁慈与惠爱，译为 benevolent 较为恰当。

【原文】 17.7 佛肸[1]召，子欲往。子路曰："昔者由也闻诸夫子曰：'亲于其身为不善者，君子不入也。'佛肸以中牟[2]畔，子之往也，如之何？"子曰："然，有是言也。不曰坚乎，磨而不磷；不曰白乎，涅[3]而不缁。吾岂匏瓜[4]也哉？焉能系而不食？"

【译文】佛肸召孔子去，孔子打算前往。子路说："从前我听先生说过：'亲自做坏事的人那里，君子是不去的。'现在佛肸据中牟反叛，你却要去，这如何解释呢？"孔子说："是的，我有过这样的话。不是说坚硬的东西磨也磨不坏吗？不是说洁白的东西染也染不黑吗？我难道是个苦味的葫芦吗？怎么能只挂在那里而不给人吃呢？"

【英译】Pi Hsi inviting him to visit him, the Master was inclined to go. Tsze-Lu said, "Master, formerly I have heard you say, 'When a man in his own person is guilty of doing evil, a superior man will not associate with him.' PiHsi is in rebellion, holding possession of Chung-Mau; if you go to him, what shall be said?" The Master said, "Yes, I did use these words. But is it not said, that, if a thing be really hard, it may be ground without being made thin? Is it not said, that, if a thing be really white, it may be steeped in a dark fluid without being made black? Am I a bitter gourd? How can I be hung up out of the way of being eaten?"

【注释】

[1] 佛肸：晋国大夫中牟的官长，是范氏的家臣。皇本、正平本作"胇肸"，下文同；定州竹简本作"佛腤"。据《史记·赵氏世家》记载，晋定公十八年，赵简子攻打中行氏和范氏，佛肸趁机以中牟为据点发动叛乱。清人崔述《洙泗考信录》认为佛肸叛变的时候，赵简子和孔子皆已不在世了。

[2] 中牟：地名，在晋国，约在今河北邢台与邯郸之间。

[3] 涅：一种矿物质，可用作颜料染衣服。

[4] 匏瓜：葫芦中的一种，味苦不能吃。

【原文】17.8　子曰："由也，女闻六言六蔽矣乎？"对曰："未也。""居，吾语女。好仁不好学，其蔽也愚；好知不好学，其蔽也荡[1]；好信不好学，其蔽也贼；好直不好学，其蔽也绞[2]；好勇不好学，其蔽也乱；好刚不好学，其蔽也狂。"

【译文】孔子说："由呀，你听说过六种品德和六种弊病了吗？"子路回答说："没有。"孔子说："坐下，我告诉你。爱好仁德而不爱好学习，它的弊病是受人愚弄；爱好智慧而不爱好学习，它的弊病是行为放荡；爱好诚信而不爱好学习，它的弊病是危害亲人；爱好直率却不爱好学习，它的弊病是说话尖刻；爱好勇敢却不爱好学习，它的弊病是犯上作乱；爱好刚强却不爱好学习，它的弊病是狂妄自大。"

【英译】The Master said，"Yu，have you heard the six words to which are attached six beclouding?" Yu replied，"I have not.""Sit down，and I will tell them to you. There is the love of being benevolent without the love of learning；-the beclouding herc leads to a foolish simplicity. There is the love of knowing without the love of learning；-the beclouding here leads to dissipation of mind. There is the love of being sincere without the love of learning；the beclouding here leads to an injurious disregard of consequences. There is the love of straightforwardness without the love of learning；the beclouding here leads to rudeness. There is the love of boldness without the love of learning；the beclouding here leads to insubordination. There is the love of firmness without the love of learning；-the beclouding here leads to extravagant conduct."

【注释】

[1] 荡：放荡。好高骛远而没有根基。理雅格将该句译为"the beclouding here leads to dissipation of mind"，"荡"指的是"心中摇荡"；辜鸿铭译为"dilettantism"，形容"好知不好学"会导致学习的"肤浅、浅薄"；刘殿爵认为，"荡"指的是偏离正确的道路，即"lead to straying from the right path"；韦利译为"lack of principle"，指好知不好学便会让人（因过分机

灵乖滑）而"缺乏原则和规矩"。此处孔安国将"荡"训为"无所适守"，朱熹解为"穷高极广而无所止"，二者皆有"摇荡不定"之义，因此我们认为此处从理雅格译本或译为"hitch one's wagon to a star"（好高骛远的）较为恰当。

[2] 绞：说话尖刻。理雅格将该句译为"The beclouding here leads to rudeness"，"荡"指的是行为上的"粗鲁无礼"；辜鸿铭译为"tyranny"，"绞"指那些"好直不好学"的人是"暴虐专横的"；刘殿爵译为"unrelenting"，形容一个人是"无情的"；韦利译为"harshness"，即"严厉的、粗糙的"。对此邢昺《注疏》认为"绞"即"讥刺太切"，意为儒者在坚持正义劝谏他人的时候也不应言辞过于激烈。由此我们认为韦利的翻译能形容人的言语是"严厉的"，较为恰当。

【原文】17.9　子曰："小子！何莫学夫《诗》？《诗》，可以兴[1]，可以观[2]，可以群[3]，可以怨[4]；迩之事父，远之事君；多识于鸟兽草木之名。"

【译文】孔子说："学生们为什么不学习《诗》呢？学《诗》可以激发志气，可以观察天地万物及人事的盛衰与得失，可以使人懂得合群的必要，可以使人懂得怎样去讽谏上级。近可以用来侍奉父母，远可以事奉君主，还可以多知道一些鸟兽草木的名字。"

【英译】The Master said, "My children, why do you not study the book of poetry? The odes serve to stimulate the mind. They may be used for purposes of self-contemplation. They teach the art of sociability. They show how to give expression to grievances. From them you learn the more immediate duty of serving one's father, and the remoter one of serving one's prince. From them we become largely acquainted with the names of birds, beasts, and plants."

【注释】

[1] 兴：激发感情。理雅格译为"stimulate the mind"，"兴"即"刺激、感发人的心灵"；辜鸿铭译为"calls out the sentiment"，即《诗经》能"唤起人的情感"；刘殿爵译为"stimulate the imagination"，即"激发想象力"。上述译本相较，辜鸿铭的翻译更为恰当。

[2] 观：观察了解风俗变化、政治得失。理雅格译为"be used for purposes of self-contemplation"，"观"即"自我沉思"；辜鸿铭译为"stimulates observation"，即"激发人的观察能力"；刘殿爵译为"endow one with breeding"，即"赋予人教养"。此处"观"更强调《诗经》能让人观察风俗人情、体察政治得失，译为"observe customs and state affairs"较为恰当。

[3] 群：合群。理雅格将"群"理解为"社交的艺术"，即"The art of sociability"；辜鸿铭译为"enlarges the sympathies"，"群"即"扩大人的同情心"；刘殿爵译为"enable one to live in a community"，即诗教能"让人群居、生活在同一个社群中"。孔安国解为"群居相切磋"，"群"指让人合群，能融入群居生活、融入共同体，可见理雅格的翻译较为恰当。

[4] 怨：讽谏上级。理雅格译为"feelings of resentment"，即《诗》能告诉人如何管理"怨恨的情感"；辜鸿铭译为"moderates the resentment felt against injustice"，指《诗》能缓解人对于不公正的怨恨情感；刘殿爵译为"give expression to grievances"，即"表达不满"。《论语》此处并非强调"管理"或"缓解"怨怼情感，而是指诗教能让人"怨而不怒"地表达怨刺、讽谏之义。对此我们认为，刘殿爵的翻译较为恰当。

【原文】 17.10　子谓伯鱼曰："女为《周南》《召南》[1]矣乎？人而不为《周南》《召南》，其犹正墙面而立[2]也与？"

【译文】 孔子对伯鱼说："你学习《周南》《召南》了吗？一个人如果不学习《周南》《召南》，那就像面对墙壁而站着吧？"

【英译】The Master said to Po-Yu, "Do you give yourself to the Chau-Nan and the Shao-Nan. The man who has not studied the Chau-Nan and the Shao-Nan is like one who stands with his face right against a wall. Is he not so?"

【注释】

[1]《周南》《召南》:《诗经·国风》中的第一、二两部分篇名。周南和召南都是地名。这是当地的民歌。

[2] 正墙面而立:面向墙壁站立着。

【原文】17.11　子曰:"礼云礼云,玉帛云乎哉? 乐云乐云,钟鼓云乎哉?"

【译文】孔子说:"礼呀礼呀,只是说的玉帛之类的礼器吗? 乐呀乐呀,只是说的钟鼓之类的乐器吗?"

【英译】The Master said, "'it is according to the rules of propriety,' they say. 'It is according to the rules of propriety,' they say. Are gems and silk all that is meant by propriety? 'It is music,' they say. 'it is music,' they say. Are bells and drums all that is meant by music?"

【原文】17.12　子曰:"色厉而内荏[1],譬诸小人,其犹穿窬[2]之盗也与!"

【译文】孔子说:"外表严厉而内心虚弱,以小人作比喻,就像是挖洞跳墙的小偷吧?"

【英译】The Master said, "He who puts on an appearance of stern firmness, while inwardly he is coward, is like one of the small, mean people; yea, is he not like the thief who breaks through, or climbs over, a wall?"

【注释】

[1] 色厉内荏：厉，威严，荏，虚弱。外表严厉而内心虚弱。理雅格将该句译为"an appearance of stern firmness，while inwardly he is weak"，形容一个人"外表严厉，内心软弱"。辜鸿铭译为"A man who is austere in his look，but a weakling and a coward at heart"，即"他外表严厉、内心软弱，是个懦夫。"刘殿爵译为"A cowardly man who puts on a brave front is"，即"一个懦弱的人装出勇敢的样子"。韦利译为"To assume an outward air of fierceness when inwardly trembling is"，即"当内心颤抖时，却装出一副凶狠的样子"。firmness 侧重"坚定"，austere 则强调人的严肃、严厉，brave 多用于形容一个人是"勇敢的"，fierceness 则侧重残暴的、无情的。此处"厉"旨在形容人的神色是严厉的、端肃的，理雅格的翻译较为恰当。辜鸿铭、刘殿爵将"荏"译为"coward"，即"胆小的、懦弱的"，trembling 形容内心因害怕而颤抖，weak 则指人是虚弱的，可见 coward 更为恰当。

[2] 窬：音 yú，洞，这里指墙洞。

【原文】 17.13 子曰："乡原[1]，德之贼也！"

【译文】孔子说："表里不一、媚时趋俗的伪君子，就是败坏道德的人。"

【英译】 The Master said，"Your good，careful people of the villages are the thieves of virtue."

【注释】

[1] 乡愿：表里不一、言行不一的伪君子。理雅格将"乡愿"译为"your good，careful people of the villages"，指乡里那些"善良却谨慎"的村民。辜鸿铭将"乡愿"译为"meek men"，即"温柔的人"，该译文没能体现出"乡愿"的贬义，不够恰当。刘殿爵译为"The village worthy"，指"乡村的价值"。韦利译为"honest villager"，即"诚实的村民"。乡愿指乡中貌似谨厚，而实与流俗合污的伪善者，译为"A man who seems virtuous，but is in

fact complicit"较为恰当。

【原文】17.14　子曰："道听而途说，德之弃也！"

【译文】孔子说："在路上听到传言就到处去传播，这是道德所唾弃的。"

【英译】The Master said，"To tell，as we go along，what we have heard on the way，is to cast away our virtue."

【原文】17.15　子曰："鄙夫，可与事君也与哉！其未得之也，患得之；既得之，患失之；苟患失之，无所不至矣！"

【译文】孔子说："可以和一个鄙夫一起事奉君主吗？他在没有得到官位时，总担心得不到。已经得到了，又怕失去它。如果他担心失掉官职，那他就什么事都干得出来了。"

【英译】The Master said，"There are those mean creatures！How impossible it is along with them to serve one's prince！While they have not got their aims，their anxiety is how to get them. When they have got them，their anxiety is lest they should lose them. When they are anxious lest such things should be lost，there is nothing to which they will not proceed."

【原文】17.16　子曰："古者民有三疾，今也或是之亡也。古之狂[1]也肆[2]，今之狂也荡[3]；古之矜也廉[4]，今之矜也忿戾[5]；古之愚也直，今之愚也诈而已矣。"

【译文】孔子说："古代人有三种毛病，现在恐怕连这三种毛病也不是原来的样子了。古代的狂者不过是不拘小节，而现在的狂者却是放荡不羁；古代骄傲的人不过是难以接近，现在那些骄傲的人却是凶恶蛮横；古代愚笨的人不过是直率一些，现在的愚笨者却是欺诈啊！"

【英译】The Master said, "Anciently, men had three failings, which now perhaps are not to be found. "The high-mindedness of antiquity showed itself in a disregard of small things; the high-mindedness of the present day shows itself in wild license. The stern dignity of antiquity showed itself in grave reserve; the stern dignity of the present day shows itself in quarrelsome ill-tempered. The stupidity of antiquity showed itself in straightforwardness; the stupidity of the present day shows itself in sheer deceit."

【注释】

[1] 狂：狂妄自大，愿望太高。

[2] 肆：放肆，不拘礼节。理雅格译为 "disregard of small things"，即 "对小事的漠视"；辜鸿铭译为 "independence"，形容古代的狂者是 "独立的"；刘殿爵译为 "impatient of restraint"，形容古代的狂者对于约束是 "不耐烦的"。从孔子的古今对比中能发现，其对于今民之疾有更深的批判，因此对于古人的形容语气较轻，译为 "disregard of small things"（对细节的漠视）更为恰当。

[3] 荡：放荡，不守礼。理雅格、辜鸿铭译为 "Wild license"，即 "放纵不羁"；刘殿爵译为 "deviate from the right path"，形容今之狂者 "偏离了正确合宜的道路"。

[4] 廉：不可触犯。理雅格译为 "grave"，即 "严肃的"；辜鸿铭译为 "modest and reserved"，即 "谦虚谨慎的"，该翻译没能体现出孔子的贬抑语气，不够恰当；刘殿爵译为 "uncompromising"，"廉" 即 "不妥协的"。上述译本相较，理雅格的翻译更能体现出古之矜者的严肃、难以接近。

[5] 戾：乖戾蛮横，不讲理。理雅格译为 "perverseness"，即 "乖戾的、倔强的"；辜鸿铭译为 "touchiness and vulgar bad-temper"，形容今之矜者 "多愁善感、有着粗俗的坏脾气"；刘殿爵译为 "ill-tempered"，形容现在的 "矜者" 是 "脾气差的"。上述译本相较，刘殿爵的翻译更为恰当。

【原文】 17.17　子曰："巧言令色，鲜矣仁。"

【译文】 孔子说："那种花言巧语，装出和颜悦色的样子，这种人的仁心就很少了。"

【英译】 The Master said, "Fine words and an insinuating appearance are seldom associated with virtue."

【原文】 17.18　子曰："恶紫之夺朱也，恶郑声之乱雅乐也，恶利口之覆邦家者。"

【译文】 孔子说："我厌恶用紫色取代红色，厌恶用郑国的声乐扰乱雅乐，厌恶用伶牙俐齿颠覆国家这样的事情。"

【英译】 The Master said, "I hate the manner in which purple takes away the luster of vermilion. I hate the way in which the songs of chang confound the music of theya. I hate those who with their sharp mouths overthrow kingdoms and families."

【原文】 17.19　子曰："予欲无言！"子贡曰："子如不言，则小子何述焉？"子曰："天何言哉？四时行焉，百物生焉，天何言哉？"

【译文】 孔子说："我想不说话了。"子贡说："您如果不说话，那么我们这些学生还传述什么呢？"孔子说："天何尝说话呢？四季照常运行，百物照样生长，天何尝说话呢？"

【英译】 The Master said, "I would prefer not speaking." Tsze-Kung said, "If you, master, do not speak, what we, your disciples, shall have to record?" The Master said, "Does heaven speak? The four seasons pursue their courses, and all things are continually being produced, but does heaven say anything?"

【原文】17.20　孺悲[1]欲见孔子，孔子辞以疾，将命者出户，取瑟而歌，使之闻之。

【译文】孺悲想见孔子，孔子以有病为由推辞不见。传话的人刚出门，孔子便取来瑟边弹边唱，有意让孺悲听到。

【英译】Zu Pei wished to see Confucius, but Confucius declined, on the ground of being sick, to see him. When the bearer of this message went out at the door, the master took his lute and sang to it, in order that Pei might hear him.

【注释】

[1] 孺悲：鲁国人，鲁哀公曾派他向孔子学礼。

【原文】17.21　宰我问："三年之丧，期已久矣。君子三年不为礼，礼必坏；三年不为乐，乐必崩。旧谷既没，新谷既升，钻燧改火[1]，期可已矣。"子曰："食夫稻[2]，衣夫锦，于女安乎？"曰："安。""女安则为之。夫君子之居丧，食旨[3]不甘，闻乐不乐，居处不安，故不为也。今女安，则为之！"宰我出，子曰："予之不仁也！子生三年，然后免于父母之怀，夫三年之丧，天下之通丧也。予也有三年之爱于其父母乎？"

【译文】宰我问："服丧三年，时间太长了。君子三年不讲究礼仪，礼仪必然败坏；三年不演奏音乐，音乐就会荒废。旧谷吃完，新谷登场，钻燧取火的木头轮过了一遍，有一年的时间就可以了。"孔子说："（才一年的时间）你就吃开了大米饭，穿起了锦缎衣，你心安吗？"宰我说："我心安。"孔子说："你心安，你就那样去做吧！君子守丧，吃美味不觉得香甜，听音乐不觉得快乐，住在家里不觉得舒服，所以不那样做。如今你既然觉得心安，你就那样去做吧！"宰我出去后，孔子说："宰予真是不仁啊！小孩生下来，到三岁时才能离开父母的怀抱。服丧三年，这是天下通行的丧礼。宰予难道就没有从他父母那里得到三年怀抱的爱护吗？"

【英译】Tsai Wo asked about the three years' mourning for parents, saying that one year was long enough. "If the superior man," said he, "abstains for three years from the observances of propriety, those observances will be quite lost. If for three years he abstains from music, music will be ruined. Within a year the old grain is exhausted, and the new grain has sprung up, and, in procuring fire by friction, we go through all the changes of wood for that purpose. After a complete year, the mourning may stop." The Master said, "If you were, after a year, to eat good rice, and wear embroidered clothes, would you feel at ease?" "I should," replied Wo. The Master said, "If you can feel at ease, do it. But a superior man, during the whole period of mourning, does not enjoy pleasant food which he may eat, nor derive pleasure from music which he may hear. He also does not feel at ease, if he is comfortably lodged. Therefore he does not do what you propose. But now you feel at ease and may do it." Tsai wo then went out and The Master said, "This shows Yu's want of virtue. It is not till a child is three years old that it is allowed to leave the arms of its parents. And the three years' mourning is universally observed throughout the empire. Did Yu enjoy the three years' love of his parents?"

【注释】

[1] 钻燧改火：古人钻木取火，四季所用木头不同，每年轮一遍，叫改火。理雅格将该句译为"in procuring fire by friction, we go through all the changes of wood for that purpose"，即"在通过摩擦取火时，我们为此目的经历了所有木材的变化"，该翻译较为平实；辜鸿铭将该句译文"in one year we burn through all the different kinds of wood produced in all the seasons"，即"在一年中，我们烧掉了一年四季生产的所有不同种类的木材"；刘殿爵译

为 "fire is renewed by fresh drilling"；韦利译为 "The whirling drills have made new fire"，即 "旋转的钻头又燃起了新的火"。《论语》此处意在通过燃烧木头的四季轮换来代指一年的时间过去，辜鸿铭的翻译体现出了 "一年" 的时间变化，较为恰当。

[2] 食夫稻：古代北方少种稻米，故大米很珍贵。这里是说吃好的。

[3] 旨：甜美，指吃好的食物。

【原文】17.22 子曰："饱食终日，无所用心，难矣哉！不有博弈[1]者乎？为之犹贤乎已！"

【译文】孔子说："整天吃饱了饭，什么心思也不用，真太难了！不是还有玩博和下棋的游戏吗？做这个，也比闲着好。"

【英译】The Master said，"Hard is it to deal with who will stuff himself with food the whole day，without applying his mind to anything good！Are there not gamesters and chess players？To be one of these would still be better than doing nothing at all."

【注释】

[1] 博弈：理雅格译为 "gamesters and chess players"，博弈指的是 "赌博" 和 "下棋"；辜鸿铭译为 "gambling and games of skill"，指 "赌博与技能游戏"；刘殿爵音译为 "bo" 和 "yi"，并在注释中补充说明为 "While yi is the game known as wei ch'i（围棋）in later ages（better known in Western countries by its Japanese reading go），po is believed to have been a board game in which the moves of the pieces are decided by a throw of dice."（"弈" 在后来被称为围棋，"博" 则被认为是一种桌面游戏，棋子的走法由掷骰子决定）韦利译为 "draughts"，即 "跳棋"，不够恰当。上述译本相较，理雅格的翻译较为恰当。

【原文】17.23 子路曰："君子尚勇[1]乎？" 子曰："君子义以

为上。君子有勇而无义为乱，小人有勇而无义为盗。"

【译文】子路说："君子崇尚勇敢吗？"孔子答道："君子以义作为最高尚的品德，君子有勇无义就会作乱，小人有勇无义就会偷盗。"

【英译】Tsze-Lu said，"Does the superior man esteem courage?" The Master said，"The superior man holds righteousness to be of highest importance. A man in a superior situation，having courage without righteousness，will be guilty of insubordination；one of the lower people having courage without righteousness，will commit robbery."

【注释】

[1] 勇：勇敢。理雅格、辜鸿铭译为"valor"，即"英勇、勇猛"，更强调战斗中的英勇、勇往直前；刘殿爵与韦利则将"勇"译为"courage"，即"勇气"，该词使用语境更为宽泛。此处并非专指作战之勇，译为 courage 更为恰当。

【原文】17.24　子贡曰："君子亦有恶乎？"子曰："有恶。恶称人之恶者，恶居下流[1]而讪上者，恶勇而无礼者，恶果敢而窒[2]者。"曰："赐也亦有恶乎？""恶徼[3]以为知者，恶不孙以为勇者，恶讦[4]以为直者。"

【译文】子贡说："君子也有厌恶的事吗？"孔子说："有厌恶的事。厌恶宣扬别人坏处的人，厌恶身居下位而诽谤在上者的人，厌恶勇敢而不懂礼节的人，厌恶固执而又不通事理的人。"孔子又说："赐，你也有厌恶的事吗？"子贡说："厌恶窃取别人的成绩而作为自己的知识的人，厌恶把不谦虚当作勇敢的人，厌恶揭发别人的隐私而自以为直率的人。"

【英译】Tsze-Kung said，"Has the superior man his hatreds also?" The Master said，"He has his hatreds. He hates those who proclaim the evil of others. He hates the man who，being in a low station，slanders his superiors. He hates those who have valor merely，and are stubborn yet unreasonable. He hates those who are forward and determined，and，at the same time，of contracted understanding." The Master then inquired，"Ts'ze，have you also your hatreds?" Tsze-Kung replied，"I hate those who pry out matters，and ascribe the knowledge to their wisdom. I hate those who are only not modest，and think that they are valorous. I hate those who make known secrets，and think that they are straightforward."

【注释】

[1] 下流：下等的，在下的。理雅格译为"being in a low station"、刘殿爵译为"being in inferior positions"，均指一个人"身处低下的位置"，较为恰当；辜鸿铭译为"Themselves living low，disreputable lives"，形容那些生活在低下耻辱生活中的人，语气微含贬义。

[2] 窒：阻塞，不通事理，顽固不化。理雅格译为"unobservant of propriety"，形容"不遵守规则"；辜鸿铭译为"narrow-minded and selfish"，"窒"即形容那些心胸狭窄且自私的人；刘殿爵译为"Whose resoluteness is not tempered by understanding"，指"决心因没有被理解而减弱"；韦利译为"violent in temper"，即"脾气暴躁"。"窒"更侧重因过于果断而导向的固执，译为"stubborn"较为恰当。

[3] 徼：窃取，抄袭。理雅格译为"pry out matters"，指"窥探事情"；辜鸿铭则将"徼"译为"censorious"，即"挑剔的"，有失文意；刘殿爵译为"unrelenting"，形容人是"无情的"；韦利将"徼"理解为"狡"并译为"cunning"，即"诡诈狡猾"之义。上述译本相较，理雅格的翻译较为恰当。

[4] 讦：攻击、揭发别人。理雅格译为"make known secrets"，指"泄露秘密"；辜鸿铭译为"ransack out the secret"，指"彻底搜查这个秘密"；刘殿爵译为"exposure of others"，指"暴露他人"。上述译本相较，理雅格、刘殿爵的翻译更为恰当。

【原文】17.25　子曰："唯女子与小人为难养也！近之则不孙，远之则怨。"

【译文】孔子说："只有女子和小人是难以教养的，亲近他们，他们就会无礼；疏远他们，他们就会抱怨。"

【英译】The Master said, "Of all people, girls and servants are the most difficult to behave to. If you are familiar with them, they lose their humility. If you maintain a reserve towards them, they are discontented."

【原文】17.26　子曰："年四十而见恶焉，其终也已！"

【译文】孔子说："到了四十岁的时候还被人所厌恶，他这一生也就终结了。"

【英译】The Master said, "When a man at forty is the object of dislike, he will always continue what he is."

微子篇第十八

【原文】18.1　微子[1]去之，箕子[2]为之奴，比干[3]谏而死。孔子曰："殷有三仁焉！"

【译文】微子离开了纣王，箕子做了他的奴隶，比干被杀死了。孔子说："这是殷朝的三位仁人啊！"

【英译】The viscount of Wei withdrew from the court. The viscount of Chi became a slave to Chau. Pi-Kan remonstrated with him and died. Confucius said，"The Yin dynasty possessed these three men of virtue."

【注释】

[1] 微子：殷纣王的同母兄长，见纣王无道，劝他不听，遂离开纣王。

[2] 箕子：殷纣王的叔父。他去劝纣王，见王不听，便披发装疯，被降为奴隶。

[3] 比干：殷纣王的叔父，屡次强谏，激怒纣王而被杀。

【原文】18.2　柳下惠为士师[1]，三黜[2]。人曰："子未可以去乎？"曰："直道而事人，焉往而不三黜！枉道而事人，何必去父母之邦[3]！"

【译文】柳下惠当典狱官，三次被罢免。有人说："你不可以离开鲁国吗？"柳下惠说："按正道事奉君主，到哪里不会被多次罢官呢？如果不按正道事奉君主，为什么一定要离开本国呢？"

【英译】Hui of Liu-Hsia, being chief criminal judge, was thrice dismissed from his office. Some one said to him, "Is it not yet time for you, sir, to leave this?" He replied, "Serving men in an upright way, where shall I go to, and not experience such a thrice-repeated dismissal? If I choose to serve men in a crooked way, what necessity is there for me to leave the country of my parents?"

【注释】

[1] 士师：典狱官，掌管刑狱。

[2] 黜：罢免不用。

[3] 父母之邦：指自己的本国。理雅格将其直译为"The country of my parents"、刘殿爵译为"The country of one's father and mother"、韦利译为"The land of my father and mother"，均为"父母之邦"之义；辜鸿铭译为"my native country"，即"我的祖国"，该翻译较为恰当。

【原文】18.3 齐景公待孔子曰："若季氏，则吾不能；以季、孟之间待之。"曰："吾老矣，不能用也。"孔子行。

【译文】齐景公讲到对待孔子的待遇时说："像鲁君对待季氏那样，我做不到，我用介于季氏、孟氏之间的待遇对待他。"又说："我老了，没有什么作为了。"于是孔子离开了齐国。

【英译】The duke Ching of Ch'i, with reference to the manner in which he should treat Confucius, said, "I cannot treat him as I would the chief of the chi family. I will treat him in a manner between that accorded to the chief of the Chil and that given to the chief of the Mang family." he also said, "I am old; I cannot use his doctrines." Confucius took his departure.

【原文】18.4 齐人归[1]女乐，季桓子[2]受之，三日不朝，孔子行。

【译文】 齐国人赠送了一些歌女给鲁国，季桓子接受了，三天不上朝。孔子于是离开了。

【英译】 The people of Ch'i sent to Lu a present of female musicians, which Chi Hwan received, and for three days no court was held. Confucius took his departure.

【注释】

[1] 归：同"馈"，赠送。

[2] 季桓子：鲁国宰相季孙氏。

【原文】 18.5 楚狂接舆，歌而过孔子，曰："凤兮！何德之衰？往者不可谏，来者犹可追。已而！已而！今之从政者殆而！"孔子下，欲与之言。趋而辟之，不得与之言。

【译文】 楚国的狂人接舆唱着歌从孔子的车旁走过，他唱道："凤凰啊，凤凰啊，你的德运怎么这么衰弱呢？过去的已经无可挽回，未来的还来得及改正。算了吧，算了吧。今天的执政者危乎其危！"孔子下车，想同他谈谈，他却赶快避开，孔子没能和他交谈。

【原文】 The madman of Ch'u, Chieh-Yu, passed by Confucius, singing and saying, "O fang! O fang! how is your virtue degenerated! As to the past, reproof is useless; but the future may still be provided against. Give up your vain pursuit. Give up your vain pursuit. Peril awaits those who now engage in affairs of government." Confucius alighted and wished to converse with him, but Chieh-Yu hastened away, so that he could not talk with him.

【原文】 18.6 长沮、桀溺[1]耦而耕[2]。孔子过之，使子路问津[3]焉。长沮曰："夫执舆者为谁？"子路曰："为孔丘。"曰："是鲁孔丘与？"曰："是也。"曰："是知津矣。"问于桀溺。桀溺曰："子为谁？"曰："为仲由。"曰："是孔丘之徒与？"对曰："然。"曰："滔滔者天下皆是也，而谁以易之？且而与其从辟[4]人之士也，岂若从辟世之士哉？"耰[5]而不辍。子路行以告。夫子怃然[6]曰："鸟兽不可与同群，吾非斯人之徒与而谁与？天下有道，丘不与易也。"

【译文】 长沮、桀溺在一起耕种，孔子路过，让子路去寻问渡口在哪里。长沮问子路："那个拿着缰绳的是谁？"子路说："是孔丘。"长沮说；"是鲁国的孔丘吗？"子路说："是的。"长沮说："那他是早已知道渡口的位置了。"子路再去问桀溺。桀溺说："你是谁？"子路说："我是仲由。"桀溺说："你是鲁国孔丘的门徒吗？"子路说："是的。"桀溺说："像洪水一般的坏东西到处都是，你们同谁去改变它呢？而且你与其跟着躲避人的人，为什么不跟着我们这些躲避社会的人呢？"说完，仍旧不停地做田里的农活。子路回来后把情况报告给孔子。孔子失望地说："人是不能与飞禽走兽合群共处的，如果不同世上的人群打交道，还与谁打交道呢？如果天下太平，我就不会与你们一道来从事改革了。"

【英译】 Ch'ang-tsu and Chieh-ni were ploughing together yoked as a team, when Confucius passed by them, and sent Tsze-Lu to inquire for the ford. Ch'ang-tsu said, "Who is he that holds the reins in the carriage there?" Tsze-Lu told him, "It is K'ung Ch'iu." "Is it not K'ung of Lu?" asked he. "Yes," was the reply, to which the other rejoined, "he knows the ford." Tsze-Lu then inquired of Chieh-Ni, who said to him, "Who are you, sir?" he answered, "I am Chung Yu." "Are you not the disciple of K'ung Ch'iu of Lu?" asked the other. "I am," replied he, and then Chieh-Ni said to him, "Disorder, like a swelling flood, spreads over the whole empire, and who is he that will change its state for you? Rather than follow one who merely withdraws from this one and that one，had you not better follow those who have withdrawn from the world altogether?" With this he fell to covering up the seed，and proceeded with his work，without stopping. Tsze-Lu went and reported their remarks，when the master observed with a sigh，"It is impossible to associate with birds and beasts，as if they were the same with us. If I associate not with these people，-with mankind，-with whom shall I associate? If right principles prevailed through the empire，there would be no use for me to change its state."

【注释】

[1] 长沮、桀溺：两位隐士。

[2] 耦而耕：两个人合力耕作。理雅格译为"work in the field together"，指二人"一起在田野里工作"；辜鸿铭译为"working in the field"，指二人"在田中工作"；刘殿爵译为"ploughing together yoked as a team"，指长沮、桀溺两人"组队在一起耕作"；韦利译为"working as ploughmates together"，即"作为犁地伙伴一起耕种"。刘殿爵、韦利译出了"耕"和"耦"的具体含义，更为恰当。

[3] 问津：津，渡口。寻问渡口。理雅格、辜鸿铭、韦利、刘殿爵均译为"ford"，即"浅滩"之义。笔者认为此处译为"ferry"（渡口）更为恰当。

[4] 辟：同"避"。

[5] 耰：用土覆盖种子。

[6] 怃然：怅然，失意。

【原文】 18.7　子路从而后，遇丈人，以杖荷蓧[1]。子路问曰："子见夫子乎?"丈人曰："四体不勤，五谷不分[2]，孰为夫子?"植其杖而芸。子路拱而立。止子路宿，杀鸡为黍[3]而食之。见其二子焉。明日，子路行以告。子曰："隐者也。"使子路反见之。至，则行矣。子路曰："不仕无义。长幼之节，不可废也；君臣之义，如之何其废之？欲洁其身，而乱大伦。君子之仕也，行其义也。道之不行，已知之矣。"

【译文】 子路跟随孔子出行，落在了后面，遇到一个老丈，用拐杖挑着除草的工具。子路问道："你看到我的老师了吗？"老丈说："你这个人，四肢不劳动，五谷不分辨，谁知道你的老师是谁！"说完，便扶着拐杖去除草。子路拱着手恭敬地站在一旁。老丈留子路到他家住宿，杀了鸡，做了小米饭给他吃，又叫两个儿子出来与子路见面。第二天，子路赶上孔子，把这件事向他作了报告。孔子说："这是个隐士。"叫子路回去再看看他。子路到了那里，老丈已经走了。子路说："不做官是不对的。长幼之间的关系是不可能废弃的，君臣之间的关系怎么能废弃呢？想要自身清白，却破坏了根本的君臣伦理关系。君子做官，只是为了实行君臣之义的。至于道行不通，早就知道了。"

【英译】 Tsze-Lu, following the Master, happened to fall behind, when he met an old man, carrying across his shoulder on a staff a basket for weeds. Tsze-Lu said to him, "Have you seen my master, sir?" The old man replied, "your four limbs are unaccustomed to toil; you cannot distinguish the five kinds of grain: -who is your master?" With this, he planted his staff in the ground, and proceeded toweed. Tsze-Lu joined his hands across his breast, and stood before him. The old man kept Tsze-Lu to pass the night in his house, killed a fowl, prepared millet, and feasted him. He also introduced to him his two sons. Next day, Tsze-Lu went on his way, and reported his adventure. The Master said, "He is a recluse," and sent Tsze-Lu back to see him again, but when he got to the place, the old man was gone. Tsze-Lu then said to the family, "Not to take office is not righteous. If the relations between old and young may not be neglected, how is it that he sets aside the duties that should be observed between sovereign and minister? Wishing to maintain his personal purity，he allows that great relation to come to confusion. A superior man takes office，and performs the righteous duties belonging to it. As to the failure of right principles to make progress，he is aware of that."

【注释】

[1] 蓧：古代耘田所用的竹器。

[2] 四体不勤，五谷不分：一说这是丈人指自己，意为"我忙于播种五谷，没有闲暇，怎知你夫子是谁？"另一说是丈人责备子路。说子路手脚不勤，五谷不分。理雅格译为"your four limbs are unaccustomed to toil；you cannot distinguish the five kinds of grain"，辜鸿铭译为"Your body has never known toil and you cannot tell the difference between the five kinds of grain"，刘殿爵译为"You seem neither to have toiled with your limbs nor to be able to tell one kind of grain from another"，以上均是将子路评价为"你的四肢不习惯劳累，你分不清这五种谷物"。

[3] 黍：黏小米。

【原文】 18.8　逸民[1]：伯夷、叔齐、虞仲、夷逸、朱张、柳下惠、少连。子曰："不降其志，不辱其身，伯夷、叔齐与？"谓柳下惠、少连，"降志辱身矣，言中伦，行中虑，其斯而已矣。"谓虞仲、夷逸，"隐居放[2]言，身中清，废中权[3]。我则异于是，无可无不可。"

【译文】 隐逸的人有：伯夷、叔齐、虞仲、夷逸、朱张、柳下惠、少连。孔子说："不降低自己的意志，不屈辱自己的身份，这是伯夷、叔齐吧。"说柳下惠、少连是"被迫降低自己的意志，屈辱自己的身份，但说话合乎伦理，行为合乎人心。"说虞仲、夷逸"过着隐居的生活，说话随便，能洁身自爱，离开官位合乎权宜。我却与这些人不同，可以这样做，也可以那样做。"

【英译】The men who have retired to privacy from the world have been Po-I，Shu-Ch'i，Yuchung，I-Yi，Chu-Chang，Hui of Liu-Hsia，and Shao-Lien. The Master said，"Refusing to surrender their wills，or to submit to any taint in their persons；such，I think，were Po-I and Shu-Ch'i." It may be said of Hui of Liu-Hsia，and of ShaoLien，that they surrendered their wills，and submitted to taint in their persons，but their words corresponded with reason，and their actions were such as men are anxious to see. This is all that is to be remarked in them. "It may be said of Yu-Chung and I-Yi，that，while they hid themselves in their seclusion，they gave a license to their words；but in their persons，they succeeded in preserving their purity，and，in their retirement，they acted according to the exigency of the times. "I am different from all these. I have no course for which I am predetermined，and no course against which I am predetermined."

【注释】

[1] 逸：隐逸。理雅格译为 "The men who have retired to privacy from the world"，形容那些 "隐退到与世隔绝的人"；辜鸿铭译为 "withdrew themselves from the world"，逸民即为 "退出了世界"；刘殿爵译为 "withdrew from society"，即 "退出、远离社会"；韦利则译为 "subjects whose services were lost to the State"，"逸民" 指那些对国家失去贡献能力的人。上述译本均将 "逸民" 理解为隐逸出世、不问世事的人。

[2] 放：放置，不再谈论世事。

[3] 权：权宜得当。理雅格译为 "acted according to the exigency of the times"，形容虞仲、夷逸能够 "根据时代的紧急情况行事"。辜鸿铭将 "权" 译为 "they rightly used their discretion"，形容上述二人能在脱离世事的同时 "正确运用自己的谨慎"。刘殿爵译为 "with the right measure for the

occasion"，指"采用正确的行为、合适的办法"；韦利译为"maintained due balance"，形容行为"保持平衡"。上述译本相较，刘殿爵的翻译突出了"权"的灵活、机变之义，更为恰当。

【原文】18.9　大师挚[1]适齐，亚饭干适楚，三饭缭适蔡，四饭缺[2]适秦，鼓方叔[3]入于河，播鼗[4]武入于汉，少师[5]阳、击磬襄[6]入于海。

【译文】太师挚到齐国去了，亚饭干到楚国去了，三饭缭到蔡国去了，四饭缺到秦国去了，打鼓的方叔到了黄河边，敲小鼓的武到了汉水边，少师阳和击磬的襄到了海滨。

【英译】The grand music master, Chih, went to Ch'i. Kan, the master of the band at the second meal, went to Ch'u. Liao, the bandmaster at the third meal, went to Ts'ai. Chueh, the band master at the fourth meal, went to ch'in. Fang-Shu, the drum master, withdrew to the north of the river. Wu, the master of the hand drum, withdrew to the han. Yang, the assistant music master, and Hsiang, master of the musical stone withdrew to an island in the sea.

【注释】

[1] 大师挚："大"同"太"。太师是鲁国乐官之长，挚是人名。

[2] 亚饭、三饭、四饭：都是乐官名。干、缭、缺是人名。

[3] 鼓方叔：击鼓的乐师名方叔。

[4] 鼗：小鼓。

[5] 少师：乐官名，副乐师。

[6] 击磬襄：击磬的乐师，名襄。

【原文】18.10　周公谓鲁公[1]曰："君子不施[2]其亲，不使大臣怨乎不以。故旧无大故，则不弃也。无求备于一人。"

【译文】周公对鲁公说："君子不疏远他的亲属，不使大臣们抱怨不用他们。旧友老臣没有大的过失，就不要抛弃他们，不要对人求全责备。"

【英译】The duke of Chau addressed his son，The duke of Lu，saying，"The virtuous prince does not treat those closely related to him casually. He does not cause the great ministers torepine at his not employing them. Without some great cause，he does not dismiss from their offices the members of old families. He does not seek in one man talents for every employment."

【注释】

[1] 鲁公：指周公的儿子伯禽，封于鲁。

[2] 施：同"弛"，怠慢、疏远。理雅格、辜鸿铭译为"neglect"，"施"即"忽略"之义。刘殿爵译为"treat those closely related to him casually"，指君子不随便对待与他关系亲密的人。韦利将"施"译为"discards his kinsmen"，即"抛弃他的亲戚"。"施"并非抛弃自己的亲属，而是强调对待亲属有正确的态度，不刻意回避、怠慢疏远。上述译本相较，刘殿爵的翻译更为恰当。

【原文】18.11　周有八士[1]：伯达、伯适、伯突、仲忽、叔夜、叔夏、季随、季骊。

【译文】周朝有八个士：伯达、伯适、伯突、仲忽、叔夜、叔夏、季随、季骊。

【英译】To Chau belonged the eight officers，Po-Ta，Po-Kwo，Chung-Tu，Chung-Hwu，Shu-Ya，Shu Hsia，Chi-Sui，and Chi-Kwa.

【注释】

[1] 八士：本章中所说八士已不可考。

子张篇第十九

【原文】19.1　子张曰：“士见危致命，见得思义，祭思敬，丧思哀，其可已矣。”[1]

【译文】子张说：“士遇见危险时能献出自己的生命，看见有利可得时能考虑是否符合义的要求，祭祀时能想到是否严肃恭敬，居丧的时候想到自己是否哀伤，这样就可以了。”

【英译】Tsze-Chang said, "The scholar, trained for public duty, seeing threatening danger, is prepared to sacrifice his life. When the opportunity of gain is presented to him, he thinks of righteousness. In sacrificing, his thoughts are reverential. In mourning, his thoughts are about the grief which he should feel. Such a man commands our approbation indeed."

【注释】

[1] 士应当有的四种德行。邢昺《注疏》云：“子张言，为士者，见君有危难，不爱其身，致命以救之；见得利禄，思义然后取；有祭事，思尽其敬；有丧事，当尽其哀，有此行者，其可以为士已矣。”朱子《集注》云：“四者立身之大节，一有不至，则余无足观。故言士能如此，则庶乎其可矣。”

【原文】19.2　子张曰：“执德不弘[1]，信道不笃，焉能为有？焉能为亡？”

【译文】子张说："实行德而不能发扬光大，信仰道而不忠实坚定，这样的人有他不为多，没他不为少。"

【英译】Tsze-Chang said，"When a man holds fast to virtue，but without seeking to enlarge it，and believes in right principles，but without firm sincerity，what account can be made of his existence or non-existence?"

【注释】

[1] 弘：大。理雅格、辜鸿铭译为"enlarge"，即"放大、扩大"；刘殿爵译为动词"hold on"，即"坚持、抓住（美德）"。上述译本相较，理雅格、辜鸿铭的翻译更为恰当。

【原文】19.3　子夏之门人问交于子张。子张曰："子夏云何？"对曰："子夏曰：'可者与之，其不可者拒之。'"子张曰："异乎吾所闻：君子尊贤而容众，嘉善而矜不能[1]。我之大贤与，于人何所不容？我之不贤与，人将拒我，如之何其拒人也？"[2]

【译文】子夏的学生向子张寻问怎样结交朋友。子张说："子夏是怎么说的？"答道："子夏说：'可以相交的就和他交朋友，不可以相交的就拒绝他。'"子张说："我所听到的和这些不一样：君子既尊重贤人，又能容纳众人；能够赞美善人，又能同情能力不够的人。如果我是十分贤良的人，那我对别人有什么不能容纳的呢？我如果不贤良，那人家就会拒绝我，又怎么谈能拒绝人家呢？"

【原文】The disciples of Tsze-hsia asked Tsze-Chang about the principles that should characterize mutual intercourse. Tsze-Chang asked，"What does Tsze-hsia say on the subject?" They replied，"Tsze-hsia says：'associate with those who can advantage you. put away from you those who cannot do so.'" Tsze-Chang observed，"This is different from what I have learned. The superior man honors the talented and virtuous，and bears with all. He praises the good，and pities the incompetent. Am I possessed of great talents and virtue？ - who is there among men whom I will not bear with？ Am I devoid of talents and virtue？ -men will put me away from them. What have we to do with the putting away of others？"

【注释】

[1] 嘉善而矜不能：能够嘉赏贤人，也能够包容不贤之人。理雅格将该句译为"he praises the good，and pities the incompetent"，形容君子能"赞美优秀的人，同情无能的人"。辜鸿铭译为"He knows how to commend those who excel in anything and make allowance for those who are ignorant"，指君子"知道如何赞扬那些在任何方面都很优秀的人，并体谅那些无知的人"。刘殿爵译为"he is full of praise for the good while taking pity on the backward"，即"他对好人赞扬有加，对后进者怜悯有加"。韦利译为"He commends the good and pities the incapable"，指"他赞扬好人，同情无能的人"。praise 的使用较为普遍，多用于对某人或某事物表现出高度评价和尊敬；commend 的使用更为正式，通常是指正式地、公开地表扬某人的品质或成就，有认可和欣赏的意味。此处"嘉"强调对君子贤人的美德品质的嘉赏，较为正式，译为 commend 更为恰当。"矜"多被理解为"同情、包容、怜悯"等含义，pity 作动词侧重"同情、怜悯"；make allowance 则强调对不能者的"体谅、谅解"。在古汉语中"矜"更强调恻隐同情之义，译为 pity 更为恰当。

[2] 包咸认为："友交当如子夏，泛交当如子张。"

【原文】 19.4　子夏曰："虽小道[1]，必有可观者焉，致远恐泥[2]，是以君子不为也。"

【译文】 子夏说："虽然都是些小的技艺，也一定有可取的地方，但用它来达到远大目标就行不通了。"

【英译】Tsze-hsia said，"Even in inferior studies and employments there is something worth being looked at；but if it be attempted to carry them out to what is remote，there is a danger of their proving inapplicable. Therefore，the superior man does not practice them."

【注释】

[1] 小道：指各种农工商医卜之类的技能。理雅格译为"Inferior studies and employments"，指那些较低等的学习和工作。辜鸿铭译为"small and unimportant branch"，指工作中那些"微小且不重要的分支"。刘殿爵、韦利的翻译简明扼要，分别译为"minor arts"、"minor walks"，形容那些微小的技艺。

[2] 泥：阻滞，不通，妨碍。

【原文】19.5　子夏曰："日知其所亡，月无忘其所能，可谓好学也已矣！"

【译文】子夏说："每天学到一些过去所不知道的东西，每月都不能忘记已经学会的东西，这就可以叫作好学了。"

【英译】Tsze-hsia said，"He，who from day to day recognizes what he has not yet，and from month to month does not forget what he has attained to，may be said indeed to love to learn."

【原文】19.6　子夏曰："博学而笃志[1]，切问[2]而近思，仁在其中矣。"[3]

【译文】子夏说："博览群书、广泛学习并且坚定自己的志向，恳切地提出疑问并且去思考，仁就在其中了。"

【英译】Tsze-hsia said，"There are learning extensively，and having a firm and sincere purpose；inquiring with earnestness，and reflecting with self-application：-virtue is in such a course."

【注释】

[1] 笃志：两种理解：1. 志同"识"。皇侃《义疏》云："笃，厚也；志，识也。言人当广学经典，而深厚识录之不忘也。"2. 志为志向。王夫之《笺解》云："笃志，专于所志也。学博而皆取其善以成其志，非徒恃泛记，非随所见闻而移其心也。"理雅格从第二种解法，译为"真诚的志向"，即"sincere aim"。辜鸿铭译为"steadfast in your aim"、刘殿爵译为"steadfast in your purpose"，"笃志"即"坚定你的目标"。韦利译为"set purpose"，即"确立目标"。aim从本义"靶子"引申而来，侧重比较具体而明确的目标，但常指短期目标；purpose既指以坚决、审慎的行动去达到的目的，又指心中渴望要实际的目标。此处"笃志"指的是长期、坚定的志向与目标，译为purpose更为恰当。

[2] 切问：切有多种解释：1. 急，急切。皇侃《义疏》云："切，犹急也。若有所未达之事，宜急咨取解，故云切问也。"2. 恳切。邢昺《注疏》云："切问者，亲切问于己所学未悟之事，不泛滥问之也。"3. 勤。戴望《论语注》云："切，勤也。不知则勤问有道，不能则近思诸身。"4. 近身之事。黄式三《论语后案》云："于切近者问之思之，所为辇近取譬也。"5. 深切、深刻。黄怀信《论语汇校集释》云："切，谓深切、深刻。《汉书·霍光传》'切让王莽'，师古注：'切，深也。'"

[3] 朱子《集注》云："四者皆学问思辨之事耳，未及乎力行而为仁也。然从事于此，则心不外驰，而所存自熟，故曰仁在其中矣。程子曰：'博学而笃志，切问而近思，何以言仁在其中矣？学者要思得之。了此，便是彻上彻下之道。'又曰：'学不博则不能守约，志不笃则不能力行。切问近思在己者，则仁在其中矣。'又曰：'近思者以类而推。'苏氏曰：'博学而志不笃，则大而无成；泛问远思，则劳而无功。'"

【原文】 19.7　子夏曰："百工居肆[1]以成其事，君子学以致其道。"

【译文】子夏说："各行各业的工匠住在作坊里来完成自己的工作，君子通过学习来掌握道。"

【英译】Tsze-hsia said，"Mechanics have their shops to dwell in，in order to accomplish their works. The superior man learns，in order to reach to the utmost of his principles."

【注释】

[1] 百工居肆：百工，各行各业的工匠。肆，古代社会制作物品的作坊。

【原文】19.8 子夏曰："小人之过也必文[1]。"

【译文】子夏说："小人犯了过错一定要掩饰。"

【英译】Tsze-hsia said，"The mean man is sure to gloss his faults."

【注释】

[1] 文：遮掩、掩饰。理雅格、刘殿爵译为"gloss"，即"掩饰他的缺点"；辜鸿铭译为"has an excuse ready"，指小人在做错事后会"准备好借口"；韦利将"文"译为"文饰、过度阐释"，即"over-elaboration"。上述译本相较，理雅格、刘殿爵的翻译更为恰当。

【原文】19.9 子夏曰："君子有三变[1]：望之俨然，即之也温，听其言也厉[2]。"

【译文】子夏说："君子有三变：远观他的样子庄严肃穆，接近他便会感觉到温和可亲，他的言辞是严厉不苟的。"

【英译】Tsze-hsia said，"The superior man undergoes three changes. looked at from a distance，he appears stern；when approached，he is mild；when he is heard to speak，his language is firm and decided."

【注释】

[1] 三变：并非君子自己要变，而是在不同时候给人不同的印象，而

且并行不悖。邢昺《注疏》云："此章论君子之德也。望之、即之及听其言也，有此三者，变易常人之事也。厉，严正也。常人，远望之则多懈惰，即近之则颜色猛厉，听其言则多佞邪。唯君子则不然，人远望之则正其衣冠，尊其瞻视，常俨然也；就近之则颜色温和，及听其言辞，则严正而无佞邪也。"朱子《集注》引谢氏云："此非有意于变，盖并行而不相悖也，如良玉温润而栗然。"

[2] 厉：严肃认真的、一丝不苟的。理雅格译为"firm and decided"，形容一个人的语言"坚毅又果断"；辜鸿铭译为"serious"，形容君子说话语气是"严肃的"；刘殿爵译为"stern"，即"严厉的"；韦利译为"incisive"，形容君子的语言是"果敢的、当机立断的"。

【原文】19.10　子夏曰："君子信而后劳其民，未信则以为厉己也；信而后谏，未信则以为谤己也。"

【译文】子夏说："君子必须取得信任之后才去役使百姓，否则百姓就会以为是在虐待他们。要先取得信任，然后才去进谏，否则君主就会以为你在诽谤他。"

【英译】Tsze-hsia said，"The superior man，having obtained their confidence，may then impose labors on his people. If he has not gained their confidence，they will think that he is oppressing them. having obtained the confidence of his prince，one may then remonstrate with him. If he have not gained his confidence，the prince will think that he is vilifying him."

【原文】19.11　子夏曰："大德不逾闲[1]；小德出入可也。"

【译文】子夏说："大节上不能超越界限，小节上有些出入是可以的。"

【英译】Tsze-hsia said，"When a person does not transgress the

boundary line in the great virtues, he may pass and repass it in the small virtues.”

【注释】

[1] 闲：木栏、栏杆，这里引申为法度、界限。理雅格译为 “the boundary line”，辜鸿铭、刘殿爵译为 “bounds”，均为 “界限” 之义。韦利译为 “cross the barrier”，“逾闲” 即 “穿越障碍”，不够恰当。

【原文】 19.12　子游曰：“子夏之门人小子，当洒扫、应对、进退则可矣，抑末也。本之则无，如之何？”子夏闻之曰：“噫！言游过矣！君子之道，孰先传焉？孰后倦[1]焉？譬诸草木，区以别矣。君子之道，焉可诬也？有始有卒者，其惟圣人乎！”

【译文】 子游说：“子夏的学生，做些打扫和迎送客人的事情是可以的，但这些不过是末节小事，根本的东西却没有学到，这怎么行呢？”子夏听了，说：“唉，子游错了。君子之道先传授什么，后传授什么，这就像草和木一样，是有所区别的。君子之道怎么可以随意歪曲，欺骗学生呢？能按次序有始有终地教授学生们，恐怕只有圣人吧！”

【英译】 Tsze-yu said, “The disciples and followers of Tsze-hsia, in sprinkling and sweeping the ground, in answering and replying, in advancing and receding, are sufficiently accomplished. But these are only the branches of learning, and they are left ignorant of what is essential.-how can they be acknowledged as sufficiently taught?” Tsze-hsia heard of the remark and said, “Alas! Yen Yu is wrong. According to the way of the superior man in teaching, what departments are there which he considers of prime importance, and delivers? What are there which he considers of secondary importance, and allows himself to be idle about? But as in the case of plants, which are assorted according to their classes, so he deals with his disciples. How can the way of a superior man be such as to make fools of any of them? Is it not the sage alone，who can unite in one the beginning and the consummation of learning?"

【注释】

[1] 倦：有多种解释：1.厌倦，见何晏《集解》、皇侃《义疏》、邢昺《注疏》等；2.教诲。朱子《集注》云："倦，如诲人不倦之倦……言君子之道，非以其末为先而传之，非以其本为后而倦教。"3.券，犹传。戴望《论语注》云："传，符传也。券，契也。古者门关出入用传，要约则用契。传以缯帛，契以牍析之，分持其一，合以为信。言君子之授教，先后有次序，信若符契然。"4.罢，停止。黄怀信《论语汇校集释》："诸说皆未尽是。言传焉、倦焉剔所传、所倦者皆当指君子之道，传、倦亦必皆为动词。《说文》：'倦，罢也。'罢止，谓不传也。先传、后倦，子夏皆谓己。子游受教晚于子夏，盖又早罢，故子夏有此言，反问之也。"今从朱子之说。理雅格将"倦"译为"无所事事"，即"allows himself to be idle about"；辜鸿铭译为"neglect"，指在那些不重要的微末知识可以被"忽略"；刘殿爵从朱熹《集注》之说，"倦"译为"taught"，即教诲之义。

【原文】 19.13 子夏曰："仕而优[1]则学，学而优则仕。"

【译文】 子夏说："做官还有余力的人，就可以去学习；学习有余力的人，就可以去做官。"

【英译】 Tsze-hsia said，"The energy that a man has left over after doing his duty to the State，should devote his leisure to learning. The student，having completed his learning，should apply himself to be an officer."

【注释】

[1] 优：有余力。理雅格译为"完成自己的任务"，即"having discharged all his duties"，指官员承担了自己的职责、学生完成了自己的学

业；刘殿爵译为"more than cope with his duties"，同样指那些完成自己职分的人；辜鸿铭译为"exceptional abilities"，"优"形容那些优秀、有特殊能力的人；韦利将该句译为"The energy that a man has left over after doing his duty to the State"，"优"即指"完成了自己的责任后仍有的多余精力"。上述译本相较，韦利的翻译更为恰当。

【原文】19.14　子游曰："丧致乎哀而止。"

【译文】子游说："丧事做到尽哀也就可以了。"

【英译】Tsze-hsia said，"Mourning，having been carried to the utmost degree of grief，should stop with that."

【原文】19.15　子游曰："吾友张也为难能也，然而未仁。"

【译文】子游说："我的朋友子张可以说是难得的了，然而还没有做到仁。"

【英译】Tsze-hsia said，"My friend Chang can do things which are hard to be done，but yet he is not perfectly virtuous."

【原文】19.16　曾子曰："堂堂[1]乎张也！难与并为仁矣[2]。"

【译文】曾子说："子张外表堂堂，难于和他一起做到仁的。"

【英译】The philosopher Tsang said，"How noble and dignified is the manner of Chang！It is difficult along with him to practice virtue."

【注释】

[1] 堂堂：仪表堂堂。理雅格将该句译为"how imposing is the manner of chang"，形容子张的态度是"威严的"；辜鸿铭译为"What a style that man carries about with him！"形容子张身上有一种"伟大的风格"；刘殿爵将"堂堂"译为"grand"，即"伟大的"；韦利译为"self-important"，形容子张是"高傲的、妄自尊大的"。《论语》此处褒奖子张，但对其评价并未至德行

"伟大"的程度。韦利的翻译贬抑色彩浓重，刘殿爵、辜鸿铭则过分高扬了子张的伟大。上述译本相较，理雅格的翻译较为恰当，或可译为"noble and dignified"，形容人仪表堂堂、高贵庄严。

[2] 难与并为仁矣：两种解释：1. 贬义。邢昺《注疏》云："曾子言子张容仪堂堂然盛，于仁道则薄，故难与并为仁矣。"朱子《集注》亦云："言其务外自高，不可辅而为仁，亦不能有以辅人之仁也。"2. 褒义，感叹子张难以企及。戴望《论语注》云："言子张行高为仁，人难与并，叹其不可及。"程树德《集释》云："《论语训》'亦言子张仁不可及也。难与并，不能比也。曾、张友善如兄弟，非贬其堂堂也。'按：子张少孔子四十八岁，在诸贤中年最少，他日成就如何虽无可考，而其弟子有公明仪、申详等，皆贤人也。其学派至列为八儒之一，非寂寂无闻者也。《集注》喜贬抑圣门，其言固不可信。如旧注之说，子游、曾子皆以子张为未仁，摈不与友，《鲁论》又何必记之？吾人断不应以后世讲朱陆异同之心理推测古人。况曾子一生最为谨慎，有口不敢人过之风，故知从前解释皆误也。王氏此论虽创解，实确解也。"倘若从后者之说，以该句为褒义，则上文辜鸿铭译为"What a style that man carries about with him"、刘殿爵译为"grand"，形容子张人格的伟大，便得以圆融解释。

【原文】19.17　曾子曰："吾闻诸夫子：'人未有自致者也，必也亲丧乎。'"

【译文】曾子说："我听老师说过，'人没有能自觉尽心尽力的事情，如果有，一定是在父母死亡的时候。'"

【英译】The philosopher Tsang said, "I heard this from our master: 'men may not have shown what is in them to the full extent, and yet they will be found to do so, on the occasion of mourning for their parents.'"

【原文】19.18 曾子曰:"吾闻诸夫子:'孟庄子[1]之孝也,其他可能也,其不改父之臣与父之政,是难能也。'"

【译文】曾子说:"我听老师说过:'孟庄子的孝,其他人也可以做到,但他不更换父亲的旧臣及其政治措施,这是别人难以做到的。'"

【英译】The philosopher Tsang said, "I have heard this from our master:'the filial piety of Mang Chwang, in other matters, was what other men are competent to, but, as seen in his not changing the ministers of his father, nor his father's mode of government, it is difficult to be attained to.'"

【注释】

[1] 孟庄子:鲁国大夫孟孙速。

【原文】19.19 孟氏使阳肤[1]为士师,问于曾子。曾子曰:"上失其道,民散久矣!如得其情,则哀矜而勿喜。"

【译文】孟氏任命阳肤做典狱官,阳肤向曾子请教。曾子说:"在上位的人脱离了正道,百姓早就离心离德了。你如果能弄清他们的情况,就应当可怜他们,而不要自鸣得意。"

【英译】The chief of the Mang family having appointed Yang fu to be chief criminal judge, the latter consulted the philosopher Tsang. Tsang said, "The rulers have failed in their duties, and the people consequently have been disorganized for along time. When you have found out the truth of any accusation, be grieved for and pity them, and do not feel joy at your own ability."

【注释】

[1] 阳肤:曾子的学生。

【原文】19.20 子贡曰:"纣[1]之不善,不如是之甚也。是以君子恶居下流^[2]，天下之恶皆归焉。"

【译文】 子贡说："商纣的不善，不像传说的那样厉害。所以君子憎恨居于下流低洼的地方，使天下一切坏名声都归到他的身上。"

【英译】 Tsze-Kung said, "Chau's wickedness was not so great as that name implies. Therefore, the superior man hates to dwell in a low-lying situation, where all the evil of the world will flow in upon him."

【注释】

[1] 纣：商代最后一个君主，名辛，纣是他的谥号，历来被认为是一个暴君。

[2] 下流：即地形低洼各处来水汇集的地方。理雅格译为 "low-lying situation"，指 "低洼的地方"；辜鸿铭译为 "low, disreputable life"，指那些 "卑微的、不体面的生活"；刘殿爵译为 "dwell downstream"，即 "住在下游"；韦利译为 "dwell on low ground"，即 "住在低的地方"。朱子《集注》云："下流，地形卑下之处，众流之所归。喻人身有污贱之实，亦恶名之所聚也。"邢昺《注疏》云："下流者，谓为恶行而处人下，若地形卑下，则众流所归。"此处指住的地方地势低洼、水流汇聚于此，因此称 "下流"，刘殿爵的翻译较为恰当。

【原文】 19.21　子贡曰："君子之过^[1]也，如日月之食焉。过也，人皆见之；更也，人皆仰之。"

【译文】 子贡说："君子的过错好比日月蚀。他犯过错，人们都看得见；他改正过错，人们都仰望着他。"

【英译】 Tsze-Kung said, "The faults of the superior man are like the eclipses of the sun and moon. He has his faults, and all men see them; he changes again, and all men look up to him."

【注释】

[1] 过：过错。理雅格、韦利译为 "faults"，即 "错误"；辜鸿铭译为

"failing"，即"弱点、缺点"；刘殿爵译为"error"，即"错误"。error 是表示"错误"使用范围最广的词，指"错误、谬误"，可以用来表示任何类型的错误，包括笔误、语法错误、操作错误、印刷错误、计算错误等等；fault 较为抽象，指道德、习惯、行为上能影响完美性的错误。我们认为，此处译为"faults"更为恰当。

【原文】19.22　卫公孙朝[1]问于子贡曰："仲尼焉学?"子贡曰："文武之道[2]，未坠于地，在人。贤者识其大者，不贤者识其小者，莫不有文武之道焉。夫子焉不学，而亦何常师之有!"

【译文】卫国的公孙朝问子贡说："仲尼的学问是从哪里学来的?"子贡说："周文王、武王的道，并没有失传，还留在人们中间。贤能的人可以了解它的根本，不贤的人只了解它的末节，没有什么地方无文王、武王之道。我们老师何处不学，又何必要有固定的老师传授呢?"

【英译】Kung-Sun Ch'ao of Wei asked Tszekung, saying, "From whom did chung-ni get his learning?" Tsze-Kung replied, "The way of King Wen and King Wu have not yet fallen to the ground. They are to be found among men. Men of talents and virtue remember the greater principles of them, and others, not possessing such talents and virtue, remember the smaller. Thus, all possess the doctrines of Wan and Wu. Where could our master go that he should not have an opportunity of learning them? And yet what necessity was there for his having a regular master?"

【注释】

[1] 卫公孙朝：卫国的大夫公孙朝。当时鲁国、郑国、楚国亦有公孙朝，因而特意指明为卫国之公孙朝。

[2] 文武之道：周文王周武王之道。朱子《集注》云："文武之道，谓文王、武王之谟训功烈，与凡周之礼乐文章皆是也。"理雅格译为"The

doctrines of wan and wu", 即"文王和武王的学说"; 辜鸿铭译为"The principles of religion and morality held by the ancients", 泛指那些"古代宗教和道德的原则"; 刘殿爵、韦利直译为"The way of King Wen and King Wu", 即"文武之道"。上述译本相较, 刘殿爵、韦利的翻译更为恰当。

【原文】19.23 叔孙武叔[1]语大夫于朝曰:"子贡贤于仲尼。"子服景伯[2]以告子贡。子贡曰:"譬之宫墙:赐之墙也及肩, 窥见屋家之好; 夫子之墙数仞[3], 不得其门而入, 不见宗庙之美, 百官[4]之富。得其门者或寡矣! 夫子之云, 不亦宜乎!"

【译文】叔孙武叔在朝廷上对大夫们说:"子贡比仲尼更贤。"子服景伯把这一番话告诉了子贡。子贡说:"拿围墙来作比喻, 我家的围墙只有齐肩高, 老师家的围墙却有几仞高, 如果找不到门进去, 你就看不见里面宗庙的富丽堂皇, 和房屋的绚丽多彩。能够找到门进去的人并不多。叔孙武叔那么讲, 不也是很自然吗?"

【英译】Shu-Sun Wu-Shu observed to the great officers in the court, saying, "Tsze-Kung is superior to Chung-Ni." Tsze-fu Ching-Po reported the observation to Tsze-Kung, who said, "Let me use the comparison of a house and its encompassing wall. My wall only reaches to the shoulders. One may peep over it, and see whatever is valuable in the apartments. The wall of my master is several fathoms high. If one do not find the door and enter by it, he cannot see the ancestral temple with its beauties, nor all the officers in their rich array. But I may assume that they are few who find the door. Was not the observation of the chief only what might have been expected?"

【注释】

[1] 叔孙武叔:鲁国大夫, 名州仇, 三桓之一。

[2] 子服景伯:鲁国大夫。

　[3] 仞：古时七尺为仞，一说八尺为仞，一说五尺六寸为仞。

　[4] 官：这里指房舍。理雅格译为"The officers in their rich array"，"官"即那些"全副武装的军官们"。辜鸿铭译为"The men that are in the holy temple"，指那些"居住在圣殿里的人"。刘殿爵将"百官之富"译为"The sumptuousness of the official buildings"，即"官方建筑的豪华富丽"，该本训"官"为"宫"，较为恰当。

【原文】 19.24　叔孙武叔毁仲尼。子贡曰："无以为也！仲尼不可毁也。他人之贤者，丘陵也，犹可逾也；仲尼，日月也，无得而逾焉。人虽欲自绝，其何伤于日月乎？多见其不知量也！"

【译文】 叔孙武叔诽谤仲尼。子贡说："这样做是没有用的！仲尼是毁谤不了的。别人的贤德好比丘陵，还可以超越过去，仲尼的贤德好比太阳和月亮，是无法超越的。虽然有人要自绝于日月，对日月又有什么损害呢？只是表明他不自量力而已。"

【英译】 Shu-Sun Wu-Shu having spoken revilingly of Chung-Ni，Tsze-Kung said，"It is of no use doing so. Chung-Ni cannot be reviled. The talents and virtue of other men are hillocks and mounds which may be stepped over. Chung-Ni is the sun or moon，which it is not possible to step over. Although a man may wish to cut himself off from the sage，what harm can he do to the sun or moon? He only shows that he does not know his own capacity."

【原文】 19.25　陈子禽谓子贡曰："子为恭也，仲尼岂贤于子乎？"子贡曰："君子一言以为知，一言以为不知，言不可不慎也！夫子之不可及也，犹天之不可阶而升也。夫子之得邦家者。所谓'立之斯立，道之期行，绥[1]之期来[2]，动之斯和。其生也荣，其死也哀'[3]，如之何其可及也？"

【译文】陈子禽对子贡说："你是谦恭了，仲尼怎么能比你更贤良呢？"子贡说："君子的一句话就可以表现他的智识，一句话也可以表现他的不智，所以说话不可以不慎重。夫子高不可及，正像天是不能够顺着梯子爬上去一样。夫子如果得国而为诸侯，或得到采邑而为卿大夫，那就会像人们说的那样，'教百姓立于礼，百姓就会立于礼；引导百姓，百姓就会跟着走；安抚百姓，百姓就会归顺；动员百姓，百姓就会齐心协力。夫子活着是十分荣耀的，死了是极其可惜的。'我怎么能赶得上他呢？"

【英译】Ch'an Tsze-ch'in, addressing Tsze-Kung, said, "You are too modest. How can Chung-Ni be said to be superior to you?" Tsze-Kung said to him, "For one word a man is often deemed to be wise, andfor one word he is often deemed to be foolish. We ought to be careful indeed in what we say. Our master cannot be attained to, just in the same way as the heavens cannot be gone up by the steps of a stair. Were our master in the position of the ruler of a state or the chief of a family, we should find verified the description which has been given of a sage's rule: -he would plant the people, and forthwith they would be established; he would lead them on, and forthwith they would follow him; he would make them happy, and forthwith multitudes would resort to his dominions; he would stimulate them, and forthwith they would be harmonious. While he lived, he would be glorious. When he died, he would be bitterly lamented. How is it possible for him to be attained to?"

【注释】

[1] 绥：安，安抚。理雅格译为"make them happy"，即让人民幸福安乐；辜鸿铭译为"beckons"，即"召唤、吸引"之义；刘殿爵译为"guide"，即"引导、指引"；韦利译为"steadied them"，指统治者能让人民"安居稳

定下来"。上述译本相较，韦利与理雅格的翻译更为恰当。

[2] 来：归服、归附。理雅格译为"resort to his dominions"，指人民纷纷"求诸于圣王的统治"；辜鸿铭将该句译为"whither he beckons，the people follow"，"来"即"跟随"之义；韦利直译为"come"，指统治者能让百姓安居乐业，人们便会纷纷前来。

[3] 其生也荣，其死也哀：有几种解释：1. 荣为荣显。何晏《集解》引孔安国云："言孔子为政，其立教则无不立，道之则莫不兴行，安之则远者来至，动之则莫不和睦，故能生则荣显，死则哀痛。" 2. 荣为尊敬亲爱。朱子《集注》云："荣，谓莫不尊亲。哀，则如丧考妣。" 3. 荣为乐。俞樾《群经平议》云："《国语·晋语》曰：'非以翟为荣'，韦注曰：'荣，乐也。'是古谓乐为荣。其生也荣，其死也哀，言其生也民皆乐之，其死也民皆哀之也。荣与哀相对，非荣显之谓。《荀子·解蔽篇》：'生则天下歌，死则四海哭。'语意与此相近。"理雅格将该句译为"while he lived，he would be glorious. when he died，he would be bitterly lamented"，即"只要他活着，他就会是光荣的。他死的时候，人们会痛惜他"，该本从孔安国之说，以荣为荣显、哀为哀痛。辜鸿铭将该句译为"while he lives，he lives honoured by the whole world；when he dies he is mourned for by the whole world"，即"只要他活着，他就会受到全世界的尊敬；他死后，全世界都为他哀悼"；刘殿爵译为"in life he is honoured and in death he will be mourned"，该翻译言简意赅，指"他生前受人尊敬，死后受人哀悼"。

尧曰篇第二十

【原文】20.1　尧曰："咨！尔舜！天之历数在尔躬，允[1]执其中。四海困穷，天禄永终。"舜亦以命禹。曰："予小子履[2]，敢用玄牡[3]，敢昭告于皇皇后帝：有罪不敢赦。帝臣不蔽，简在帝心[4]。朕躬有罪，无以万方；万方有罪，罪在朕躬。"周有大赉[5]，善人是富。"虽有周亲，不如仁人。百姓有过，在予一人。"谨权量[6]，审法度[7]，修废官，四方之政行焉。兴灭国，继绝世，举逸民，天下之民归心焉。所重：民、食、丧、祭。宽则得众，信则民任焉。敏则有功，公则说。

【译文】尧说："舜！上天的大命已经落在你的身上了，诚实地保持中道吧！假如天下百姓都隐于困苦和贫穷，上天赐给你的禄位也就会永远终止。"舜也这样告诫过禹。商汤说："我小子履谨用黑色的公牛来祭祀，向伟大的天帝祷告：有罪的人我不敢擅自赦免，天帝的臣仆我也不敢掩蔽，都由天帝的心来分辨、选择。我本人若有罪，不要牵连天下万方，天下万方若有罪，都归我一个人承担。"周朝大封诸侯，使善人都富贵起来。周武王说："我虽然有至亲，不如有仁德之人。百姓有过错，都在我一人身上。"认真检查度量衡器，周密制定法度，修复已废弃的官职部门，全国的政令就会通行了。恢复被灭亡了的国家，接续已经断绝了家族，提拔被遗落的人才，天下百姓就会真心归服了。所重视的四件事：人民、粮食、丧礼、祭祀。宽厚就能得到众人的拥护，诚信就能得到别人的任用，勤敏就能取得成绩，公平就会使百姓高兴。

【英译】Yao said, "Oh! you, Shun, the heaven-determined order of succession now rests in your person. Sincerely hold fast the due mean. If there shall be distress and want within the four seas, the heavenly revenue will come to a perpetual end." Shun also used the same language in giving charge to Yu. T'ang said, "I the child Li, presume to use a dark-colored victim, and presume to announce to Thee, o most great and sovereign god, that the sinner I dare not pardon, and thy ministers, o god, I do not keep in obscurity. The examination of them is by thy mind, o god. If, in my person, I commit offenses, they are not to be attributed to you, the people of the myriad regions. If you in the myriad regions commit offenses, these offenses must rest on my person." Chau conferred great gifts, and the good were enriched. "Although he has his near relatives, they are not equal to my virtuous men. The people are throwing blame upon me, the one man." He carefully attended to the weights and measures, examined the administration and laws, restored the discarded officers, and the good government of the kingdom took its course. He revived states that had been extinguished, restored families whose line of succession had been broken, and called to office those who had retired into obscurity, so that throughout the kingdom the hearts of the people turned towards him. What he attached chief importance to was the food of the people, the duties of mourning, and sacrifices. By his generosity, he won all. By his sincerity, he made the people repose trust in him. By his earnest activity, his achievements were great. By his justice, all were delighted.

【注释】

[1] 允：真诚、诚信。理雅格译为 "sincerely hold"，即 "真诚地坚

守"；辜鸿铭译为"Hold fast with thy heart and soul to the true middle course of right"，指圣王需要用"心与灵魂"来坚守正确的道路；刘殿爵将"允执其中"译为"holdst thou truly to the middle way"，"允"做副词，形容"真正的、真实的"。上述译本相较，理雅格的翻译较为恰当。

[2] 履：这是商汤的名字。

[3] 玄牡：玄，黑色谓玄。牡，公牛。孔安国云："殷家尚白，未变夏礼，故用玄牡。"皇侃《义疏》云："玄，黑也。牡，雄也。夏尚黑，尔时汤犹未改夏色，故犹用黑牡以告天，故云果敢用于玄牡也。"

[4] 简：阅，这里是知道的意思。正平本"简"作"萠"，俗字。帝臣不蔽，简在帝心；有多种理解：1.帝臣指桀；蔽，隐瞒，简即阅，明白了解之义。邢昺《注疏》云："帝，天也。帝臣，谓桀也。桀是天子，天子事天，犹臣事君，故谓桀为帝臣也。言桀居帝臣之位，罪过不可隐蔽，以其简阅在天心故也。"2.帝臣指天下贤人。朱子《集注》云："简，阅也。言桀有罪，已不敢赦。而天下贤人，皆上帝之臣，已不敢蔽。简在帝心，惟帝所命。"3.帝臣乃汤之自谓也。韩愈云："帝臣，汤自谓也，言我不可蔽隐桀之罪也。"又简，察也，见黄怀信《论语汇校集释》。理雅格译为"o god，I do not keep in obscurity. the examination of them is by thy mind"，该句意为"我没有默默无闻，对他们的考察是由上天的思想来完成的"。辜鸿铭译为"Thou wilt let me know Thy will and pleasure"，即"让我知道上天的旨意和快乐"；刘殿爵译为"I shall present thy servants as they are so that the choice rests with Thee alone"，意为"我要将他们的本来面目摆在上天面前，上天就可以独自作出选择"。

[5] 赉：赏赐。周有大赉，善人是富。两种理解：1.周受到上天的恩赐，善人也多了起来。何晏《集解》云："周，周家。赉，赐也。言周家受天大赐，富于善人，有乱臣十人是也。"2.周大封天下，善人因而富有。朱子《集注》云："此以下述武王事。赉，予也。武王克商，大赉于四海。见周书武成篇。此言其所富者，皆善人也。《诗序》云'赉所以锡予善

人'，盖本于此。"理雅格译为"chau conferred great gifts，and the good were enriched"，即"周公大封天下，善就丰富了"；辜鸿铭译为"The country was greatly prosperous；but only the good were rich"，即"这个国家非常繁荣；但只有好人才是富人"；刘殿爵从朱熹《四书章句集注》的观点，译为"The Chou handed out great gifts and good men alone were enriched"，即"周大封天下，好人因此而变得富有"。本书从朱子之说，认为刘殿爵、理雅格的翻译更为恰当。

[6] 权量：权，秤锤，指量轻重的标准。量，斗斛，指量容积的标准。理雅格、辜鸿铭、刘殿爵等均译为"The weights and measures"，指度量衡。

[7] 法度：指量长度的标准。理雅格译为"The body of the laws"，指具体的法律、法度；辜鸿铭译为"The administration and laws"，指行政规定与法律条例；刘殿爵将"审法度"译为"government measures will be enforced everywhere"，指在各地强制执行政府措施。我们认为，辜鸿铭译为"The administration and laws"更为全面。

【原文】20.2　子张问于孔子曰："何如，斯可以从政矣？"子曰："尊五美，屏四恶，斯可以从政矣。"子张曰："何谓五美？"子曰："君子惠而不费，劳而不怨，欲而不贪，泰而不骄，威而不猛。"子张曰："何谓惠而不费？"子曰："因民之所利而利之，斯不亦惠而不费乎？择可劳而劳之，又谁怨！欲仁而得仁，又焉贪！君子无众寡，无小大，无敢慢，斯不亦泰而不骄乎！君子正其衣冠，尊其瞻视，俨然人望而畏之，斯不亦威而不猛乎！"子张曰："何谓四恶？"子曰："不教而杀谓之虐，不戒视成谓之暴，慢令致期[1]谓之贼，犹之与人也，出纳之吝，谓之有司[2]。"

【译文】子张问孔子说："怎样才可以治理政事呢？"孔子说："尊重五种美德，排除四种恶政，这样就可以治理政事了。"子张问："五种美德是什么？"孔子说："君子要给百姓以恩惠而自己却无所耗费，使百姓劳作而不使他们怨恨，要追求仁德而不贪图财利，庄重而不傲慢，威严而不凶猛。"子张说："怎样叫要给百姓以恩惠而自己却无所耗费呢？"孔子说："让百姓们去做对他们有利的事，这不就是给百姓以好处而自己却无所耗费吗？选择可以让百姓劳作的时间和事情让百姓去做，这又有谁会怨恨呢？自己要追求仁德便得到了仁，又还有什么可贪的呢？君子待人，无论多寡，无论势力大小，都不怠慢他们，这不就是庄重而不傲慢吗？君子衣冠整齐，目不斜视，使人见了就让人生敬畏之心，这不也是威严而不凶猛吗？"子张问："什么叫四种恶政呢？"孔子说："不经教化便加以杀戮叫作虐，不加告诫便要求成绩叫作暴，不加监督而突然限期叫作贼，同样是给人财物，却出手吝啬，叫作小气。"

【英译】Tsze-Chang asked Confucius, saying, "In what way should a person in authority act in order that he may conduct government properly?" The master replied, "Let him honor the five excellent, and banish away the four bad, things; -then may he conduct government properly." Tsze-Chang said, "What are meant by the five excellent things?" The Master said, "When the person in authority is beneficent without greatexpenditure; when he lays tasks on the people without their repining; when he pursues what he desires without being covetous; when he maintains a dignified ease without being proud; when he is majestic without being fierce." Tsze-Chang said, "What is meant by being beneficent without great expenditure?" The Master replied, "When the person in authority makes more beneficial to the people the things from which they naturally derive benefit; -is not this being beneficent without great expenditure? When he chooses the labors which are proper, and makes them labor on them, who will repine? When his desires are set on benevolent government, and he secures it, who will accuse him of covetousness? Whether he has to do with many people or few, or with things great or small, he does not dare to indicate any disrespect; is not this to maintain a dignified ease without any pride? He adjusts his clothes and cap, and throws a dignity into his looks, so that, thus dignified, he is looked at with awe; is not this to be majestic without being fierce?" Tsze-Chang then asked, "What are meant by the four bad things?" The Master said, "To put the people to death without having instructed them; -this is called cruelty. To require from them, suddenly, the full tale of work, without having given them warning; -this is called oppression. To issue orders as if without urgency, at first, and, when the time comes, to insist on them with severity; -this is called injury. And, generally, in the giving pay or rewards to men, to-do it in a stingy way; -this is called acting the part of a mere official."

【注释】

[1] 致期：克期，限期。慢令致期谓之贼，有两种理解：1. 指懈怠政令，对民不信，设了期间，却提前责罚。邢昺《注疏》云："谓与民无信，而虚刻期，期不至则罪罚之，谓之贼害。"2. 指起初懈怠政令，后面却限期完成，这叫作贼害。朱子《集注》云："致期，刻期也。贼者，切害之意。缓于前而急于后，以误其民，而必刑之，是贼害之也。"

[2] 有司：指负责具体事务的官员。何晏《集解》引孔安国云："谓财物俱当与人，而吝啬于出犹之纳惜难之，此有司之任耳，非人君之道。"本章所述之事乃君王之事，君王送人财物像个官员而已，意指其小家子气。

【原文】 20.3　子曰："不知命[1]，无以为君子也。不知礼，无以立也。不知言[2]，无以知人也。"

【译文】 孔子说："不懂得天命，就不能做君子。不懂得礼，就不能立身处世。不善于分辨别人的言语，就不能真正认识人。"

【英译】 The Master said，"Without recognizing the ordinances of heaven，it is impossible to be a superior man. Without an acquaintance with the rules of propriety，it is impossible for the character to be established. Without knowing the force of words，it is impossible to know men."

【注释】

[1] 命：天命。理雅格、韦利译为 "the ordinances of heaven"，即"上天的条例"；辜鸿铭将"命"译为 "religion"，即"宗教信仰"，一定程度误解了儒家之"命"；刘殿爵译为 "destiny"，即"命运"，该本侧重"时命"而非"天命"，不够恰当。上述译本相较，理雅格的翻译更为恰当。

[2] 知言：善于辨析语言中的是非善恶。刘殿爵、韦利直译为 "understands words"，即"懂得语言"；辜鸿铭译为 "knowledge of the use of language"，即"关于语言使用的知识"；理雅格译为 "knowing the force of words"，即"了解语言的力量"。我们认为，此处将"知言"翻译为"分辨语言"（distinguish between languages）更为恰当。

后　记

　　《论语》是一部十分重要的中华文化原典，是孔子思想的集中展现。一方面，《论语》在汉唐经学时代与宋明理学时代，均是儒家经典系统中的重要典籍。在汉唐经学时代，《论语》与《孝经》都是"五经"的羽翼，而在宋明理学时代，《论语》则是"四书"之一。所以，《论语》是研究孔子思想乃至传统儒学思想绕不开的一部重要典籍。另一方面，《论语》所蕴含的思想价值，对于重塑现代君子人格、重建儒家美德伦理、重构传统人文精神，具有积极的借鉴意义。

　　本书对《论语》的通解，与以往一般意义上的英文翻译、现代汉语翻译，有一定的区别。由于现存的历代《论语》注解、现代汉语翻译、英文翻译十分丰富，本书的通解思路，主要是建立在这些丰富成果的基础上，即对这些丰富成果进行比较、筛选和评价。首先，也是最重要的部分，对《论语》中的疑难、重点字词，本书在注释里面主要参考何晏《论语集解》、皇侃《论语义疏》、邢昺《论语注疏》、朱熹《四书章句集注》、王夫之《四书笺解》、刘宝楠《论语正义》、戴望《论语注》等古代注解，以及理雅格（James Legge）、韦利（Arthur Waley）、刘殿爵（Din Cheuk Lau）、辜鸿铭等英文翻译，并且予以义理上的比较与评价。其次，现代汉语翻译部分，本书主要参考杨伯峻、钱穆等译文，并且融入本人在注释中的评判结果。再次，英文翻译部分，本书以理雅格的译文为主。由此，形成对整部《论语》的通解。

　　本书的撰写和出版，得到曾振宇先生提供的思路以及殷殷督促和全力支持，在此深表谢忱！由于本人的学力不济，研究能力有限，尤其是在跨语种的英译上，常有力不从心之处，如今却斗胆撰写些许文字，难免存在诸多疏漏与错谬，恭请方家达贤、读者朋友批评指正。

蔡杰于山东大学儒学院

2023 年 6 月 15 日